# Face-to-Face Diplomac

MW01092268

Face-to-face diplomacy has long been the lynchpin of world politics, yet it is largely dismissed by scholars of International Relations as unimportant. Marcus Holmes argues that dismissing this type of diplomacy is in stark contrast to what leaders and policy makers deem as essential and that this view is rooted in a particular set of assumptions that see an individual's intentions as fundamentally inaccessible. Building on recent evidence from social neuroscience and psychology, Holmes argues that this assumption is problematic. Marcus Holmes studies some of the most important moments of diplomacy in the twentieth century, from "Munich" to the end of the Cold War, and by showing how face-to-face interactions allowed leaders to either reassure each other of benign defensive intentions or pick up on offensive intentions, his book challenges the notion that intentions are fundamentally unknowable in international politics, a central idea in IR theory.

MARCUS HOLMES is Assistant Professor of Government at The College of William & Mary, Virginia. He is coeditor of *Digital Diplomacy: Theory and Practice* (2015, with Corneliu Bjola) and has written articles for multiple journals including *International Organization, International Studies Quarterly*, and *Journal of Theoretical Politics*.

# Face-to-Face Diplomacy

*Social Neuroscience and International Relations*

Marcus Holmes

*The College of William & Mary, Virginia*

CAMBRIDGE
UNIVERSITY PRESS

CAMBRIDGE
UNIVERSITY PRESS

University Printing House, Cambridge CB2 8BS, United Kingdom

One Liberty Plaza, 20th Floor, New York, NY 10006, USA

477 Williamstown Road, Port Melbourne, VIC 3207, Australia

314-321, 3rd Floor, Plot 3, Splendor Forum, Jasola District Centre, New Delhi - 110025, India

79 Anson Road, #06-04/06, Singapore 079906

Cambridge University Press is part of the University of Cambridge.

It furthers the University's mission by disseminating knowledge in the pursuit of
education, learning and research at the highest international levels of excellence.

www.cambridge.org
Information on this title: www.cambridge.org/9781108404440
DOI: 10.1017/9781108264761

First published 2018
First paperback edition 2019

*A catalogue record for this publication is available from the British Library*

ISBN 978-1-108-41707-5 Hardback
ISBN 978-1-108-40444-0 Paperback

*Dedicated to Lindsay, Maxi, and Lexi*

# Contents

# Acknowledgments

This book began with a simple observation made in graduate school. Leaders, diplomats, and other high-level decision-makers spend considerable time and money, and occasionally put their own safety on the line, in order to personally meet face-to-face with allies, adversaries, and even enemies. And yet, despite this ubiquitous practice of international politics, our theories seemed to discount the activity as relatively unimportant at best, and downright dangerous at worst. Analogies to Yalta or Munich, cases where face-to-face diplomacy went terribly wrong, dominate. This seemed puzzling. If face-to-face diplomacy is so fraught with peril, why has the practice continued and why do many leaders swear by the benefit of personally sitting down to have a conversation?

I was very fortunate that just as I was asking these questions, several pieces were falling into place that allowed me to come to some provisional answers. First, as I entered the dissertation phase of my graduate program there was something of a renaissance occurring in the study of diplomacy. Paul Sharp, Vincent Pouliot, Corneliu Bjola, Costas Constantinou, Iver Neumann, Rebecca Adler-Nissen, Halvard Leira, Brian Rathbun, Markus Kornprobst, Brian Hocking, Christer Jönsson, Noe Cornago, Ole Jacob Sending, Jan Melissen, Jennifer Mitzen, Stuart Murray, Keren Yarhi-Milo, Todd Hall, and many others were all publishing work that revitalized the study of diplomacy, particularly in the American context. These scholars both challenged me to think about how I could make my own contribution, often eventually reading chapters or responding to the argument at conferences, and inspired me to think deeply about what specifically about face-to-face interaction was important to diplomacy.

At the same time, new exciting discoveries in psychology and neuroscience were challenging long-held assumptions about the nature of social interaction and specifically the importance of face-to-face. My father, Gregory L. Holmes, is a research neuroscientist and clinical neurologist, and perhaps because of genes and/or socialization, I have long been interested in how knowledge of the brain informs our understanding of social (and political) behaviors. I was also very fortunate that at The Ohio State University, where I did my Ph.D. work, Gary Berntson, one of the leading authorities in social neuroscience, was not only approachable and helpful in answering my questions, but allowed me, a nonneuroscientist, to take his year-long graduate sequence in social neuroscience. Gary turned me on to the work of Jean Decety on the neuroscience of empathy, Marco Iacoboni on the mirroring system in the brain, John Cacioppo on social brain paradigms and the emerging new field of "social neuroscience," and many others who would be influential as I put my dissertation together.

Finally, the most important lynchpin during this time was Alex Wendt's mentorship as my dissertation advisor. Alex encouraged me to forge ahead with a dissertation project that attempted to ask big questions and tried to break new ground in bringing social neuroscience to IR. I suspect that many others would have tried to persuade me to take a more traditional approach. To my mind Alex is the best dissertation advisor one could hope for: always willing to read carefully, provide stringent critique, and allow one to make one's own mistakes while providing support along the way. He continues to be a mentor and a source for inspiration as he continually pushes all of us to think harder and ask bigger questions.

My committee at Ohio State also included Jennifer Mitzen, who pushed me to continually refine the implications for the argument and address counter-explanations, and Richard Herrmann, who was terrific in identifying flaws in my logic or argumentation. It was a genuine pleasure to be put through the fire by this group and this book would not exist without their insights and help. Randy Schweller at Ohio State ran the dissertation colloquium where the first traces of my argument began to take shape. He provided the right mix of encouragement and criticism. Ted Hopf was instrumental, particularly in the early stages of the argument's development, pushing me to think about broader ramifications for the theory for IR theory. I had a tremendous cohort of peers. Eric Grynaviski, John Oates, Erin Graham, Zoltan Buzas, Joshua Kertzer, David Traven, Fernando Nunez-Mietz, Bentley Allan, Xiayou Pu, Jason Keiber, Austin Carson, Tom Dolan, Ryan Phillips, Caleb Gallemore, Chaekwang You, Nina Kollars, Katy Powers, Burcu Bayram, and Tim Luecke all provided insights, criticisms, ideas, and most of all encouragement, in a noncompetitive environment. It was great fun working with this group of fine scholars and I cherish those relationships. Finally, I received financial support from the Mershon Center at Ohio State for interviews and fieldwork.

Prior to starting at Ohio State, I began my graduate work at George-town University. J. P. Singh, Dale D. Murphy, and Daniel Nexon were not only fabulous teachers, but mentors and friends as well. JP chaired my Master's thesis on media framing, showing me how to take a project from initial idea to completed thesis, an invaluable experience for any scholar. Dale's classes were not only incredibly eclectic (and challenging) but his teaching style, a soft Socratic discussion style, is one that I have stolen from him. Finally, Dan made me appreciate the intricacies of IR theory and introduced me to all sorts of literatures I had not encountered. The inspiration and insight from all three of these friends have certainly made it into this book.

In fall 2013, I received an email from Nicholas J. Wheeler at the University of Birmingham with an invitation to present my research at the Institute for Conflict, Cooperation and Security at the University of Birmingham, which he directs. Nick had read my dissertation and saw relevance for his own work in trust building at the interpersonal level between enemies. I presented two chapters of the book at the ICCS conference and received extremely valuable feedback from his colleagues, including Naomi Head, Josh Baker, Harmonie Toros, David Dunn, Daniel Hucker, Paul Schulte, Kim Shapiro, Adam Quinn, Jan Ruzicka, and many others. I also benefitted tremendously by gaining access to the Chamberlain papers at the Cadbury Research Library, which Nick Wheeler facilitated. More recently Nick hosted a book workshop for our two books where I was fortunate to have been put through the fire by Ken Booth, Nicholas Wright, Tereza Capelos, and many others. The presentations in Birmingham have been foundational and the book would not be nearly as good without them. Since that initial email Nick and I have developed the type of working relationship any academic would love to have, but is rare. We push and encourage one another to continually refine, sharpen, and expand our arguments. I view this book, and his book on trust written often contemporaneously with this one, *Trusting Enemies*, to be in conversation with each other. These two books, I hope, represent the first steps in a productive research program on the dynamics of interpersonal interactions in international politics.

This book also benefitted tremendously from a book workshop organized and hosted by Mike Tierney through the Institute for the Theory & Practice of International Relations (ITPIR) at The College of William & Mary. Under the leadership of Mike Tierney and Sue Peterson, and with support from the Reves Center for International Studies, ITPIR is facilitating path-breaking research in international aid, security, and the dynamics of the international relationship discipline itself. I was fortunate to have several highly distinguished scholars at the workshop, drawn from faculty at William & Mary, as well as outside institutions. Nick Wheeler, Brian Rathbun, Steve Hanson, Mike Tierney, Sue Peterson, Jaime Settle, Amy Oakes, Hiroshi Kitamura, Jennifer Stevens, and Daniel Maliniak all provided fantastic feedback and helped to sharpen the arguments in the book. I received generous financial support from the Reves Center and College of Arts and Science at The College of William & Mary.

I benefitted greatly from several presentations of various aspects of the book. In particular, Roland Bleiker and Emma Hutchison graciously hosted me at The University of Queensland. They not only provided encouragement and sharp suggestions on the text, but continue to be a source of inspiration. In Brisbane I also received fantastic feedback from several scholars, including Constance Duncombe, Renee Jeffery, Wes Widmaier, Matt McDonald, and Barbara Keys.

Several other individuals have read and commented on different parts of the book over the years. My notes are most certainly incomplete, but include: Jeff Cohen, Jon Crystal, Robert Jervis, Melissa Labonte, Annika Hinze, Ida Bastiaens, Bob Hume, Nick Tampio, James Wilson, Len Seabrooke, Costas Panagopoulos, Sarah Lockhart, Alex Thompson, Andrew Ross, Jon Mercer, Gunther Hellman, Vincent Pouliot, Jeremie Cornut, Alastair Iain Johnston, Michal Onderco, Ursula Stark, Manu Duran, Jarrod Hayes, Sean Wong, Janice Bially Mattern, Maurits van der Veen, Tristen Naylor, Maria Konnikova Hamilton, Erik Dahl, Jonathan Renshon, Geoff Bird, Adam Richardson, Andy Kydd, Elizabeth Saunders, Rose McDermott, Nuno Monteiro, Dale Copeland, Brandon Yoder, Avery White, Srdjan Vucetic, Austin Knuppe, Jon Pevehouse, John McGlennon, Tuomas Forsberg, and John Park. Apologies to anyone I have left off, of whom I am sure there are many.

I have had a number of fantastic research assistants that have helped with this book. Kathleen Bryant, Caper Gooden, and Hannah Gourdie read every chapter and provided detailed feedback on each. Bailey Hall, Sarah Hong, Emily Ruhm, Barrett Mills, Nora Logsdon, and Jacob Nelson also provided very helpful assistance. I would also like to thank Cambridge University Press for allowing me to reprint with permission portions of "The Force of Face-to-Face Diplomacy: Mirror Neurons and the Problem of Intentions," *International Organization* 2013 67(Fall): 829–61, and Oxford University Press for the same regarding "The Psychological Logic of Peace Summits: How Empathy Shapes Outcomes of Diplomatic Negotiations," *International Studies Quarterly* with Keren-Yarhi-Milo (2016), "Believing This and Alieving That: Theorizing Affect and Intuitions in International Politics," *International Studies Quarterly*

(2015) 59(4):706–720, "Acting Rationally Without Really Thinking: The Logic of Rational Intuitionism for International Relations Theory" *International Studies Review* with David Traven (2015) 17(3): 414–440, and "You Never Get a Second Chance to Make a First Impression? First Encounters and Face-Based Threat Perception," *Journal of Global Security Studies* (2016) 1(4): 285–302. I also thank the National Science Foundation for supporting my attendance at the *Institute for Genomic Biology* in 2009 and the *Belgrade Security Forum* for inviting me to present my research in 2013. Lastly, the staff at the British National Archives was tremendously helpful during my archival research on Neville Chamberlain.

Finally, my brother Garrett patiently listened to, and critiqued, several arguments related to the book for the better part of a decade. My parents have been very supportive and, in particular, my mother Colleen provided invaluable proofreading and research help. My wife Lindsay is a source of both support and daily inspiration. During the writing of this book our precious two children, Max and Lexi, were born. This book is dedicated to our little family.

# 1    The Puzzle of Face-to-Face Diplomacy

> Your face, my thane, is as a book where men may read strange matters.
> – Shakespeare (*Macbeth*, Act I, Scene 5)

## The Puzzle and Argument

The journey was one of the most secretive in American history.[1] On January 20, 1945, ten days before his sixty-third birthday, the president of the United States, Franklin Delano Roosevelt, took the oath of office for the fourth time. His health was poor. His eldest son, James, remarked to his father shortly before taking the podium, in a vote of confidence, that he looked like hell. Despite this, a few days later Roosevelt embarked on a long voyage that would involve armored trains, a dangerous wartime Atlantic ship crossing, a circuitous airplane voyage, and finally, a Soviet limousine. At his destination, Yalta, Roosevelt would, together with Winston Churchill, negotiate the postwar world order with Joseph Stalin. Like many leaders before them, both Roosevelt and Churchill were believers in personal diplomacy, proponents of traveling to meet with friends and adversaries face-to-face in order to establish relations, build understanding, reassure one another, hash out deals, and ultimately find cooperative solutions to political problems.[2] This trip, however, would ultimately leave Roosevelt disappointed. As the politics unfolded over the coming months and years, "Yalta" became an infamous symbol, rivaled perhaps only by "Munich," for the perils of personal diplomacy and the naiveté of taking the words of other leaders at face value.

This, at least, has been the received wisdom. In recent years the tripartite negotiations at Yalta have been reanalyzed through the lens of the ending of the Cold War and the opening of the archives. An examination

---

[1] See Plokhy 2010, 3–35 for an excellent and thorough rendition of the history of this trip. I return to the Yalta summit in more detail in the concluding chapter of the book.
[2] Larres 2002; Reynolds 2009; Plokhy 2010.

1

of newly available evidence suggests that the notion that Yalta was a diplomatic failure is based more on subsequent disappointment with Soviet intervention in Eastern Europe at the beginning of the Cold War, specifically the 1940s and 1950s, than what happened at the summit itself.[3] The eventual political outcome has overshadowed both the poor negotiating position of the West as well as what Roosevelt and Churchill got right in their reading of Stalin. The Western leaders knew that Soviet cooperation would be required for peaceful postwar organization, but the most that they could offer was providing Stalin with autonomy in dealing with his territorial acquisitions and allowing Stalin to keep German war booty. In exchange, Roosevelt was able to secure a commitment for his two most significant aims: for the Soviet Union to fight in the war with Japan and to join the fledgling United Nations Organization. Stalin kept both promises. Further, on the specific intention regarding Poland, a main source of future dismay, little was actually settled at Yalta. Disagreements over Poland were not resolvable in a week-long mid-war conference, nor was this the intention. Indeed the Soviets had no clear discernible intentions regarding Eastern Europe at the time. In other words, specific intentions regarding Poland were not present at Yalta and they were therefore not communicated in the face-to-face diplomacy that Roosevelt, Churchill, and Stalin engaged in.

Thus one of the greatest and persistent myths from the Cold War, which has been codified in powerful analogy that is used to evoke the dangers of face-to-face personal diplomacy, that Stalin lied to a naive and all-too-trusting Churchill and Roosevelt and thereby started the Cold War, is problematized by the record. This is not to suggest that Western leaders could not have engendered more from their negotiations with Stalin at Yalta. They likely could have. But what is often lost in the symbol and analogy of Yalta as a failure of face-to-face diplomacy is how much both sides were able to communicate and read from each other *and* how the persistent myths that are told about these interactions may be misleading. While Roosevelt was ultimately disappointed that he could not reassure Stalin, the evidence suggests that he did ultimately read him, in large part, correctly. The story of Yalta should be focused as much on what Roosevelt and Churchill got right in their reading of Stalin's intentions, as what would happen subsequently during the Cold War.

I argue in this book that leaders like Roosevelt and Churchill are right in their belief that face-to-face diplomacy aids intention understanding and can often result in the transformation of relationships, whether it be in conveying peaceful intent to adversaries or reassuring nervous allies.

---

[3] See, for example, Plokhy's 2010 account.

While they may not be able to articulate precisely what it is, whether a "sense" or a "gut instinct" or an "intuition," practitioners of international politics who privilege the interpersonal are on to something. This stands in stark contrast to much of received international relations (IR) theory. Many scholars of IR take cases such as Yalta to highlight the futility, at best, and danger, at worst, of personal diplomacy. Diplomacy of the type practiced in Yalta, the *face-to-face meeting*, has long been the lynchpin of international politics. Yet, as analysts such as Sol Sanders have often argued, "personal diplomacy, whether practiced by Franklin D. Roosevelt with the cool disdain of a Hudson River patroon or Henry Kissinger with his accent 'mit schlag,' has largely led to disaster."[4] Indeed this interpretation of Yalta as something of a disaster for the West fits this narrative nicely and contributes to a healthy amount of skepticism in IR regarding diplomacy's place. This pessimism has different sources.

First, many argue that diplomacy generally, and face-to-face diplomacy specifically, is cheap talk. Costless communication that is expected to reveal preferences often fails to do so because diplomats and leaders have incentives to deceive during crisis bargaining.[5] Since leaders can lie, there is often little reason to trust what they say, particularly in personal encounters where there is less of an audience to worry about. This gets at the heart of what many IR scholars refer to as the "problem of intentions," and is responsible for creating potential conflict, in relation to the security dilemma.[6] Since we cannot read the minds of other people in order to ascertain or divine their intentions, individuals are always susceptible to misperception and deception.[7] And, as IR theorists point out, in the worst cases this can lead to catastrophe.[8] Roosevelt and Churchill allegedly read Stalin's intentions regarding Poland incorrectly, in the received narrative of the summit, foreshadowing the Cold War. Similarly, Neville Chamberlain famously read Adolf Hitler incorrectly in the run-up to the Munich agreement. These high-profile failures, where

---

[4] Sanders 2008.    [5] Fearon 1994.

[6] I view the security dilemma *as* the problem of intentions, though there is divergence of opinion on this issue in the literature. See Booth and Wheeler 2008 for a systematic analysis of the links between the problem of intentions and the security dilemma and Tang 2009 for a conceptual review of the security dilemma.

[7] The problem of intentions has both synchronic and diachronic dimensions, since intentions are always subject to change in the future due to simply changing minds, changing leadership, or other reasons (see Mearsheimer 2001; Copeland 2006). This book is primarily concerned with the synchronic dimension of the problem, though for reasons to be discussed in the following chapter face-to-face diplomacy also helps to undercut some forms of the diachronic dimension as well.

[8] Though it does not have to, necessarily, as I discuss in the next chapter. See Rosato 2015 for a pessimistic take.

the costs of getting the intentions wrong were extremely high, loom large, and cloud, for many, the very prospect of face-to-face diplomacy serving any beneficial purpose in world politics. Put simply, since the stakes are so high, face-to-face interactions, without anything costly to back them up, cannot be trusted.[9]

Second, traditional structural considerations, such as power and economic disparities, are believed to account for most of the variation in international politics outcomes. From this perspective diplomats and leaders are essentially "along for the ride," willing participants in a game that they have little control over. They may believe that they make a difference, and report in their memoirs and diaries that they were central to important outcomes during their time in power, but at the end of the day their activities are epiphenomenal to more important and powerful processes at work. Even those who think that diplomacy might make a difference often concede that it is what occurs *before* diplomacy takes place that is the relevant part of the process. This line of argument suggests that a necessary condition for having diplomacy, in other words, is the strong prospect for agreement.[10] You do not get personal meetings without all sides believing that agreement is likely (or perhaps as a last resort after everything else has failed), and therefore the personal meeting is less important than what happened before it. This leads to a selection bias problem that bedevils many studies of diplomacy: since instances of diplomacy exist because agreement was likely, the study of diplomacy is biased toward viewing diplomacy as successful. In other words, it is difficult to address "the dogs that don't bark," the instances where diplomacy does not happen because it would never have a chance of succeeding. These critiques of diplomacy are important reasons to think that personal diplomacy, as practiced by diplomats and leaders for centuries, is largely secondary to more powerful material processes.

On the other hand, minimizing diplomacy as secondary or irrelevant puts scholars in the uncomfortable position of having to argue that a

---

[9] See the large literature on "costly signaling," e.g. Fearon 1994. It should be noted that the "costs" that scholars typically have in mind when it comes to costly signaling is of the domestic audience variety, where leaders will theoretically have to pay for not living up to a commitment, not necessarily a personal variety. While FDR and Churchill undoubtedly paid significant costs in making the annoying and dangerous travel to Yalta, particularly in FDR's case because of his health, this is not a type of cost that necessarily would communicate truthfulness since it is the costs of *backing down* from the agreement that really matter. Though see Snyder and Borghard 2011 for more skeptical views of the traditional "audience cost" perspective from a variety of empirical perspectives.

[10] This notion is similar to William Zartman's (1986) insight that some conflicts might be "ripe" for agreement and settlement. For more on this line of argument and responses to it, see Ramsay 2011; Rathbun 2014.

prevalent variable of political practice does not much matter when leaders tell us that it often matters a great deal. Ronald Reagan, on realizing that the Soviets harbored beliefs about US intentions that were inaccurate, desperately sought a face-to-face meeting with Soviet leadership in order to clarify intentions and "get beyond the stereotypes."[11] Jimmy Carter believed that if he could just get Anwar Sadat and Menachem Begin in the same room together, they would see each other as equals and cooperate on important matters in the Middle East. This is not merely a twentieth century invention. Rather, the personal face-to-face meeting has been a cornerstone of world politics at least since the fourteenth century, with institutionalized face-to-face meetings dominating since the Congress of Vienna, with some arguing the origins go back far longer, perhaps to antiquity.[12]

This creates an important puzzle. Is face-to-face diplomacy actually important, as many leaders believe and, if so, what is it specifically that sometimes results in mutual understanding and in other cases creates misperception or even the perpetration of deception? If diplomacy is helpful to cooperation and developing understanding, why is it perceived by many non-diplomats and non-leaders as unimportant or irrelevant? Or is this simply a case of decision-makers displaying naiveté or overconfidence in their ability to persuade and read others? Further still, could the positive cases of personal diplomacy be explained by leaders overemphasizing their influence for posterity? After all, it is easy to highlight the virtues of face-to-face once one is out of office and "the results are in." It is harder to make such determinations when the stakes of failure are high. Outcomes in international politics often depend on the personal meeting, and the success or failure of diplomacy often hinges on what occurs in those meetings and the decisions that are made based on the information exchanged in those encounters. A theory of face-to-face diplomacy must be able to explain not only *why* leaders engage in this type of diplomacy but also the *outcomes* that obtain from such interactions.

I argue that face-to-face diplomacy is important to world politics because it is a sui generis form of communication. Face-to-face interaction represents a unique signaling mechanism that allows leaders to escape the problem of intentions, and thus the security dilemma, by communicating their intentions to each other with a very high degree of specificity. Put simply, face-to-face interaction is an unrivaled mechanism for intention understanding. Drawing from recent insights in social

---

[11] Massie 2013, 174.
[12] Finnemore 2003, 114 and Mitzen 2013 on the Concert, Bederman 2001 on Antiquity.

psychology, philosophy of mind, and especially social neuroscience, I argue that face-to-face meetings allow individuals to actively *simulate* the *specific* intentions of others. We know the intentions of others by automatically simulating what we would be thinking and intending if we were in the position of the other. This type of intention understanding is quick, intuitional, and, it turns out, supported by discrete architecture and mechanisms in the brain that are devoted to parsing others' intentions via cues that exist only in face-to-face interaction. This brain architecture, referred to broadly as the *mirroring system*, enables advanced neural synchronization between individuals, which in turn enables actors to directly access the intentions of others with a higher degree of certainty than economic or game-theoretic models of bargaining predict. Put simply, in face-to-face interaction the mirroring system increases, all else being equal, the prospects for intention understanding and deception detection.

The mirroring system is highly nuanced. It is able to pick up on microchanges in facial expressions and realize subtle shifts in the emotional states of others, which conveys their level of sincerity. This means they are applicable to a wide range of diplomacy settings. In certain instances leaders wish to convey their sincere intentions as clearly as possible. During the Cold War it was a series of personal face-to-face meetings between Mikhail Gorbachev and Ronald Reagan that helped to reassure each other of their benign intentions. Both sides sought to signal to the other, in the clearest way possible, their sincere intentions to cooperate. The face-to-face diplomacy between the two allowed both sides to read the sincerity of the other.

In other cases leaders do not wish to convey their intentions, preferring instead to keep their plans close to the vest. At the end of the Cold War, Gorbachev found himself again negotiating with US and European leadership over the fate of Germany, in particular on the question of whether Germany would remain divided or be reunified. Gorbachev, in negotiations with President George H.W. Bush, sought a solution to the Germany problem that would be favorable to Soviet interests and therefore sought to not let his reluctant intentions for a unified Germany be known to the American delegation. Yet the face-to-face meetings, particularly those that occurred during the Malta Summit, belied that strategy. Bush and others read from Gorbachev that he could be pushed on German unification, which was a correct understanding of Gorbachev's intentions, a reading that was likely only possible because of the face-to-face meetings that occurred.

Under certain conditions face-to-face interactions may also allow individuals to overcome long-standing intractable conflicts where distrust is abundant. At the beginning of the Camp David Summit in 1978, Jimmy Carter quickly realized that lack of trust and personal animosity between Menachem Begin and Anwar El Sadat, leaders of Israel and Egypt respectively, meant that the two could not stand to be in the same room with each other after the first two days of the summit. Yet, less than two weeks later the two signed monumental accords, which brought a lasting peace between the two states. Crucially, while there was an overt lack of trust between the protagonists, in particular between Sadat and Begin but also between Carter and Begin, Carter was able to use face-to-face interactions in such a way that the sincere intentions of both were conveyed to each other.

The mirroring system has also been shown to play a role in detecting deceptive intentions. The human brain comes equipped with resources to help individuals detect when they are being lied to, a skill that improves greatly in face-to-face interactions because of the wealth, and richness, of information being transmitted. In one of the most infamous cases of deception in the twentieth century, Neville Chamberlain traveled to Germany to meet with Adolf Hitler in an attempt to negotiate a settlement that would avert war on the continent. Hitler told Chamberlain that his aims were modest and he could be trusted to keep his word; Chamberlain bought it, telling his Cabinet back home that he felt Hitler could be trusted. Ultimately this deception contributed to the timing, if not the onset, of World War II. This case is taken to be an example *par excellence* of the futility of personal diplomacy precisely for all the reasons mentioned above, namely the problem of intentions and inherent cheap talk quality of diplomacy. Yet, a careful reading of Chamberlain's experience in Germany suggests a much more nuanced reading of the case. There is evidence to suggest that while Chamberlain did not ultimately conclude that Hitler was being deceptive he did get the impression that something was amiss. More specifically, he identified the very precise characteristics that are often present in people who are being deceptive. Therefore, even in the hardest case for the utility of diplomacy, deception, there is value that comes from the face-to-face interaction.

Ultimately this argument problematizes the notion that intentions are fundamentally unknowable in international politics, a common and important assumption made in international relations theory, and provides a way out of the security dilemma at the interpersonal level by providing a new mechanism for *intention understanding*. More broadly the book contributes a new understanding of the latent uncertainty problem in international politics. Rather than individuals operating under uncertainty, face-to-face interactions allow them to be much more certain in their assessments of the other. This suggests that uncertainty as the default position under anarchy needs to be re-examined. Under certain conditions, it can be escaped.

Importantly, leaders and diplomats often intuitively understand precisely what I argue in this book. They often *insist* on meeting face-to-face, arguing that this arrangement allows them to achieve outcomes they would not be able to achieve otherwise. As Vincent Pouliot has persuasively argued, they have a "feel for the game."[13] They know what to do and when to do it, even if they cannot pinpoint precisely why or how face-to-face works. How did interacting face-to-face become part of the feel for the game? What do diplomats and leaders often understand at an intuitive level that IR scholars have not yet appreciated? Most importantly, what is the mechanism by which face-to-face interactions sometimes result in mutual understanding and other times in continued misperception? Historians, like leaders, have also extolled the virtues of leaders and diplomats meeting personally with one another to resolve conflict. Yet, IR has been slow to appreciate these claims, arguably because there is, as of yet, no theory of face-to-face diplomacy that is generalizable beyond particular cases.[14] This book attempts to answer these questions and provide theoretical and generalizable support for claims regarding the value of face-to-face diplomacy, made by historians and leaders alike.

## The Renaissance of Diplomacy Studies: Diplomacy as Agency and Structure

In so doing this book contributes to something of a renaissance in diplomacy studies. Despite serving a central role in world politics, the study

---

[13] Pouliot 2010, 35–36. See also Adler-Nissen and Pouliot 2014.

[14] One of the closest to doing so among historians is Frank Costigliola (2012, 98), who notes the importance of personal politics, including interpersonal interactions, in shaping the beginning of the Cold War. In particular he highlights the importance placed by Roosevelt, Churchill, and Stalin in using face-to-face encounters to "reveal inner thoughts and ultimate intentions." He does not, however, theorize the extent to which this belief is validated or create a generalizable theory that can be applied to other individuals and cases. Other IR scholars have noted the importance of face-to-face interaction in diplomatic history, without theorizing its importance in a systematic way. Martha Finnemore (2003, 114–115) notes, for example, that the "face-to-face personal [meeting] as a means of interstate diplomacy emerges from largely unintended and unexpected experiences at [The Concern of] Vienna," with negotiators and leaders such as Castlereagh alike extolling the virtues of sitting down together. Finally, Booth and Wheeler (2008) have come the farthest in an IR context to theorize the "human factor of international politics, while stopping short of a full-fledged theory of face-to-face interaction (though see Wheeler 2018 for follow-up work on the links between face-to-face interaction and trust-building, which I discuss in detail in the concluding chapter of the book).

of diplomacy has historically been relatively marginalized in the discipline of IR, particularly in the American context, limiting what we know about both what diplomacy is and how it works.[15] Diplomacy has been variously defined, though most accounts include some notion of "communication between states," and "peaceful conflict resolution through negotiation when interests diverge or do not wholly overlap."[16] The marginalization of these processes has several sources. One is the systemic and structural focus of the discipline since the Cold War.[17] Another relates to the aforementioned problems of sending/receiving costly signals and deception. Perhaps even more importantly, accounts of diplomacy in the literature have traditionally often been comprised of personal reflections and anecdotes, sometimes bordering on autobiography, with statesmen or diplomats describing the virtues of diplomacy while paying little attention to the other important forces mentioned above, or downplaying the times when it did not work out.[18] This work, while interesting and important, comes from a "very hands-on" vantage point, one that makes it difficult to both generalize across different types of cases, and to evaluate diplomacy's effects relative to other causes of outcomes. That is to say, diplomacy "has been particularly resistant to theory."[19]

This has begun to change recently, however, with a turn toward theorization of diplomacy from diverse perspectives, a renaissance to which I seek to contribute.[20] Two broad approaches in particular have emerged: diplomacy as agency and diplomacy as structure. While in some cases these approaches may overlap, the contours are distinct and highlight the ways in which diplomacy as an object of inquiry has evolved over the last

---

[15] I am far from the first to argue that diplomacy has been relatively marginalized in IR, particularly American IR, and therefore remains poorly understood. For recent work conceptualizing diplomacy and explaining this marginalization, see Neumann 2005; Neumann 2008; Neumann 2012; Adler-Nissen 2014; Adler-Nissen and Pouliot 2014; Rathbun 2014; Sending, Pouliot, and Neumann 2015. On the other hand, not everyone agrees that what is occurring in diplomacy studied now constitutes a renaissance or revival, since, "strictly speaking ... [r]ather than a *revival* of interest in diplomacy ... it is perhaps more accurate to refer to an *expansion* of interest" (Constantinou, Kerr, and Sharp 2016, 8) as there was never a great deal of diplomacy study in IR, at least that which would resemble what is being studies in diplomacy studies today. Though, as I elaborate below, diplomacy has long been at the heart of the English School theory of IR.

[16] Rathbun 2014, 11.    [17] Holmes and Bjola 2015.

[18] Sharp 2009, 1–2; Der Derian 1987, 91; Sending, Pouliot, and Neumann 2015. Nicolson 1939 is a prominent example of this type of work.

[19] Der Derian 1987, 91.

[20] Trager 2017 provides an excellent overview of the recent diplomacy literature, delineating two traditions which he terms "diplomatic communication" and "rhetorical-argumentative." My delineation of diplomacy as agency and diplomacy as structure shares many commonalities with this approach.

several decades. Agentic approaches tend to highlight the causal effects of individuals in diplomatic social interactions, such as negotiations. The emphasis tends to be on the ways in which decision-makers, typically leaders and statesmen, but also diplomats and ambassadors, communicate, and process information they are able to gather in diplomatic encounters in order to make political decisions and achieve outcomes. Diplomacy is agentic because, as Rathbun argues, individual actors "go about achieving [their interests] in very different ways."[21] Negotiation style, form of communication, and the individual characteristics of those taking part in diplomacy each have causal effects, suggesting that diplomacy and diplomatic outcomes are not endogenous to attributes of the material environment, such as the distribution of power.[22] Rather, actors possess significant ability to intentionally engage in goal-directed action that is not determined solely by structure.[23] This set of approaches has greatly contributed to our understanding of the force of leaders and statesmen in acting against structural constraints.

Another perspective highlights diplomacy's constitutive effects on international politics. This approach agrees that diplomacy cannot be reduced to structural or systemic forces, but rather "produces effects of its own" as a *socially* emergent phenomenon.[24] Put another way, diplomacy is a social structure, which in turn has effects. The structure in mind here is not the distribution of power or material resources, but rather the practices of diplomats and other representatives. The English School, for instance, viewed diplomacy as one of the key social institutions of the "international society" of states.[25] More recently the *practice* of diplomacy has come into focus as an area of inquiry, recognizing the power of individuals, groups, and movements to structure international politics.[26] Sending, Pouliot, and Neumann, for example, argue that the practices of diplomats constitute world politics, "making and remaking" the international in a number of ways through social processes. As such, diplomacy is a social and historical institution that provides a communication channel, reduces transaction costs, and provides a permanent infrastructure that often stretches beyond state boundaries. It also institutionalizes hierarchies.[27] For example, in his recent book on

---

[21] Rathbun 2014, *x*.

[22] On negotiation style see Rathbun 2014. On forms of communication, see Yarhi-Milo 2014. See also Rathbun 2014; Yarhi-Milo 2016 on individual-level characteristics.

[23] Agency is a "thick" concept in that it is multifaceted and multidimensional; see Mitzen 2013, 3–4 for a discussion of the use of agency in IR.

[24] Sending, Pouliot, and Neumann 2015, 17.    [25] Bull 1977.

[26] Neumann 2003; Constantinou 2006; Sharp 2009; see also Sending, Pouliot, and Neumann 2015.

[27] Sending, Pouliot, and Neumann 2015.

international pecking orders, Pouliot shows "how social stratification," a structural property, "emerges as a normal, basic condition of diplomacy."[28] Paul Sharp argues that precisely because IR theory has tended to be written from a systemic vantage point, diplomacy is given little causal weight. In contrast, he builds a diplomatic theory of international relations from the ground up, rather than shoehorning diplomacy *into* IR theory.[29] The international is the diplomatic, in effect. Iver Neumann similarly brings the diplomat *qua* diplomat into focus, highlighting the work conducted by members of the diplomatic corps, how they experience the world on a daily basis, and their institutionalizing effects.[30] While there is considerable diversity and heterogeneity in the ways in which diplomacy structures international politics, one of the key insights that is often made is that diplomacy should not be viewed as an alternative to structure, but rather the work of diplomats *creates* structure itself. Diplomacy is about structuring, rather than working against structures.

There is perhaps no greater indication of a thriving research area than healthy disagreement. While there is much upon which to agree between these two broad approaches, including the importance of diplomatic communication and interaction, a debate has emerged on a number of key issues, including just how agentic the agentic view actually is, the source of preferences, and the relevant unit of analysis. First, Pouliot has recently argued that the diplomacy as agency perspective often "[reinforces] the pervasive view in IR that diplomacy is epiphenomenal – except in cases where agency takes over . . . " The reason for this, in his view, is that the agentic perspective has tended to demonstrate diplomacy's effects "[by] focusing on instances of 'unlikely success.'"[31] That is, "agentic accounts end up focusing on exceptional individuals (who punch above their country's weight), unexpected outcomes (that depart from structural distributions) or both . . . [leading to] a rather restrictive starting point . . . " In contrast, the structural approach suggests that we take seriously the everyday quotidian practices of diplomats and other actors, even if the actors are particularly ordinary (in the non-pejorative sense) and the subject matter mundane, as *they* create social institutions through which actions, policies, and responses are routinized and normal, rather than focusing on the exceptional or unlikely.[32] Pouliot shows how the everyday operation of diplomats results in the aforementioned social stratification and becomes accepted "as a normal, basic condition

---

[28] Pouliot 2016, 8.    [29] Sharp 2009.    [30] Neumann 2005.    [31] Pouliot 2016, 8.
[32] Practice theory represents a broad set of approaches that interrogates IR by investigating the "embodied, materially interwoven practices centrally organized around shared practical understandings" (Schatzki et al. 2001, 3). See Pouliot 2010.

of diplomacy."[33] More generally, a growing number of scholars have demonstrated the utility of thinking about diplomacy "as a bundle of practices" that serve as a force in world politics, with significant identifiable effects, bringing practice theory from sociological studies to bear on IR.[34] Finally, it may also be the case that agentic theories actually explain outcomes "through preexisting distributions," further limiting the extent to which they are actually agentic. Pouliot, in critiquing Rathbun's agentic approach, notes that negotiators tend to enter an interaction with particular preferences, ones that are given exogenous to the interaction itself, from "preexisting distributions" such as personality traits or payoff matrices, and thus ironically end up downplaying the role of interaction. One significant reason for this downplaying of interaction, as I will elaborate in the next chapter, is that agentic theories of diplomacy lack the rich account and theory of interaction that would satisfy the Pouliot critique. Put another way, by not having a theory of face-to-face interaction, one that includes how intentions may be communicated or changed, it is difficult for agentic theories to posit what precisely is occurring when individuals personally meet one another.

In their own ways, both of these perspectives to diplomacy, agentic and structural, highlight the importance of communication and interaction, without providing a specific and generalizable theoretical account for the most ubiquitous form of interaction in diplomacy throughout its evolution as a social institution through time: the face-to-face encounter. I situate this book squarely in this debate, creating an agentic theory of diplomacy that attempts to deal with the critiques posed by structural accounts, while positing an explanation of face-to-face diplomacy that is relevant for structural approaches to diplomacy as well. By focusing on the intention understanding that is engendered in face-to-face interactions, I contribute to the significant role played by leaders and statesmen to develop rapprochement, settle disputes, or clarify differences, which is to say I highlight the agency of the powerful individuals involved against the material forces they are operating with or against. At the same time, the theory of face-to-face interactions as intention understanding I develop here is as applicable to everyday interactions of diplomats as it is to the monumental moments in diplomatic history conducted by statesmen.

As I will demonstrate in the empirical chapters, it is often the face-to-face interactions of ambassadors and diplomats, operating within a thick social diplomatic structure, that provide crucial intention understanding.

---

[33] Pouliot 2016, 8.
[34] Pouliot and Cornut 2015; Sending, Pouliot, and Neumann 2015.

Further, as alluded to above, face-to-face interaction has been part and parcel of the development and maintenance of diplomacy as structure, both in terms of historical and social institutions, from Antiquity to the development of the ambassador system, to the rise of permanent representatives, pecking orders, and high-level summitry. As Pouliot recently put it, "[p]ermanent representation truly is a form of 'face-to-face diplomacy.'"[35] To understand the nature of the institutions of diplomacy, we need a theory of what is occurring in the face-to-face interactions that help to create them. Lastly, as I develop in the following chapter, agentic accounts of diplomacy need not assume stable and exogenously given intentions. Intentions are often dynamic: they can change within a social interaction, and it is precisely through the mirroring system in the brain that dynamic intentions are received and understood. Ultimately, one of my aims is to provide a bridge between the agentic and structural approaches to diplomacy by refocusing attention back on the process of interaction itself and in so doing provide a theory that helps to explain landmark outcomes of world politics while explaining the ubiquity of face-to-face diplomacy throughout time, particularly in the development of the social institution of diplomacy.

## Challenges

A theory of face-to-face diplomacy that bases its argument in philosophy of mind, psychology, and neuroscience has many different theoretical hurdles to overcome. Most importantly, it must be able not only to explain diplomatic outcomes but also to justify explaining political behavior by looking at the mind and brain. After all, the "distance" between brain functioning and higher level functioning, such as state decision-making, is quite large. Why not just stay at the level of political interaction and assess the efficacy of face-to-face diplomacy relative to what extant IR theories would expect?

At the outset it is important to highlight precisely what it is that neuroscience brings to the table from an international relations standpoint and why learning about the brain and how it operates is worthwhile for our endeavors. I adopt a position of *rational reductionism*.[36] This position posits that there can be insights derived from lower levels of analysis, such as brain functioning, but these lower levels interact with, and affect, rather than replace or determine, higher levels of analysis. The aim of rational reductionism is not to substitute higher levels of analysis,

---

[35] Pouliot 2016, 123.
[36] Cacioppo and Berntson 2004a; Cacioppo and Berntson 2004b.

such as political behavior, with biochemicals and neurons, but rather to *include* lower levels in order to generate testable hypotheses *about* the higher levels.[37] The reason for this is simple: by only analyzing behavior at the political level it is difficult to understand variation in outcomes. This is because causal mechanisms often exist at lower levels of aggregation.[38] As Elster argues, "To explain is to provide a mechanism, to open up the black box and show the nuts and bolts, the cogs and wheels of the internal machinery."[39] It is difficult to understand *why* some face-to-face encounters result in intention understanding while others fail to produce the same outcome if we cannot identify the mechanism at work. Put simply, the philosophical position taken in this book is that investigating causal mechanisms at the biological level allows us to better understand how intention understanding works in the first place, which in turn helps to explain variation in diplomacy outcomes.

It also allows us to problematize and test previously untested assumptions. One of the assumptions that nearly all schools of thought within the international relations discipline make is that political intentions are fundamentally unknowable. This is the case because intentions are mental states. That is, they exist not in tanks, weapons, speeches, or Gross Domestic Product, but rather in the minds of leaders and diplomats. And since individuals cannot read the minds of others, they are forced to approximate intentions by looking at observables such as tanks and weapons. Capabilities, behaviors, and words serve as the basis for the attempts by state leaders to understand each other's intentions: not able to see directly into each other's minds, they resort to theorizing, often systematically and scientifically, about the meaning of behaviors. The origin of this assumption is a particular view on the nature of social interaction, drawn from folk psychology, that suggests individuals' sincere intentions are fundamentally inaccessible, locked in the mind of another individual, a mind we do not have access to. Without the power to read minds, individuals must fall back on interpreting behavior and deducing intentions by theorizing about the meaning of statements and actions, which in turn can fuel the security dilemma. Until now, such a position has been on safe ground, since there has been little evidence to suggest that the underlying assumption is untrue. However, the mirroring system suggests that there is a causal mechanism at the micro-level that suggests that we *can* know the intentions of others, which in turn provides strong support for the claim that the initial folk psychology assumption was

[37] On rational reductionism's self-conscious approach to the determinist criticism, see Holmes 2014; Holmes and Panagopoulos 2014. Also relevant is Bell's 2006 and 2015 criticism of approaches that privilege deterministic perspectives.
[38] Elster 1983; Elster 1998, 47–48.    [39] Elster 1983, 24.

wrong. The value added of going to the neuroscientific level, in other words, is that the micro-level can help us to test this previously untested assumption.

Yet, any theory that involves psychology and neuroscience must be able to stand up against the skeptic's critique. Neuroscience and psychology continue to evolve and the meaning of scientific studies continues to be debated, with controversy abounding regarding just how far the limits of using neuroscientific insights to inform social behaviors might stretch. This is true of the mirroring system, as will be discussed in detail in the next chapter. Further, the advent of new technologies continually refines, updates, and causes us to reassess what we know about how the brain works. Today's knowledge of the brain may well be outdated in the future. Indeed, science progresses in a non-linear fashion and history is rife with examples of findings science once suggested to be true and no longer do. And, as skeptics are quick to point out, it is one thing to study neural behavior in the safe confines of a sterile and simple experiment, it is another to show the same mechanisms are operative in the messy political world with actual diplomatic actors. In order to satisfy the skeptic, it is not enough to show that a causal mechanism in the brain problematizes an untested assumption, but the propositions that are generated from neuroscience must ultimately be able to be validated in the *political* world even if the assumptions and insights behind them are rooted in the realm of psychology and the brain, since those are typically not directly testable. Lastly, but no less importantly, psychology-based theories must also be able to deal with the problem of aggregation, since individuals, even leaders, are just one part of a large state decision-making apparatus. For all their power, leaders are not able to pull *all* of the levers, and the insights they draw upon in choosing which levers to pull come from different sources. Aggregating all of this together is a significant challenge.

Second, any agentic theory of diplomacy must also be able to articulate why the behaviors of the individuals involved are not reducible to the environment or structure that they are operating within, as discussed earlier. To be agentic, diplomacy must matter to the outcome and stand up to the counterfactual analysis that were it not for diplomacy, the outcome would be different. I will illustrate in the case studies that follow that the outcomes were not pre-determined before the diplomats or leaders arrived on the scene; but rather, what occurred in the personal meetings, particularly the ability of each side to read each other, was important not only to the negotiation process but the outcome itself. In some cases, such as with Camp David, the prospects for cooperation were so low that many in Jimmy Carter's administration were advocating against such a summit. Nevertheless, establishing that diplomacy made a difference relative to other factors is a daunting task since material and social structure are *always* present and are difficult to hold constant, since agents, such as leaders and diplomats, and structure are mutually constituted and affect one another. Relatedly, rationalist explanations for diplomatic successes and failures typically revolve around "costly signaling." In order to demonstrate that it was the face-to-face interaction, and not something else correlated with those interactions such as a signal that ultimately led to a particular outcome, these rationalist explanations need to be dealt with in each of the cases investigated.

Ultimately, however, these limitations and theoretical challenges can be overcome. In the following chapters, I will seek to show just how unique face-to-face interactions are as a form of human communication, why this uniqueness matters a great deal for international politics as it helps to overcome the most important deleterious aspects of the security dilemma, and how this understanding helps to shed new light on some of the most salient moments in twentieth-century diplomatic history.

### Structure of the Book

In this introductory chapter, I have laid out the puzzle of face-to-face diplomacy and provided a general overview of the arguments in the book. Chapter 2 investigates the puzzle and situates its roots in the international relations literature. I suggest that IR theorists have assumed that intentions are unknowable because they take a very specific view of the problem of other minds. They have essentially made a wager, based on an assumption that is very logical, regarding the inaccessibility of intentions. I develop this argument and provide my own theoretical approach in more detail, introducing the intricacies of the mirroring system in the brain, which constitutes my own wager, one that problematizes the inaccessibility position. While the science may be complex, the claim is simple: face-to-face facilitates intention understanding. The chapter concludes with a brief discussion of research methods and an outline of the propositions that will be investigated in the case studies to follow.

Chapters 3–6 are concerned with demonstrating the importance of face-to-face interactions in real-world politics. As discussed in detail in the following chapter, I have purposefully chosen cases that are both difficult for the theory, present useful *within-case* variation to explore multiple forms of communication, are unsettled in the sense that they continue to generate debate and discussion, and most importantly, represent salient moments in diplomatic history. A theory is most useful, in my view, if it can contribute an understanding to the most pressing cases, while also shedding light on the quotidian. To foreshadow my findings, in each of the cases we see a prominent role for face-to-face diplomacy in developing intention understanding. I utilize detailed process tracing paired with counterfactual analysis to attempt to isolate the causal effect of face-to-face encounters. One of the striking observations that represents a recurring theme in the chapters to follow is that those who engage in face-to-face interactions the most tend to understand their counterparts' intentions better than those who attempt to understand intentions from afar. This is particularly true for specific intentions, and therefore face-to-face diplomacy represents nothing less than a truly transformative force in international politics.

Chapter 3 deals with the beginning of the end of the Cold War. I trace the US–Soviet Union relationship through the lens of individual leaders and diplomats through the mid-1980s, focusing specifically on the face-to-face interactions between Mikhail Gorbachev and Ronald Reagan where both sides attempted to reassure the other of their benign defensively minded intentions. I show that through a series of summits, beginning in Geneva in 1985 and culminating in Moscow in 1988, the interpersonal relationship between Gorbachev and Reagan developed to such a degree that Reagan goes from terming the USSR an "evil empire" in 1983 to crediting Gorbachev with essentially ending the Cold War in 1988. What was particularly key to this relationship were the face-to-face encounters, where both sides were able to read sincerity from the other side. I contrast these interactions with the intention assessments that were conducted in Washington and Moscow, and show how the individuals who engaged with their counterparts face-to-face were much more likely to come to an accurate understanding of the others' intentions than those attempting to assess intentions from afar.

Chapter 4 continues this point by investigating the so-called intentional "Bush pause" in US–USSR relations in 1989, instituted by the newly installed President George H.W. Bush. When Bush entered office he eschewed offers from Gorbachev to continue the summitry Reagan had engaged in, preferring instead to take time to review US policy and assess Soviet intentions from indicators other than interpersonal interactions. The fall of the Berlin Wall changed this calculus decidedly as the major powers scrambled to determine the fate of the "two Germanys." Faced with this change in structural conditions and environment, the Bush administration engaged in a flurry of interactions that ultimately allowed Bush, and others such as James Baker, to accurately assess Soviet leadership's private intentions regarding a unified Germany. This information provided the necessary catalyst to push for a unified Germany in NATO, despite Gorbachev's public protestations.

Chapter 5 deals extensively with a particular set of countervailing conditions that make for a particularly hard test of the theory: intractable conflict, where long-standing hatred, mistrust, and a lack of empathy characterize the relationship and create important priors that are thought to impinge cooperation. These are the hardest cases for a theory of diplomacy, specifically one focused on intention understanding. I demonstrate that even in these instances there is value in face-to-face interactions in communicating intentions. Substantively, I track the interactions that occurred in the lead-up to, and during, the 1978–1979 Camp David Accords between Israel and Egypt, mediated by Jimmy Carter. While Israeli and Egyptian leadership did not get along and had to be separated at the summit, Carter was able to overcome these hostilities by working with each party individually to understand their intentions and arbitrate an agreement based on that understanding. This case is particularly useful in illuminating the scope of the theory with respect to countervailing prior-held beliefs.

Chapter 6 tackles another important countervailing condition: the problem of deception. While this book began with a discussion of Yalta, "Munich" is perhaps the most well-known moment of deception in modern diplomatic history and it occurred when Neville Chamberlain was looking in Adolf Hitler's eyes in a face-to-face encounter. There can be no harder case for a theory of face-to-face intention understanding. Nevertheless I demonstrate that the predictions that stem from an understanding of the social brain are validated even in this overt case of deception. Additionally, I illustrate how the individuals who understood Hitler's aims and intentions the clearest, the British foreign officers and diplomats who were stationed in Berlin and had the benefit of encounters with Hitler on a regular basis, gained that understanding through face-to-face diplomacy.

I conclude the book with a chapter that returns to international relations theory. I assess the security dilemma and the problem of latent uncertainty in the international system and suggest that face-to-face diplomacy transcends the problem of the security dilemma at the interpersonal level and thus increases the amount of certainty, rather than uncertainty, in the system. This has important ramifications for international relations theory as well as future research, which I outline. I also utilize the Conclusion to address, and theorize, two important areas at the intersection of political psychology and international relations. First, I address the "meta" question of how bridges can be built between the two disciplines, which traditionally have been separated by a rather wide, and often unsurpassable, gulf. Second, I attempt to theorize the relationship between intention understanding and interpersonal trust, two discrete concepts that are often found together in case studies of inter-personal relationships. Lastly, I identify a number of further questions that emerge from the theory and cases presented, such as how to account for instances in diplomatic history that do not seem to fit the theory, and highlighting fruitful areas for additional theoretical and empirical research.

I begin, in the following chapter, by assessing the problem of inten-tions in IR theory.

# 2 Face Value
## The Problem of Intentions and Social Neuroscience

> In general I do not surmise fear in him – I *see* it. I do not feel that I am deducing the probable existence of something inside from something outside; rather it is as if the human face were in a way translucent and that I were seeing it not in reflected light but rather in its own.
>
> – Wittgenstein 1980, §170

In this chapter, I present a theoretical explanation of the value of face-to-face diplomacy. Face-to-face diplomacy is conducted for many different reasons and for many purposes, including efforts to avert crisis, build trust between adversaries, break a cycle of enmity, collect information, manage an impression, signal resolve, or a desire to appease domestic constituencies.[1] My aim is not to provide a theoretical account of all of these plausible reasons why diplomats or leaders might engage face-to-face, but rather to identify a particularly important mechanism that often occurs through face-to-face interactions: intention understanding. Intentions represent a hard problem for IR. Under anarchy it is believed that states can never be certain of the intentions of others and therefore, depending on how pessimistic one is, intentions may serve as a reason for states to think twice before cooperating, since they worry about others reneging on their commitments, or cause states to find themselves in violent conflict, even if neither side sought conflict in the first place.[2]

I argue that the basis of this *problem of intentions* in IR theory is ultimately the philosophical *problem of other minds*. To be sure, there are many practical roadblocks to understanding another state's intentions. These often result from state sovereignty, where it is difficult to see inside states and their decision-making apparatus. States such as North Korea illustrate this very well: one of the reasons why it is difficult to predict what North Korea will do, or even intends to do, is that gaining access to valuable information inside the state, such as decision-making

---

[1] See Saunders and Lebovic 2016 on the determinants of high-level diplomacy.
[2] Waltz 1979; Keohane 1984; Wendt 1999; Mearsheimer 2001; Booth and Wheeler 2008.

procedures, is difficult.[3] Yet, these practical issues ultimately reduce to a simple philosophical position: it is difficult, if not impossible, to look inside the minds of other people in order to experience what they are thinking. After all, if we could access the intentions of individuals, such as leaders, directly, then opaqueness caused by sovereignty would be less problematic. Since we cannot access the minds of others, statesmen and stateswomen must resort to interpreting behaviors and approximating what they believe the intentions of others to be, a very imprecise process that can lead to misperceptions and errors.[4]

The problem of other minds has garnered significant attention in cognitive science, philosophy of mind, psychology, and social neuroscience in recent decades because of growing recognition that, at least under certain conditions, the problem may be overstated. Studies in empathy – the capacity to recognize the emotions, perspectives, and experiences of others – have demonstrated that individuals possess a refined ability to understand the intentions of others; indeed we do so routinely and automatically every day, making social life possible.[5] A number of brain systems, collectively referred to as "the social brain," because they facilitate social interaction, contribute to this understanding.[6] The mirroring system, in particular, supports the hypothesis that the way we understand the intentions of others is by simulating their intentions in our own brains. When interacting with others in face-to-face contexts we mirror what the other is doing in a type of "as if," or "pretend"[7] portrayal of their own intentions. Crucially, the mirroring system is not simplistic or naive, but rather highly nuanced and, under certain specific conditions, can aid individuals in unconsciously picking up on deception as well. These systems together ultimately suggest three very important theoretical points for international politics. First, face-to-face interaction is a unique mode of communication that brings with it special properties.

---

[3] Holmes and Wheeler 2017.     [4] Jervis 1976.

[5] Importantly, my theory is about intention understanding, which represents a relatively thin version of empathy. This is different from the thick, robust version that is normally analyzed in IR (see, for example, Booth and Wheeler 2008, 237–41; Head 2012; Crawford 2014), where empathy is often conceived as a multi-level dynamic *process* rather than outcome or stable state. The use of the term empathy is somewhat unavoidable since it is used in neuroscience and many psychology studies to mean intention understanding. It is only in this context that I use the term where appropriate. I also do not use the term to connote one of empathy's related concepts, sympathy. Finally, the term "empathic accuracy" is often used in the literatures I investigate below to refer to high-level mentalizing/mindreading. My argument relates to this in the sense that I consider political intentions to be high-level, rather than low-level. See Goldman and Jordan 2013 on this important distinction.

[6] On the social brain paradigm, see Humphrey 1976; Cosmides and Tooby 1992.

[7] The pretend language is not mine but that of philosophers of mind Alvin Goldman and Lucy Jordan (2013, 449–53).

Second, these properties problematize the notion that we cannot gain access to the minds of others in order to read their intentions and thus, third, severely undercut the hard problem of intentions that dominates many strands of international relations theory and underlies the security dilemma. Face-to-face diplomacy, under certain conditions, mitigates the security dilemma.

In order to make my case, I first develop the problem of intentions as a manifestation of the philosophical problem of other minds. I provide an overview of the problem of intentions, how different IR theories have addressed it, and connect it with the broader philosophical problem, which has also been addressed in a variety of ways. I then turn to the evidence that suggests that the two problems can be overcome through a better understanding of face-to-face interactions in diplomacy. From this understanding I develop propositions and articulate conditions under which intention understanding is most likely to occur in world politics, and importantly, when it is not. Finally, I outline the methodology and cases I use to assess the theory in subsequent empirical chapters.

## The Problem of Intentions

The problem of intentions is central to IR theory. As Brian Rathbun has argued, it forms the basis for much of the uncertainty inherent to a system under anarchy.[8] Uncertainty, in turn, leads to many roads of potential conflict, often in the form of security dilemmas and a disincentive to cooperate. Many realists argue that states are necessarily uncertain about each other's intentions, because they exist not in capabilities, such as tanks or airplanes, which may be empirically verified, but in the minds of leaders which are difficult to access. And since intentions exist in the minds of leaders, they are very difficult to credibly communicate.

In addressing this difficulty, scholars have looked at the ways in which actors navigate this central problem. Conceding that it is impossible to read the minds of others, states pursue other avenues in order to communicate their intentions, such as sending "costly" signals with the assumption that if signals are costly enough, they can be read as sincere indications of a state's intentions. The costly signaling logic suggests that not all signals are created equally. Talk is cheap and therefore states need to pay some cost in order to back up their statements; otherwise, they are not credible. Thomas Schelling recognized this problem during the Cold War, noting that it is difficult for states to communicate credible deterrence threats, without some type of cost attached to them.[9]

---

[8] Rathbun 2007.    [9] Schelling 1966, 150; Fearon 1994.

While the direct intentions of the leader are still not accessible, others can reasonably interpret behavior and approximate his or her intentions through inference, an imperfect process that often leads to error. Similarly, Andrew Kydd has argued that cooperation signals a state's trustworthiness, since it provides reassurance in the form of a payoff to the other party.[10] As Kydd argues, states "would hesitate to send [such signals] if [they] were untrustworthy."[11] There are several difficulties here. First, cost is often treated unproblematically, as a type of measuring stick of sincerity. This implies that cost is viewed objectively, that senders of signals and receivers of signals view the cost in similar terms. Similarly, Wheeler argues that signals are not correctly interpreted absent some underlying trust. If trust is a causal variable that is required for costly signals, what explains the development of trust in the first instance?[12] And, importantly, as the stakes of defection rise, how and why do levels of trust similarly rise? Here too, actor intentions are approximated by an understanding of what it *means* to cooperate, rather than accessed directly.

Liberal institutionalists, constructivists, and social theorists are more optimistic than realists and rationalists about the ability to successfully approximate intentions. For institutionalists the problem of intentions and the uncertainty that follows is essentially based in ignorance, a non-pejorative lack of information about other states.[13] Institutions can, under certain conditions, provide clues or inferences to state intentions through information-sharing mechanisms.[14] The institution serves as a method of stabilizing expectations regarding intentions and behavior.[15] By establishing rules and expectations, creating compliance and grievance procedures, sanctioning misconduct, and increasing transparency, institutions and regimes help states to gain reputations for honesty and trustworthy behavior, ultimately helping states to overcome their anxiety about the intentions of others.

Constructivists take a social-learning approach and suggest that states can approximate the intentions of others through social interaction.[16] States can overcome their anxiety of being cheated through common identity formation and by reflecting on the interactions they have with others, which can lead to common expectations regarding future behaviors. As Wendt notes, states *learn* to view each other as friends or enemies based on how significant others treat them.[17] Through interactions

---

[10] Kydd 2005.    [11] Kydd 2000, 326.    [12] Wheeler 2018.
[13] Rathbun 2007.    [14] Keohane 1984.    [15] Keohane 1993, 288.
[16] Checkel 2001; Adler 2005.
[17] Wendt 1999, 171. On recent developments in socialization and identity, also see Rathbun 2007.

over time, states learn more about each other such that they can more accurately interpret their actions and intentions through intersubjectivity.[18] Wendt explains how this works by invoking aspects of the state of nature thought experiment and positing a first encounter between two actors, Alter and Ego.[19] The first encounter takes place in a world "without shared ideas" (since his aim is to highlight the role of identity formation), though he notes that the "base model [of Alter and Ego] can be readily extended to situations in which culture already exists," such as modern politics.[20] Even in a state of nature, the two actors are not completely blank slates for a couple of reasons. First, they bring with them different types of material and ideational priors or "baggage." One is the body, the physical manifestation of the actor. Another is an identity, a sense of who they are. Second, Alter/Ego, by virtue of not having ever met, do not know much about the *specific* other they are to interact with, though they likely do have preconceived ideas about the other, given their previous interactions with other human beings.[21] As such the two actors bring ideas, formed by previous social interaction with other actors, that are exogenous to this first encounter.

As their interaction begins, both Ego and Alter engage in actions that are interpreted, understood, and then acted upon. The perception of the other and the relationship that they end up cultivating is determined by the interaction. Two processes are particularly important. First, each actor engages in role-taking, which "involves choosing from among the available representations of the Self who one will be, and thus what interests one intends to pursue, in an interaction."[22] Second, each actor also "casts" the other into a corresponding counter-role. Ego, for example, "alter-casts" Alter into a particular role, thus making Ego's own identity meaningful.[23] The result is that "they will get to know each other, changing a distribution of knowledge that was initially only privately held... into one that is at least partly shared."[24] The content of this knowledge may be threatening or it may be reassuring, depending on the interaction itself.

---

[18] Wendt 1999, 334.     [19] Wendt 1999, 328–36     [20] Wendt 1999, 328.

[21] In a pre-social environment, the literal "first encounter," where little is shared between Alter/Ego, it would be difficult to see how behaviors could even be interpreted; after all, on what basis does the interpretation rest? As Blaney and Inayatullah (1996, 73) argue, first encounters carry with them "the motivations, ideas, purposes, intentions, and images actors bring to contact." The problem therefore is not the interaction itself, but rather what came before it. From this perspective, there can be no pre-social blank slate; Alter/Ego have interacted with each other (albeit indirectly), through shared history, memories, ideas, and so on, throughout time. See also Doty 1997; Fierke and Wiener 1999.

[22] Wendt 1999, 329.     [23] Wendt 1999, 329.     [24] Wendt 1999, 331.

The Alter/Ego first encounter is a useful way to highlight the importance of interaction and identity on social relations. Wendt's point is that the metaphor provides a different way of thinking about the state of nature that does not rely on assuming characteristics of the actors, such as a human nature defined by *animus domandi*, or results in actors feeling threatened by others a priori to an interaction. Rather than focusing on the possibility of harm that actors may pose to each other in the state of nature, as realists would suggest, since individuals or states are unable to read the minds of others in order to ascertain their intentions, actors need not *necessarily* assume the worst about others. Rather, as Wendt argues, there is simply no reason for Alter to assume prior to Ego's first gesture that Ego is threatening in the absence of other information that would indicate it as such. Each actor understands the other through a learning process; it is only through the interaction, and not anarchy itself, that "Ego and Alter are . . . jointly defining who each of them is."[25]

One of the implications of this model is that intentions may be provided exogenously to the interaction, or they emerge *through* the interaction, and they might change in the course of interaction as well through social learning. I term this *intention dynamism*: the potential for intentions to emerge and change through social interaction and will return to it later.[26] For our purposes here, it is important to note that the mechanism of intention understanding that underpins the social learning is approximation through theorizing. As Wendt puts it, "who Alter is, in this interaction, depends on who Ego *thinks* Alter is." Both sides are engaged in processes of deducing and interpreting, making inferences, of what the other side is up to.[27]

One final point is worth mentioning. Wendt envisages Alter/Ego as relatively ambiguous "actors," presumably done so the metaphor can extend to collectivities, such as states. This ambiguity is useful because it allows generalizability across different units of analysis, such as states or

---

[25] Wendt 1999, 335.

[26] It is important to note, however, that even when actors arrive at an interaction with a particular intention, that is, it is "exogenous" to the particular interaction at the outset, from a social constructivist perspective the intention is still the product of interaction broadly defined. As I will elaborate in the next chapter, to use Mikhail Gorbachev as an example, as it is one used by Wendt, Gorbachev's intentions vis-à-vis Ronald Reagan prior to their first face-to-face encounter were a product of the social interactions he has had with others, his travels, his education, the books he has read, interactions with domestic constituencies, and so on. Intentions are thus always, at some level, social and endogenous to interaction.

[27] See Zehfuss 2002, 48 as well as Wheeler 2018 on this point.

regimes.[28] The downside of this move, however, is that it is unclear precisely *how* the interaction between Alter/Ego takes place. After all, state interaction, regime interaction, or individual human being interactions are each very different and engage different processes. The rich interactionist account is missing precisely because the units are left vague. This becomes problematic as we attempt to assess how processes such as social learning, a process that emphasizes "people's interactions with other people,"[29] are carried out in a world where the actors are underspecified. If we are more specific on the units, and posit Alter/Ego as individuals, we can be more detailed on theorizing their interaction in face-to-face contexts and provide more richness to Wendt's account that ultimately supports his conclusions, a task I will turn to below.

Finally, social psychology, cognitivist, and practice-theory approaches address the problem of imputing intentions by looking at the social identities, heuristics, images, "feel for the game," and habits individuals rely on to make sense of the actions of others. For example, image theory provides a method for understanding how states perceive each other by providing a framework for interpreting behaviors.[30] The difficulty, as cognitivists point out, is that information processing and provisioning is fraught with complexity – cognitive biases make it difficult to accurately read the intentions of others. Even worse, certain cognitive biases, such as the certainty bias, can lead individuals to believe that they are *certain* of the intentions of another actor even if they objectively are not.[31] This does not suggest that individuals cannot overcome these biases under certain conditions, though they face significant constraints in doing so with respect to accurately processing intention information.[32] Some of these approaches have explicitly dealt with face-to-face and will be assessed in more detail below.[33] Finally, practice theory approaches highlight the "everyday" habits and routines that "bring order to the complexity of social interaction."[34] The day-to-day engagement with one another can stabilize expectations and inference of intentions, often through social learning mechanisms.[35] For example, Pouliot highlights this in the day-to-day world of the NATO-Russia Council (NRC) where joint programs ensure that civilian and military personnel from both Russia and Allied countries work together

---

[28] See, for example, Wendt's use of different units, variously referred to as Gorbachev, the Gorbachev regime, and the Soviet Union, during his discussion of the end of the Cold War. Wendt 1999, 76, 129, and 375.
[29] Adler 2005, 20.    [30] Herrmann and Fischerkeller 1995.
[31] See, for example, Mitzen and Schweller 2011.    [32] Herrmann and Choi 2007.
[33] Goffman 1959; Jervis 1970; Yarhi-Milo 2014.    [34] McCourt 2016, 478.
[35] See, for example, Adler 2005, 19–22.

productively. The result, according to a British practitioner, was reassurance about Russia's intentions, or as one German official put it, "[p]eople stop thinking about the possible threat of the Russian army."[36] Thinking does not go away, of course, but the everyday practices of both parties provide intuitions and inferences regarding the other.[37]

Each of these perspectives, at root, shares a mechanism of intention approximation. Whether through interpretation of signals, balance of power, capabilities, regime type, iterative interaction in an institutional setting, reflected appraisals, or practices, actors approximate intentions through inference by theorizing about them given available data. Capabilities, behaviors, practices, and words serve as the basis for attempted intention understanding; not able to see directly into the minds of diplomats and leaders, scholars and states alike fall back on theorizing about the meaning of material and actions. This theorizing might be systematic, rigorous, or even scientific.

Realists counter these optimistic arguments by pointing out that power politics explains institutional design and intentions can change. Mearsheimer argues that institutions represent a "false promise" because they may appear to aid cooperation but in reality the dominant states use institutions to further their own goals.[38] Put simply, institutions aid cooperation when the dominant states want to cooperate. Further, realists argue that intentions are always subject to change. This is the diachronic critique. While it may be the case that states can more or less approximate the present intentions of others through a variety of mechanisms, the core problem that they may change in the future remains: "today's alliance partner might be tomorrow's enemy."[39] Most fundamentally, with an uncertain future conflict is always, at least ostensibly, a possibility.[40]

Finally, while different types of intentions are often conflated, an important distinction should be made between those that are fundamentally *distributive* in nature and those that are based on *reassurance* questions. While these two are often related, reassurance intentions involve

---

[36] Pouliot 2010, 128.
[37] On the link between practice theory/logic of habit and inference/intuition, see Holmes and Traven 2015.
[38] Mearsheimer 1994.    [39] Mearsheimer 2001, 33.
[40] Copeland 2006; Copeland 2011. As noted in the previous chapter, this book predominantly concerns itself with the synchronic dimension of the problem of intentions. The diachronic dimension largely remains even if individuals are able to know the *current* intentions of others, since those intentions are subject to change or the individual leaders might change. On the other hand, evidence below suggests a role for face-to-face in anticipating future long-term intentions as well as short-term intentions, as I discuss below and demonstrate in the empirical chapters. Since the argument is rooted at the interpersonal level, the problem of changing leadership remains, however.

existential or ontological security concerns of the actors involved. The Cuban Missile Crisis, for example, highlights the extent to which both the United States and Soviet Union were concerned about the defensive or offensive intentions of the other vis-à-vis their own security. Distributive intentions, on the other hand, may involve security issues but typically are rooted in the assumption that actors may prefer different outcomes in a bargaining situation and therefore understanding what they intend to pursue is an important aspect of negotiations. For example, actors involved in a multilateral trade negotiation will want to understand what each party intends to accomplish (their intention to negotiate in good or bad faith, for example) and predict what their reservation price is (their specific intention in the negotiation, in other words), in order to craft a favorable outcome.

Despite these important distinctions of intention type, whether distributive or reassurance-based, in the present or the future, the problem of intentions remains a problem because it is believed to be impossible to access the intentions that reside in the minds of others. State intentions are individual intentions since it is individuals who create them.[41] Extrapolating intentions from behavior, words, or prior actions, are all *approximations* of intentions based on inference. One can never confirm how another state is intending to act as states allegedly do not have access to the minds of decision-makers; they only have access to behaviors and words that may or may not be correlated well with actual intentions. As Wendt notes, "It is hard to read individual minds because we cannot see inside them. Lacking telepathic powers, we have to fall back on context and behavior to infer what others are thinking."[42] This is one area where Mearsheimer agrees, noting "intentions . . . are ultimately in the minds of policymakers, making them impossible to observe and measure."[43] Thus, the ultimate cause of the intentions problem in world politics, and the uncertainty from it that causes conflict, stems from the inability of individuals to read the minds of others. Even when states *want* to sincerely communicate their benign intentions, the problem of other minds presents a formidable roadblock.

Ultimately then, if we could solve the problem of other minds, then the problem of intentions, and consequently the uncertainty that follows from it, would also be solved. Solving the problem of other minds would also solve the opposite problem of misplaced certainty, where leaders are unaware of the intentions of others yet nevertheless act as if they are. In the next section, I will develop the problem of other minds and

[41] Byman and Pollack 2001, 114.    [42] Wendt 1999, 222.
[43] Mearsheimer 2011, 29.

present recent neuroscientific evidence that fundamentally undercuts the problem.

## The Problem of Other Minds

The philosophical problem of other minds poses two questions. First, how is it possible to know that others think like I do? Second, how is it possible to be able to understand the mental states of others when they exist in minds of other people, hidden from view behind the cranium? John Austin frames the problem simply: "How do we know that another person is angry? . . . Do we ever know?"[44] We often take as a given that all humans experience states of mind similar to what we experience: pain, pleasure, fear, and so forth. Yet, what justifies that certainty? Assuming that we can be justified in thinking that others have similar minds to our own, how do actors, through the course of interaction, come to understand those states in others? The problem of other minds occurs precisely because there is a large disconnect between the access we have to our own inner experience and our access to the experience of others. We can often tell when we are in serious pain, yet we do not have access to the mental states of other humans to tell whether or not *they* are in serious pain; maybe they are being particularly stoic or faking the pain. This creates an information asymmetry between what we know about ourselves and what can be known about others.

To illustrate how this problem manifests itself in international politics, consider again the example of Alter/Ego above. Wendt's "mirror theory of identity formation"[45] has been critiqued from different angles, but the most forceful criticism has been made from the perspective of the other minds problem. For Dale Copeland, Wendt's theory of intention suffers from three "serious flaws."[46] First, while some states, perhaps even the majority, have a pretty good sense of the intentions of others today, history suggests that uncertainty has been a significant problem in the international system, accounting for war and widespread conflict. Second, the problem with the gestures that Alter/Ego engage in is that "behavior does not speak for itself."[47] Linking this criticism to the problem of other minds, Copeland argues that "[b]ecause leaders cannot observe directly what the other is thinking, they are resigned to making inferences from its behavior."[48] This critique amounts to a claim that the social learning aspects of the theory remain undertheorized and underspecified. At the end of the day, for Copeland, Wendt's

---

[44] Austin 1979, 76.    [45] Wendt 1999, 407.
[46] Copeland 2006, 11.    [47] Copeland 2006, 12.    [48] Copeland 2006, 12.

formulation does not provide us with a basis for distinguishing sincere gestures from insincere ones.

Relatedly, Zehfuss and others have pointed out that while Wendt acknowledges the importance of language, the actors in the Ego/Alter interaction do not speak, rather, they signal to each other through behavioral actions.[49] According to Zehfuss, "a social act consists in sending a signal, interpreting it and responding on the basis of interpretation. A 'conversation of gestures' develops."[50] Ego/Alter are unlikely to share a common language, since they do not acquire characteristics from participating in a society. Therefore the symbolic interactionist framework, from which Wendt seeks to draw, and for which shared language may be vital, loses one of the core ways in which actors communicate. More generally, Zehfuss and Copeland agree that the "actors cannot communicate about their behavior; they communicate *through* their behavior."[51] On what basis can Ego or Alter's behavior be judged in a first encounter?

Finally, third, Copeland notes that there is a strategic aspect to interaction that Wendt does not discuss, namely the problem of impression management. The concern here is that a strategic actor will have strong incentives to make conciliatory gestures in order to deceive the other. "When we consider the implications of a Hitlerite state deceiving others to achieve a position of military superiority, we understand why great powers in history have tended to adopt postures of prudent mistrust."[52] Equally problematically, even if for some reason a particular actor could be trusted, the diachronic problem of future intentions remains ever present. This means that not only are deceptive intentions unknowable because of the problem of other minds, the problem of intentions persists into the future as well; solving the synchronic problem does not necessarily solve the diachronic problem. The philosophical problem of other minds thus constitutes the foundation upon which the problem of intentions is built.

Research into this philosophical problem falls into two theoretical camps and is broadly referred to as "theory of mind."[53] The first, termed "theory-theory" (TT) suggests that we rely on theories of mental states

---

[49] Zehfuss 2002; Booth and Wheeler 2008; Wheeler 2018.    [50] Zehfuss 2002, 48.
[51] Zehfuss 2002, 49.    [52] Copeland 2006, 13.
[53] The theory of mind literature is very diverse and too broad to be fully explored here. Each of the perspectives that follow, including TT and ST, has engendered significant literatures. There are also recent phenomenological accounts of social perception that reject many of the assumptions of the theory of mind literature, namely that mental states are not directly observable. On this view phenomenologists argue that we can indeed "directly perceive" the mental states of others through their behaviors. When we see people behaving in particular ways we are, in essence, seeing their minds in action. See, for example, the debate between Zahavi 2008; Krueger 2012; Bohl and

that we have derived throughout life.[54] In this view we hold personal theories of psychology that we use to infer the mental states – including emotions, beliefs, intentions, desires, and so forth – of others. These inner theories allow us to understand the present actions of people as well as predict their future actions. A simple example illustrates this perspective. A person witnessing someone sitting in a restaurant crying, holding their face in their hands, may well infer from their own life experiences, such as being taught by a parent, that the crying individual is sad. TT suggests that in these instances we are essentially applying a folk psychology theory, honed and updated since childhood, of how others think and behave to the situation. The mechanisms of understanding others at work in this example are reasoning and observation, a form of "scientific theorizing" about the intentions of others.[55] While one can never be certain of one's reading of another, after all the person in the restaurant may be crying out of happiness or suffering from allergies, the TT perspective provides a probabilistic and approximating route to understanding the mental states of others; and, context and situational factors provide clues to help us refine our predictions.

Recently a second perspective on the problem of other minds has garnered significant attention by philosophers, psychologists, and neuroscientists. This approach, "simulation theory" (ST), proposes that we come to understand the mental states of others and their intentions not through theorization and approximation, but rather through simulation. ST stems from skepticism about TT's claim that individuals possess a database complete with vast theories of social behavior, which would not only be biologically expensive but seemingly impractical from an evolutionary standpoint. Rather, ST proponents suggest that understanding the mental states of others involves activating mental processes that, if actually carried out, would produce similar behaviors. In this sense they are "pretend" versions of the mental states of others that occur in one's own mind.[56] This simulation, for many neuroscientists, is the basis for a specific form of empathy, the ability for individuals to know what it feels like to be someone else and in another's position both analytically and emotionally.[57] The ST insight is that we often do not need to theorize, either scientifically or through folk psychology, about what someone else

---

Gangopadhyay 2014. See also Wendt 2015, 232 which engages with this literature from a quantum perspective.

[54] For an excellent synopsis of the theory of mind literature, see Goldman 2006 as well as Goldman and Jordan 2013.

[55] Wendt 2015, 231.        [56] Goldman and Jordan 2013.

[57] The neuroscientific notion of empathy does not carry the positive normative bias that is often implied in common colloquial usage, as I mentioned above. Here the context of empathy is biologically self-serving and distinct from sympathy, which I conceive as

is experiencing – we simply know because we can experience it automatically for ourselves.

For example, individuals who watch a video of a spider crawling on the back of another human being often report that they get the "chills" watching the video. The participants do not need to theorize or think about what the experience feels like – they know, because they are simulating, or mirroring, in their own bodies, in real time, what the experience actually is. Similarly, individuals watching a horror movie in a theater often report physiological emotional changes, such as accelerated heart rates, as they experience the fear that the character in the film is experiencing. ST proponents point out that in these instances it seems unlikely that the individuals involved are *theorizing* about the experience others are going through; rather, they seem to be *simulating* the experience for themselves.

ST proponents also argue that this type of empathy, the very quick simulation of experience of others, is precisely the type of ability that is required in social life, where instantaneous evaluation of the social environment and quick decisions are necessary to get through life. As de Vignemont and Singer argue, "[e]mpathy might enable us to make faster and more accurate predictions of other people's needs and actions and discover salient aspects of our environment."[58] Much of what humans do on a day-to-day basis, indeed what social life requires, as Marco Iacoboni, a leader in investigating simulation and the neurological structures that support its processing argues, is the ability to quickly make important inferences about the actions and accompanying mental states of others:

One glance at my eleven-year-old daughter at the breakfast table tells me to tread carefully and sip my espresso in silence. When a colleague reaches for a wrench in the laboratory, I know he's going to work on the magnetic simulation machine, and he's not going to throw his tool against the wall in anger. When another colleague walks in with a grin or a smirk on her face – the line can be fine indeed, the product of tiny differences in the way we set our face muscles – I automatically and almost instantaneously can discern which it is. We all make dozens – hundreds – of such distinctions every day . . . Nor do we give any of this a second thought.[59]

We know these things because we *simulate* them for ourselves, in our own brains, in automatic fashion. From a ST perspective, a smirk or grin are

---

an emotional response of sorrow or concern for the condition of someone else. In this way empathy can be entirely egoistic or self-serving: successful chess playing arguably requires empathy in order to anticipate an opponent's moves but does not necessarily involve sympathy for the opponent. See also Bloom 2016.

[58] de Vignemont and Singer 2006, 440.     [59] Iacoboni 2008, 3–4.

not theorized from past experience, but are simulated in present experience. Put another way, if social life required constantly checking behavior against a database of experiences and theorizing about the motivations of that behavior, it would be an exhausting and comparatively slow way of understanding others. Social life requires quick judgment. This does not mean that TT does not have a place in understanding the mental states of others, but ST provides another account, and arguably a more plausible one given the complexities of social life, of how intention understanding might occur.

One way to understand the key differences between TT and ST is to consider the activities associated with each proposed process by which we understand others. At root, TT is a detached theoretical activity, with emphasis on individuals observing others and interpreting through the use of inner databases and folk-psychology perspectives, not unlike the ways states interpret the intentions of other states in IR theory. ST, on the other hand, implies a much more *direct* attempt to replicate or mimic the mental states of others in one's own mind. ST is not detached in the sense that there is a "correspondence between the mental activity of the simulator and target,"[60] and not theoretical in the sense that individuals are not using honed theories of psychology to draw inferences about intentions. Some have suggested that the ST perspective implies something of a "shared circuit" or "coupling" between individuals where the distance between individuals is minimized.[61] Since the minds of individuals are actively experiencing what the other is experiencing, there is a sense in which the two become congruent and the perception of others' mental states is done automatically and directly. In that sense we often do not need a theory at all to understand the mental states of others.[62]

Importantly, these very different perspectives on understanding others imply important empirical differences that can be investigated. If ST is correct, for example, we should expect to find evidence of mental mimicry, the literal simulation of the other, in the body. Since TT does not claim to have a mimicry component to its process, evidence of mental mimicry would support ST. Lastly, while the two theories of mind are delineated analytically, it is likely that both are involved, at some level, in understanding others. I will return to this point in more detail later.

---

[60] Gallese and Goldman 1998, 497.    [61] Hurley 2008.

[62] This is not to say that theorizing never comes into play about intentions. There are undoubtedly situations where we do not have a clue as to what someone else is thinking and therefore require theorizing about them. Or, perhaps more common, as I will discuss below, theory comes into play *after* interpersonal social cognition as part of reflection back on the interaction that took place.

While these different models of understanding actors exist, IR theory has largely been developed from a TT perspective, as has positivist social science in general. As behaviorism declined in the 1950s and 1960s, cognitive scientists looked inward rather than outward for explanations of mental states. Cognitivists argued that individuals possessed inner representations of the world and that the word *theory* described what these representations constituted and how they operated. If we knew how such representations and symbols were created, we could understand and deduce them through probabilistic rules. The differing views of behaviorists and cognitivists become clear in the following basic situation: a person leaves the house carrying an umbrella. A behaviorist might suggest "X believes that it is raining, if X takes an umbrella when X goes out." This logic works only if the rain believer does not like getting wet. A person might not take an umbrella, yet still believe that it is raining. Behavior does not necessarily reflect a person's underlying mental state. Cognitivists attack this problem by suggesting it is not solely behavior that matters, but that inner beliefs and desires explain mental states. There is no straight line from behavior to mental state. We invoke a theory of desire plus belief, in conjunction with behavior, to understand mental states. Therefore, from a TT perspective one might possess a folk theory about individuals who enjoy walking in the rain and those who do not, a theory constantly updated by experience.

Realist, liberal, and constructivist perspectives invoke, either implicitly or explicitly, these cognitivist perspectives.[63] The traditional rationalist model of desire + belief = action,[64] for example rests on this TT perspective of attributing mental states to actors in order to understand their behavior. Just as individuals engaged in a social interaction interpret the presentation of the other's behaviors, signals, and so forth against theories they hold of behavior, states do the same thing. When realists argue that states interpret costly signals as a way to reveal intentions, it means that states are using their own folk theories of signal sending/receiving to interpret the behavior and intentions of other states. Liberal institutionalists argue that states have a theory of state reputation that they use to interpret the actions of states embedded in institutions. Finally, constructivists, by suggesting that states can understand the meaning of the actions of others through identity, are arguing that states possess an innate theory of identity, and how it works, that has been honed through time and iterative interactions with salient others.

---

[63] Tetlock 1998.

[64] Fearon and Wendt 2002. It should be noted that there is some disagreement amongst the rationalist school regarding how accessible the beliefs and desires may be, independent of outcomes. See Frieden 1999.

What this suggests is that there has been a parallel between, on the one hand, the ways some psychologists and philosophers of mind approach the problem of other minds, and on the other, the ways in which IR theories have approached the problem of intentions. Both have largely adopted a TT perspective, where each side, be it an individual or a state, in an interaction responds to presentations of the other's signals, identity, and so forth, and deduces an explanation of behavior through a theoretical or (non-pejorative) folk-psychology perspective.[65] The incoming data is then subconsciously checked against the database of experiences that the individual or state has amassed over time to come to a conclusion about the present actions and future intentions of others. Put simply, IR theory is TT-dominated and, as of yet, has not incorporated the ST perspective into its theorizing. It is therefore not surprising that extant IR scholarship has viewed the problem of other minds as something of an unsurpassable problem: from a folk psychology or scientific theorizing (i.e. TT) perspective, other minds really are unknowable. And crucially this amounts to something of a wager. If the TT perspective is correct, and the only way to know intentions is to theorize about them, then this places the pessimists on firm ground.

In the next section, I review efforts by psychologists, neuroscientists, and philosophers of mind to understand when, and under what conditions, these two conceptions of theory of mind might be operating. In particular, face-to-face interactions have become the topic of very intense study when it comes to how we understand the mental states of others, in part because new findings suggest that simulation is abundant in face-to-face interactions, which supports a rich set of findings and arguments in social theory and psychology that face-to-face is a unique form of social interaction. It is to that discussion that I will now turn in order to construct a ST-based theory of intention understanding in world politics.

## Face-to-Face as a Unique Simulation Opportunity

### A Typology of Behavioral Face-to-Face Effects

Scholars in a variety of domains have long understood that face-to-face interaction is a particularly rich information environment that allows

---

[65] The term *folk psychology*, despite its unfortunate and misleading name, refers to a sophisticated and highly complex theory about the interaction of desires and beliefs, despite carrying an unfortunate label that implies amateurish post hoc rationalization of the crudest sort. In fact, "folk-psychology" is quite difficult to undermine theoretically. See Horgan and Woodward 1985.

individuals to communicate on multiple levels, including dialog, nonverbal actions, and emotions. Erving Goffman famously theorized this in his 1959 treatise on dramaturgical theory applied to social interactions, noting the importance of these various information levels in conveying overt and subtle clues:

> When an individual enters the presence of others, they commonly seek to acquire information about him or to bring into play information about him already possessed... many sources of information become accessible and many carriers (or "sign-vehicles") become available for conveying this information. If unacquainted with the individual, observers can glean clues from his conduct and appearance which allow them to apply their previous experience with individuals roughly similar to the one before them or, more important, to apply untested stereotypes to him.... [T]he "true" or "real" attitudes, beliefs, and emotions of the individual can be ascertained only indirectly, through his avowals or through what appears to be involuntary expressive behavior.[66]

One of Goffman's contributions was to highlight the ways in which face-to-face interactions are rich environments of information sharing, including information that may not want to be shared, but *is* through involuntary expression. Robert Jervis applied this insight to international politics and introduced the importance of indices, signals that bring with them some sign of inherent credibility, such as the expressive behavior in interpersonal interactions that may be difficult to conceal.[67] The insight here is particularly important for understanding the value of personal face-to-face interactions in diplomacy: since expressive behaviors are often involuntary and can reveal "true" or "real" mental states, the interaction itself brings with it a certain credibility that may elevate it to an index.[68] As Jervis notes, these are ultimately perceptual in nature, so they may be prone to error, but nevertheless are important to the actor because he or she views them as credible.

This framework has been applied specifically to the problem of intentions. Keren Yarhi-Milo argues that there are a variety of ways that states

---

[66] Goffman 1959, 1.

[67] Jervis distinguishes an index from a signal in the following way: "*Signals* are statements or actions the meanings of which are established by tacit or explicit understandings among the actors... In contrast to signals, *indices* are statements or actions that carry some inherent evidence that the image projected is correct because they are believed to be inextricably linked to the actor's capabilities or intentions." Jervis 1970, 18.

[68] Many authors implicitly endorse this perspective, even if they do not explicitly invoke the Goffman/Jervis perspective. Jenny Edkins (2015, 1) opens her book on face politics by noting "[w]e pay attention to reading each other's faces – reading people's moods, personalities and origins into their facial appearance. We search for clues as to who the person opposite us may be and what they may be thinking... face-to-face encounters are seen as potentially more honest and open than those conducted by other means."

may attempt to assess the intentions of other states, including interpreting capabilities, current and past behaviors, as well as the subjective experiences of individual decision-makers. In this latter process,
individuals "tend to rely on kinds of information that are particularly
*vivid*... [referring] to the 'emotional interest of information, the con-
creteness and imaginability of information, and the sensory, spatial, and
temporal proximity of information.'"[69] Face-to-face interactions are particularly good sources of vivid information, for the reasons Goffman and
Jervis allude to, namely the difficulty of manipulation. For Yarhi-Milo,
decision-makers often rely on this information, even if it is costless, to
derive conclusions about the intentions of others. The vividness theory
is still in the realm of approximating and theorizing intentions since it
relies, at root, on the "selection and interpretation of signals" in the face-
to-face interaction, though the insight that face-to-face encounters provide credible information even if the interaction is costless, is of critical
importance. One drawback of the vividness hypothesis is that it is difficult to predict *a priori* what types of information decision-makers will
find to be vivid, since it is not clear what mechanism makes information
vivid. That is, the emotional interest of information or the imaginability
of information is highly subjective and largely dependent on individual
personalities and prior-held beliefs, and therefore it becomes difficult in
any one particular instance to determine whether decision-makers will
find a face-to-face encounter relevant from an intention understanding
perspective.

In addition to signaling and information gathering, face-to-face contact has been of particular interest to IR scholars for some time because
of the perceived benefits it produces with respect to humanization, emotional bonding, and, potentially, reduction of prejudice. Roland Bleiker's
study of reconciliation in Korea, between North and South Kore-
ans, highlights the importance of face-to-face encounters in "removing
entrenched stereotypes and threat images," contributing "to the creation of a culture of reconciliation, which is an essential – and so far
lacking – precondition for a significant diplomatic breakthrough on the
Korean peninsula."[70] The Sunshine Policy by South Korea in the late
1990s and early 2000s seemed to internalize this logic, attempting to
increase face-to-face contacts among ordinary citizens in an effort to,
as Bleiker puts it, find a *sustainable* way to accept difference between
the two Korean identities without appealing to violence.[71] While the

---

[69] Yarhi-Milo 2014, 3.     [70] Bleiker 2004, 152.
[71] Bleiker 2005, *xlii*; also Bleiker 2004, 153–55 and Bleiker 2010, 235–55 connecting the
   North Korea case with literature on "sustainable diplomacies" which seek to focus on

precise mechanism by which face-to-face encounters work to reduce threat images and increase constructive dialogue remains unexplored, Bleiker's perspective resonates with a large research paradigm in sociology on the "contact hypothesis," which provides relatively clear conditions, such as the existence of equal status and common goals among individuals, that foster improved relations between groups.[72] Finally, a critical product of the humanization process may be the growth of trust between actors. I address trust more directly in the concluding chapter of the book, but at this point it is worth noting that scholars have identified face-to-face contact as that which "makes possible the growth of trust between... key actors."[73] Precisely how, and under what conditions, this trust development occurs remains in dispute, though it is likely the case that face-to-face interactions play a strong role in building trust between adversaries at the interpersonal level.[74]

Face-to-face interactions have also featured prominently in both the relational and practice "turns" in IR theory. From a relational perspective, IR has embraced a substantialist tendency, the conflation of an object with the outcomes of its actions.[75] As Patrick Jackson and Daniel Nexon argue, this tendency or bias assumes particular entities existed prior to interaction, "or that entities are already entities before they enter into social relations with other entities rather than being created and shaped by the process of interaction..."[76] A relational perspective, in contrast, suggests that we take seriously the notion that it is social *relationships* that make up world politics. States, for example, do not come into being *qua* states and then have interactions with other states; rather, states are made through relations with both other states and non-state actors. With reference to diplomacy, Rebecca Adler-Nissen argues that "... most diplomats know... that world policy is deeply relational. Their job is to make those relationships 'work.'" Face-to-face interactions, as the most ubiquitous form of diplomatic interaction in many environments, often are the starting point for relational diplomatic studies.[77]

Practice theorists, who highlight the quotidian processes of building and maintaining relationships, have similarly highlighted the importance of face-to-face interactions in structuring diplomatic practice. Pouliot,

"long-term reconciliation and/or coexistence of competing entities and ways of living." Constantinou and Der Derian 2010, 2. On reconciliation more generally see Hutchison and Bleiker 2013.

[72] There is a very large literature on the contact hypothesis, beginning with Allport 1954. For more recent developments, see: Pettigrew and Tropp 2006; Pettigrew and Tropp 2013. While there are obvious connections between the theory in this book and the contact hypothesis, my interest is specifically on intention understanding rather than prejudice reduction.

[73] Wheeler 2013, 479.    [74] See Wheeler 2018.    [75] Holmes and Rofe 2016, 6.
[76] Jackson and Nexon 1999, 293.    [77] Adler-Nissen 2015, 286.

for example, argues that it is the "thick face-to-face environment" of multilateral diplomacy, specifically in relation to UN Security Council diplomacy, that provides structures of appropriate behavior, calling to order failure to conform with norms of the game.[78] Permanent representation follows a similar logic. "The small world of permanent representation, feeding on regular and face-to-face interaction, heightens the probability that breaching the rules will spark an immediate social reaction."[79] Mitzen finds similar behavior in the forum effects of face-to-face in the Concert of Europe.[80] Face-to-face interactions thus serve to aid the creation and maintenance of routine and expected behaviors.

Parallel to these developments in IR and sociology, psychologists developed face-to-face interaction research programs, investigating in great detail at the behavioral level how interpersonal social interactions are conducted. As Wilson wrote in 1972, the study of human communication "surely must be one of the most important of all emerging scholarly fields," with the importance of face-to-face as a discrete type of interaction serving as a cornerstone.[81] Duncan and Fiske systemized this face-to-face research and cataloged the early effects of face-to-face, including empirical studies in the ability to pick up on emotions, the ability to send and receive signals through nonverbal communication, gender differences in the ways face-to-face interactions are conducted, the tendency of individuals to mimic each other and so forth.[82] The development of these studies in the 1970s, both in IR and psychology, laid the foundation and inspiration for sophisticated experimental designs that could both delineate what it is precisely about face-to-face that makes it unique as well as predict under what conditions its effects obtain.

One of the first disciplines to investigate this empirically was business administration and organizational behavior, where understanding the dynamics of negotiation, particularly face-to-face negotiation, may lead to more beneficial (and profitable) outcomes. Early experiments in the 1980s and 1990s demonstrated that face-to-face negotiation, relative to negotiation conducted via computer terminals, for example, increased the prospects for cooperation and minimized the pernicious aspects of the prisoner's dilemma.[83] One of the reasons hypothesized for this was that face-to-face allows for the reading of emotions, which serves to *provide information* to help individuals know others' emotions, beliefs, and intentions."[84] Morris and Keltner conclude that "emotional expression helps individuals solve one of the basic problems of social

---

[78] Pouliot 2016, 61.     [79] Pouliot 2016, 125.     [80] Mitzen 2013.
[81] See, for example, Duncan and Fiske 1977.     [82] Duncan and Fiske 1977.
[83] Raiffa 1982.     [84] Morris and Keltner 2000, 16.

interaction: reliably knowing the thoughts and feelings of others."[85] Put another way, they are alluding to the possibility of face-to-face interactions undercutting the problem of other minds through emotional signaling.

Face-to-face signaling has been shown to be particularly important because of its *unconscious* information exchange. As Alex Pentland has argued, building on Goffman, Jervis, and this initial wave of psychology studies, signals become "honest" when they are processed unconsciously and are otherwise uncontrollable.[86] These signals include mimicry, "the reflexive copying of one person by another during a conversation."[87] Individuals engaged in face-to-face interactions will often begin to copy each other. If one person nods their head frequently, the other will do so; if one smiles frequently, the other will often do so as well.[88] "Laughter is contagious," but so are many other behaviors, including emotions, nonverbal physical behaviors, tone of voice, mannerisms, and so forth.[89] Studies suggest that face-to-face interactions, all else being equal, also increase the amount of the empathy displayed between participants. For instance, in experiments where individuals interact face-to-face versus in online environments, individuals in face-to-face report more favorable impressions of the other (greater rapport) as well as greater perceived union (or "oneness," and coupling) with the other individual. Put simply, there was more self–other overlap in identity in the face-to-face condition than in the online condition, suggesting increased empathy in the face-to-face condition.[90] This greater overlap with the other allows for better understanding of the intentions of the other. For instance, in a business negotiation experiment where the participants were asked to predict the pricing intentions of others in the experiment, accuracy of intention-reading was much higher in the face-to-face negotiating group than other groups, such as computer-mediated groups.[91]

Similarly, comparisons between face-to-face environments and online environments suggest behavioral differences in face-to-face interactions relative to other modalities, such as e-mail and online auctions.[92] E-negotiators have a harder time trusting each other than those who engage in face-to-face negotiation, possibly because of the difficulty in understanding intentions in the online context.[93] The cues associated

---

[85] Morris and Keltner 2000, 16.    [86] Pentland 2008, 4.    [87] Pentland 2008, 4.
[88] Chartrand and Bargh 1999; Chartrand, Maddux, and Lakin 2005; Tummolini et al. 2006.
[89] For a review, see Chartrand, Maddux, and Lakin 2005.
[90] See, for example, Okdie et al. 2011.    [91] Rockmann and Northcraft 2008.
[92] See, for example, Moramarco et al. 2013.
[93] Naquin and Paulsen 2003; Rockmann and Northcraft 2008.

with cooperative intentions, including pitch and cadence of voice for example, are difficult to convey in non face-to-face communication modalities.[94] Studies also indicate that e-negotiators engage in more deception and less truth telling than their counterparts interacting face-to-face.[95] In the aggregate, face-to-face interaction "is at the heart of a process of building trust, mutual respect...[and] shared understanding."[96] At this point it is important to note that while these studies mainly focus on the salutatory effects of mimicry and face-to-face, they should not imply anything about a normative dimension to this type of intention understanding. As will be made clear in subsequent chapters, face-to-face interaction and the intention understanding that engenders from it can also be strategic, or deceptive, in nature.

In sum, as Jane Mansbridge suggests, face-to-face contact "seems to increase the actual congruence of interests by encouraging the empathy by which individual members make one another's interests their own."[97] These insights, particularly the automatic unconscious mimicry in face-to-face interactions, also lend support to the ST theory of mind perspective. If we develop a type of empathy with each other and understand the perspectives and intentions of the other through simulation, then mimicry suggests behavioral simulation of the other. Mimicry and development of empathy, in other words, are a reflection of the internal simulation that is occurring in the mind of the other. This important insight has not only been studied behaviorally but also in the brain through a series of experiments which have important ramifications for theory of mind, to which I will now turn.

### The Mirroring System in the Brain

As Marco Iacoboni argues, we rarely give much thought to our ability to read and understand quite clearly the mental states of others in our day-to-day lives. Indeed "[i]t all seems so ordinary."[98] Yet for centuries philosophers have been befuddled by the problem of other minds – how could something so extraordinary feel so ordinary? As Iacoboni points out, this "befuddlement was reasonable: they had essentially no science to work with." Now, however, sophisticated tools have changed that baseline. "No one could begin to explain how it is that we know what

---

[94] Ekman 1992.      [95] Rockmann and Northcraft 2008.
[96] Ansell and Gash 2007, 558. As they note, and I will discuss later in the book, face-to-face provides the potential for trust-building and empathy-building, but it certainly is not a panacea, as the possibility for deception looms large. See also Naquin & Paulson 2003, Purdy et al. 2000, Thompson & Coovert 2003.
[97] Mansbridge 1983, 33.      [98] Iacoboni 2008, 4.

others are doing, thinking, and feeling...Now we can achieve our very subtle understanding of other people thanks to certain collections of special cells in the brain called mirrorneurons."[99] The mirror neurons that Iacoboni refers to have an interesting story behind their discovery.

Recently, neuroscience researchers in Parma, Italy were amazed at a discovery involving macaque monkeys, a species of monkey whose brain, while much smaller than that of the human, corresponds well with the human brain. The researchers were investigating motor actions and were specifically interested in the brain functioning involved in planning and executing motor acts, such as grasping, holding, bringing objects to the mouth, and so on.[100] One day between experiments, with a monkey sitting quietly waiting for the next experiment to begin, neurophysiologist Vittorio Gallese reached out for an object and was startled by the burst of activity coming from the computer that was monitoring the brain activity of the monkey. The monkey was sitting quietly, not grasping for anything, yet the neurons in the monkey's brain associated with hand grasping were firing all the same. The neurons were firing based on the mere perception of the researcher reaching out to grasp an object. This was an amazing discovery. As Iacoboni points out, "[c]ells in the monkey brain that send signals to other cells that are anatomically connected to muscles have no business firing when the monkey is completely still, hands in lap, watching somebody else's actions. And yet they did."[101]

Subsequent research revealed that a distinctive class of neurons fires when a monkey executes a motor act and also when it observes another monkey, or a human researcher, performing the same motor act.[102] If a monkey saw someone else eating an ice cream cone, neurons would fire in the monkey's brain as if the monkey itself was eating an ice cream cone. These neurons have been termed "mirror neurons" because of the functional role they play in the brain: they actively replicate, or mirror, the actions of others. Subsequent research has demonstrated that humans possess these mirror neurons as well.[103] One of the reasons this discovery was remarkable is that it demonstrated that the very same neurons could be involved with both perception (such as seeing objects) and action (grasping objects). Rather than these two domains remaining separate, as received neuroscientific knowledge suggested,[104] they are "two sides of the same coin, inextricably linked to each other." This is a very important finding because it links action, and models of action in the brain, with abstract behaviors such as perception. Put another way, the

---

[99] Iacoboni 2008, 3–4.     [100] Iacoboni 2008.     [101] Iacoboni 2008.
[102] See Gallese et al. 1996; and Iacoboni 2009a and 2009b.
[103] For a review of the literature, see Iacoboni 2009a and 2009b.
[104] Keysers 2011, 14.

mirror neuron discovery suggested a more holistic interpretation of how the brain works, with motor actions and the goal of those actions, linked together. Action is not just action or physical behavior; rather, actions are linked with perceptions and intentions.

The discovery of the mirroring system in the brain provides a physiological basis for the ST perspective approach to the problem of other minds. Since perception and action are coupled together in the functioning of the neuron, there is not a separate theorizing activity that needs to occur in order for an individual to gain access to the mental states of another; they are instead simulating the experience for themselves. One may wonder, however, whether this type of experience is the same as being able to *read* the mental states of others. The initial mirror neuron studies did not ask monkey participants about their beliefs regarding the mental states of others, of course, nor did they ask participants to predict what their future actions might be. Put simply, is mirroring the same thing as mindreading?

Neuroscientists attacked this problem by examining the experience of witnessing pain in others. Individuals were shown depictions of hands and feet in two conditions: one where it was obvious that the hands and feet were in a painful position and another in a neutral position. They asked participants to attribute the intensity of pain the other was experiencing. The study illustrated that watching others in painful situations triggered the neural network involved in self-pain processing. This confirms the mirroring of experience. But more importantly, the attributions that individuals had regarding the level of pain in others were strongly correlated with the level of activity in the self-pain processing network, confirming the idea that individuals not only mirror the experience of others but also use that mirroring to produce mindreading.[105]

In addition to supporting the ST perspective on other minds with respect to present actions and behavior, mirror neurons are also critical to intentions. The studies mentioned so far suggest that the neurons allow for individuals to mirror the experiences of others and make attributions about their mental states based on that experience, but it may be that the neurons simply are mirroring the actual motor acts, i.e. the grasping or bringing to mouth, but do not mirror the intention of that act. Neuroscientists have identified the "what" and the "why" as two distinct, but linked, elements that characterize each intentional action and are processed by mirror neurons. The "what" refers to a simple observation of the action. Actor A grabs a basketball. The "why" represents an inference of intention. Actor A grabs a basketball because A

---

[105] Goldman 2006, 138.

intends to shoot it at the basketball hoop. Since our actions are normally associated with a particular intention, it is important to know whether the mirroring system is involved with the mere action or the intention.

In a seminal experiment that illustrates many of the nuances of the mirroring system, Leo Fogassi assessed the neural activity of monkeys during the execution of a grasping task as well as the observation of a grasping task, but in different contexts with respect to the goal of the action. In one execution condition the monkey reached for a piece of food and then brought it to its mouth in order to eat it. In another condition the monkey reached for an inedible object and placed the object in a container. The experimenters attempted to ensure that the actions were as close as possible by placing the container as close to the mouth of the monkey as possible, thereby matching the grasping-to-eat and grasping-to-place-in-container conditions (the experimenter even rewarded the monkey with a treat after placing the inedible object in the container so that there would be little difference in reward between the two conditions). Fogassi wanted to know whether the mirror neurons would fire in the same way with these very similar actions, or whether the neurons would be able to pick up on the intention difference. Does the intention of the act, in other words, matter? Fogassi found that while a small percentage of the neurons fired equivalently in both conditions, the majority of the neurons fired differently between the two setups. Grasping in order to eat caused approximately seventy-five percent of these particular neurons to fire vigorously, whereas grasping to place caused twenty-five percent of the neurons to fire vigorously.[106] The same was found when the experimenters changed the placing condition such that the monkey was placing food in the container and not an inedible object. This suggested that the difference in firing was not about the object itself but rather had something to do with the goal of the action.[107]

Fogassi's team then tested the monkeys as they observed the same experimental setup, but this time the human experimenter conducted the action. In one condition, with the container visible to the monkey, the experimenter grabbed food and placed it in a container. In another

---

[106] The actual percentage of neurons firing is less important (most of the neurons seemed to "prefer" eating (Iacoboni 2008, 32)) than the *difference* in firing, which is attributable to the distinction in specific intention.

[107] The differential firing between grasping-to-eat and grasping-to-place may seem inefficient, since "a large number of neurons with similar properties are required for executing different types of actions," but as Rizzolatti and Fogassi (2014) point out, it is like "that neurons encoding specific motor acts within an action form pre-wired intentional chains, in which a neuron encoding a motor act is facilitated by the neuron encoding the previous one."

condition, with no container, the experimenter grabbed food and ate it. The container provided a clue to the monkey about the future movement of the experimenter. The results were striking. The intention of the experimenter made a difference. The pattern of firing during observation very closely mirrored the pattern of firing during the monkey's execution of the same act.[108] The same was true if the monkey was observing the human grasping food to place it in the container. These results are striking because they demonstrated that the mirroring system was not merely aiding in recognizing action, but they provided a way of recognizing intentions as well. Importantly, the neuron discharges are measured during grasping, *before* the monkey knows whether eating or placing of the food is going to take place. When there is no intention associated with a particular act, such as with an experimenter pantomiming a grasping action, the neurons do not fire, suggesting that they are able to discern intentional from non-intentional behavior.

The neurons also play a role in inferring specific intentions even when intentions are shielded from view. In one of the most influential mirror neuron studies, experimenters demonstrated that the neurons in a monkey fired when the monkey observed an experimenter's hand moving toward a piece of food to grasp it. They did not fire nearly to the same extent, however, when the hand made the same motion without the food present, as this was a pantomiming action. This replicated the finding mentioned above, where the neurons correctly identified if there was a specific intention present, such as reaching for food. The researchers then placed an opaque screen in front of the food. While the monkey could no longer see the food, the memory of the food being there was enough to cause a subset of the neurons to fire when witnessing a hand reach behind it to grab the food. Similarly, if the screen was placed in front of the bare table and the experimenter reached their hand behind the food then the neurons would not fire. This finding suggests that the mirroring system is involved not only in discriminating intentions, but also in inferring intentions that are partially shielded or hidden from the participant. The only difference between the conditions was the monkey's knowledge of the object on the table; the monkey was still able to discern a pantomime from an actual intentional action. Put another way, the neurons are filling in gaps when information is omitted. Or, as the authors argue, "For these neurons, 'out of sight' was therefore not 'out of mind.'"[109]

Contributing to this "out of sight" aspect of the mirroring system may be the ability to predict future unknown actions, or the diachronic

[108] Iacoboni 2008, 32.     [109] Umilta et al. 2001, 156.

problem of intentions. One study at Harvard Medical School placed monkeys into a prisoner's dilemma situation where cooperation was rewarded with apple juice and defection punished by a lack of juice. When the monkeys played against a computer program, they rarely chose to cooperate. Yet when they played the game with another monkey that they were able to see, they were more likely to cooperate. This finding replicates the earlier finding I discussed above, where face-to-face interaction helps to overcome the prisoner's dilemma. In this case, however, the scientists were also measuring brain activity. As the monkey was deciding what to do, a particular set of neurons that predict an actor's unknown decisions during social interaction was activated. In effect the neurons were coding unknown actions, anticipating cooperation based merely on the fact that the monkeys could see each other, even though the action of cooperation/defection remained in the future.[110] As Haroush and Williams argue, this means that a particular set of neurons is able to predict the covert intentions of others.[111]

For decades there was limited evidence of the mirroring system in human brains since studying single neurons in the human brain requires invasive procedures that are not typically available to neuroscientists interested in mirroring. Mirror neurons were therefore traditionally studied in humans from a distance, using brain-wave activity and functional magnetic resonance imaging (fMRI), to identify particular areas of the brain associated with mirroring. For example, participants that are scanned using fMRI while observing and executing actions showed intense activity in the regions of the brain where mirror neurons are believed to reside,[112] particularly the inferior frontal cortex and superior parietal lobe. More recently, researchers have been able to study the mirror neurons directly. Using brains of twenty-one patients who were being treated for intractable epilepsy, and therefore required implanted electrodes to identify where the seizures were originating, the researchers were able to use the same electrodes to study mirror neurons. The researchers found specific neurons that fired when individuals performed a task and observed the task, providing evidence that the mirroring system exists in humans as well.[113] I will now turn in more detail specifically

[110] Haroush and Williams 2015.
[111] This is the first set of findings with respect to these particular neurons, though it remains unclear if these should be considered mirror neurons or a different set altogether. As Mukamel et al. 2010, 1 argue, there is increasing evidence that there are "multiple systems in humans [that] may be endowed with neural mechanisms of mirroring," and therefore thinking about a mirror neuron system as one discrete entity may be misleading. For this reason I prefer to use the language of "mirroring system" to capture the holistic and multi-region essence of mirroring in the brain.
[112] Keysers and Gazzola 2009.     [113] Mukamel et al. 2010.

to what these neurons might mean for human communication and inter-action.

### *Face-to-Face Interaction and Mirroring: Blurring the Distinction between Self and Other*

The prominent neuroscientist V. S. Ramachandran has termed these mirror neurons in humans "'Gandhi neurons' because they blur the boundary between self and others – not just metaphorically, but quite literally, since the neuron can't tell the difference."[114] As we have seen, the mirroring system in the brain actively simulates the actions and intentions of others, providing a physiological mechanism by which it is possible for individuals to be able to understand and read the mental states of others. This is the basis for the version of empathy discussed earlier, the ability to feel what it is like to be someone else and understand their cognitive mental states. It also provides philosophical support for a ST understanding of reading others minds. And, importantly, if Ramachandran is right, then empathy is not causing the neurons to fire, but rather the neurons firing *constitutes* empathy. Put another way, empathy has an observable mechanism in the brain.[115]

One of the questions that arises, however, is why we do not *literally* feel the pain of others or literally mimic the actions of others when we see action being performed. One explanation is that mirror neurons are operating in a bodily system comprised of many other types of neurons and processing systems. The mirroring system is not the only one in play in social interactions. For example, when we watch someone being touched the mirror neurons in the brain will fire as if we were being touched, but our skin receptors are sending "null signals" that tell the brain that we are not literally being touched. This suggests a further sophistication of the mirroring system: it helps individuals to empathize with others and be aware of their experiences without having to always literally feel what another is experiencing. Ramachandran supports this interpretation by noting that individuals with phantom limb syndrome, situations that occur when an individual loses a limb but still feels pain in that region as if the limb were still present, when watching another person who still has the limb, are able to feel what occurs with the limb that they are observing. If the observed limb is touched the individual without the limb will feel it. This suggests that the mirroring system is

---

[114] Ramachandran 2011, 124.
[115] See also Singer 2006; Corradini and Antonietti 2013 on this issue of the neural under-pinnings of empathy and philosophical debates connecting mirror neurons to empathy.

actively simulating the literal feeling on the limb but there are no "null signals" that are sent because the limb is physically missing.

As the preceding studies indicate, there is a strong role for visuality in the mirroring system. Much of what is occurring is replication of action and intention based on *observing* that behavior. This has led neuroscientists to become particularly interested in face-to-face interactions in humans, particularly since the behavioral studies mentioned above seem to suggest a coupling or congruence between individuals in face-to-face encounters, ostensibly suggesting that face-to-face is a prime candidate for mirror neuron activity. As Schulte-Rüther and colleagues have shown in a study of the mirroring system involved in face-to-face interaction, the process of recognizing the other's affective and cognitive states strongly invokes the mirroring system and, as they hypothesize, this system allows for interpersonal cognition.[116] They point out that face-to-face interaction involves constant firing of mirror neurons, likely because each side in the interaction, both the self and other, are simulating each other in an effort to understand the other person's overt and inferred meanings.[117] This finding suggests a significant difference between face-to-face and other communication modalities: during face-to-face interaction we move from private to shared experiences.[118] "During conversation, the participants focus or orient toward the other person's mind, inferring meanings and relevancies rather than just decoding the verbal messages. The interaction involves, as probably the most important part, the recognition of the other person's affective and cognitive states."[119] Verbal communication is clearly part of the exchange, but it is not just the verbal aspect that is relevant.

One study explored the relative importance of verbal communication between the face-to-face modality and other modalities by asking participants to communicate in a variety of conditions, including face-to-face and back-to-back. The study utilized a new hyper-scanning technique, where multiple subjects can interact with each other while simultaneous fMRI is conducted.[120] The researchers found in this study that there were significant differences in "neural synchronization" between these conditions. Put simply, the same biological brain processing occurred simultaneously between individuals. This finding suggests, as the authors point out, that compared to other forms of communication, face-to-face "is characterized by a significant neural synchronization between partners based primarily on multimodal

---

[116] Schulte-Rüther et al. 2007, 1369.     [117] Schulte-Rüther et al. 2007, 1369
[118] Hari and Kujala 2009.     [119] Hari and Kujala 2009, 461.
[120] Montague et al. 2002.

sensory information integration."[121] In reviewing the relevance of this study for our understanding of communication, Yun points out that the findings suggest that this was not simply about mirroring the action of speaking, such as mouth movements, but rather a much greater and broader neural synchronization.[122] This testing method is important because it allows researchers to isolate various action-related movements from other forms of intentions, creating an index of indicators. Face-to-face therefore includes neural features that other forms of communication do not have, leading the authors to conclude "that people should take more time to communicate face-to-face."[123] Therefore there is some neural truth to the notion of being "on the same wavelength."[124]

Therefore in addition to allowing individuals to understand another person's "*visual* vantage point," they also enable "us to adopt the other person's *conceptual* vantage point."[125] Put another way, as Ramachandran argues, "[t]he only thing separating your consciousness from another's might be your skin!"[126] While we should not take this metaphor too far, since individuals are indeed separate autonomous beings with their own sentience and consciousness, the notion of sharing and simulating experiences helps to drive home the point of shared experiences that occur when individuals are observing each other, and arguably the potential for shared identity as well. Neuroscientists have referred to this as the "shared network" hypothesis, connoting the extent to which the brains of individuals are linked by the mirroring system. These findings point to what Leonhard Schilbach and colleagues have termed a "second-person" neuroscience.[127] The implication here is that in face-to-face interaction, and the social cognition that goes along with it, individuals form a congruent "I–You" relationship rather than a detached "I–She" relationship, suggesting that the *second person* stance is the appropriate one for thinking about face-to-face interpersonal cognition, including intention understanding.[128]

Scholars have also found evidence to suggest that the mirroring system is activated not only with simple low-level instrumental action understanding, but through higher-level abstract thinking, such as propositional attitudes and links to consciousness, as well.[129] Abstract thinking may be derived from the same simulation and mirroring processes involved with perception of action, making abstract thinking a

---

[121] Jiang et al. 2012, 16069.      [122] Yun 2013.      [123] Jiang et al. 2012, 16069.
[124] Yun 2013.     [125] Ramachandran 2011.     [126] Ramachandran 2011, 125.
[127] Schilbach et al. 2013.     [128] See Schilbach et al. 2013; Wendt 2015, 232.
[129] See Iacoboni 2009a and 2009b; Keysers and Gazzola 2007; and Rizzolatti and Craighero 2004.

form of an inner motor action.[130] "Activation of mirror neurons in a task relying on empathic abilities without explicit task-related motor components supports the view that mirror neurons are not only involved in motor cognition but also in emotional interpersonal cognition."[131] Additionally, researchers have found that empathic accuracy, the ability to *accurately* judge the mental states and emotions of others, is associated with increased activity of the mirror neuron system, suggesting an important role for mirror neurons and higher-level mentalizing.[132] As I will suggest below, these findings suggest that unconscious signaling, of the type Pentland suggests, enters conscious reasoning somewhere in the process of interpersonal exchange.

### Mirroring Emotions and Deception

One area of particular importance for empathy is the affective component, specifically the ability to recognize and understand the emotions of others. Neuroscientists hypothesize that the mirroring system plays an important role in allowing individuals to "feel" the emotions of others when looking at their faces by imitating the emotion in their own body. On this view, emotions are not only reflected in the face, but individuals are able to feel the emotions of others by simulating, through observation, the emotional experience another is going through. As Iacoboni argues, "this simulation process is not an effortful, deliberate pretense of being in somebody else's shoes. It is an *effortless*, automatic, and unconscious inner mirroring." Or, put another way, "[h]umans are 'walking mood inductors,'" continuously resonating with others at a neural level.[133] Much of this simulation occurs at a "micro" level.

---

[130] Keysers and Gazzola 2007, 4. This type of argument is typically referred to as embodied cognition. With respect to mirror neurons it would suggest that "it is the embodied imitation of the observed body in action that directly enables us to recognize other as persons like us, not an abstract, inferential and theory-like process. The hypothesis that action understanding is based on a resonance mechanism does not exclude the possibility that other processes, based on movement descriptions, could influence this function. It simply highlights the primacy of a direct, automatic and prereflexive matching between the observation and the execution of action. By accepting this premise the traditional tension between acting and thinking considerably shrinks, as the capacity to detect the meaning of the behaviors of others consists in employing the same resources used to model our motor behavior." See Wilson and Foglia 2011.

[131] Schulte-Rüther et al. 2007, 1354.    [132] Zaki, Weber, Bolger & Ochsner 2009.

[133] Christov-Moore and Iacoboni 2016.

Microexpressions are very brief involuntary facial expressions that accompany an emotional experience.[134]

One of the early questions raised regarding this type of shared experience that individuals may engender when observing each other is to what extent that experience allows individuals to perceive deception, bad faith, or flat-out lying. Can the mirroring system help individuals differentiate sincere intentions from deceptive intentions? Might the ability to read microexpressions aid in detecting deception since the expressions reveal a true emotional state? Just as there is an evolutionary reason to need to read others' intentions, there is a similar evolutionary need to differentiate sincerity from deceit. As Putnam has noted in his review of the values of social interaction, "[i]t seems possible that the ability to spot nonverbal signs of mendacity offered a significant survival advantage during the long course of human evolution."[135] Or, as Jay explains, "[S]pecies who can't tell the difference between what is true and what is not are unlikely to prosper for very long. The ability to detect deception is, after all, just as functional in evolutionary terms as the ability to deceive."[136] Clearly, deception-detection capabilities help to ensure the survival of the species. This insight led researchers to ask whether discrete brain architecture exists that has evolved for that particular purpose.[137]

A seminal experiment in face-to-face deception detection conducted by Grèzes has provided important answers. Her findings demonstrate that individuals routinely perform better than chance in the detection of deceptive intentions and that distinct brain architecture is invoked when making judgments about those intentions.[138] The study asked participants to view other individuals lifting boxes and assess how heavy the boxes appeared to be. By watching how the individuals picked up the boxes, the observers could infer the boxes' weight, because the movements required for heavy boxes differed from light boxes. The researchers then instructed the individuals lifting the boxes to pretend

---

[134] There is a large literature on microexpressions which were first described in the 1960s investigating nonverbal communication. Paul Ekman and colleagues later connected microexpressions with deception. For an overview see Ekman and Rosenberg 1997; Ekman 2009; Porter and ten Brinke 2008.

[135] Putnam 2001, 175. See also Mehrabian 1981.          [136] Jay 2010, 24.

[137] It should be noted that there is some disagreement as to what constitutes a lie or deception. Sissela Bok in a seminal book on lying referred to a lie, for example, as "any intentionally deceptive message which is stated" (1978, 13). Ekman and O'Sullivan (1991) and Ekman and Rosenberg (1997) added an important notification criteria: lies require the target to be unaware that there is an intention to mislead, thereby explicitly linking deception to intention.

[138] Grezes, Frith, and Passingham 2004.

they were lifting a heavy box when it was actually light. The participants who recognized the deception were able to do so because they inferred the mental state of the person trying to deceive. The finding allows neuroscientists to begin theorizing about the ways in which the brain processes deceptive intentions. Ekman and O'Sullivan, whose research specializes in deception detection, identify this type of mirroring as "emotional." They suggest that human beings detect lies in face-to-face encounters by understanding the emotions on display.[139]

This research is particularly important for refining the conditions under which individuals can simulate sincere intentions and detect deception. Psychologists have long known that, while it is difficult to detect deception, face-to-face interaction makes it easier to do so, because individuals can utilize nonverbal behavior in making judgments about deception.[140] For example, in economic dyadic negotiations individuals display better accuracy in detecting deception face-to-face than in computer-mediated conditions.[141] Building on the work of Ekman and others, Buller and Burgoon synthesize an "Interpersonal Deception Theory" (IDT), where deception is modeled as a dyadic and dynamic process between individuals. Deceivers expend considerable cognitive resources in an attempt to mask deception and unwittingly perform unconscious nonverbal actions during those attempts. It is these nonverbal actions that can provide evidence of deception. These "behavioral markers" suggest that deception literally plays out in the deceiver's physical expression.[142] This "leakage" of intention is part of the, according to some estimates, roughly ninety percent of meaning that is conveyed nonverbally.[143]

Economic models of exchange implicitly adopt these IDT insights and often emphasize face-to-face engagement as a truth-detection device. As Storper and Venables put it, "[F]or complex context-dependent information, the medium *is* the message. And the most powerful such medium for verifying the intentions of another is direct [face-to-face] contact."[144] People with the best deception-detection skills rely on nonverbal cues more than verbal ones. This may be one reason why deception studies, using strangers as participants, often find a weak ability to detect deception. As Frank argues, many of the expressive clues to deception become available through repeated exposure. While individuals have difficulty detecting deception among strangers based on short

---

[139] Ekman and O'Sullivan 1991.
[140] See Frank 1988, Chapter 6; Bond et al. 1992; Ekman and O'Sullivan 1991; Frank and Ekman 1997; Vrij et al. 2004; Giordano et al. 2007.
[141] Giordano et al. 2007.     [142] Barry and Rehel 2014.     [143] Mehrabian 1972.
[144] Storper and Venables 2004, 356.

exposure, such as in an experimental setup, "[i]t takes time to recognize a person's normal pattern of speech, gesturing, and other mannerisms," suggesting that separating honest cues from deceptive ones requires experience with that individual, something that is typically not present in experimental designs involving deception detection.[145] In sum, while deception detection is certainly not easy nor foolproof, the evidence suggests that it is easier in a face-to-face context than it is in other interaction modalities. The discovery of brain regions associated with that detection helps to define the precise conditions where detection is successful.[146]

There is another important link between face-to-face interactions and deception: individuals tend to engage in deception *less* when they are interacting face-to-face versus other modalities. As Rockmann and Northcraft show in an innovative experiment where they conduct business negotiations between strangers, individuals who wish to engage in deception when interacting face-to-face confront an uphill battle since they have to control both verbal and nonverbal signals, any one of which may divulge the intention to deceive. As such negotiators may intuitively be aware, or "have a feel," that allows them to pick up on deception and realize that "face-to-face is the most difficult environment" to deceive, since "the deceiver must control all aspects of communication and must present a consistent and believable story even when questioned. The increased cognitive load present when attempting to accomplish such a task impairs one's ability to project a believable lie."[147] The effect of more honesty in face-to-face interactions is seen even with very minimal interaction where there is no back-and-forth conversation; reading from a script in a distributive economic game face-to-face leads participants to be more honest.[148] Face-to-face interactions therefore might serve as an important check on deception, by decreasing the likelihood that it is attempted at all.[149] This is particularly true in "high-stakes" environments, presumably such as high-level diplomacy, where the deceiver has a strong motivation to be successful and consequently becomes *less* effective at controlling nonverbal behavior and therefore is, all else being equal, worse at deceiving.[150] This also resonates with Mearsheimer's claim that lying is not particularly ubiquitous in international politics due to fear of being caught.[151]

Lastly, individuals vary in their ability to perceive deception through expressive cues, just as they vary in their ability to empathize more

---

[145] Frank 1988, 136–37.     [146] Langleben, Willard, and Moriarty 2012.
[147] Rockmann and Northcraft 2008.     [148] Van Zant and Kray 2014.
[149] See also Valley et al. 1998 on individuals telling the truth more in face-to-face negotiations versus telephone and written communications.
[150] Depaulo et al. 2003.     [151] Mearsheimer 2011.

generally. Deception detection is a manifestation of emotional and social intelligence.[152] This type of intelligence refers to the ability to understand one's own, and others', emotional states and the capacity to successfully navigate social relationships.[153] Indeed, the individuals best at detecting deception are those that score highly on emotional intelligence measures and consequently are able to interpret nonverbal cues accurately.[154] Interestingly, some studies suggest that successful leaders in general possess high levels of emotional intelligence.[155] On the other hand, individuals routinely express overconfidence in their ability to detect lies. In fact, in a range of tasks, including sensitivity to lies and reading emotions, across multiple dimensions, including controlled video stimuli and face-to-face interactions, the individuals with the *least* sensitivity tended to substantially overestimate their capabilities. For example, those in the lowest quartile on actual empathic ability rated themselves at or above average.[156] Importantly, overestimation is somewhat predictable based on individual characteristics. Narcissism, for example, predicted self-estimated performance. Put simply, individuals with narcissistic tendencies toward self-aggrandizement overestimated their ability to read others.[157]

All of this suggests that there is variation in deception detection and there is reason to believe that leaders, all else being equal, may be in a better position than most to pick up on deception unless they possess particular characteristics, such as high levels of narcissism in their personality. Deception is therefore not as devastating to a theory of intention understanding as the problem of dissembling might initially suggest, though as the Munich case to be discussed later illustrates, it remains a difficult problem for face-to-face diplomacy.

### What Kind of "Knowledge" is Brain-Based Knowledge?

The preceding discussion has suggested that brain systems are involved in the understanding of others' intentions, and these integrated systems allow for individuals to experience what the other experiences, suggesting a way around the problem of other minds, such that others are conceived "not as bodies endowed with a mind but as persons like us."[158] A question remains, however, regarding how we should think about mirroring from an epistemological perspective. Put most simply, what do these studies *mean*? Since brain data is confined to the laboratory, how do we fill in the gaps between fMRI experiments and real-world politics?

[152] O'Sullivan 2005, 237.     [153] O'Sullivan 2005, 237     [154] O'Sullivan 2005, 248.
[155] Goleman 2005.     [156] Ames and Kammrath 2004, 205.
[157] Ames and Kammrath 2004, 205–08.     [158] Gallese 2001, 43.

This is the scientific realism challenge: unable to observe mirror neurons in actual politics, how can we know whether or not they are indeed a causal mechanism of import? The first step in answering these important questions is understanding how we should conceive of the type of inferences that are supplied through face-to-face interaction. After all, it may be that the brain is simulating the intentions of others, but if that simulation remains inaccessible to the individual's conscious thoughts, then it is less clear how useful the mirroring is in political situations, though current research points toward mirroring occurring in conscious thought as well as subconscious thought.[159]

While it may be the case that what we call the simulation is less relevant than what it allows individuals to do, what is important is determining the extent to which the mirroring is accessible in consciousness, since political decisions in diplomacy are presumably conscious ones.[160] As Corradini and Antonietti point out, neuroscientists refer to the type of intention understanding that occurs quite variably, including: "non-predicative,"[161] "without verbal mediation,"[162] "without the need of theorising,"[163] "without propositional attitudes,"[164] "non-inferential,"[165] "without any knowledge operation,"[166] "not needing cognitive processes,"[167] "pre-reflective."[168] Further, the adjectives used to describe these types of understanding also vary, including: "direct,"[169] "immediate,"[170] "effortless,"[171] "automatic,"[172] "implicit,"[173] "unconscious,"[174] "subpersonal."[175] One curious observation regarding this survey of terminology is that "knowledge" is absent; on this view the mirroring system is providing the self with a pre-reflective unconscious and automatic mental picture of what is going on in the mind of the other, but we should stop short of calling that sense knowledge, even if it does influence decision-making.

There is reason to believe, however, that the pre-reflective picture does constitute, at least for some, a special type of knowledge. The problem

---

[159] See, for example, Christov-Moore et al. 2016 that demonstrates a correlation between conscious decision-making in economic games and brain activity that occurs during mirroring-related tasks, such as the use of facial headshots.

[160] Though there is a growing recognition in IR that many decisions may be habitual, intuitive, or otherwise automatic in nature. See, for example, Pouliot 2008; Hopf 2010; Holmes 2015; Holmes and Traven 2015.

[161] Gallese 2001, 44.  [162] Rizzolatti and Sinigaglia 2006, 120.

[163] Gallese 2001, 41.  [164] Gallese 2001, 41.

[165] Gallese 2001, 41; Rizzolatti and Sinigaglia 2006, 174.

[166] Rizzolatti and Sinigaglia, 2006, 127.  [167] Rizzolatti and Sinigaglia, 2006, 174.

[168] Iacoboni 2009a, 666.  [169] Gallese 2001, 41.

[170] Gallese 2001, 41; Rizzolatti and Sinigaglia 2006, 127.  [171] Iacoboni 2009a, 666.

[172] Gallese 2001, 41; Iacoboni 2009a, 666.  [173] Gallese 2001, 41.

[174] Gallese 2001, 41.  [175] Gallese 2001, 42 and 46.

with traditional knowledge terminology, as Alvin Goldman points out, is that "knowledge is a thick epistemological concept, connoting more than just attribution or belief."[176] Philosophers tend to view knowledge "as something like justified true belief, or reliably formed true belief."[177] Since it would be difficult to objectively justify what engenders from the mirroring system without first checking up on its accuracy empirically, it is difficult to see how the mental picture constitutes traditional knowledge and this is likely the reason that neuroscientists do not refer to the picture in knowledge terms. Yet, many philosophers argue that the traditional view of knowledge does not account for the distinctiveness of "self-knowledge." Self-knowledge is knowledge of one's own mental states, including one's own beliefs, desires, sensations, and so forth.[178] What makes self-knowledge unique is that the self has "privileged access" to what occurs in one's own mind. This doctrine suggests that there is a fundamental difference between experiencing something for oneself, in one's own mind, and relying on something that comes from the outside, such as a third-person report. In self-knowledge, the justification for having the belief is that one is experiencing it for oneself. From this perspective it may be that the mirroring system provides a type of knowledge that is quite unique and, as some argue, potentially the basis for consciousness.

I conceptualize the direct and automatic product of the mirroring system as an intuition. Intuition is often viewed pejoratively in decision-making as the source of bias or irrationality; after all, *homo economicus* is a rational cost-benefit calculating individual,[179] not one prone to gut reactions and decisions based on instincts. Work in psychology and philosophy of mind takes a different view, however, suggesting that automatic intuitions play a vital role in social interaction and decision-making. While there is disagreement on exactly how to conceptualize intuitions, there is widespread agreement that intuitions serve a *belief-like* function that is likely antecedent to belief and other cognitive states. The functions include "the speed of knowing something, knowing without knowing how you know, and also knowing without a conscious step-by-step process."[180]

Intuition can have many sources, including learned experience, emotional or affective responses, or gut reactions that may not have identifiable sources, and is often referred to in different forms and is linked to a number of similar concepts in the literature. For instance, practice theory and the logic of habit, which have recently been applied

---

[176] Goldman 2006, 223–24.    [177] Goldman 2006, 223–24.
[178] Gertler 2003 for review of this literature.    [179] Frantz 2004.    [180] Frantz 2004.

to international politics, and suggest non-conscious non-deliberative sources of behavior, have strong resonance with intuitions. On both views individuals do not act on conscious reasoning but rather on unthinking practices and habits.[181] These practices and habits, which are automatic in nature and resistant to change, share many of the same properties of intuitions, though they are not necessarily referred to as such. Therefore when leaders, for example, have a "feel for the game" that guides their decision-making, they are likely operating on an intuition about how to proceed in a given context.[182] Recent work in psychology also suggests a role for intuition in creating moral judgments. Haidt has argued that contra rationalist models of moral judgment, individuals often use quick automatic affective evaluations, or intuitions, to come to moral conclusions.[183]

One way of understanding intuition is to view it as a heuristic that bypasses conscious rational thought processes but is nevertheless accessible by consciousness. A familiar example of this concept is found in Kahneman and Tversky's research program in prospect theory. As Kahneman notes, "[our research] was guided by the idea that intuitive judgments occupy a position – perhaps corresponding to evolutionary history – between the automatic operations of perception and the deliberate operations of reasoning."[184] The different types of processing that Kahneman refers to are exemplified by the difference between "System 1" and "System 2." System 1 is the fast and automatic processing that provides quick judgments; System 2 is the more deliberate, reasoned, and reflective processing that is much slower in nature.

The intuition framework is helpful because it captures much of what the mirroring system is doing, as articulated by neuroscientists, and how it is useful to individuals engaged in social interactions, as articulated by psychologists and philosophers of mind. Intuition represents a very general category of pre-analytical non-reasoning based on "knowing without knowing how you know." This "self-knowledge" intuition that is produced by the mirroring system constitutes a belief-like mental state that is antecedent to further cognitive processing and therefore is in the realm of System 1 automatic processing, but can move to System 2 upon reflection. What begins as an automatic experience-based *intention intuition* becomes an *intention belief* once the content of the intuition is reflected upon and the individual reasons and deliberates about its content. This formulation also helps to bridge the divide between

---

[181] Hopf 2010; Pouliot 2008; Adler and Pouliot 2011a; Pouliot 2010; Adler-Nissen and Pouliot 2014.
[182] Pouliot 2010, 35; Holmes and Traven 2015.       [183] Haidt 2001.
[184] Kahneman 2003, 697.

ST and TT approaches. The evidence presented in this chapter suggests that ST is a largely automatic mirroring process in the body, creating a quick intuition about the mind of the other, and TT involves reflection about that intuition, forming a belief. Crucially, in this move from the automatic to the reflective there is an opportunity for other psychological mechanisms, or what Wheeler calls "psychological drivers" to enter the equation, providing an important scope condition for the theory. Doubt, latent mistrust, bad-faith models and images, stress, anxiety, hubris, and so on, all likely have an effect on the formation of *intention beliefs*. The privileged access doctrine discussed above implies that individuals will be likely to privilege intention beliefs over other types of information. As Jervis puts it, leaders may believe "that their rise to power was partly dependent on a keen ability to judge others."[185] This does not imply that the individual's reading of the other will be accurate, however, only that it will be privileged.

### Intention Beliefs: Accuracy and Change

One of the greatest challenges that psychologists, neuroscientists, and philosophers face when researching intention understanding is delineating why it sometimes engenders, or "works," and why in other cases it does not. For every example of President Ronald Reagan and Russian President Mikhail Gorbachev creating an emotional bond of common understanding, what Gorbachev called "the human factor," and former US diplomat Jack Matlock said was essential in overcoming the Cold War,[186] there are salient examples of the precise opposite occurring. President George W. Bush visited Russia's president Vladimir Putin and argued that by looking him in the eye he was able to "get a sense of his soul." Whereas Reagan would find that his intention beliefs regarding Gorbachev's intentions to end the Cold War were accurate, Bush later found that his reading of Putin was flawed. Was this a case of poor empathic accuracy or a lack of mirroring in the first place?

Psychologists have found a variety of factors that can affect empathic accuracy. First, the perceiver's familiarity with the target is important.[187] Practice with a particular target can increase accuracy.[188] The intuition that ambassadors often have, for example, that it is their familiarity with counterparts on the ground that helps to explain their understanding of the political dynamics in a given culture,[189] is supported by these studies. Gender differences have also been suggested to play an important role in

---

[185] Jervis 1970, 33.    [186] Matlock 2004.    [187] Stinson and Ickes 1992; Ickes 1997.
[188] Marangoni et al. 1995.    [189] See, for example, Pouliot 2016.

empathic accuracy, though interestingly only if the woman is made aware that her ability to empathize is being measured: "If a woman is aware that the task she is completing is assessing her empathic capabilities, it may be important for her to perform well. She therefore may be more successful than a man completing the same objective measurement of empathy because of her increased level of motivation."[190] Put simply, it seems that it is not a difference in ability, but rather a difference in motivation, that accounts for higher empathic accuracy in women.[191]

Empathy is also affected by group dynamics.[192] Participants in empathy studies show less simulation for members of different races, thus supporting the existence of a so-called "empathy gap" that suggests empathic accuracy may be mediated by social groups.[193] In one study individuals showed significantly less simulation of actions and intentions when viewing members of the out-group when compared to members of the in-group (in this study the groups were defined by ethnic identity).[194] Others studies have suggested that it is more difficult to recognize faces of those in the out-group,[195] including recognition and interpretation of facial expressions.[196] On the other hand, the mirroring system is also implicated in being able to *reduce* the empathy gap. In an innovative study Michael Inzlicht, Jennifer Hutsell, and Lisa Legault found that they could reduce racial prejudice in experiment participants by having them mimic the movements of a member of the group that they are prejudiced against.[197] The authors hypothesize that part of what defines prejudice is the lack of empathic connection with others; by explicitly invoking the mirroring system individuals are able to empathize more with others. Put another way, prejudice reduces the ability to resonate with out-groups, but resonating with the actions of the out-group can also reduce prejudice. Visuality reduces prejudice. Similarly, as mentioned earlier, emotional intelligence is correlated with empathy and deception detection while narcissism is inversely correlated with deception detection. Further, as Hall and Yarhi-Milo argue, readings of others through empathy may be particularly important in times of information scarcity, ambiguity, or cognitive stress, where leaders are searching for ways to understand one another.[198]

---

[190] Klein and Hodges 2001, 721.     [191] Klein and Hodges 2001, 727.
[192] See, for example, Emile Bruneau's work on parochial empathy, the difference between ingroup empathy and outgroup empathy. Cikara, Bruneau, and Saxe 2011; Bruneau et al. 2012.
[193] See Gutsell and Inzlicht 2011; and Xu et al. 2009; Bloom 2016.
[194] Gutsell and Inzlicht 2010.     [195] Sporer 2001.
[196] Elfenbein and Ambady 2002.     [197] Inzlicht et al. 2012.
[198] Hall and Yarhi-Milo 2012.

The mirroring system is, however, also universal in a number of important, and surprising, respects. Neuroscientists and philosophers of the mind have suggested that the simulation circuit created between individuals is a universal phenomenon, with most individuals possessing the architecture required for simulating the mental states of even dissimilar others. Deficits to the mirroring system limit empathic capabilities, and it is also likely that individual differences on the other side of the spectrum, individuals with more robust mirroring systems, are capable of a type of "super-empathy," with most individuals falling somewhere in the middle of the empathy bell curve.[199] As mentioned above, empathy can, to a certain extent, also be practiced and learned. Lutz et al. found that Buddhist monks, who had years of training, practice, and meditation devoted to developing empathy and compassion for others, displayed greater activation of empathy networks than untrained control groups;[200] long-term meditation practice has also been linked to thicker brain regions associated with empathy tasks.[201] Even individuals who are very different from those they are observing, such as individuals born without hands and feet, are able to mirror the actions of those born *with* hands and feet.[202] More generally, however, subjects who score highly on standard empathy measurement scales also tend to show higher activation with empathy-circuit and mirroring systems in the brain.[203]

Finally, returning to the early mirroring experiments, specificity of intention plays a very important role in the ability to successfully intuit intentions. Mirror neurons fire the most when they are engaged in simulating a specific intention act, rather than a vague one, even if that specific intention is shielded or deceptive in nature. This implies an important scope condition for empathy generated in face-to-face interactions: we should expect the level of intention specificity to matter for intention understanding. Put another way, one reason why Bush may have read Putin incorrectly has to do with specificity. The mirroring system does not mirror "senses," or general trustworthiness; it mirrors specific intentions and specific actions. Whereas Gorbachev and Reagan iterated over a series of meetings where very specific intentions were discussed and conveyed, Bush's gleaning of a sense from Putin did not involve a similar level of intention specificity. Bush thought that he could look Putin in the eye and judge his trustworthiness; the error was not in thinking that others can be read, but rather *what* can be read. Reading specific intentions is a different activity than reading the generalized soul.

[199] Baron-Cohen 2011, 177-181.  [200] Lutz et al. 2004.
[201] Lazar et al. 2005.  [202] Keysers and Gazzola 2007.
[203] Singer et al. 2004; Singer et al. 2006.

The iteration of interaction becomes particularly important when it comes to belief change. As noted earlier, since intuitions are the realm of System 1 and beliefs the realm of System 2, belief represents a stickier, and less conducive to change, mental state. Further, because System 2 includes the "psychological drivers" discussed above, intuitions face a particularly uphill battle in changing beliefs. A question emerges from this discussion as to how intention beliefs may change or update over time. While the question of belief change, particularly with respect to how it comes about, is far from settled in psychology and philosophy of mind, there is often a distinction made between belief updating and belief revision. With belief updating new information is taken into account in the present and old beliefs are changed to take account of the new information. Revision, on the other hand, occurs when new information shows an inconsistency between new and old information and the belief is changed in such a way to account for the inconsistency. Belief revision represents more minimal change than belief updating. In the case of intention intuitions changing intention beliefs, it is likely the case that we are more often dealing with belief revision than updating. Since beliefs are sticky, and intuitions may represent inconsistencies between old beliefs and new information, they are likely to require several iterations of revising before they are fully changed. Returning to the Gorbachev and Reagan example, which will be the focus of the next chapter, the iteration that occurred in their meetings led to a series of belief revision over time. Beliefs were not updated and changed completely when the first face-to-face intention intuition was engendered, but rather the beliefs required incremental revising in order to change.[204]

### Special Problems for Individual-Level Psychological Arguments

Theories of international politics that are based in the individual-level of analysis, or "first image," necessarily run up against special problems of causal inference. These include the problem of aggregating individuals upward to the state decision-making apparatus, identifying the relative causal weight of individuals versus structural factors such as power, the

---

[204] In this way the incremental process of System 1 intuitions changing System 2 beliefs is consistent of an interpersonal socialization perspective where individuals come to understand each other better through iterative interactions, though importantly in my case the intention intuitions are accessible without socialization. Iterative interaction and the socialization that often follows, in other words, is not necessary for the creation of intention intuitions, though as discussed above with deception may indeed make those intuitions more accurate.

theoretical and empirical difficulties of accessing internal beliefs that motivate individuals, and dealing with the limits of psychology and neuroscience evidence. In this section I focus on the issues of psychology, in particular, and attempt to deal with the aggregation and causal inference problems both in the case studies themselves as well as the concluding chapter of the book.

### *Accessing Beliefs Theoretically and Empirically*

It is often stated that it is difficult to attribute behavioral causality to a particular belief or set of beliefs. As a mental state, beliefs are difficult to access and even if one could be reasonably sure that one had a correct read of another's mental state, behavior that follows does not necessarily imply that the underlying belief served as the motivation for that action.[205] O'Mahoney refers to this as the "fundamental problem of reason attribution" in IR.[206] This creates a difficult problem as it relates to investigating intuitions, or the intention beliefs that may follow, since it is difficult to gain access to one of the main causal variables identified in this book.

While this critique, raised recently in response to the burgeoning constructivist literature on framing and rhetoric, is an important one, there are reasons to believe that the fundamental issue of attribution here is overstated.[207] First, most analysts of international politics are interested in making probabilistic accounts of motivation, and therefore would concede certainty at the outset. Second, without attempting to theorize the mental states that drive behavior we are often left with an unsatisfying account of political action. While it is certainly true that attributions of motivation can be unsatisfying because of the uncertainty problem, so too are accounts that eschew the endeavor entirely. Ultimately if we think that beliefs matter and that actor behavior can be partly attributable to those beliefs, at least some of the time, then explanations that are devoid of beliefs will be inherently unsatisfying since they are missing an important piece of the puzzle.

---

[205] Note that here I use the term motivation only with reference to understanding the action that follows from an *intention belief*. That is, empirically if one wants to demonstrate that a particular belief was the basis of an action, as I will suggest in the subsequent chapters regarding intention beliefs, then it is important to have some way of articulating how an intention belief motivates action. Motives and intentions should not be conflated, though they often are. Motives are "primitive" and useful for determining state type. Intentions are action-oriented and "result from the interaction of a state with its international environment." See Glaser 2010, 38 and O'Mahoney 2015, 235.

[206] O'Mahoney 2015, 232.     [207] Krebs and Jackson 2007.

Further, political psychologists have documented the predictable ways in which individual behaviors relate to cognitive biases, emotional processing, simulation of intentions, and so forth, all of which problematize the notion that we never get an accurate sense of what is motivating behavior.[208] Nevertheless, the core of the Krebs and Jackson critique is an important one that can be divided into two versions, hard and soft. The hard problem of motive attribution is that we can never be certain in our appraisal of action; the soft version posits that while motive attribution is difficult, we can be probabilistic in our attempts to understand motivations. Accepting the existence of the hard problem does not necessarily imply that we should give up as long as we are willing to settle for solving only the soft version. Innovative empirical designs, including triangulation of multiple sources on beliefs and other motivating factors can help to overcome the soft, if not the hard, version of the problem, as I detail below.

### *The "Big Debate": The Limits of Empathy, Neuroscientific Evidence, and Mirroring*

In addition to challenges posed by levels of analysis and accessing the motivations of actors, there are other challenges that face utilizing brain systems in particular. For example, there is still disagreement on the precise *meaning* of the mirroring system, particularly mirror neurons. While many leading neuroscientists tout their remarkable qualities and suggest profound meaning for understanding social relations, others vigorously dispute the importance of the neurons and believe many of the findings are little more than hype when it comes to complex social behaviors. Put another way, there is healthy skepticism that we can learn anything meaningful about complex social and political behaviors from mirror neurons.

Part of the disagreement relates to the debate above about how to conceptualize precisely what the mirroring system is providing, be it knowledge or intuition or something else. Relatedly, it is often difficult to understand what precisely the activation of a mirror neuron *means*. As Glenberg asks, "If a cell responds to visual stimulation with, say, 50% of the activity observed when the action is produced, does that count as mirroring?"[209] In other words, in many instances researchers can identify mirror neurons activation, but interpreting this activation and

---

[208] For example, with respect to emotional processing, see Bleiker and Hutchison 2008; Mercer 2010; Hutchison and Bleiker 2014; Bially-Mattern 2011; Ross 2014; Hall and Ross 2015.

[209] Glenberg 2011a.

the role the activation plays in social cognition requires theory building and development.

When it comes to theory building, a critical question revolves around the extent to which a focus on mirror neurons, with their latent link to motor actions, may be overemphasized with respect to social cognition.[210] That is, most of the mirror neuron studies to date have focused on relatively simple motor tasks and not the more abstract beliefs that are an integral part of social relations.[211] Some have suggested that present evidence only points directly to mirroring in motor actions and therefore making the link between motor and higher level abstract intentions is tantamount to putting the cart before the horse.[212] Put simply, mirror neurons might be necessary in understanding actions, but they may not be sufficient to explain inference of unobservable mental states. On this view, the simulation that is occurring may be at the facial expression and emotional level, but not of higher-level intentions, and thus a heavy dose of skepticism is warranted.

Skeptics of mirror neurons supporting higher-level intention understanding often point to the difficulties of isolating simulation of facial effects from simulation of intentions in face-to-face interactions, since both are occurring simultaneously. Others counter by noting the strong evidence for very sophisticated high-level belief understanding, particularly with respect to emotion and the effects of deficiencies in the mirror neuron system.[213] Further, there are links between more robust forms of empathy, such as those that require high-level mindreading, and the mirror neuron system.[214] Those that report "being more empathic in life," measured by empathy questionnaires, are often associated with greater mirror neuron system activation. The same is true for individuals who are observing facial expressions – more MNS activity is associated with higher scores on empathy scales.[215] Research into the mirroring system,

[210] Hickok 2014 has provided one of the strongest critiques against this type of analysis, determining mirror neurons to be a "myth." Hickok actually does not argue that mirror neurons do not exist, but rather that many of the assumptions underlying some of the claims made about mirror neurons are problematic and this leads to unfounded hype surrounding the neurons. I am sympathetic to this perspective, particularly given the attention mirror neurons have been given in popular media. In this section I address the assumptions that Hickok finds to be problematic and note that his perspective is instructive in assessing the types of claims we should be making based on mirror neuron evidence. I also argue, however, that despite the problems Hickok identifies, there is still very good reason to believe that mirror neurons play a crucial role in face-to-face intention understanding. For a strong critique of Hickok, see Keysers 2015.

[211] Jacob and Jeannerod 2005.    [212] See, for example, Spunt et al. 2011.

[213] Dapretto et al. 2006; Iacoboni and Dapretto 2006.

[214] See Baird, Scheffer, and Wilson 2011 for a review of this literature.

[215] As Keysers, Thioux, and Gazzola (2013, 244) point out, this literature is still developing and not all studies have been able to replicate the same findings, but the links that

and mirror neurons in particular, is still in its relative infancy and consequently scholars are still debating the wide-ranging ramifications of the system. These debates will presumably continue for some time and all of the answers are not in.

While there is much that we do not know about the mirroring system, and future research will continue to refine, and perhaps even refute our current understanding, one aspect of the debate deserves clarification before proceeding. It is sometimes stated that the "jump," or as Marco Iacoboni terms it "long reach," between simple laboratory experiments with monkeys and bananas to humans with politics and social life is simply too big of a leap. When making that leap the theoretical claims quickly outpace what is available to test experimentally. While this is an important point, and one that needs to be made at the outset as an underlying assumption to the theory, the fact that mirror neurons and other systems are tested in relatively simple laboratory environments does not mean that they are *only* activated or implicated in those simple designs. Indeed, the epistemology and methodology of psychology and social neuroscience relies on using simple designs to identify core features of a system and then using theory to extrapolate those features for more complex environments, where the interaction of genes, environment, and brain makes for an incredibly complex social brain to navigate.[216]

Many of the insights that we have from social neuroscience are based in animal models, where researchers can manipulate neural systems in order to understand the mechanisms that underlie social processes.[217] Therefore, just as psychology, and increasingly political science, utilizes simplified laboratory experiments in order to identify core causal factors, so too does social neuroscience. In addition, social neuroscience has utilized deficit models, instances where individuals with unfortunate diseases or physical limitations have overt deficits in particular brain regions. This allows researchers to identify function of brain regions by comparing the individual with the deficit to a distribution of behaviors.

Despite the absence of a comprehensive theory of mirror neurons and lack of knowledge about their role in social cognition, there is much agreement that mirror neurons challenge the mainstream view in cognitive science that action, perception, and cognition are separate domains.[218] Mirror neurons suggest that these elements are intimately connected, with simulation serving as the mechanism that ties them

do exist provide a correlation between mirror neurons and intentions (the thin version of empathy) as well as a thicker, more robust, high-level form of empathy.

[216] See, for example, Decety 2011.     [217] Cacioppo et al. 2007.
[218] Glenberg 2011b.

together. This has led many to reconsider the ways we think about the problem of other minds. Rather than consulting a database of experiences and constructing a folk psychology theory about the mental states of others, an act of approximating the intentions of others, the mirroring system suggests that we come to know what others are thinking by simulating their intentions, beliefs, and so forth, in our own brains. While some may remain skeptical that simulation and mental mimicry of high-level mental states are possible in the same way that they are with low-level action intention understanding, a review of the evidence suggests that they are. As Goldman and Jordan conclude about this critical question: "Is there really evidence for a tight enough similarity between pretend and genuine states to support high levels of mindreading accuracy? Yes."[219]

This is *not* to say that theorizing about the mental states of others has no place, but rather there is another mechanism that explains how individuals are able to understand, and predict, the behaviors of others. Theorizing and reflection are part of this process, but mirroring and simulation are antecedent to them and provide the important raw material for intention belief-creation. Ultimately face-to-face interaction is critical to intention understanding because it is there that simulation of intentions takes place; previous takes on intention understanding from afar are based on a TT mode of reasoning and approximation.

Nevertheless, it remains true that studying the mirroring system in complex environments and in a messy social world is difficult. Constructing experiments that definitively show a strong role for mirroring in actual interactions among leaders, or even experiment participants, is not easy. Disaggregating mirroring of the specific intentions, for example, from other types of mirroring, such as facial expressions, emotions, and so forth, is a particularly challenging proposition (though mere mirroring of facial expressions and emotions is also useful for understanding intentions).[220] These difficulties are paralleled in any discipline where simple experimental designs are utilized to gain insights into more

---

[219] Goldman and Jordan 2013, 453.

[220] What follows from this discussion is that there are different types of experimental evidence required for two different activities that are important to understanding intentions. Evidence of emotional and facial expression simulation supports the claim that face-to-face interactions aid individuals in reading intentions because they allow individuals to interpret behavioral clues to sincerity and deception. Evidence of intention simulation in the brain would support the claim that face-to-face interactions aid individuals in reading intentions because they are able to simulate the intention for themselves when interacting in a face-to-face encounter. There is more evidence to support the first claim than the second, though largely because of the difficulties of disaggregating the two activities experimentally.

complicated behavior, though the introduction of brain and biological systems complicates the matter further. Therefore, in interpreting brain and other biological evidence one must decide for oneself how comfortable one is extrapolating from simple designs to more complex environments.

At some level, basing a theory on neuroscientific evidence requires, in the scientific realism tradition,[221] placing a *theoretical bet* on the innerworkings of the human mind in action, since we cannot draw a direct causal arrow between the hypothesized functioning of neurons to complex political behaviors, nor can we observe the hypothesized mechanism in real-world politics. Indeed any approach to IR that either seeks to systematically incorporate theoretical findings into a complex and messy environment, or seeks to provide a theoretical mechanism that explains observable findings, must make a similar wager; neuroscience is not special in this regard. Consider work that incorporates psychological or sociological principles, such as emotion, identity, or rationality, and attempts to appropriate that concept into IR. Doing so *necessarily* requires that a theoretical bet be made, either regarding an assumption or unobservable mechanism. Work in emotion is not just wagering that emotions play a role in decision-making in the external "real-world" environment just as they do in the sterile confines of the social psychology laboratory, but also that there is some mechanism in the body, as of yet largely unidentified, that produces particular emotions under certain conditions and other emotions under other conditions. And, once this occurs, a second bet is often placed that such emotions can "scale up" to the social/group level.[222] Positing the existence of emotions that emerge as a group-level property and have specific effects is necessarily making a very large theoretical wager. Similarly, rational choice theorists largely agree that they are making a wager that individuals in political environments operate, under identifiable conditions, in a goal-oriented manner. They are not only betting that we can translate what occurs in simplified economic games to the real world environment with individuals but that this can scale up to the aggregate level as well, similar to emotion. These bets do not just apply to psychological or sociological-based theories. Nexon

---

[221] By scientific realism I refer to a particular style of reasoning that includes the stipulation of "the existence of mind-independent entities – observables and unobservables alike – that provide the ontological basis which constrains and enables human action" (Michel 2009, 401). Put simply, there exists a world "out there" independent of our minds and it can be studied. A point of emphasis in the scientific realist tradition is the role for causal mechanisms, even those that might be unobservable in nature. This is in contrast to "a postfoundationalist perspective that suggests that mechanisms are not 'real' or existing 'out there'" (Pouliot 2007, 374).

[222] Sasley 2011; Mercer 2014.

argues that balance of power theory is "defined by a core wager: that systemic balances of power represent some kind of natural tendency of international politics."[223] Further Wendt has recently placed a theoretical bet regarding the nature of physical, including social, systems.[224] And, as argued earlier, IR theorists have made the bet that intentions are fundamentally unknowable.

The key point is that any approach to IR needs to make certain theoretical bets in order to generate testable theory. It may be that we cannot yet see the proposed mechanism (in this case neural mechanism) operating at the level of real-world politics and we may never be able to see it, but that is a type of bet that is made routinely in IR – for we cannot directly see emotions in the body, emotions as a social property, goal-oriented behavior in the body, quantum mechanics, or the "natural tendency" of systems to seek balance – as well as the other social and natural sciences. Neuroscience itself is not immune from needing to make bets, but it has a significant advantage in identifying a mechanism that one can look for in the brain and thus allows the theory to be falsifiable. While it is exceedingly difficult to falsify the existence of group emotions, it is theoretically possible to demonstrate that mirror neurons are not involved in the processing of high-level political intentions in face-to-face interactions with technology.

In the end, however, no amount of future research and evidence will likely allow us to draw the causal arrows as neatly and cleanly as we would like. The mechanism is observable in the laboratory while not observable outside of it, creating a disjuncture between what we can see. Rather, in my view, the best we can do is to take what we know based on current neuroscientific evidence (the mirroring system), determine what that evidence likely means, and the limitations of it, for social interaction based on our current understanding of such processes (support for ST and the importance of face-to-face), and use those insights to bootstrap a theory and develop propositions regarding political interaction. This allows us to create a falsifiable theory that is open for investigation in real world politics. Phil Tetlock has argued that this ultimately is the value of psychology: combining its insights with "independent evidence that the hypothesized psychological processes are indeed operating in the political world."[225] Insights from brain systems, such as the mirroring system, can provide useful hypotheses about social behavior that are testable in the political world. Therefore, even if the theoretical bet does

---

[223] Nexon 2009, 335; quoted in Monteiro 2014, 87.     [224] Wendt 2015.
[225] Tetlock 1998, 870.

not pay off, the insights gained by investigating its hypothesis in the real world should pay dividends.

Lastly, there is value in engaging in debates in other disciplines that are not yet settled. If we are to build meaningful bridges between psychology/neuroscience and international relations, there is no better way than to actively engage with debates that are occurring in both disciplines. The unsettled science, in other words, is beneficial to more productive dialogue between our fields. As Rose McDermott has argued, neuroscience and international relations are often interested in the same questions, the origins of theory of mind, our beliefs, intentions, desires, and so forth, being chief among them. International relations can bring a unique perspective to this debate because we have our own understanding of the origins of these concepts. Our debates are not settled, nor are theirs, but the parallel in question with divergence in approach aligns neatly for bridges to be built.[226] Or as Ralph Adolphs, one of the leading figures on theorizing the social brain puts it, "mapping social processing onto social brain structures may be an iterative way to make progress, bootstrapping our understanding of both even though each requires revision."[227] We need not be afraid of revising our theories and understanding as new evidence becomes available, either on the neuroscientific side or the social side.

In particular, one of the calls neuroscientists studying mirror neurons have made recently is the need for more interdisciplinary debate and discussion.[228] The reason for this is intentionality is not, at its root, a biological construct. It is largely a philosophical one. As Bonini et al. argue, there is simply not a general consensus regarding how we think about, describe, or explain intentions in human beings.[229] Patricia Churchland, for example, has expressed skepticism about mirror neurons because they are based on assumptions that involve unresolved philosophical issues.[230] The answers to these questions will not come from neuroscience alone, but will rather be drawn from dialogue with other disciplines. International relations can help to clarify this debate by providing how we think about intentions, both individual and collective, which will help neuroscience to refine its theories and measurement.[231] Put another

---

[226] On the contribution of political science to neuroscience specifically, see McDermott 2009.

[227] Adolphs 2010.     [228] See, for example, Antonietti 2013.

[229] Bonini, Ferrari, and Fogassi 2013.     [230] Churchland 2011, Chapter 6.

[231] Or, as one leading neuroscientist working on mirror neurons recently told me at a conference, "We need you [international relations scholars] to tell us how you think about these things and what *you* need to know from us!"

way, neither neuroscience nor international relations can, or should, wait until we, or they, believe we have everything figured out.

### Revisiting Alter and Ego: Propositions Regarding Face-to-Face Diplomacy

Bringing these diverse findings on face-to-face interaction, from behavioral outcomes to identification of psychological and neural processes, together, a number of specific propositions regarding face-to-face diplomacy can be identified. In particular, the mirroring system and its related processes suggest a very different interpretation of the Alter/Ego problematique discussed above. In this section I first will re-examine the Alter/Ego interaction in light of the mirroring system and delineate specific propositions that will be empirically investigated in the remainder of the book. Ultimately, while we cannot test brain systems directly in action in actual politics, we can derive expectations and predictions about the effects of those systems in social environments that can be investigated empirically.

Absent knowledge of the mirroring system and its ability to simulate specific intentions, the interpretation of Alter and Ego, engaged in a face-to-face interaction, is that they are forced to interpret the behavioral moves of the other with little to go on. As discussed, social constructivists are more sanguine about the ability to correctly interpret these moves than others. As Copeland argues, "Wendt's analysis offers no basis for saying when peaceful gestures should be taken at *face value*, and when they should be discounted as deceptions."[232] Put another way, there is not a theory provided that links behavioral gestures to intentions. Or, as Checkel puts it succinctly, "constructivists offer no theory of social learning,"[233] which serves as the main promise for approximating intentions in Wendtian constructivism. Without a mechanism to understand the meaning of gestures and to be able to differentiate sincere from deceptive moves, this approach is open to such a line of critique. Subsequent constructivist analyses have theorized social learning from a number of different angles, such as argumentation and persuasion.[234] The mirroring system in individuals, however, provides a different and two-pronged response to this problem: a very robust way to simulate the intentions of the other and, at least under certain conditions, detect deception as well. The analysis above suggests that behavior *can*, in some instances, speak for itself. This suggests that Wendt's "mirror theory" of identity

---

[232] My emphasis.     [233] Checkel 2001, 561.     [234] Risse 2000; Checkel 2001.

formation has material support in the brain and body in the form of an actual mirror, the mirror neuron.

Additionally, given the mirroring system's ability to interpret intentional behavioral actions, the lack of a shared linguistic basis need not necessarily be as problematic for engendering understanding as some have suggested. The mirroring system is tied to language; it is also tied, however, to visuality. The visual experience of face-to-face contact, replete with facial expressions, micro-expressions, honest signals, and indices, combined with the cross-cultural, and cross-linguistic findings suggest the ability to simulate intentions even in the absence of a robust, thick shared cultural or linguistic framework. The ability to communicate linguistically is still crucial, as others have pointed out, but the analysis here suggests that the visual experience of Alter/Ego can often overcome the problem of not having that ability. Finally, Alter and Ego's intentions may not necessarily be given exogenously, but rather emerge and change through the course of interaction. The visuality of the mirroring system provides the crucial ability to detect the dynamism of intentions, meaning that Alter and Ego are not stuck in a one-off game where intentions are communicated and then each goes their separate ways. Indeed, to the extent that intentions might change as a result of discussion, rhetoric, or even coercion, the mirroring system provides a mechanism for recognizing those changes that are endogenous to the face-to-face interaction itself.

Alter and Ego, however, at the end of the day, are only a thought experiment. Determining the extent to which insights from the experiment travel to real world politics requires specific propositions and empirical investigation. First, all else being equal and at its most basic, face-to-face diplomacy should provide a better route to intention understanding than through other means, both in terms of modality (such as cable wires or letters) and means, such as assessment of intentions from afar based on approximation, theorization, and folk psychology. Relatedly, individuals who have the opportunity to interact with others face-to-face, such as policymakers in country, should derive better understanding of intentions than those who are left to approximate intentions from afar. And, given the dynamic nature of intentions in social interactions, face-to-face interaction should serve to provide an understanding of intention change, should it occur through the interaction.

The literature on the neural mirroring system suggests that simulation of *specific* intentions will be more effective than simulation of broad or general intentions. Similarly, the literature does not suggest that face-to-face diplomacy is a panacea; putting individuals in a room together to "work it out," in a very general sense, is likely to not get very far from a mirroring perspective. Finally, the literature suggests that while deception detection is difficult, face-to-face interactions provide clues and inferences to deception, including the simulation of facial microexpressions, mimicry of behavioral mannerisms, and so forth, that may be picked up on only in face-to-face interactions. Importantly, we should expect that deception detection accuracy will increase with repeated exposure and interactions.

These propositions, like most social scientific claims, are affected by a number of scope and contextual conditions, such as psychological and personality mechanisms, biases, and drivers. These include possessing defensive self-images, ideological fundamentalism, bad faith models of the adversary, long-standing intractable conflict, and narcissism. High levels of narcissism, as mentioned earlier, are particularly important as they negatively affect the accuracy of intention beliefs. Put simply, narcissists are more likely to be fooled in face-to-face interactions. Before continuing with the case studies, it is worth laying out with some precision what these conditions are and their likely effects.

### Countervailing and Supporting Conditions

The preceding theory and propositions that follow from it are bounded by particular context-setting conditions. As Ragin argues, "context-setting conditions," or "scope conditions," abound when studying social phenomena.[235] These conditions "enable or disable" theoretical relationships.[236] In the theory I have tried to identify the boundaries, such as the focus on specific intentions and the role of narcissism, and incorporate them into the theory itself. These serve as conditions that disable the relationship between face-to-face diplomacy and intention understanding.

In this section I will identify what I term countervailing and supporting conditions, those that serve to have a moderating effect on the proposed relationship.[237] The first set of conditions has to do with individual differences and idiosyncrasies. As noted above, face-to-face interaction provides a route to deception detection through the simulation of the interlocutor's intentions. Nonverbal communication is crucial here as it provides clues to the sincerity of the other. As argued earlier, there are some conditions that make face-to-face deception detection more difficult, such as narcissism. In this instance higher levels of narcissism, an

---

[235] Ragin 2009, 73.     [236] Ragin 2009, 73.
[237] As Ragin points out, in more formal terms, if one is positing a relationship between X (face-to-face) and Y (intention understanding), then the question of conditions occurs when a particular level of Z affects the connection between X and Y.

individual trait, moderate the success of face-to-face leading to an accurate intention intuition and subsequent belief. There are other potential conditions that exist at the individual level, however, which may affect the relationship, though may be difficult to test directly. Emotional or social intelligence, the ability to understand one's own, and others', emotional states and the capacity to successfully navigate social relationships,[238] has been linked with the ability to perceive and interpret the expressive cues of others. Indeed, the individuals best at detecting deception are those that score highly on emotional intelligence measures and consequently are able to interpret nonverbal cues accurately.[239]

Relatedly, psychopathy and "Machiavellian intelligence" have historically been characterized by a lack of empathy or shallowness of affect.[240] Importantly, however, psychopaths also possess a strong ability to manipulate others because they often have superior perspective-taking abilities.[241] Indeed new models suggest that cognitive-perspective taking is not impaired in psychopathy, though affective empathy (understanding of emotional states) may well be impaired. What this suggests is that deception detection may be more difficult when the interlocutor possesses individual characteristics that bring a proclivity toward deception. Machiavellian intelligence has also been linked with the ability to use empathy strategically, such as the ability to appear that one possesses great empathic capacity, even if one does not. Lastly, other individual characteristics such as personality likely provide scope conditions as well. For example, as the studies investigating a lack of deception attempts in face-to-face interaction point out, there is likely some type of concern regarding being identified directly as a liar that is moderating deception attempts in a face-to-face setting. Similarly, since individuals presumably care about their reputations and do not want to be discovered as lying, they put considerable cognitive effort into controlling their behaviors which work precisely in the wrong direction of their target, since it is the attempt to control behaviors that often leaks insincerity. Individuals who discount their reputations, or do not believe that they can be discovered as liars, will likely not face the same pressures and therefore be able to deceive more easily. Put more simply, individuals who are not constrained by social norms or are driven by the sui generis nature of their ideology may be better at deception than others.[242]

The second set of conditions has to do with the psychological drivers that may affect the formation of an intention belief from an intention

---

[238] O'Sullivan 2005, 237.    [239] O'Sullivan 2005, 248.
[240] On psychopathy see Hare 2003; Lockwood et al. 2013. For a recent review of Machiavellian intelligence, see Jonason et al. 2014.
[241] Lockwood et al. 2013.    [242] Thanks to Brian Rathbun for pointing this out.

intuition. As mentioned earlier, I suggest that this occurs during the movement from System 1 (intuitions) to System 2 (beliefs). The difficulty arises in that there are a number of different psychological drivers that affect the formation of political beliefs. Consider long-standing intractable conflict where leaders have long histories of disappointment and perhaps perceived unethical behavior. In such instances, individuals may come to face-to-face interactions with a pre-formed set of beliefs about the intentions of the other. Over the course of interaction they may gain an intuition that stands in contrast to their prior-held beliefs, but *changing* that belief likely requires more than a single intuition. The neuroscientific and psychological studies referenced above are normally conducted with complete strangers, individuals without the type of experience and history with others that is quite common in international politics, particularly in intractable conflicts. As Wheeler has noted, bad-faith models, for example, may serve to point individuals toward particular beliefs because the past is influencing the present.

These System 2 psychological drivers can be very hard to overcome. Belief perseverance, while a powerful psychological principle, does not imply that individuals simply reinforce their beliefs upon meeting face-to-face, however. Rather, because of the privileged access doctrine discussed above, where individuals feel more certainty in their intuitions since they are experiencing them for themselves, simulating the intuition in their own physical body, individuals are more likely to privilege the intuition they generate in ST face-to-face than TT intention approximation. Put another way, the empirical cases that follow often demonstrate instances of individuals arriving to an interaction with a pre-formed belief about the intention of the other, generated from afar through approximation, and either confirming or revising that belief based on the intuition that follows from the face-to-face interaction. Prior-held beliefs might predispose individuals to feel a particular way regarding the other's intentions, but they do not preclude face-to-face interaction from providing an entirely different understanding since the mechanisms of ST and TT are entirely different.

In addition to the problems of individual differences and psychological drivers, there are a number of counter-arguments that need to be addressed. Rather than deal with all of them in a single place, I will address them individually as they often appear as counter-explanations of the empirical cases to follow. Three common counter-arguments that will be found in each of the cases that follow are folk psychology/TT approximation of intentions, costly signaling, and trust. The theory presented in this book suggests that ST represents the method by which diplomats and leaders come to understand the intentions of others in face-to-face diplomacy and that this explains their ultimate decisions. If, instead, they privilege intention approximation from afar, or learn little from their face-to-face encounters with respect to intentions, then this would be a problem for the theory and a strong counter-argument to what I am proposing. Similarly costly signaling has been identified as an effective way for states to convey their intentions. If costly signals explain the intention understanding engendered, rather than face-to-face diplomacy, this too would be problematic for the theory. Finally, trust is a particularly thorny problem since the development of intention understanding and the development of trust often go hand-in-hand. If it is indeed trust, or perceptions of trustworthiness of one's counterpart, that explain the decisions made in diplomacy, rather than the face-to-face intention understanding, then this would be problematic. In each of the cases that follow, as well as the concluding chapter in the case of trust, I deal explicitly with these counter-arguments.

### Case Selection and Measurement

Empirically investigating these propositions in diplomacy is challenging for a number of reasons. First, it requires an independent measure of intentions. If "intention" is defined as a diplomat's reading of intentions, the key question becomes how to measure that reading's accuracy. For a compelling empirical case, the intentions of the interlocutor need to be available as well as what intentions the diplomat is reading from the interlocutor. For example, it is important to demonstrate that diplomats not only believe that face-to-face interaction makes a difference from an intention understanding perspective, but to provide evidence that it actually does. This is difficult since the ideal evidence, an independent measure of the mental state of an actor, is not attainable. Nevertheless, what we can do is reconstruct, through triangulation of sources and evidence, with a relatively high level of precision what the diplomat believed the other's intentions to be and what the interlocutors intentions were at the time. Because leaders may not be able to articulate precisely what face-to-face diplomacy is doing for them, they often cannot express precisely what it was that caused them to infer a particular intention. As such, much of what we are looking for is reference to claims of "having a sense," or "feeling," which speaks to intuition. Clearly this is subject to error, and at root the process of knowledge-creation is based on approximation. In any case, such a standard of evidence creates arguably a high bar for empirical research.

Investigating these propositions faces another hurdle: the analysis of face-to-face interactions themselves. Researchers may be able to empirically demonstrate the sincere intentions of the interlocutor as well as the diplomat's reading of those intentions, but it is far more difficult to prove that it was the face-to-face interaction that led to that assessment. One interaction as a source of information cannot be isolated easily from other sources of information. If, for instance, a diplomat has an interaction with another diplomat and uses that meeting as a data point together with data points from classified documents, military intelligence, and so forth, how can the researcher determine that the face-to-face meeting was the decisive factor? Scholars face serious empirical problems in distinguishing the source of intention understanding when there are many potential sources that need to be disaggregated.

On the other hand, if we take what diplomats have to say about their interactions seriously, and we can check up on what they say through triangulation and consilience, then we can gain insight into what was occurring in their minds at the time. Records of conversations with others, meeting minutes, contemporaneous memoirs, and so forth, all provide ways to buttress, or falsify, the claims that leaders and diplomats make. Further, recent evidence suggests that the distance between public statements and private beliefs may not necessarily be that great.[243] Put another way, we need not naively take the words of diplomats at face value in order to reconstruct what was occurring at the time of interaction – other sources of evidence allow for corroboration and gain an assessment of what they were likely thinking, and importantly feeling, at the time.[244] This does not absolve us of the problems of post-hoc rationalization or the value-laden nature of interpreting the past, but it does allow us to combine different types of evidence to revise, or update, our understanding of the past.

Lastly, if face-to-face diplomacy aids in intention understanding, which represents a core problem under anarchy, then it is precisely moments where much is at stake in the international system that the problem of intentions is particularly relevant. This means that a theory of intentions necessarily must grapple with some of the bigger moments in diplomatic history. At the same time, focusing on the "big moments" of international politics may give the false impression that face-to-face diplomacy only matters when there is a lot on the line or an unexpected

---

[243] See, for example, Renshon 2009; Schafer 2000.

[244] One of the more intriguing strategies for assessing mental states in historical cases come from piecing together emotional states experienced by the individuals and communities involved. While difficult to pinpoint what individuals were thinking at any given time, uncovering emotion through letters, deeds, chronicles, and so forth help to uncover the patterns of emotions and "feeling rules" tell individuals how to feel and express feelings. See Hochschild 1979 and Rosenwein 2005.

outcome obtains.[245] This is both an opportunity and a challenge. The opportunity is in providing a potentially new understanding of salient moments in world history. The challenge is that most, if not all, of these moments are likely causally overdetermined.

These methodological obstacles require a specific strategy. Following the advice from John Gerring, who has perhaps done the most to provide a detailed analysis of the usefulness of the case study method and articulated a precise strategy for choosing cases, when it comes to studying decision-behavior, "case study research may offer insight into the intentions, the reasoning capabilities, and the information-processing procedures of the actors involved in a given setting," even if they are inherently unobservable. Importantly, in order to do this we need to identify the causal implications of the theory and find corroborating evidence, through process tracing, for the causal argument.[246] As Gerring suggests, process tracing is "akin to detective work," where "multiple types of evidence are employed for the verification of a single inference – bits and pieces of evidence that embody different units of analysis."[247] Or as Mahoney puts it, "The search for decisive clues and the use of other diagnostic evidence makes process tracing somewhat like the method of discovery employed by detectives, the reasoning carried out by juries, and the guidelines used by physicians when diagnosing illnesses."[248] The aim is to solve a puzzle;[249] this requires a number of steps.

First, in order to deal with problems of selection bias and endogeneity, I am interested in cases where the likelihood of agreement or overall success was low but policymakers nevertheless chose to pursue face-to-face diplomacy, while noting that the theory does not just apply to surprising or unusual outcomes. For example, Jimmy Carter faced tremendous skepticism from some in his administration with respect to the idea of bringing Israeli and Egyptian leadership together in order to craft an unprecedented peace agreement. Given the level of hostility and deep suspicion each side shared for the other, the likelihood of success was low. Indeed in this case, the dogs were not barking until Carter engaged in a series of face-to-face interactions that allowed him to understand the potential for cooperation. The aim of each case study is to answer a relatively simple question: would the outcome of intention understanding (or misunderstanding) be the same were it not for face-to-face interaction? Each case is structured around this counterfactual

---

[245] See, for example, Pouliot's (2016, 8) critique of the "widespread bias toward extraordinary individuals or outcomes" in many existing studies of diplomacy.
[246] Gerring 2007, 45.     [247] Gerring 2007, 173.     [248] Mahoney 2015.
[249] On the virtues of puzzle-based research, see Shapiro 2002; Bleiker 2009, 178–80.

in order to provide as much evidence as possible that it was the face-to-face interaction itself that led to a particular outcome. I follow Levy, who argues that counterfactuals are useful additions to case studies in identifying causal processes. As Levy notes, the "statement that $x$ is a cause of $y$ implies that if the value of $x$ were different, the outcome $y$ would be different."[250] Counterfactuals are always theory-driven, since we can never be certain about the thought-process outcome, but they can provide more analytical leverage than case studies alone. In short, "the more explicit the counterfactual implications of a theory, the better the theory."[251]

Second, dealing with epiphenomenality requires demonstrating that face-to-face diplomacy itself made a difference. In order to deal with this we need cases where the type of interaction varied but other structural considerations, such as power and economics, remained relatively static. Within case variation, where differences in interaction modality occur in a relatively short period of time, such as in the case of the German unification process at the end of the Cold War, is particularly useful. This allows for controlling, to the extent possible in a case study, the structural material environment.

As my theory is one that posits a causal relationship between two variables, specifying and measuring the variables is paramount. In terms of measurement, we should expect variation in interaction modality, i.e. whether the interaction occurs face-to-face or not (the independent variable), to have an effect on intention understanding (dependent variable). The outcome of a diplomat or leaders attempting to understand an interlocutor's intentions that are communicated in a letter, cable wire, or through costly signaling should be different from a diplomat attempting to understand intentions through a face-to-face interaction. We therefore need cases where significant variation of the interaction modality exists in order to measure difference in intention understanding. Ideally, the information provided in both interaction modalities should be the same. For instance, an interlocutor sends the diplomat a cable wire with a proposal at time $t_1$. The interlocutor then meets the diplomat in a face-to-face interaction and presents the same proposal at time $t_2$. We would then look for independent measures of the intentions of both the interlocutor and diplomat at $t_1$ and $t_2$ to measure any change in the dependent variable that resulted from the change in interaction modality. There are many confounding variables that need to be accounted for in such cases, such as preference change between $t_1$ and $t_2$, the presence of actions that may be construed as costly signals, or intention dynamism within an

[250] Levy 2008, 629.     [251] Levy 2008, 631.

interaction itself. Systematic discourse analysis of the meetings, contemporaneous writings, memoirs, and so forth will aid in identifying signals and preference changes as a result of new information. Lastly we will want some indication of the theory's limits through an analysis of scope conditions. This of course is the ideal research design. History presents more ambiguity, making the identification of actual intentions at any given time difficult. But it also presents more dynamism and nuance that can be investigated.

Finally, a note about sources is worthwhile. Given the emphasis in this book on individuals, I take what the individuals involved in the cases *say* about the interactions seriously. The drawback with doing so is that one can never be sure that what is said reflects the truth as it is understood by the individual. There are multiple challenges here. Memoirs, diaries, and so forth are always written for an audience (even if the audience is the author) and as such need to be understood in that context. Additionally, there may be a propensity to funnel historical insights into what Tilly calls a "standard story," a simplified linear representation of a causal sequence of events that, in all likelihood, was nonlinear and complex when it played out. However, the upside of utilizing the words of actual leaders is that we can gain insight into what they were thinking, and saying, as the events unfolded, allowing for process tracing that is impossible to reconstruct without an understanding of what was going through the minds of the individuals involved at the time. In order to deal with the drawbacks associated with taking the words of leaders at face value, I adopt a strategy of triangulation and consilience, the notion that a theory "gains in credibility to the extent that the several pieces of evidence in its favor are unrelated," whenever possible.[252] Put simply, evidence from independent or unrelated sources can often converge on particular conclusions. Comparison of personal accounts with official declassified documents provides further opportunities to deduce the perspectives of the individuals involved at the time. The problems associated with memoirs still remain, but triangulation and consilience severely undercut the issue.

Each of these steps, from careful linking of laboratory findings to real world politics in theory-building and proposition-construction, to triangulation of evidence, appropriation of a consilience strategy, and counterfactual analysis in the cases, contributes to a research design that seeks to make the case for the importance of face-to-face interaction

---

[252] O'Mahoney 2015, 248. On the use of consilience as a strategy for assessing unobservables in actors, such as motives and reasons for actions, see O'Mahoney 2015, especially 248–49.

while avoiding the logical fallacy of inference to the best explanation. Precisely because the mirroring system is difficult to observe in real world politics, the focus here is on demonstrating, through a rigorous empirical strategy, that which is observable in the lab also occurs in the real world.

## The Value of Face-to-Face: An Old Idea, Refreshed

In the end the value of face-to-face diplomacy is an old idea brought into the twenty-first century by new insights from psychology and neuroscience. Social theorists in the 1950s, 60s, and 70s were right to point out that face-to-face is saliently different from other types of communication modalities. We are now in a better position, with the benefit of new technologies and experimental designs, to understand potentially why. In the following four chapters, I assess these new insights, and the propositions that I have derived from them, in four of the most salient cases of diplomatic history in the twentieth century: Cold War reassurance, the unification of Germany, the Camp David Accords of 1978, and "Munich."

# 3     Reassurance at the End of the Cold War

## Gorbachev and Reagan Face-to-Face

### Face-to-Face with the End of the Cold War

Why and how did the Cold War end? Most importantly, why did it end peacefully? These questions continue to be debated and the ramifications of the ending of the Cold War continue to affect current geopolitics. It has become commonplace to hear commentators and scholars, both in the United States and Russia, suggest that the particulars of the Cold War, including unification of Germany[1] in NATO and subsequent NATO expansion Eastward through Poland and other Eastern European states, represent some of the most important causal factors in modern international politics. The relationship of mistrust between the United States and Russia that characterizes much of the first part of the twenty-first century, for example, is often argued to be rooted in the particular circumstances of Mikhail Gorbachev's final negotiations with the United States at the end of the twentieth. Put simply, many believe that Russia was duped by the United States. Others contest this interpretation of the history, noting that a promise regarding NATO expansion was never made. This has created a competition of narratives that may be fueling current conflict, such as the escalation of hostilities in Eastern Ukraine in 2014.[2]

---

[1] There are a number of different framings used to refer to the reestablishment of a unified German state. The process by which this occurred is the subject of the next chapter, but as it will be referenced in this chapter it is worth addressing the various formulations used, including "unification," "reunification," and "Germany unification," "German unification." While these are used interchangeably they often are used to imply different meanings or connotations. Spohr (2000) notes that "reunification" implies the pre-WWII German state being brought back together. The issue with this formulation is that in 1990 this was not the aim, as eastern territories (including Silesia and East/West Prussia) would remain part of Poland. The German government chose to use the term "re-establishing Germany's unity" or "German unification" in order to refer to the post-Cold War Germany initiative. Following this convention I have attempted to use "German unification" throughout this book. For further discussion of the history of this issue, see Spohr 2000, 869.

[2] See, for example, Mearsheimer 2014.

There is also a lingering question about what *specific* role individual leaders played in breaking the cycle of enmity. Recent work has highlighted the importance of the relationship between the Soviet Union's General Secretary Mikhail Gorbachev and US President Ronald Reagan in building empathy and trust between each other.[3] What was it specifically about that relationship, and the face-to-face interactions that helped to create it, that transformed the US–Soviet conflict? Further, what role did interactions among other leaders play? After all, when Ronald Reagan left office at the beginning of 1989, the Cold War was not yet over. The Berlin Wall was still standing and the ramifications of it falling would have to be dealt with. Did the goodwill that existed between Gorbachev and Reagan spill over to relations between Gorbachev and George H.W. Bush, or were those interactions qualitatively different? These questions serve as the motivating inspiration for the next two chapters.

Any complex political outcome is likely to be the result of many causal factors. The end of the Cold War is certainly no exception. The outcome is, as some argue, over-determined because one could provide many very different causal arguments or multiple causal pathways that seek to explain, for example, German unification and indeed all of the arguments could be right, assuming they were not mutually exclusive.[4] They could all be explaining the various processes that come together to produce a complex political outcome and in doing so help to make sense of the larger picture.[5] As one might expect, these explanations vary considerably on the causal factors privileged in the analysis and have engendered significant debate.[6] Soviet economic decline, particularly the economic situation in East Germany, has led many to conclude that ending the Cold War on terms favorable to the United States was the most probable outcome.[7] Others cite the role of leadership, particularly the "Gorbachev Factor," in changing views about where the Soviet Union should be headed, particularly with respect to relinquishing control of East Germany.[8] Still others look at ideas more generally, suggesting that "Gorbachev's New Thinking was a deep, conceptual reassessment of what the US-Soviet relationship 'was.'... It may be that objective conditions were such that the Soviets 'had' to change their ideas about the Cold War but that does not change the fact that in an important sense those ideas *were* the Cold War, and as such changing them by definition changed the reality."[9] Finally, and most recently, there has been a turn

[3] Booth and Wheeler 2008; Wheeler 2013; Wheeler 2018; Gorbachev 1996; Reynolds 2009; Yarhi-Milo 2013; Brands 2015.
[4] Lebow and Stein 2004.    [5] Herrmann and Lebow 2004.    [6] Forsberg 1999.
[7] Brooks and Wohlforth 2002; Brooks and Wohlforth 2003; Davis and Wohlforth 2004.
[8] Brown 1996.    [9] Wendt 1999, 375.

toward understanding the transformation of the international system at the end of the Cold War in *interpersonal* terms. Growing trust, engendered through a series of iterative moves, between Ronald Reagan and Mikhail Gorbachev ultimately resulted in suspension of calculation that helped costly signal interpretation.[10] Thus in addition to power, economics, and leadership, it may be that the meaning of the relationship between the United States and Soviet Union itself changed through the interpersonal, reconstituting what the Cold War, and its ending, meant.

In the following two chapters, I take an interpersonal perspective on the ending of the Cold War and argue that it was successful intention understanding and intention beliefs that followed from face-to-face diplomacy that explain both the timing and outcome of, first reassurance between the US and USSR, and second, German unification in NATO. The opening of the Soviet archives, declassification of US material, recent oral histories, and interviews with high-level decision-makers in office during the period, provide rich primary evidence to draw upon in order to revisit the process by which the Cold War ended. Through careful process tracing of the face-to-face diplomacy that occurred during the lead-up to the Berlin Wall falling, as well as the context and events surrounding those interactions, I illustrate how interpersonal interactions aided in transmitting and clarifying intentions. In so doing, I posit and address a simple counterfactual: would intention understanding between Reagan and Gorbachev, specifically with respect to their peaceful intentions of reassurance, have been obtained were it not for face-to-face interactions?

In this chapter I focus on the critical meetings between Gorbachev and Reagan that ultimately served to reassure both sides of each other's intentions, specifically to pursue a nonviolent end to their states' long-standing conflict. This chapter ends with the George H.W. Bush administration taking office and subsequent "pause" in the deepening of endgame discussions with Gorbachev and the fall of the Berlin Wall that occurs shortly thereafter. In the following chapter, I examine the events that occur in quick succession after the fall of the Wall that ended, ultimately, with Germany's unification and membership in NATO. In both chapters I contend that it is difficult to explain the outcome and timing of the events that followed without taking into account the face-to-face diplomacy between Reagan/Bush and Gorbachev.

Before turning to the salient interpersonal face-to-face meetings between 1985 and 1991 that would ultimately reshape the structure of the international system, it is worth noting the epistemological stance I

---

[10] Wheeler 2018.

take in this chapter, and indeed all of the case studies that follow, with respect to other explanations. Brooks and Wohlforth have aptly identified and termed a "straw man bias" that is particularly strong when it comes to the end of the Cold War, where explanations abound. This bias occurs when scholars "cast others' arguments as deterministic in order to high-light the significance of their own otherwise unremarkable finding that a different causal factor is necessary to explain a given event."[11] My aim here is to investigate whether intention intuitions and beliefs are remark-able *in the first place*. In doing so I do not dismiss or downplay the role of other factors, such as Soviet economic decline, changing ideational structures in Europe, or the development of trust between the main protagonists. As I will suggest at the conclusion of the following chap-ter, face-to-face interactions and the intention beliefs engendered often *complement* and help to refine these existing explanations. As Robert Hutchings, who was at the National Security Council for much of the period discussed in these two chapters, recently put it when examining the role of diplomacy at the end of the cold war, "the contention . . . is not that diplomacy was *more* important than the deeper structural forces at work, but that structure and agency were *both* important."[12] My aim here is to demonstrate the importance of face-to-face interaction as an agentic force that helped to end the Cold War.

### The Puzzle

The puzzle I address in this chapter is two-fold. First, how did Presi-dent Reagan go from calling the Soviet Union an "evil empire" in 1983, with a threat of nuclear war a being very real possibility, to "produc-tive partner" in 1988, where an agreement between the two banned an entire class of nuclear weapons? Second, how did General Secretary Gorbachev come to understand Reagan's sincere designs for the United States' relationship with the Soviet Union? Would it have been possible to engender a similar outcome without face-to-face interactions with one another?

As I will argue, Reagan and Gorbachev both entered office with par-ticular intentions regarding the other's state. Gorbachev possessed a dif-ferent approach to Soviet security than his predecessors. He understood how the security dilemma worked and realized that the Soviet Union viewed itself in a very different way than the United States viewed it. His intentions focused on resolving this disjuncture in image by conveying to the United States that the Soviet Union represented a peaceful actor.

---

[11] Brooks and Wohlforth 2002, 96.    [12] Hutchings 2015, 149–50.

Few in the United States or Europe saw him this way, preferring instead to view him as a cunning wolf in sheep's clothing. It was only after a series of face-to-face interactions with Gorbachev that Reagan was able to see Gorbachev's sincerity regarding his own intentions of not pursuing deceptive practices or, more importantly, aggressive offensive policies.

For his part, Reagan entered the White House with a particular view of Soviet intentions, but he also understood the need to convey the United States' intentions in a personal way. The Able Archer episode of 1983 made it clear to Reagan that successfully communicating intentions was critical. And therefore it was this conjunction of two leaders, both of whom believed in the utility of the personal meeting as a way to convey and understand intentions, that ultimately paved the way for a series of interactions that would effectively end the Cold War.

*The Road to Face-to-Face Interactions*[13]

When asked in May 1988 in Moscow if he deserved credit for positive changes in Soviet behavior since 1985, US President Ronald Reagan responded that "Mr. Gorbachev deserves most of the credit, as the leader of this country."[14] After Reagan's death in 2004, the question was renewed, with American and British media outlets such as *Time* magazine and *The Economist* suggesting that Reagan was "The Man Who Beat Communism."[15] Understanding the dynamics of how the Cold War ended requires going beyond giving credit to one side or the other. Both sides deserve credit for engaging in a series of face-to-face interactions that between 1985 and 1988, beginning at the Geneva Summit, allowed both sides to clarify their intentions to one another, leading to intention beliefs that ultimately reduced mutual insecurity. As David Reynolds recently argued, the Reagan–Gorbachev encounters "helped ensure that the Cold War ended not with a bang or a whimper, but with a handshake."[16]

That such a handshake between US and Soviet leaders would even occur seemed extremely unlikely just a few years earlier. When Ronald Reagan entered the White House as President in January 1981, his administration's approach to the Soviet Union was one of creating

---

[13] The Reagan and Gorbachev interpersonal interactions during the second half of the 1980s have engendered significant scholarly, in addition to former practitioner, attention. See Garthoff 1994; Oberdorfer 1998; Rhodes 2007; Booth and Wheeler 2008; Skinner 2008; Reynolds 2009; Mann 2009; Yarhi-Milo 2014; Pfiffner 2013; Wilson 2014; Brands 2015; Wheeler 2018.

[14] Gorbachev 1996, 457.

[15] *The Economist*, June 12, 2004. Quoted in Blanton 2010, 50.       [16] Reynolds 2009.

aggressive policies that would "[take] the long-term strategic offensive." This was contrasted with previous attempts of "reactive and defensive strateg[ies] of containment."[17] This strategy had multiple components. On the material capabilities side, Reagan would engage in massive defense spending, compelling the Soviet Union to respond in kind, which increased its share of defense spending, and would in turn have salient effects on the Soviet economy. Importantly, however, the aim was not to force the USSR into spending beyond its means, but rather to "provide ourselves with adequate defenses."[18] As Jack Matlock would later argue, "None of the key players were operating from the assumption that we were going to do the Soviet Union in ... Our goal was always to give the Soviets incentives to bring the Cold War to an end."[19] Ideationally, Reagan made clear how the United States interpreted its relationship with its counterpart in the Cold War. In a March 1983 speech, Reagan famously declared the Soviet Union "an evil empire," and "the focus of evil in the modern world."[20]

Two weeks after the "evil empire" speech, Reagan doubled down on the material advantage by publicly proposing the "Strategic Defense Initiative" (SDI), also dubbed "Star Wars," partly due to the fantastical-sounding architecture of the initiative, a program ostensibly designed as a defensive measure to intercept and destroy nuclear weapons. Edward Teller, one of the original architects of the hydrogen bomb, had provided Reagan with an intriguing idea in September 1982: "nuclear weapons can be used in connection with Lasers to be nondestructive except as used to intercept and destroy enemy missiles far above the earth."[21] The core of the program was a plan to use both ground and space-based systems to protect the United States against intercontinental ballistic missiles as well as submarine-launched ballistic missiles. Reagan maintained that the program was a defensive one in nature that replaced the logic of mutually assured destruction (MAD). Though, as is often the case with the defense/offense distinction,[22] the program immediately escalated concerns in the Soviet Union and Europe that the system could be used for mounting a nuclear first-strike.[23]

In order to understand how a president championing a nuclear defense system with strong rhetoric could ultimately engage in productive

---

[17] Schweizer 2003, 130.     [18] Shultz quoted in Rhodes 2007, 190.
[19] Matlock quoted in Rhodes 2007, 190.
[20] Speech to National Association of Evangelicals, Orlando, Florida, March 8, 1983.
[21] Quoted in Wilson 2014, 72.
[22] See, for example, Hopf 1991; Van Evera 1998; Glaser and Kaufmann 1998; Jervis 1978; Glaser 2010.
[23] Reynolds 2009, 346.

negotiations that transformed conflict, Reynolds argues that it is necessary to understand Reagan's passion against nuclear weapons. Central to this was a belief, formed relatively early in Reagan's presidency, "that the Cold War policy of deterrence based on mutually assured destruction was truly insane."[24] Reagan reportedly told the then Deputy National Security Advisor Robert "Bud" McFarlane that "[this] inexorable building of nuclear weapons on our side and the Russians' side can only lead to Armageddon. We've got to get off that track."[25] Thus Reagan was likely sincere when he announced that the ultimate goal of US policy was to "render these nuclear weapons impotent and obsolete."[26]

Importantly, however, any personal views that might lend themselves toward transformative processes necessarily brushed up against contradictions within Reagan's own administration. Casper Weinberger, Secretary of Defense; William Casey, head of the CIA; Robert Gates, Deputy Director for Intelligence at the CIA; and, William Clark, National Security Advisor, were all skeptical of Soviet intentions. In a memo sent from William Clark to President Reagan, though drafted by one of Clark's young advisors, John Lenczowski, he wrote that "So long as our leaders deliver this message [of strength], the Soviets will know that we are not spiritually weak, that we are not Finlandized and that we have not permitted wishful thinking to obscure a clear understanding of Soviet intentions."[27] National Security Decision Directive 75 (NSDD-75), endorsed by Clark, reflected this logic and explicitly invoked Soviet aggressive intentions:

To contain and over time reverse Soviet expansionism by competing effectively on a sustained basis with the Soviet Union in all international arenas – particularly in the overall military balance and geographical regions of priority concern to the United States . . . The U.S. recognizes that Soviet aggressiveness *has deep roots in the internal system*, and that relations with the USSR should therefore take into account whether or not *they help to strengthen this system and its capacity to engage in aggression*.[28]

Reagan signed the directive on January 17, 1983. It did not, however, represent the views of the entire administration.

George Shultz, Secretary of State, was more optimistic.[29] Shultz, two days later, sent Reagan a memorandum entitled "U.S.-Soviet Relations in 1983." The memo argued that "new Soviet activism" could be

---

[24] Reynolds 2009, 346.
[25] Quoted in documentary, "The Reagan Legacy: Star Wars." See also Hey 2006, 83.
[26] March 8, 1983 speech. See also Lettow 2005; Reynolds 2009.
[27] Quoted in Wilson 2014, 68.     [28] NSDD-75. Italics added.
[29] Reynolds 2009, 348.

countered "by starting an intensified dialogue with Moscow."[30] Shultz' view was that the Soviets could be persuaded, were open to negotiation, and could be dealt with on a human level. As Secretary of the Treasury, Shultz had traveled extensively to Leningrad and Moscow and "had learned something of the human dimension to the Soviet Union... the Soviets were tough negotiators but... you could negotiate successfully with them... I respected them not only as able negotiators but as people who could make a deal and stick to it."[31] A few months after the signing of NSDD-75, Shultz told US Senators in a speech that, "Strength and realism can deter war, but only direct dialogue and negotiation can open the path toward lasting peace."[32] Shultz based his argument on the understanding that he gained through experience, by meeting with Russian leaders and attaching particular significance to the human dimension of international affairs.

One of the greatest sources of disagreement between Shultz and others in the administration stemmed from Shultz' desire to have Reagan meet face-to-face with Soviet leadership. As Robert Gates told me, Shultz was a believer in the "personal touch" and, in particular, culling information from personal meetings that could be reported back to the CIA: interests, likes and dislikes, body language, all of these small pieces of information represented important data to Shultz. Getting to know someone personally, he believed, could pay large dividends. Shultz recalls a comment made to him by Helmut Schmidt, the then chancellor of West Germany, when Shultz entered office: "The situation is dangerous; there is no human contact."[33] In February 1983, in an attempt to rectify that, Shultz arranged for Reagan to meet with Ambassador Anatoly Dobrynin, a Washington D.C. resident and by most accounts, someone who "possessed a cosmopolitan outlook and a gregarious demeanor."[34] The plan was to have Shultz and Dobrynin meet with Reagan at the White House. Clark was "furious," but his disapproval did not prevent the plan from moving forward.[35] "We talked for 2 hours," Reagan notes in his diary, "Sometimes we got pretty nose to nose. I told him I wanted George [Shultz] to be a channel for direct contact with [General Secretary of the Communist Party of the Soviet Union, Yuri] Andropov – no bureaucracy involved."[36] It was an important face-to-face meeting with Soviet leadership, not because of any particular content that was discussed

---

[30]  Shultz 1993, 164.    [31]  Shultz 1993, 119.
[32]  Statement to Foreign Relations Committee June 15, 1983; quoted in Matlock 2004, 61.
[33]  Shultz 2013.    [34]  Wilson 2014, 69.    [35]  Wilson 2014, 69.
[36]  Reagan 1990, 558.

but because it paved the way forward for future face-to-face interactions. This was a view that was shared on the Soviet side. "George tells me that after they left the Ambassador said 'this could be an historic moment.'"[37]

Despite the success of this encounter, disagreements between Shultz, on the one hand, and Weinberger and Clark on the other were fierce, leading Shultz to consider resignation at least four times.[38] Disagreements on foreign policy in Reagan's administration are perhaps best exemplified by the succession of six national security advisors, the most in any presidential administration to date.[39] This included William Clark's quiet resignation in October of 1983, precipitated by attempts by Clark to work around Shultz, as well as alleged growing concern in the White House (including that of Nancy Reagan, the First Lady) that Clark's aspirations were more personal than administration-based.[40]

On the Soviet side, succession was also occurring. Brezhnev's death in 1982 signaled the potential for reform with Yuri Andropov, but he died just two years later in February 1984. Andropov was followed by Konstantin Chernenko, who served only a year before dying, in March 1985. During this period of successive leadership in the USSR, Reagan found it difficult to provide a clear account of sincere US intentions from afar. Part of the problem was the incessant turnover; more importantly, however, the United States lacked a personal relationship with the individuals that were coming in and out of office that they could utilize for relationship-building. As Reagan once pointed out with respect to meeting his Soviet counterparts, "You don't just call up and say, 'Yes, let's get together and have lunch,"[41] in order to talk things over. Or, more to the point, "How am I supposed to get anyplace with the Russians if they keep dying on me?"[42]

One of the major catalysts that forced the issue of the personal meeting occurred in November 1983 with the Able Archer episode, a NATO military exercise that included 40,000 US and NATO troops moving across Western Europe. Designed as a training exercise, the event induced tremendous fear in Moscow that an attack from the United States might be imminent. Recently declassified materials suggest that US and British intelligence agencies were very concerned that the Soviets had misinterpreted the exercise. A British Joint Intelligence Committee report notes, for example that "we cannot discount the possibility that at least some Soviet officials/officers may have misinterpreted Able Archer 83

---

[37] Reagan 2007, 131.     [38] Oberdorfer 1998, 41–42, 490; Reynolds 2009.
[39] Reynolds 2009, 349.     [40] See Wilson 2014, 75.     [41] Fischer 1997, 24.
[42] Maureen Dowd editorial, *New York Times*, November 18, 1990.

and possibly other nuclear CPXs [command post exercises] as posing a real threat."[43] What concerned British intelligence is that the Soviet response was uncharacteristic of a war games scenario. They did not respond in the way that indicated a training exercise: it "took place over a major Soviet holiday, it had the form of actual military activity and alerts, not just war-gaming, and it was limited geographically to the area, central Europe, covered by the NATO exercise which the Soviet Union was monitoring."[44] Much of the intelligence the British authorities were working with at this time was supplied by Oleg Gordievsky, a Soviet defector who had intimate knowledge of the Moscow psyche. Margaret Thatcher, recognizing the danger invoked by Able Archer, ordered officials to "consider what could be done to remove the danger that, by miscalculating western intentions, the Soviet Union would over-react."[45] The British reports were shared with Reagan and, according to reports, swayed him into a new understanding of the importance of personally clarifying US intentions. It is likely at this moment that Reagan appreciated the deleterious effects of the security dilemma, developing a sensibility toward it, witnessing its effects first hand: an exercise aimed at increasing US security led to increased insecurity, and by some accounts, narrowly missed nuclear war.[46] Able Archer further instilled in Reagan a need to sit down and talk with Soviet leadership.

After Able Archer, Reagan believed that the United States and Soviet Union understood each other in divergent terms. The Soviets did not look at the United States in the same way that the United States did and this would have to change if the security dilemma was to be transcended or escaped. Reagan had the intuition that this type of clarification was best done face-to-face with the Soviet Union's new leader, Chernenko, who took office in February 1984 after Andropov's death. "I have a gut feeling I'd like to talk to him about our problems man to man & see if I could convince him there would be a material benefit to the Soviets if they'd join the family of nations."[47] This meeting was beginning to take shape in March–April 1984 as letters were exchanged which broached the idea of talks. In Reagan's April 7 letter to Chernenko, he laid out the US position clearly: "I want you to know that neither I nor the American people hold any offensive intentions toward you or the Soviet people."[48]

---

[43] British Intelligence Document E14, "Soviet Union: Concern About a Surprise NATO Attack," May 8, 1984.

[44] British Intelligence Document E10, "Draft Minute to [redacted] From Sir Robert Armstrong," undated.

[45] British Intelligence Document E12, "Soviet Concern About a Surprise NATO Attack," April 10, 1984.

[46] cf. Booth and Wheeler 2008, 52–53.    [47] Quoted in Wilson 2014, 82.

[48] Quoted in Wilson 2014, 83.

Chernenko responded by noting that it was difficult for the Soviet Union to believe this, as "the Soviet Union is encircled by a chain of American military bases. These bases are full of nuclear weapons. Their mission is well known – they are targeted on us."[49] Rather than dismissing the letter, Reagan seemed to internalize their logic. "Do you suppose they really believe that? I don't see how they could believe that – but it is something to think about."[50] Reagan notes in his diary regarding a potential summit, "I have a gut feeling we should pursue this . . . His reply to my letter is in hand & it lends support to my idea that while we go on believing, & with some good reason, that the Soviets are plotting against us & mean us harm, maybe they are scared of us & think we are a threat. I'd like to go face to face & explore this with them."[51] As James Graham Wilson argues, "Reagan always yearned for a man-to-man meeting with a Soviet leader." Now the need seemed as high as ever. The Soviets were convinced that the United States had offensive intentions and Reagan was beginning to appreciate how this could be the case from afar. Clarifying US intentions would require, as Reagan intuited, a face-to-face meeting with Soviet leadership at the highest level.

Mikhail Gorbachev's rise to leadership of the Soviet Union in 1985 therefore came at an important time for the United States with respect to a desire to clarify intentions. After Chernenko's death in March, both Vice President George H.W. Bush and Shultz traveled to Moscow for the funeral and to meet Gorbachev for the first time. They brought with them a letter of invitation for Gorbachev to travel to Washington for a summit. "You can be assured of my personal commitment to work with you and the rest of the Soviet leadership in serious negotiations. In that spirit, I would like to invite you to visit me in Washington at your earliest convenient opportunity."[52] Understanding the crucial need to clarify intentions, Gorbachev was very candid with the two US leaders: "The USSR has never intended to fight the United States and does not have such intentions now. There have never been such madmen within the Soviet leadership, and there are none now."[53] Shultz' impressions based on the face-to-face interaction were positive: "[T]he result was a certain Gorbachev euphoria in the air."[54] Further indications of being able to work with Gorbachev come from Shultz' aide's notes: "[C]onfident but not overbearing. Can decide things. Businesslike and bright. Sense of humor. Can be provoked but keeps control." In summation a "very different kind of person from the others."[55]

[49] Quoted in Wilson 2014, 83.    [50] Quoted in Fischer 1997.    [51] Reagan 2007, 287.
[52] Quoted in Wilson 2014, 92.    [53] Shultz 1993, 530.    [54] Shultz 1993, 532.
[55] Quoted in Oberdorfer 1998, 110.

*Gorbachev and Reagan Face-to-Face*

Almost immediately upon ascending to power, Gorbachev demon-strated that Shultz' intuitions of being a "very different kind of per-son" were in fact accurate. Gorbachev ushered in a sequence of uni-lateral arms reductions proposals and concessions. Coinciding with the fortieth anniversary of the Hiroshima bombing in August 1985, the Soviet Union announced that it would "unilaterally end any nuclear explosions,"[56] meaning an effective ban on nuclear testing. Many in Washington questioned whether Gorbachev actually intended anything new or whether the Soviet Union was simply buying time. Shultz, for example, was skeptical and rejected the ban on nuclear testing, noting that "history has shown when [the Soviets] feel they need to test, they'll break out of it with a bang."[57] There was reason for the United States to be skeptical. After all, the end of nuclear testing announcement was made in conjunction with the conclusion of a series of nuclear tests. It would be easy for the Soviets to proclaim an end to testing, since another round would presumably not be required again for some time. The United States was engaged in a process of theorizing about Soviet intentions from afar and attempting to interpret the costly signals sent from Moscow. They were interpreting public discourse and the actions that the Soviets were taking and used folk psychology principles to gather their intentions. It was a commonsense position that an enemy would say that they are going to ban testing precisely when they no longer need test-ing. To take such an action at face value would be foolish, the argument went. In the end, many in Washington concluded that the Soviets were engaged in continued gamesmanship.

The United States would respond in kind. After inviting Soviet inspec-tors to Nevada to examine the US' nuclear testing sites, the United States conducted its own nuclear test days later, on August 17. Shortly after that the United States tested antisatellite missiles and created a new US Space Command for coordination of military operations in outer space.[58] As Wheeler argues persuasively, these moves are best under-stood as attempts to continue development of Reagan's SDI.[59] Reagan might have understood the security dilemma, but he was still ultimately unsure of Soviet intentions and justified SDI as a way of ridding the world of nuclear weapons. For his part Gorbachev showed a remark-able sensibility in understanding how Soviet moves could lead to "con-fusion . . . uncertainty [and] anxiety" with respect to Soviet intentions.[60]

---

[56] Quoted in Goldstein and Freeman 1990, 112.    [57] Quoted in Evangelista 2002, 265.
[58] Goldstein and Freeman 1990, 117.    [59] Wheeler 2018.
[60] Goldstein and Freeman 1990, 118.

During this period, from March 1985 to November 1985, both leaders were unsure of the other's intentions but also wanted to break the
cycle of gamesmanship. A series of letters were exchanged that conveyed
the desire from both sides to have a frank face-to-face discussion. The
letters, starting with Reagan's to Gorbachev are cordial, respectful, and
make clear that while significant differences between the two sides exist,
sitting down together can help to overcome them. Reagan in the first
letter invites Gorbachev to Washington for serious negotiations. Two
weeks later Gorbachev responds, noting the "great importance [of] contacts at the highest level. For this reason I have a positive attitude to the
idea you expressed about holding a personal meeting between us . . . The
main thing is that it should be a meeting to search for mutual understanding on the basis of equality and account of the legitimate interests of each other." Shortly thereafter Reagan responded in a manner
that reaffirmed the importance of a "new opportunity for a high-level
exchange of views between our two countries . . . I believe meetings at
the political level are vitally important if we are to build a more constructive relationship between our two countries." In effect, both leaders were conveying their intuition that a face-to-face meeting would be
important, and potentially transformative, for the US–Soviet relationship, setting the stage for their first interaction in Geneva in November
1985.

It is important to note that while both leaders were looking forward
to the interaction with each other, the baseline upon which they viewed
each other was skepticism and caution. Gorbachev noted of the American team he saw at the Chernenko funeral, "The general impression
that the American delegation left is, I tell you honestly, quite mediocre.
This is not a very serious team."[61] Gorbachev also found some of
Reagan's letters to be "amorphous and general."[62] For his part Reagan
was still not convinced that Gorbachev was as different as many were
conveying to him. "If he wasn't a confirmed ideologue he never would
have been chosen,"[63] further noting that "I'm too cynical to believe that
[Gorbachev is different than past Soviet leaders]."[64] Matlock did his best
to disabuse Reagan of this belief, noting in a psychological profile provided in the run-up to Geneva that Russia possesses an "abiding fear of
war," which influences many of their statements and policies, but importantly one needs to look behind the stated discourse to understand true
intentions. "Matlock recalled instances when Soviets had told him privately that none of them actually believed the official rhetoric. They said

[61] Conference of Secretaries of the CC CPSU, March 15, 1985.
[62] Quoted in Wilson 2014.      [63] Reagan 2007, 317.      [64] Reagan 2007, 337.

certain things publicly because they had to."[65] This insight, derived from Matlock's personal interactions, instilled in Reagan a sense that perhaps the deep-seated anti-American ideology was not as deep-seated as Reagan had previously assumed. Just as importantly, other intentions lay behind the public rhetoric.

Nevertheless, some of the skepticism verged on overt worry of deception, reflected most clearly in a December 17, 1984 document prepared by the NSC and forwarded on to Reagan. "The principal theme of Soviet strategic deception is to convince us that the political transformation of the US is not a Soviet objective." To the extent that Gorbachev and other Soviets were speaking in terms of change, this was a ploy and a trick. "The very act of sitting at a negotiating table accomplishes this task by leading us to believe that a live-and-let-live policy . . . is acceptable to the Soviets, when in fact it is not acceptable whatsoever." Gorbachev, like Reagan, had hardliners in his administration, but Gorbachev chose to discount them, or if necessary, reassign them.[66] Shultz once again believed that the intelligence report written in Washington was wrong, but Reagan would soon have a chance to find out for himself in Geneva.

## Geneva – November 1985

The Geneva Summit served as the first in a series of steps that would eventually break this cycle of gamesmanship and interpreting the intentions of the other from afar. Declassified transcripts of the Reagan–Gorbachev interactions, which occurred over two days, illustrate the great extent to which the meetings were about trying to gain a specific understanding of the other. Indeed references to intention understanding permeate the transcripts. At their first private meeting, on November 19th, which had been booked by the handlers for fifteen minutes but lasted an hour,[67] Reagan began by offering a specific goal for the summit: "to eliminate the suspicions which each side had of the other."[68] Reagan argued that substantive discussions on complex topics such as arms, for example, could not occur if both sides remained suspicious of one another. As he was fond of saying, Reagan argued that "countries don't mistrust each other because of armaments; they build up their armaments because they mistrust each other."[69] For Gorbachev, it was crucial to convey to Reagan that he was being sincere. As Rhodes argues, "The Soviet Union wasn't playing a game with the United States.

---

[65] Wilson 2014, 97.    [66] See, for example, Wilson 2014, 96.    [67] Rhodes 2007, 187.
[68] Memorandum of Conversation, Reagan–Gorbachev Meeting in Geneva, November 1985. Available: http://nsarchive.gwu.edu/NSAEBB/NSAEBB172/Doc15.pdf.
[69] Rhodes 2007, 188.

It wasn't being duplicitous. If it were, if it harbored secret intentions, then the relationship couldn't be improved."[70]

Invoking the concept of empathy generally, and simulation specifically, Gorbachev notes in his *Memoir* that one of the functions of these meetings, in attempting to relieve these suspicions and convey his sincerity, had been providing an ability to "put myself in Reagan's place."[71] Referencing the meeting in Geneva specifically, Gorbachev notes that he and Reagan were able to develop an "intuition" about the other.[72] "Our dialogue was very constructive . . . and increasingly friendly the better we got to know each other."[73] This perspective is validated by officials on both Soviet and US sides that discussed the importance of the summit in encouraging Reagan and Gorbachev to believe that they could work together.[74] Pavel Palazhchenko, the Soviet interpreter from 1985 to 1991, notes the particular role of intuition played by both men, but particularly Gorbachev:

For both Reagan and Gorbachev, intuition played an important role in shaping their attitudes and actions. Of particular interest in this regard is the remark Mitterrand made to Gorbachev in the summer of 1986, quoted by Cherniaev: "Reagan is among those leaders who intuitively want to put an end to the existing status quo." I think intuition made Reagan support the inclusion in the final communiqué of the Geneva summit in 1985, of the phrase, "Nuclear war cannot be won and must never be fought," although at least the first part of it contradicted the views of some of his advisers. Gorbachev is usually regarded as a politician for whom instincts were less important, but I believe that without trusting his instincts he would not have been able to accomplish as much as he did.[75]

The key interaction from an intention sincerity intuition perspective, for both sides, came on the second day in Geneva when Reagan was posed a direct question by Gorbachev regarding Soviet intentions:[76]

"Why don't you believe me when I say the Soviet Union will never attack?" demanded Gorbachev . . . "Please answer me, Mr. President. What is your answer? I want an answer from you. Why won't you believe me?"

Reagan responded, "Look, no one can say to the American people that they should rely on personal faith rather than sound defense."

Gorbachev: "Why should I accept your sincerity on your willingness to share SDI research when you don't even share your advanced technology with your allies? Let's be more realistic. We're prepared to compromise."

---

[70] Rhodes 2007, 194.    [71] Gorbachev 1996, 405–08.    [72] Gorbachev 1996, 405–08.
[73] Gorbachev 1996, 405–08.
[74] Cf. Shultz 1993, 606–07; Matlock 2004, 169–73; Wheeler 2018.
[75] Palazhchenko 2007, *xiii*.
[76] Quotations from Reynolds (2009, 380) which are based on Oberdorfer's account (149) and are triangulated against the memcon summary. Dobrynin (1995, 590) uses the same questions as Reynolds.

After clarification of the Soviet offer, cuts to the nuclear arsenal if the US were to give up on SDI, there was a pause of at least thirty seconds according to Shultz. Gorbachev reflected and responded, "Mr. President, I don't agree with you, but I can see you really mean what you say." Softening the tone, "Maybe this has all grown a little heated. I was just trying to convey to you the depth of our concerns on SDI." Both sides had clarified their intentions to the other. "Gorbachev apparently realized that Reagan no more intended to use nuclear weapons than he did. Both men, each in his own way, were scouting a path out of the Minotaur's lair."[77] The US saw this as a turning point as it was the first time that the Soviets "had blinked," allowing the US to get a sense of their sincere intentions. Gorbachev was clearly thinking long-term, according to Reagan, and would not let disagreement over SDI jeopardize the relationship transformation that Gorbachev had in mind. Similarly the Soviets understood from the US that their intention was *not* offense, but rather defense. As Deborah Larson argues, this moment was particularly important also because it signaled that Gorbachev sought to go above Reagan's advisors, many of whom who had been known to possess "adversarial, zero-sum" views,[78] and appeal to the President directly.[79]

Gorbachev might have thought that SDI was a misguided policy, but he understood Reagan's sincerity regarding it.[80] "The 'human factor' had quietly come into action. We both sensed that we must maintain contact and try to avoid a break,"[81] alluding to a desire not to break the momentum that was occurring. Reagan felt similarly. With respect to crucially conveying intentions, Reagan used the face-to-face meetings as a way "to convince Gorbachev that we wanted peace and they had nothing to fear from us."[82] The sticking point for Gorbachev was not necessarily Reagan, but who would replace him. Invoking the diachronic problem, Gorbachev asked Reagan to put himself in Soviet shoes, to try to simulate his position, and realize the feeling of insecurity that such a position entails. After all, neither Gorbachev nor Reagan could guarantee anything about the future relationship of the two countries or who would be making decisions in the future. Future uncertainty was ultimately about trust, a trust that had not yet developed between the two leaders. They were gaining intuitions of the other, but had not yet formed solid intention beliefs.

The joint communiqué that followed the end of the summit put into words what both sides had agreed to at the meeting: "a nuclear war cannot be won and must never be fought," and neither would "seek

---

[77] Rhodes 2007, 210.     [78] Rhodes 2007, 238.     [79] Larson 2000, 206.
[80] Reynolds 2009, 375.     [81] Gorbachev 1996, 408.     [82] Fischer 1997, 48.

to achieve military superiority."[83] While Geneva had been an important first step, it did not completely resolve differences or engender significant trust. As Jack Matlock, Special Assistant to the President for National Security Affairs, puts its, Reagan and Gorbachev "had different ideas of what it would take to build trust." Gorbachev was looking to Reagan to pull back SDI, and Reagan believed that SDI was a defensive measure that was precisely what both sides needed in order to enhance the prospects for peace. The distance between the two was still significant, but as Shultz points out, an understanding between the two was growing. "I was surprised and encouraged, as much by the obvious rapport between the two men as by their quick agreement without hesitation on reciprocal visits for two follow-on summit meetings."[84]

Shortly after the summit, Gorbachev reported to Anatoly Chernyaev, Deputy Head of the International Department of the Communist Party of the Soviet Union (CPSU), that "a spark of electric mutual trust... ignited between us, like a voltaic arc between two electric poles."[85] Clarifying what this trust was based on, Chernyaev notes that Reagan was able to move beyond "rhetoric" and convey his "actual sincere belief in the possibility of dealing with the Soviet Union."[86] Most importantly, Chernyaev realized that the assessments the USSR had made of Reagan, and US intentions, were likely wrong. "For a Soviet leader, for Gorbachev, for the first time he got the sense that there is something deeply wrong in our general evaluation of the American administration and American life, that our class analysis is failing and does not give us an answer that would provide a good basis for any kind of realistic politics."[87]

Reagan and Gorbachev were building an understanding of each other. Gorbachev "is a somewhat different breed even though he solidly believes in their system," Reagan wrote, a changed perspective from his earlier belief that Gorbachev was not all that different.[88] Reagan's beliefs about Gorbachev were changing. Shultz, in reflecting on the summit, notes the importance of the meetings in getting both Reagan and Gorbachev to see each other as people, not simply objects or policies. Reagan echoed these sentiments in a February 10, 1986 letter to advisor and Russian specialist Suzanne Massie, "I'm not going to let myself get euphoric, but still, I have a feeling that we might be at the point of beginning. There did seem to be something of a chemistry between the

---

[83] Joint Soviet-United States Statement on the Summit Meeting in Geneva, November 21, 1985. Available: www.reagan.utexas.edu/archives/speeches/1984/112185a.htm.
[84] Shultz 1993, 601.      [85] Morris 2001, 568 and 823.      [86] Savranskaya 2010, 189.
[87] Quoted in Rhodes 2007, 210.      [88] Quoted in Wilson 2014, 101.

General Secretary and myself."[89] With respect to Gorbachev's sincerity, and reflecting on his interactions with the Soviet leader, Reagan had a new belief: "The guy means it. He is going to put his money where his mouth is," in reference to a private discussion Reagan had had with Gorbachev on the need "to teach our children to love each other."[90] Massie credits Reagan's confidence in his instincts, particularly after the assassination attempt on his life, with the success of the personal diplomacy in Geneva.[91] Citing instincts specifically, Matlock argues, "Once Reagan met Gorbachev [at Geneva], he did not need an intelligence officer to tell him whether he was a guy he could deal with. He felt it instinctively."[92] For his part, Gorbachev felt similarly. As Dobrynin puts it, "Gorbachev found it possible to establish contact with [Reagan] and discovered a man who was not as hopeless as some believed," likely referencing officials back in Moscow.[93] According to Arthur Hartman, US ambassador to the Soviet Union at the time and present at the meetings, upon returning to Moscow, Gorbachev "decided that Reagan meant what he said at Geneva . . . [Reagan] did want to rid the world of nuclear weapons, and he was deadly serious about SDI."[94]

Shortly after Geneva, with this new base of mutual understanding intact, the two leaders renewed the exchange of letters. The form of the letters was different, however. After the face-to-face interactions in Geneva, Reagan pursued a strategy of providing Gorbachev with a handwritten letter, friendly in tone and confirming that both sides wanted to eliminate nuclear weapons, while maintaining opposition to issues related to cutting back SDI. "Obviously there are many things on which we disagree," Reagan wrote, "and we disagree very fundamentally. But if I understand you correctly, you, too, are determined to take steps to see that our nations manage their relationship in a peaceful fashion. If this is the case, then this is one point on which we are in total agreement – and it is after all the most fundamental one of all."[95] While both seemingly wanted eventual agreement on the abolishment of nuclear weapons, Reagan demurred that there was not yet enough trust built between the two leaders for such a move and a nuclear weapons agreement would have to be part of a comprehensive peace settlement that included verification mechanisms, progress on human rights, and solving various regional issues. As Wheeler documents, the letters that followed in the ensuing months displayed a crucial lack of ability to convey empathy for the other's position. At each turn they were unable to replicate the type

---

[89] Massie 2013, 189.    [90] Quoted in Massie 2013, 190.
[91] See Massie 2013, 174 and 190.    [92] Quoted in Savranskaya and Blanton 2017, 15.
[93] Dobrynin 1995, 592.    [94] Quoted in Newhouse 1989, 58.    [95] Reagan 1990, 643.

of intention understanding they had gained face-to-face in Geneva and Gorbachev became more disillusioned with Reagan during this period, even implicitly questioning Reagan's sincerity about desiring peace.[96] On the other hand, Gorbachev did admit, on SDI specifically, that his reading of Reagan in Geneva was that the President was sincere about SDI's intended purpose of not relating to "obtain[ing] military superiority." Most importantly, Gorbachev appealed to Reagan for a follow-up face-to-face meeting, intuiting that he needs understanding whether "the U.S. leadership [is] really willing to seek agreements which would lead to the termination of the arms race and to genuine disarmament..."[97] Reagan agreed to meet with Gorbachev again in Reykjavik from October 11 to 12, 1986.

## Reykjavik – October 1986

In the lead-up to the meetings in Iceland, the NSC prepared a document to brief the President on beliefs regarding what Gorbachev's ultimate aims vis-à-vis the talks would be. The paper warned that:

We go into Reykjavik next week with very little knowledge of how Gorbachev intends to use the meeting. The same was true of Geneva of course, but the uncertainty is perhaps greater this time around.

Gorbachev's long-term goals are clear enough: to unravel the Western consensus behind tougher policies toward the Soviet Union, to stabilize US-Soviet relations in a way that gives him greater latitude in his domestic policies, and over time to regain a more favorable position in the global balance of power. Arms control negotiations play a central role in this strategy.[98]

This pessimism was misplaced. As Matlock had predicted, Reagan need not worry. Sitting down with Gorbachev and interacting with him one-on-one, on a human level, would provide significant dividends.[99] Gorbachev knew, based on their interaction in Geneva, that Reagan was not the "sort of person who would buy a used car sight unseen from a fast-talking salesman without having your mechanic check it out... both Gorbachev and the Soviet people as a whole respect you as a real leader."[100] While the venue was different, the Reykjavik talks continued the aims generally and specific language of Geneva.

In their first and only private discussion, Reagan opened with a very similar line to the one that he had delivered in Geneva: the two leaders

---

[96] The letters are available: www.thereaganfiles.com/letters-between-president.html.

[97] Gorbachev September 15, 1986 letter.

[98] Declassified memo: "Gorbachev's Goals and Tactics at Reykjavik." Available: http://nsarchive.gwu.edu/NSAEBB/NSAEBB203/Document06.pdf.

[99] Wilson 2014, 111.       [100] Quoted in Wilson 2014, 112.

"had to find a way to bolster confidence and reduce suspicion between them."[101] What followed "astonished" Reagan. Gorbachev laid out unprecedented proposals and concessions, including cuts to strategic nuclear arms, including radical cuts to the Soviet ICBM force. Gorbachev sensed this disbelief and claims that Reagan was concerned about "some sort of trick" in the proposal. In fact there was no trick and Reagan responded positively to Gorbachev's proposal, telling him that he was encouraged by the proposals.[102] Subsequent discussions over the next day in many ways continued the momentum of the initial discussions. Reagan, in his memoirs notes that "George [Shultz] and I couldn't believe what was happening. We were getting amazing agreements. As the [second] day went on I felt something momentous was occurring."[103] SDI would present a significant stumbling block, however.

Gorbachev's bottom line on SDI was that it must be researched and tested in a laboratory, not in outer space. Gorbachev told Reagan that he would be willing to abolish all nuclear weapons if they could agree that "the testing in space of all space components of the missile is prohibited, except research and testing conducted in laboratories."[104] Gorbachev's fear was that SDI would inevitably lead to a space-based arms race; Reagan believed the opposite. Appreciating Gorbachev's concern and fears, Reagan offered sharing of SDI with the Soviet Union, a proposal that Gorbachev did not favorably act upon, but there is evidence suggesting that he believed Reagan's sincerity.[105] "I may believe you, Mr. President . . . but would your successors repeat the offer,"[106] invoking the diachronic future uncertainty problem initially brought up in Geneva. Put another way, Gorbachev might have a good understanding of Reagan's intentions, and believe his sincerity about SDI, but this was not something on which he could base his policies, at least not yet. Perhaps the biggest reason for this was Gorbachev's perceived inability to convince decision-makers in Moscow of the understanding he had engendered from Reagan. Gorbachev argues that the Politburo would label him "a fool" if he were to go back to Moscow with an agreement that the US would test missiles in space. Gorbachev believed based on his initial reading of Reagan in Geneva that he had "no intention of

---

[101] Matlock 2004, 219.     [102] Matlock 2004, 220.     [103] Reagan 1990, 677.
[104] Matlock 2004, 223.
[105] There is also evidence that Reagan was sincere on the sharing of SDI. A November 1, 1985 CIA paper entitled "Sharing SDI Technology with the Soviets" suggests at the very least that the administration was taking the idea seriously. Gorbachev does not seem to trust that Reagan can deliver on this, noting that "sharing SDI would be a second American revolution. And revolutions do not occur all that often." Savranskaya and Blanton 2017, 132.
[106] Palazchenko 1997, 56.

using the SDI program to obtain military superiority,"[107] but convincing others of this would be no easy task.

For Reagan's part, despite Gorbachev's insistence that his intentions were to limit, rather than ban, SDI, Reagan read from Gorbachev something different. Leffler argues that Reagan was not convinced by Gorbachev's claims and, as Wheeler argues, "it appears that Reagan's intuition was correct."[108] According to Sergei Akhromeyev, Marshal of the Soviet Union and Gorbachev's top military advisor,[109] "it was Gorbachev, not his military, who made the word 'laboratories' a stumbling block."[110] Palazhchenko claims that SDI testing in the laboratory was a "neuralgic point" for Gorbachev.[111] It was not fear in Moscow that was driving Gorbachev's position, but rather Congressional politics and Gorbachev's strategic thinking. Weinberger and others told Reagan that Congress would not fund SDI if it was only a laboratory exercise. Gorbachev, recognizing this, knew that insistence on the laboratory would be a route to killing SDI altogether. Put simply, Reagan was intuiting from Gorbachev that the latter's intention was to kill SDI, despite his protests, and there is good reason to believe that Reagan's reading was correct. Indeed Gorbachev continued to insist on the laboratory condition through their final meeting in Iceland, noting that if no agreement on the topic could be readied then they both could "forget everything they had discussed."[112]

Some in Reagan's administration believed that this had all been a trap. As Gates argues, Gorbachev made concession and concession in the lead-up to, and during, the summit, "[then] Gorbachev sprang the trap. Surveying all that was on the table, all the progress that had been made, a smiling Gorbachev said: 'This all depends, of course, on you giving up SDI.' He had taken Reagan to the mountaintop, showed him a historic achievement, and tempted him... The President got mad. He realized he had been set up."[113] For their part Soviet leadership was concerned about the level of trust between the two states. Georgy Arbatov, advisor to Gorbachev, told Paul Nitze, one of Reagan's lead negotiators, that "Accepting your offer would require an exceptional level of *trust*... We cannot accept your proposals."[114]

The summit ultimately ended with no agreement, and though the experience seemed to complicate the notion that significant trust was building between the two protagonists, important intention understanding *had* occurred. Gorbachev intuited once again Reagan's sincerity

---

[107] Saltoun-Ebin 2013, 62.      [108] Wheeler 2018.      [109] Adelman 2014, 279.
[110] Matlock 2004, 236.      [111] Palazchenko 1997, 55.      [112] Lettow 2005, 225.
[113] Gates 1996, 408.      [114] Quoted in Massie 2013, 242. Italics are Massie's.

regarding SDI intentions and Reagan intuited from Gorbachev an intention to kill SDI. And, it appears that this was a correct reading. Palazhchenko has argued that Gorbachev's intention at that time was to push for the end of SDI and if Reagan did not agree, Gorbachev would "mount a campaign accusing the United States of not [being] willing to negotiate in good faith."[115] Reagan, however, was still not ready to give up on SDI: "The price was high but I wouldn't sell [SDI] & that's how the day ended," Reagan wrote in his diary.[116] Importantly, despite the palpable disappointment, both sides resisted the urge to blame each other in a final press conference, preferring instead to view the face-to-face diplomacy in Reykjavik as an important development in their relationship. Indeed Chernyaev, reflecting on the summit, wrote "a spark of understanding was born between them, as if they had winked to each other about the future."[117] Reagan wrote that "it's clear there was a chemistry between Gorbachev and me that produced something very close to a friendship."[118] This feeling was apparently somewhat mutual, with a marked change in Gorbachev's stance toward Reagan, something "he never spoke about...in his inner circle as he had before."[119] This reflects the *belief* that Gorbachev developed during this period that, as Wheeler argues, "Reagan was not preparing an attack against the Soviet Union, and that far from being a representative of US capitalist imperialism, Reagan was, in Grachev's words, 'a trustworthy partner, who shared similar hopes and ideas.'"[120] Shultz' executive assistant, Charles Hill, in reflecting back on this period notes the importance of the humanization that occurred: "[it is as if] suddenly somebody at the top [of the Soviet hierarchy] said, 'It's okay to be a human being again.' And their officials from top to bottom changed."[121]

Reykjavik is also remarkable for how close Reagan and Gorbachev came to agreement. As the Soviet notes from the summit suggest, "Everybody saw that agreement is possible. From Reykjavik, we drew the

---

[115] Palazhchenko 2014 comments during "Dialogue & Diplomacy in the Reagan-Gorbachev Era" panel discussion, April 12, 2014. Available: www.c-span.org/video/?318818-1/dialogue-diplomacy-reagangorbachev-era. Importantly, however, Gorbachev does not go ahead with this plan, even though it was his intention to do so. Palazhchenko recalls that Gorbachev saw the horde of reporters waiting for the press conference and changed his mind at that moment, not wanting to disappoint a world that was hoping for good news, or at the very least not horrendous news that all progress had been stalled because the United States was not acting in good faith.

[116] Reagan 2007, 482.     [117] Chernyaev 2000, 85.

[118] Quoted in Reynolds 2009, 363.     [119] Chernyaev 2000, 85.

[120] Wheeler 2018; Grachev quote from Grachev 2008, 95; see also Blanton and Savranskaya 2011.

[121] Wilson 2014, 114.

conclusion that the necessity for dialogue has increased even more."[122]
In Reagan's view "one lousy word," laboratory, prevented agreement. A
final document, perhaps written on the last day of the summit, entitled
"Lessons of Reykjavik," neatly captures just how wrong the US side had
been, with respect to Soviet intentions for the summit, as they entered it:
"Reykjavik demonstrated once again how poor we are at guessing what
the Soviets will do. The widespread prediction was that the Soviets would
concentrate on INF and shun START, would hit hard on interin [sic]
restraint, and press testing . . . None of this was much in evidence."[123]
   Several changes to Soviet policy occurred after Reykjavik. Perhaps the
most significant was the so-called "untying of the package," referring to
the package of proposals the Soviets had proposed in Iceland. Since SDI
was a stumbling block, and Gorbachev feared that progress would stall
without interjecting new ideas, Gorbachev, allegedly much to the chagrin
of many of his advisors,[124] proposed delinking an agreement on missile
reduction (the intermediate-range nuclear forces or INF) from an agreement on SDI. This would allow for Reagan to maintain his stated intention of pursuing defensive SDI, which Gorbachev read as being a sincere
intention, while continuing progress with a dramatic step of significantly
cutting the number of missiles both sides possessed. Additionally Gorbachev moved his position to allow for on-site inspections, as part of a
potential INF deal, and announced that the Soviet Union would adopt
a proposal by NATO entitled "global double zero," which eliminated
INF in Europe and Asia as well as all short-range intermediate forces
(SRINF).
   There are many explanations for why these changes occurred after
Reykjavik. Wheeler, for example, argues that Reagan and Gorbachev
had built significant interpersonal trust and this allowed Gorbachev to
suspend concerns that Reagan would not use concessions against him
domestically.[125] Plokhy suggests that one of Gorbachev's leading scientific advisors, Andrei Sakharov, "father of the Soviet hydrogen bomb
and a prominent political dissident," convinced Gorbachev that SDI
was nothing more than imaginative fiction.[126] SDI, for Sakharov, was a
"Maginot line in space – expensive and ineffective." The all-or-nothing
"package principle" at Reykjavik, according to Sakharov, should be disaggregated, since it "would create a new political and strategic climate
in which the US would not deploy antimissile defenses in space," or if

---

[122] Anatoly   Chernyaev's   Notes.   Available:   http://nsarchive.gwu.edu/NSAEBB/
      NSAEBB203/Document19.pdf
[123] The Secretary's Post-Reykjavik Media Events Briefing. Available: http://nsarchive.gwu
      .edu/NSAEBB/NSAEBB203/Document18.pdf
[124] See Oberdorfer 1992, 230.     [125] Wheeler 2018.     [126] Plokhy 2014, 13.

they did, "we would simply revert to the current situation [of MAD], with appreciable political gains for the USSR."[127] Gorbachev therefore arguably had little to fear in SDI becoming a reality and advantage for the United States. Perhaps most simply, Gorbachev read Reagan's sincerity with respect to intention and tenacity in terms of defending his bottom line; realizing that insistence on laboratories was not going anywhere, Gorbachev made the prudent choice to uncouple SDI from the rest of the negotiated package in order to keep the negotiations from stalling. All of these changes ultimately resulted in the pieces falling into place for the historic INF treaty to be signed in Washington in December, 1987.

## Washington – December 1987

Shortly upon arrival in Washington, Gorbachev and Reagan signed the INF treaty. There was little to negotiate after the Soviet moves following Reykjavik and though the two leaders had not met personally for over a year, "the easy and friendly relationship between the two leaders came through their words and their body language."[128] This did not imply that all remaining issues had been worked out, however. Gates warned Reagan before the summit that to the extent that Moscow is seeking changes, the purpose "remains to further increase Soviet military power and political influence . . . 'dynamic diplomacy,' [threatens] to make the USSR a more competitive and stronger adversary in the years ahead."[129] Further, before the signing of the treaty Gorbachev and Reagan sparred over the USSR's approach to human rights. Gorbachev did not take these moments of disagreement as indications of failure, rather noting that "now and then, there appeared to be a feeling of mistrust and we would exchange biting remarks – but these moments gradually grew fewer."[130] As Wheeler argues, empathy was deepening between the two protagonists.[131]

In fact, in a profound statement in front of the Politburo in December 1987, Gorbachev remarked that there was something special he found in Reagan at the Washington Summit that was productive for the US–USSR relationship:

In Washington, probably for the first time we clearly realized how much the human factor means in international politics. Before . . . we treated such personal

---

[127] Sakharov 1991, 22–23.    [128] Shultz 1993, xxx.
[129] Quoted in Wilson 2014, 135.    [130] Gorbachev 1996, 447.
[131] Wheeler 2018, xxx.

contacts as simply meetings between representatives of opposed and irreconcilable systems. Reagan for us was merely the spokesman of the most conservative part of the American capitalism and its military-industrial complex. But it turns out that politicians, including leaders of governments if they are really responsible people, represent purely human concerns, interests, and the hopes of ordinary people – people who vote for them in elections and who associate their leaders' names and personal abilities with the country's image and patriotism. The people are guided by the most natural human motives and feelings. In our age, it turns out, this has the biggest impact on political decisions . . .[132]

Importantly, Gorbachev is quite specific on what the "human factor" meant in this context, referring to the growing humanization of the relationship, the distance between the two having been lessened by a bridge that was growing between them through the summitry process. Gorbachev noted that the summit was "a landmark," and Reagan called it "the best summit we've ever had with the Soviet Union."[133] It was Gorbachev's specific hope that Reagan would come to Moscow so that "the two sides of the bridge should be locked together."[134] In the end, the INF treaty eliminated more weapons than any agreement in history,[135] but there was still work to be done.

## Moscow – May 1988

Having reached agreement on INF, Gorbachev was eager to maintain momentum and forge agreement on Strategic Arms Reduction, what would be known as START, in Moscow. Substantive discussions regarding START had taken place in Washington, but neither side wanted an INF agreement to be put in jeopardy by disagreement over START and therefore the latter was left for future negotiations. The stumbling block to an agreement on START was precisely the same stumbling block that previously presented itself with the INF treaty: SDI. Laboratory versus space discussions had not abated and, as Wheeler argues, a consequence was the belief in the minds of both leaders that a START agreement would not be signed in Moscow.[136] The other problem for Reagan resided in domestic political concerns. As Wilson argues, "[a]ttacks came . . . from the self-professed 'realists,' to whom Soviet willingness to sign a treaty indicated it must not be in US interest," referencing

---

[132] Chernyaev 2000, 142–43.
[133] Iceland Chronology. Available: http://nsarchive.gwu.edu/NSAEBB/NSAEBB203/Document19.pdf. Also see Reagan 2007, 557.
[134] Iceland Chronology. Available: http://nsarchive.gwu.edu/NSAEBB/NSAEBB203/Document19.pdf.
[135] Wilson 2014, 138.          [136] Wheeler 2018; see also Shultz 1993, 1101.

the INF treaty.[137] Or, in the words of William Clark, "For the foresee-able future, it will not be realistic to pursue agreements to eliminate all nuclear weapons ... The [Warsaw] Pact is not well positioned to launch a surprise attack, and in the coming decade it could enhance this capability."[138] Reagan may have been assured of Gorbachev's sincere intentions, but the hardliners in the administration, witnessing behaviors from afar, were still unconvinced.

The Moscow summit is perhaps most notable not because of any particular agreement reached or issue raised (though there were some extraordinary ones, such as Reagan's request that Gorbachev include religious freedom in the peoples' rights), but rather the atmosphere of the exchanges. As Gorbachev recalls, "the significance of those first Moscow talks lay not so much in the subjects we discussed as in the friendly atmo-sphere and mutual desire to strike a well-meaning, trustful tone from the start."[139] Gorbachev also noted to Nancy Reagan during their visit he and Reagan shared "a certain chemistry" that Gorbachev felt was "very rare."[140] In Gorbachev's memoir he notes the importance of this sum-mit in overcoming stereotypes and misconceptions, not just with Reagan but with Shultz as well.[141] For his part Reagan recalls that "despite our differences, it was not a contentious meeting."[142]

The chemistry between Reagan and Gorbachev was best exemplified during a press conference where the "body language told the story: a dangerous cold war era was ending."[143] It was at this press conference that Reagan credited Gorbachev with the moves that he had made to reassure the world of the Soviet Union's peaceful intentions. Reagan also admitted to having changed his mind about the nature and char-acter of the Soviet Union. When asked, "do you still consider this an evil empire," Reagan responded, "No. That was another time, another era."[144] For Gorbachev this was a critical moment. It signaled to him that Reagan had, perhaps finally, understood his true intentions. As argued above this is a process that began in Geneva, and there is evi-dence that Reagan had a good reading of Gorbachev even after their first interactions, but now it was Gorbachev who was able to realize this fact. Reagan was not shielding his understanding of Gorbachev any longer for political gain and negotiation strategic reasons. Gorbachev would later reflect back on this, noting, "for me, Ronald Reagan's acknowledgement was one of the genuine achievements of his Moscow visit. It meant that he had finally convinced himself that he had been right to believe, back in

[137] Wilson 2014, 139.    [138] Quoted in Wilson 2014, 140.
[139] Gorbachev 1996, 453.    [140] Reynolds 2009, 366.
[141] Gorbachev 1996, 447–48.    [142] Reagan 1990, 709.    [143] Shultz 1993, 1103.
[144] Matlock 2004, 302.

Reykjavik, that you could 'do business' with the changing Soviet Union – the hopeful business of preventing a nuclear war."[145]

The rest of the talks in Moscow were focused on continuing to alleviate misconceptions of the other on a variety of topics, including human rights. Reagan noted that he and Gorbachev "agreed that we had both begun our relationship with misconceptions about the other, and that it had taken these one-on-one sessions to build trust and understanding."[146] Reagan reportedly told Gorbachev at one point that "you don't get in trouble by talking to each other, and not just about each other."[147] In the end the Moscow summit was more notable for the human dimension and affirmation of correct intention understanding than substantive agreements on policy issues. Gorbachev noted that there were indeed "missed opportunities" in Moscow because the US and Soviet Union were simply not aligned on a number of issues, but the summit had nevertheless served to further correct misperceptions. In a letter to Reagan sent shortly after the summit, "our meeting in Moscow has been given an encouraging human dimension – not only in terms of our personal liking for each other, but also in terms of warmer relations between our peoples and their more correct perception of each other."[148]

Before turning to Gorbachev's significant post-Moscow move at the United Nations, it is worth highlighting the various face-to-face interactions that occurred at other levels of government in tandem with the Reagan–Gorbachev interactions. In particular, face-to-face interactions between US Secretary of State George Shultz and his Soviet counterpart Eduard Shevardnadze, as well as with Gorbachev, helped to clarify intentions and the importance of these meetings cannot be overstated. Gorbachev notes, for example, that both sides used these meetings to determine intentions. With respect to a meeting between Gorbachev and Shultz in April 1987, Gorbachev reflects that "[i]t seemed that the American's main objective had been to learn more about our views and intentions – an entirely justified purpose. But what was to follow? Another round or propaganda campaigns and battling for public support? Or were these soundings a prelude to real politics?"[149] Gorbachev used the meetings to attempt to answer that question: "my own aim had been to find out what lay behind the Reagan administration's rhetoric. I wanted to see whether there was any chance of improving relations with Washington . . . the talks had shown that underlying considerations and intentions were far more important [than accusations]."[150] Similarly Shultz and Shevardnadze would spend hundreds of hours together

[145] Gorbachev 1996, 457.      [146] Reagan 1990, 709.      [147] Mann 2009, 304.
[148] Reagan 1990, 712.      [149] Gorbachev 1996, 440.      [150] Ibid.

between 1985 and 1989 attempting to derive, among other things, what lay behind the rhetoric (or what the Soviet team called the "phrase book") in terms of intentions. As Palazhchenko notes of their first meeting in Helsinki in 1985, "Shultz was watching Shevardnadze closely, in a sharply appraising way. One could see that he was keenly interested – there was none of that characteristic cool and even seemingly indifferent look of his . . . I don't know whether on that day in Helsinki they believed they would establish a personal and very human relationship, and whether they wanted such a relationship then . . . Shultz and Shevardnadze were not in the combative mood that had characterized US-Soviet relations in the previous years."[151] According to Wilson, Palazchenko's note that Shultz was watching Shevardnadze closely is accurate; Shultz was grateful that Shevardnadze allowed the use of simultaneous translation, because it allowed both sides to read the body language and facial expressions of the other.[152]

Robert Gates, who served as Deputy Director of Central Intelligence from 1986 to 1989, personally met face-to-face with his counterpart in the Soviet Committee for State Security (KGB), Victor Kryuchkov, three times and the meetings instilled in Gates a better understanding of what lay behind the scenes at the KGB. In their first meeting, which occurred shortly before the Washington summit, on December 4, Gates remarked to Kryuchkov that "although each side certainly is intimately familiar with the daily lives of the other in the two capitals," this face-to-face meeting was an important step in understanding each other. Kryuchkov admitted to Gates that "Perestroika is proceeding much more slowly than [he] had anticipated two years ago," and implied, at least according to Gates, that the Soviet Union was concerned about their power. As Gates notes in a "stunning revelation . . . At one point he turned to me and, in a statement that admitted much, said, 'I hope CIA is telling the US leadership that the Soviet Union is not a weak, poor country that can be pushed around.'"[153] As Gates told me, the impression that Kryuchkov gave off was one of confidence, though one could see hints of the insecurity in his face.[154] Months later at the Moscow summit Gates met Kryuchkov again, though this time the "tone, demeanor, and whole approach were very different."[155] There was less candid discussion, "[no] more talk about the need for reform or support for perestroika. He spoke at length of problems in the USSR, of the nationalities and the dismal conditions in Russia."[156] By this point

---

[151] Palazhchenko 1997, 34.    [152] Wilson 2014, 93.    [153] Gates 1996, 425.
[154] Interview with Robert Gates, May 14, 2015.    [155] Gates 1996, 491.
[156] Gates 1996, 491.

Kryuchkov could not bely his feelings and was open about his opposition to Gorbachev. Reflecting back on the difference between the two meetings, Gates notes the importance of body language, demeanor, and tone, which all told a particular story to Gates, information and data that would be difficult to pick up on from afar.[157] As Jack Matlock, former US diplomat who was present at most of the executive-level summits argues in summation, these "face-to-face meetings between the Soviet and American leaders and their policy makers were essential to move the US-Soviet dialogue in a constructive direction."[158]

### Contemporaneous Intention Understanding from Afar: Observable Implications of Face-to-Face

To fully address the counterfactual regarding whether the intention understanding could have occurred without the face-to-face interactions, it is necessary to understand activities in intention approximation that were occurring contemporaneously from afar. Despite these auspicious exercises in face-to-face diplomacy, where Reagan, Gorbachev, Shultz, Shevardnadze, and so forth, were clarifying their intentions, Washington was continually slow to react to the changing relationship. In a classic example of the "two-level game" that states play,[159] the interaction among leaders and the machinery of the bureaucratic state were not in sync. The frustration reached a boiling point for Gorbachev a year after Geneva when he had noted that despite all of the progress made personally, little substantively was changing, particularly on the US side. As Reynolds sums up the situation nicely, progress was being "sabotaged by free-ranging bureaucrats."

Part of the reason was a difficulty in changing long-held beliefs about the intentions of the USSR. As Deputy Secretary of State John Whitehead said in a speech in January 1988, the empire's intentions had not changed: "Let us be clear, the long-run Soviet interest in maintaining a hegemonic relationship with Eastern Europe has not changed."[160] Because of differing views on intentions, policy prescriptions differed as well, with many in Washington maintaining that nuclear disarmament should proceed alongside the development of SDI, a point of significant disagreement with Gorbachev.[161] In a November 1987 memo to Reagan, then Deputy Director of the CIA Robert Gates concluded

---

[157] Interview with Robert Gates, May 14, 2015.
[158] Matlock 2004, 319. See also Chernyaev 2000, 85; Gorbachev 1996, 420.
[159] Putnam 1988.
[160] Speech by John Whitehead, January 19, 1988 Department of State.
[161] Booth and Wheeler 2008, 150.

that the reforms Gorbachev was implementing amounted to "breathing space" that would simply buy time before "further increase in Soviet military power and political influence," with Gorbachev only agreeing to arms reductions that protected "existing Soviet advantages."[162] Decision-makers in Washington were making approximations from afar and applying theories to Gorbachev in order to understand what his intentions might be.

Just as importantly, 1988 represented a transition year in the United States, as George H.W. Bush, Reagan's Vice President, was elected into office in November. Despite Soviet concessions, US officials were slow to react to what Gorbachev was proposing. Gorbachev interpreted this as an unfortunate reality of democratic politics. In a conversation with Hungarian communist party leader Janos Kadar, Kadar gives his interpretation of what is happening: "It seems they are following a policy of delaying agreement for the reduction of offensive weapons. It looks like they do not want to give this issue to Reagan, they want to save it for the new president." Gorbachev responded, "I can only express my complete agreement and understanding. I have neither questions nor doubts about this."[163]

Despite Washington pushing back on agreements and not reflecting the progress that had been made at an interpersonal level, 1985–1988 represented a period of gradual mutual understanding and empathy building between Gorbachev and Reagan, an understanding that helped to "undercut the hard-line tendencies on both sides," thus literally transforming positions, indicative of progress in the US–USSR relationship that inspired hope for further progress in the coming new year.[164]

*Gorbachev's UN Speech and the Bush "Pause": 1989–1990*[165]

George H.W. Bush, despite being a member of the same Republican political party as Reagan, possessed very different views on Gorbachev and the Soviet Union. Despite the progress that had been made during

---

[162] William Webster Memorandum, November 24, 1987. Available: http://nsarchive .gwu.edu/NSAEBB/NSAEBB238/usdocs/Doc%2011%20%28Memo%20from %20Webster%2011.24.87%29.pdf.
[163] Savranskaya 2010, Doc 23.    [164] Blanton 2010, 52.
[165] The period of 1989 to 1990 has garnered, perhaps, as much scholarly attention as any single two-year span in history. Excellent secondary sources related specifically to the Germany reunification that I draw from for use in this chapter and the next include: Sarotte 2009; Szabo 1992; Leffler and Westad 2010; Anderson 1999; Jarausch 1994; Goldgeier and McFaul 2003; Lange and Pugh 1998; Görtemaker 1994; Gaddis 2005; Engel 2009; Brown 1996; Bozo 2009; Anderson 1999; Zelikow and Rice 1995; Lévesque 1997; Moens 1991; Merkl 2010. Chollet and Goldgeier 2003.

the Moscow Summit, Bush, still campaigning for the Presidency, declared during the summer of 1988 that "The Cold War is not over."[166] Shortly before Bush assumed office in January 1989, Gorbachev effectively sought to end the Cold War by giving a speech at the United Nations on December 7, 1988 that would serve as the conclusion to what Winston Churchill had begun with his "Iron Curtain" speech in Fulton, Missouri in 1947. Internal Soviet documents suggest that Gorbachev told his advisors that the UN speech should be "an anti-Fulton, Fulton in reverse."[167] In the speech Gorbachev announced unilateral cuts to Soviet forces and the withdrawal of thousands of tanks and troops from Eastern Europe. From an ideological perspective Gorbachev spoke of the need to endorse "common interests of mankind," "the compelling necessity of the principle of freedom of choice" as "a universal principle in which there should be no exceptions."[168] Gorbachev was saying the right things and attaching a significant cost, in the proposed reductions of arms and troops, to his words. The reaction in the West to the speech was swift. The *New York Times* argued in its editorial page:

Perhaps not since Woodrow Wilson presented his Fourteen Points in 1918 or since Franklin Roosevelt and Winston Churchill promulgated the Atlantic Charter in 1941 has a world figure demonstrated the vision Mikhail Gorbachev displayed yesterday at the United Nations.[169]

In testimony to the Senate Intelligence Committee that was occurring at the moment when Gorbachev was speaking, Douglas MacEachin confesses that assumptions regarding Soviet behavior and intentions among many in government made it difficult to foresee this type of monumental shift:

Now, we spend megadollars studying political instability in various places around the world, but we never really looked at the Soviet Union as a political entity in which there were factors building which led to the kind of – at least the initiation of political transformation that we seem to see. It does not exist to my knowledge. Moreover, had it existed inside the government, we never would have been able to publish it anyway, quite frankly. And had we done so, people would have been calling for my head. And I wouldn't have published it. In all honestly, had we said a week ago that Gorbachev might come to the UN and offer a unilateral cut of 500,000 in the military, we would have been told we were crazy. We had a

---

[166] LA Times, June 30, 1988. "Bush Warns That 'Cold War Is Not Over.'"
[167] NSA Electronic Briefing Book 261. Available: http://nsarchive.gwu.edu/NSAEBB/NSAEBB261/.
[168] For the full text of the speech see FBIS-SOV-99–236, December 8, 1988: 11–19.
[169] *The New York Times*, December 8, 1988: 34.

difficult enough time getting air space for the prospect of some unilateral cuts of 50 to 60,000.[170]

MacEachin's words echoed official reports, such as the NIE that was issued a week before the speech and stated clearly: "to date...we have not detected changes under Gorbachev that clearly illustrate either new security concepts or new resource constraints are taking hold."[171]

Perhaps most importantly however, President-elect Bush had a relatively muted response to the speech. On Governors Island after the speech President Reagan and Gorbachev engage in their final official meeting, discussing their nostalgia for the series of summits they had participated in since Geneva in 1985 and the progress that had been made. Reagan presented Gorbachev with a photograph of their meeting in Switzerland inscribed with hand-written words that spoke of the two together clearing "a path to peace."[172] As Reagan noted, while there was still much to do, an important foundation had been laid. For his part Bush noted that he hoped the progress could continue and that a similar photograph could be taken one day with the same significance, but importantly he "would need a little time to review the issues."[173] Bush noted that "he had no intention of stalling things," but nevertheless needed time. As Blanton points out this was a bit of an odd statement as Bush had been Reagan's Vice President for the previous eight years and therefore should have been well versed on all of the issues. There is evidence to suggest that Gorbachev shared this view based on their face-to-face interaction. Noting to the Soviet Politburo, Gorbachev said: "[W]hen I managed to tear myself away from Reagan, I spoke to Bush about this indecisiveness. He snapped back: You must understand my position. I cannot, according to American tradition, come to the fore until a formal transfer of power has taken place."[174] Gorbachev's intuition that Bush intended a pause would turn out to be correct. Nevertheless, despite this statement to the Politburo, Gorbachev's reflections on his first interaction with Bush, face-to-face, was that an important beginning had been made, laying "a foundation stone of mutual understanding and trust."[175]

---

[170] NSA Briefing Book 261. Available: www2.gwu.edu/~nsarchiv/NSAEBB/NSAEBB261/us07.pdf

[171] NIE 4–3/8–88. Quoted in Haines and Legget 2003, 176.

[172] NIE 4–3/8–88. Quoted in Haines and Legget 2003, 176.

[173] Memcon, "The President's Private Meeting with Gorbachev," December 7, 1988, 1:05–1:30pm, Commandant's residence, Governors Island, New York. In NSA Electronic Briefing Book No. 261, document 9. Available: http://nsarchive.gwu.edu/NSAEBB/NSAEBB261/.

[174] Savranskaya 2010, Doc. 35.    [175] Gorbachev 1996, 449–50.

As Blanton argues, "[t]o a remarkable degree only obvious in hind-sight, the transition from the Reagan administration to the Bush admin-istration in January 1989 was one from doves to hawks."[176] In sharp contrast to Reagan, Bush and his top officials were skeptical about Gorbachev. As Bush recounts in his *Memoir* (jointly written with his National Security Advisor Brent Scowcroft):

To oversimplify, I believed that Gorbachev's goal was to restore dynamism to a socialist political and economic system and revitalize the Soviet Union domes-tically and internationally to compete with the West. To me, especially before 1990, this made Gorbachev potentially more dangerous than his predecessors, each of whom, through some aggressive move, had saved the West from the dan-gers of its own wishful thinking about the Soviet Union before it was too late.[177]

While Reagan had clarified intentions with Gorbachev, Bush's reaction to him is one characterized by a lack of understanding of his intentions. Scowcroft echoes these concerns, suggesting that Gorbachev might have been attempting to deceive the US and take advantage of a newly elected President. As such, Scowcroft, in contrast to the Reagan team, was very much against a summit with Gorbachev.[178] Richard Cheney, Bush's sec-retary of defense, concurred. As Ackerman and Foer report, "Cheney believed that, with a gust of aggressive support for alternatives to Gorbachev, the United States could dismember its principal adver-sary once and for all."[179] While Cheney was ultimately unsuccessful in pushing Bush away from Gorbachev, his words of skepticism regarding Gorbachev, even after the prolonged summitry, speak to the continued level of concern over Gorbachev's intentions among those who did not spend much time with him.

Indeed, the prevailing attitude of the Bush administration, in contrast to that of Reagan's, was summed up on national television by Brent Scowcroft on January 22, 1989: "I think the Cold War is not over."[180] As Robert Hutchings, National Security Council member, later noted, there was "no such thing as a 'Reagan-Bush' foreign policy. Before 1989 there was Reagan; afterwards there was Bush."[181]

---

[176] Blanton 2010, 61.      [177] Bush and Scowcroft 1998, 13.
[178] Bush and Scowcroft 1998, 46.      [179] Ackerman and Foer 2003, 3–4.
[180] It is important to note, however, that in addition to potentially revealing what the US administration believed about USSR intentions, there were practical reasons for US policymakers to not declare victory. First, once a war has been declared over it is diffi-cult to rescind that statement, should the need arise. Second, Scowcroft in particular was well aware of Congressional politics. Referring to the Cold War as having been won might translate to slashed defense budgets. See Rhodes 2007, 288.
[181] Hutchings 1997, 6. Quoted in Sarotte 2009, 22.

While it is difficult to assess precisely why the Bush administration viewed Gorbachev and the Soviet intentions so skeptically, one of the concerns some in the administration faced was preventing previous failures in personal diplomacy. For instance, one idea that was floated once it became clear that stability in Eastern Europe was beginning to crack, was to send Henry Kissinger to Moscow to serve as a secret liaison between Washington and Moscow. The idea had appeal, particularly given the administration's shared realpolitik views with Kissinger. However, they also wanted to avoid "[n]egotiating the future of Eastern Europe," which was, "the last thing we needed to do," recalling the failed Yalta conference at the end of the Second World War. The plan was even referred to by some in diplomatic corps as "Yalta II," highlighting not just a skepticism regarding Soviet intentions but a skepticism over the notion of personal diplomacy more generally. This skepticism is arguably one reason why Bush and Gorbachev would not have a summit until Malta, which occurred nearly a year after their meeting on Governors Island, and is the subject of the following chapter of the book.

Thus whereas Reagan had pursued vigorous and sustained relationship-building successive meetings, Bush instituted a "pause" in the process. Matlock would later describe this period as one where "Washington Fumbles," and Chernyaev would declare the period as "The Lost Year," referring to the missed opportunities after Reagan's departure from office.[182] To be sure, part of the problem was party politics. As Douglas MacEachin notes, the administration "had to be constantly looking over their back, because everybody from the tougher line of their party was waiting for them to make their first capitulations ... [T]here politics delayed a lot of steps that could have been taken with more confidence by, for example, President Reagan ... "[183] Bush was also concerned, as Richard Hermann puts it, with "coming out from under the shadow of Reagan," such that he was viewed as his own leader and not simply as an extension of the previous President.[184] There was also the legitimate concern that should Gorbachev leave office, it was not at all certain that he would be replaced with a leader who possesses similar sensibilities toward the US.[185]

Further, Bush's review of interests and positions ultimately relied on intelligence estimates rather than face-to-face interactions. As alluded to above, throughout Reagan's second term high-level interactions were aiding Reagan in understanding Gorbachev's intentions, but the NIEs portrayed a different view. As Garthoff notes, "the greatest

---

[182] Matlock 2004, 177; Chernyaev 2000, 201.    [183] Savranskaya 2010, 185.
[184] Savranskaya 2010, 196–97.    [185] Chollet and Goldgeier 2003.

shortcoming of the NIEs on Soviet military power from 1987 to 1991 was the failure to give even cautious recognition to the radical changes already underway in Soviet outlook, doctrine, policy and strategy."[186] As Yarhi-Milo argues, through Reagan's second administration, "most agencies believed that the Soviet motivation for the short-term pursuit of a benign posture vis-à-vis the West reflected Gorbachev's need for breathing room to execute domestic economic reforms."[187] Even overt and costly moves, such as arms reductions, withdrawal from Afghanistan, cuts to conventional forces, and so on were interpreted as moves to strengthen the Soviet position, not moves to convey benign intentions. Importantly, as MacEachin argues, "The fact of the matter is, the NIEs – this is the unfortunate part of it – are a sort of doctrinal showcase. This is what we 'declare' we believe ... That is the only stuff that ever affects anything."[188] As such if Bush was relying on intelligence assessments, and the doctrinal nature of them makes that likely, rather than personal interactions, to derive Soviet intentions, it is unsurprising that he began his first term in a skeptical position.[189]

By April 1989 divisions in the administrations' understanding of Soviet intentions were beginning to mount. One CIA document referred to "The Gorbachev Challenge," which included a section entitled "Disagreements," reflecting the various positions regarding Gorbachev's intentions:

Some analysts see current policy changes as largely tactical, driven by the need for breathing space from the competition ... They judge that there is a serious risk of Moscow returning to traditionally combative behavior when the hoped for gains in economic performance are achieved.[190]

Contrarily, "Other analysts believe Gorbachev's policies reflect a fundamental re-thinking of national interests and ideology as well as more tactical considerations ... " considerations that amount to "historical shifts in the Soviet definition of national interest" and "lasting shifts in Soviet behavior."[191] Among those in the second category was Jack Matlock, a holdover from the Reagan administration and someone who was in Moscow interacting with Yakovlev on a regular basis. Matlock

---

[186] Haines and Leggett 2003, 175.     [187] Yarhi-Milo 2014, 238.
[188] Savranskaya 2010, 187.
[189] Beschloss and Talbott 1993, 43–45, 47–49; Chollet and Goldgeier 2003.
[190] NIE 11–4–89. Available: www.cia.gov/library/center-for-the-study-of-intelligence/csi-publications/books-and-monographs/at-cold-wars-end-us-intelligence-on-the-soviet-union-and-eastern-europe-1989–1991/16526pdffiles/NIE11–4–89.pdf.
[191] NIE 11–4–89. Available: www.cia.gov/library/center-for-the-study-of-intelligence/csi-publications/books-and-monographs/at-cold-wars-end-us-intelligence-on-the-soviet-union-and-eastern-europe-1989–1991/16526pdffiles/NIE11–4–89.pdf.

was concerned that there were "mistaken ideas [about Gorbachev] float-ing around Washington" that would make progress difficult and sent three cables to Bush officials urging that they not delay in continuing to make progress with Gorbachev and that the ideology behind the Cold War, from a Soviet perspective, really was dead.[192] Bush officials read the cables (they are referenced in the Bush-Scowcroft *Memoir*)[193] but they were not enough to convince the administration to change their views. Instead the administration was concerned with "[strengthening] the image of America's foreign policy as driven by clear objectives" and "[appearing] confident about our purposes and agenda."[194] As Blanton argues, the overarching theme of this period is one of competition, rather than cooperation, with Gorbachev.[195] In the Bush-Scowcroft *Memoir*, "Scowcroft pointed out that the United States was losing the battle with Gorbachev over influencing the direction of Europe ... The President agreed that Gorbachev had undermined US leadership, and he wanted to go to the NATO summit in May with a series of bold proposals that would put us out in front."[196] This interpretation of Gorbachev's moves as competition even extended to concessions. In May 1989 Baker inter-prets Gorbachev's proposal of withdrawing 500 tactical nuclear weapons from Eastern Europe as a public diplomacy surprise meant to "[split] the alliance and [undercut] us in Western Europe, by appealing past West-ern governments to Western publics."[197] This was an offer that the Bush administration would eventually agree to, in the fall of 1991, an indi-cation that "in 1989, one can only conclude that American insecurity created a major missed opportunity."[198]

Finally, it is interesting to note that in April and May of 1989 the Bush administration drafted National Security Directive 23, which called for various steps that should be pursued from the Soviet side in order to, in the words of Robert Hutchings, "lead to a new coopera-tive relationship."[199] As Blanton points out in reviewing the document, "Gorbachev had already met every one of its major 'conditions,'" includ-ing reduction of forces announced at the UN in December 1988, agree-ing to self-determination for Eastern Europe, and the rejection of class struggle in international relations.[200] The Bush administration was not only misreading Soviet intentions, they are also misreading, or misinter-preting, statements and actions that had already been taken, pointing to a very strong hesitancy, derived largely from intention reading from afar, to take Gorbachev at face value.

---

[192] Savranskaya 2010, 68.    [193] Bush and Scowcroft 1998, 39–40.
[194] Busch and Scowcroft 1998, 40.    [195] Savranskaya 2010, 69.
[196] Bush and Scowcroft 1998, 43.    [197] Baker and DeFrank 1995, 70.
[198] Blanton 2010, 69.    [199] Hutchings 1997, 34.    [200] Blanton 2010, 71.

A few months after National Security Directive 23 is drafted, uprisings in Eastern Europe soon gave way to the Berlin Wall falling. The new Bush administration was still trying to get a handle of Gorbachev's intentions regarding security concerns, but a new host of distributive issues would soon take precedence. It is those issues, and the face-to-face interactions that resolved them, that serve as the topic of the next chapter.

## Conclusion

In this chapter I have argued that the process of reassurance at the end of the Cold War, overcoming the security dilemma that many argue the US and Soviet Union found themselves in, was aided in very specific ways by face-to-face diplomacy. Over the course of several interactions, Reagan and Gorbachev were able to clarify and convey their sincere specific intentions to each other. This intention understanding ultimately helped to ensure that the Cold War ended with a handshake rather than war. As I have illustrated, the evidence suggests that Reagan was serious about intending SDI as a defensive system. At the same time, the evidence also suggests that Gorbachev intended to kill the SDI program, not because he necessarily questioned Reagan's sincerity, but because of crucial domestic pressures at home and his beliefs regarding the destabilizing nature of the program. Reagan picked up on this in their interactions and ultimately used it to his advantage. By walking out of the room in Reykjavik, Reagan did, as Gorbachev once told Henry Kissinger, the one thing the Soviets had not anticipated. "We had thought of everything except that Reagan might leave the room."[201] Reagan was intent on not using SDI as a bargaining chip and by realizing Gorbachev's aims to kill it, he knew he could not give in. Finally, precisely because Gorbachev knew that Reagan was serious about SDI's defensive orientation he felt comfortable in "untying the package" that connected SDI to other arms reduction agreements and was confident that Reagan would not exploit the move. Reagan read Gorbachev's sincerity and Gorbachev read the same from Reagan.

In reflecting back on this period, Shultz makes an important observation regarding the relationship between Reagan and Gorbachev: "One reason they respected each other was that they both could see that the other guy was saying what he thought. Maybe you did not agree with him and maybe you did. But there it was. It wasn't maneuvering and manipulating and trying to make some obscure point. It was right there.

---

[201] Kissinger 1994, 783.

It was real. What you saw was what you got."[202] This statement captures succinctly what this chapter, and indeed the book, is about: *seeing what the other is thinking*, in a very real and tangible way, through diplomacy.

As will become a recurring theme in this book, those that did *not* have the same face-to-face access to Reagan and Gorbachev routinely misperceived and misinterpreted the intentions of these two leaders. On the American side, for instance, William Clark and Caspar Weinberger routinely suggested that Gorbachev was a wolf in sheep's clothing, interpreting his discourse and concessions as mere cheap talk, at best, and cunning ploys at worst. These amount to theories regarding Gorbachev's aims. Those in the administration that had regular access to Soviet policymakers, and Gorbachev in particular, such as Jack Matlock and eventually George Shultz, come to an entirely different understanding of Gorbachev. Most importantly, Reagan himself undergoes a significant revision of his beliefs regarding Gorbachev. Not only is the Soviet Union interpreted as an evil empire, Gorbachev himself is interpreted as just another Soviet leader. These beliefs only change once Reagan is able to intuit Gorbachev's specific intentions and reflect upon that new information. And ultimately the "pause" in relations between the US and Soviet Union is based, at least in part, on George H.W. Bush's lack of confidence in Gorbachev's sincerity with respect to his intentions. Not having the same opportunity to read Gorbachev as his predecessor did, Bush enters office with uncertainty and beliefs regarding Gorbachev that were more costly aligned with Gates than Reagan.

Thus in the end, what we see in the ending of the Cold War, from a reassurance perspective, is a series of face-to-face interactions providing leadership at the highest levels, specifically Reagan and Gorbachev, with the ability to intuit the intentions of the other and eventually revise their beliefs about the intentions of the other. And, it should be mentioned, particularly with Reagan's beliefs about Gorbachev, they were deeply ingrained. In this case it is very difficult to see how intention understanding could have engendered to the degree it did without the face-to-face interactions in which the two engaged.

One of the remarkable aspects of the summits that Reagan and Gorbachev engaged in was that there was relatively little deception occurring between the two protagonists. Recalling the discussion in the previous chapter, realists in particular worry about diplomacy as an intention understanding mechanism because of incentives to dissemble. Yet in this case an analysis of the face-to-face interactions demonstrates a remarkable amount of sincerity.

---

[202] Quoted in Wohlforth 1996, 105.

Perhaps because of this lack of overt deception on either side, it is tempting to read this case as a story of interpersonal trust, as others have done.[203] While there is much in the interactions to support such a reading, after all Gorbachev's move in 1987 to "untie the package," seemingly requires trust that Reagan will not take advantage of that move and exploit Gorbachev for domestic political gain, there are also significant moments in time that suggest Reagan and Gorbachev are reading each other correctly but interpersonal trust has not developed. For example, in Rejkyavik the ultimate agreement for arms reduction was on the table. As Deborah Larson argues, the fact that an agreement did not occur represents a "stunning missed opportunity."[204] Ultimately the reason why they could not find the will to finalize an agreement at Reykjavik relates to their inability, at that time, to fully trust the other. In their first meeting on October 11, Reagan makes this clear: "There is a Russian saying: *doveryai no proveryai*, trust but verify. How will we know that you'll get rid of your missiles as you say you will?" Reagan is explicitly stating that he cannot trust Gorbachev on this point without verification – a point that Gorbachev understands and accepts, suggesting on-site inspections of weapon facilities. Later that day Reagan tells Gorbachev that SDI technology would be shared with the Soviet Union, at which point Gorbachev demurs that "If you will not share oil-drilling equipment or even milk-processing factories I do not believe that you will share SDI." Both Reagan and Gorbachev are explicitly *rejecting* interpersonal trust in this crucial interaction.[205]

Yet, they are able to read the intentions of one another. The crucial next step to trusting, however, has not yet occurred. According to Gates, Reagan felt like he had been trapped at Reykjavik and left angry both because of the lack of agreement *and* because Gorbachev had laid a trap with the flurry of concessions leading into the summits. Palazhchenko's argument that Gorbachev had been planning a public

---

[203] Wheeler 2018 is the exemplar here.          [204] Larson 2000, 212.

[205] A somewhat related difficulty for the interpersonal trust argument is the series of issues on which there seemed to be a lack of trust between Reagan and Gorbachev. For example, in October 1987 Reagan, in a speech at West Point, states that he still believes the USSR is an expansionist power, which belies what Gorbachev had told him of his intentions in Geneva and Reykjavik. "It is in regional conflicts where Soviet performance has been most disturbing. Anyone searching for evidence that the Soviets remain expansionist – indeed, imperialist – need look no farther than Nicaragua or Afghanistan." This may be a speech intended for a particular domestic audience, so it is easy to read too much into it, but it does suggest that on issues other than weapons, interpersonal trust might not be a significant causal factor. Finally, Matlock outlines a number of important areas of controversy, from Libya to the Daniloff arrest, where Reagan seemed to be personally outraged at the behavior of the Soviet Union. See Matlock 2004 182–83; 199.

campaign of accusing the US of acting in bad faith further illustrates the point that, at least at Reykjavik trust was not in abundance, though it may have been at later summits, such as Washington. Though, as Robert Gates told me in a recent interview, ultimately when reflecting back on those summits, "I would not go so far as to say trust occurred."[206] Thus the empirical record on trust between Reagan and Gorbachev is somewhat mixed, with actors close to the negotiations putting their stakes down on both sides of the debate. I do not doubt that trust eventually developed between the two; for my purposes however, the key is that trust is not doing *all* of the work in transforming enemies into partners at the end of the Cold War. More important, in my view, is the intention understanding that developed between the two sides as a result of interpersonal face-to-face interactions. Ultimately, the question of how intention understanding and trust development are linked is an important issue that I will further develop in the concluding chapter of the book.

I now turn to the other side of the Cold War coin: the distribution realignment problem that manifests once the Berlin Wall falls, specifically the decisions that had to be made with respect to what to do about an unstable, and divided, Germany.

---

[206] Interview with Robert Gates, May 14, 2015.

# 4    Unification and Distribution after the Wall Falls
## A Flurry of Face-to-Face

### Face-to-Face with a Changing Europe

The pause would be short-lived. Events in late summer and fall of 1989, merely months after Bush takes office in January, changed the decision-making calculus of the incoming administration considerably. Once the Wall falls, the administration engages in face-to-face diplomacy as a way of understanding what Soviet and European leadership intended with respect to German unification. From this understanding the administration crafts a particular strategy and plan on how to proceed. The first aim of this chapter is to understand the mechanics of how the Bush administration came to understand that the Soviet Union would accept a unified Germany in NATO. Second, as others have argued, there has been a tendency to view German unification as a US-led process;[1] I intend to demonstrate, in contrast, that face-to-face interactions among European leaders were some of the most important in pushing the process forward. While Gorbachev and Bush were undoubtedly at the heart of the process, and it would be difficult to overstate their importance, one of the aims of the chapter is to highlight the importance of lower-level face-to-face interactions, such as those between the seasoned diplomats in Europe, in providing intention intuitions and beliefs that were critical to the process. I will argue that the outcome was largely contingent on the specific intention intuitions, and eventually beliefs, that were generated in face-to-face interactions. Put simply, the counterfactual test is whether similar intention understanding vis-à-vis Germany and NATO would have obtained without the flurry of face-to-face interactions that accompanied both processes.

While it is easy, in hindsight, to view German unification and integration into NATO as inevitable, the events at the time were far from predetermined. As Robert Hutchings, who was the National Security

---

[1] Blanton 2010.

Council's director for European affairs at the time puts it, "Those building a simple narrative structure for understanding such historic turning points [such as the end of the Cold War] tend to omit, or dismiss as mere bureaucratic detail work, the role of diplomacy... By succumbing to what the French philosopher Henri Bergson has called 'illusions of retrospective determinism'... [they ignore] the contingencies that might have turned events in a different direction, they are ahistorical."[2] Dennis Ross, chief peace negotiator and diplomat in the George H. W. Bush and Bill Clinton presidential administrations, notes that if one had queried leaders in Europe, the State Department, journalists, pundits, and most foreign policy experts around 1988, they would have claimed that it was simply inconceivable that Soviet leadership would accept an end to the Cold War outcome of a unified Germany that was integrated into NATO.[3] If there was one red line in the Cold War, it surely "ran between East and West Germany."[4] Indeed as late as October 1988 Helmut Kohl, Chancellor of Germany from 1982 to 1998, responded to the notion that Gorbachev may permit unity to Germany in the following way: "I do not write futuristic novels... What you ask now, that is in the realm of fantasy."[5] As Philip Zelikow and Condoleezza Rice, both negotiators and diplomats who took part in the process, recount the history, there was practically no indication in late 1988 that German unification would even be on the agenda of negotiation topics for the coming year. After all, there were far more pressing concerns, such as arms reduction agreements that had begun under the Reagan administration that needed attention. Yet, less than one year later the Berlin Wall fell and German unification and NATO membership quickly followed in 1990. What was once believed to be fantasy had become real, and in very short order. What explains this drastic change of course in world history?

### The Wall Falls

While US–Soviet relations were pausing, unrest in Eastern Europe was fomenting. This meant that the US found itself on its "back foot" as events began to quickly unfold in Eastern Europe.[6] While events on the ground were changing rapidly, the Bush administration sought to reinforce the status quo. This was reflected most clearly at the May 1989 NATO conference where the US pushed for the modernization of eighty-eight Lance missiles in West Germany, a modernization that sought to maintain US force in Europe and prevent what Baker referred to as

---

[2] Hutchings 2015, 149.    [3] Ross 2008, 29–30.    [4] Beschloss and Talbott 1993.
[5] Zelikow and Rice 1995, 62.    [6] Sarotte 2009, 25.

"slipping down a path of denuclearization of our defense . . ."[7] The modernization push would have to be dealt with later as the issue remained unresolved, but the European trip was an opportunity to publicly reaffirm the status quo. In Mainz, Germany, the President reminded the world that the Cold War was not over and that it would not be over until Europe was whole and free: "Our overall aim is to overcome the division of Europe and to forge a unity based on Western values . . . The Cold War began with the division of Europe. It can only end when Europe is whole. Today it is this very concept of a divided Europe that is under siege."[8]

The events of the following months would reinforce the notion that East Europeans also believed that the old order, one of a divided Europe, was no longer sufficient. Protests, rallies, and other forms of relatively peaceful mobilization in Hungary, Poland, and East Germany gained intensity while the US and USSR largely watched from afar, a consequence of the pause. In effect, US desires to maintain the status quo were rubbing up against very strong desires on the ground for change. As Sarotte aptly puts it, "Western Europe might have had a good Cold War, but Eastern Europeans most definitely had not, and they wanted fundamentally different life choices, now that the threat of violent repression was gone."[9] The events in the fall of 1989 reflected this perspective and ushered in a new era. The status quo was over, the division of Germany was also over. What would replace it?

The vision for a reunified Germany that the Bush administration had in mind was one that needed to avoid the pitfalls of Versailles. As Robert Zoellick, one of the key architects of policy that the administration would negotiate, put it, "President Bush, Secretary Baker, and National Security Advisor Brent Scowcroft and their colleagues recognized that their decisions would shape Europe for decades to come . . . The U.S. aim was to unify Europe in peace and freedom, while seeking to avoid a 'Versailles victory' that invited its own destruction."[10] What Zoellick meant here is that "any limits imposed from the outside would create the potential for future grievances."[11] At the same time, however, the Bush administration firmly believed that Germany's past could not be ignored. "The president and his advisors believed that if Germany was not embedded in NATO, it would be a source of danger. If neutral, it would seek security by gaining its own nuclear capability, which would put Europe on a nuclear hair-trigger and cause the nuclear nonproliferation regime to unravel as other states capable of developing nuclear weapons chose to

---

[7] Quoted in Sarotte 2009, 27.      [8] Zelikow and Rice 1995, 31.
[9] Sarotte 2009, 47.      [10] Ross 2008, 33.      [11] Quoted in Ross 2008, 34.

do so."[12] As such the US found itself in a difficult position with respect to negotiating for German unification. It had to, on the one hand, push for unification, which would include its addition in Western institutions such as NATO (President Bush had, in the Mainz speech in May 1989, begun to allude to this possibility in the future using the language of "A Europe whole and free")[13], but not give in to the perceived Soviet desire to create a weakened German state. On the other hand, if the US wanted to bring about an end to the Cold War, it would likely have to make concessions to the Soviets.

It is also important to note at the outset that while the US had a vision for the future of Germany, nearly all of the parties involved had their own metaphors for understanding what was occurring in Europe and a vision for how to move forward. As Sarotte argues persuasively, what defined the relatively short period from the Berlin Wall opening to unification was contestation regarding what the post-Cold War order would look like.[14] The results were not predetermined, with each of the major powers, and leaders, proposing "competing blueprints for the future."[15] In fact, the US faced significant skepticism over the prospects of a unified Germany. The Soviets, British, and French were not enthusiastic about the prospect; all parties involved worried about the destabilizing force of a unified Germany. As Robert Gates told me, it is hard to overstate how skeptical nearly everyone was about the prospects for unification in these early stages. While a divided Germany was far from ideal, and each side had a desire to see the Cold War come to a close, the process of it occurring could have tremendous disruptive effects on the continent. As Bob Blackwell pointed out, the domestic situation in Germany could have significant consequences for the domestic situation in the USSR: "If it were to appear that Soviet troops were being forced to retreat from the GDR, [Gorbachev] had 'lost' Germany, and the security environment for the USSR was now more threatening, the domestic fallout – when combined with other complaints – could pose a threat to his position."[16] Put another way, the prospect of German unification was one that could significantly hamper the US–USSR relationship by putting Gorbachev in a politically difficult position.

This type of destabilization of Europe is something the French and British would rather avoid. Gorbachev agreed. He noted to Francois Mitterrand in November 1989 that the day Germany became unified

---

[12] Ross 2008, 34.
[13] Bush speech in Mainz, Federal Republic of Germany, May 31, 1989.
[14] Sarotte 2009, 5.    [15] Sarotte 2009, 5.    [16] Ross 2008, 35.

was the day that "a Soviet marshal will be sitting in my chair."[17] Margaret Thatcher laid out why Gorbachev should be concerned in a meeting with Bush: "Reunification means Gorbachev is lost. He loses the integrity of the Warsaw Pact. A unified Germany would be a country of eighty million in the middle of Europe, one with a strong balance of trade."[18] Thatcher reportedly told as much to Gorbachev directly, "[leaving] him with the clear impression that she not only did not welcome the reunification of Germany, but ardently hoped that Gorbachev would block it."[19] Thatcher's position on unification was complicated by a number of issues. First, British troops were based in West Germany, forcing involvement at some level. More importantly, however, memories of the Second World War were still relatively fresh. Rapid change in Germany was not a prospect that she, or many others in Britain, welcomed. Further, with the change in administrations from Reagan to Bush, Thatcher lost a strong personal ally. As Sarotte notes, her relationship with Bush was not nearly as strong as that with Reagan.[20] Ironically her closest ally in preventing, or at least slowing down, a unified Germany was Gorbachev. Sarotte describes how as early as September 1989 Thatcher had begun the process of "[stiffening] his spine with regard to divided Germany."[21]

Gorbachev, perhaps not needing the reinforcement, understood the stakes and at various times repeated that a unified Germany was "absolutely ruled out."[22] At the beginning of the process the Soviet Union favored a *restoration model*, one in which quadripartite governing mechanisms, as existed in 1945, would return.[23] Part of Gorbachev's thinking was that he believed at this early stage that none of the Western powers, perhaps even the United States, wanted to see a united Germany given the recent collective memories of the past.[24] Indeed as of late October 1989 the United States was signaling, in the form of a visit by Zbigniew Brzezinski that "[b]oth blocs should not be disbanded right now. I do not know what will happen if the GDR ceases to exist. There will be one Germany, united and strong. This does not correspond to either of your interests.[25] Even Helmut Kohl originally preferred a *revivalist model*, one where a confederation of German states would exist, "two states in one German nation," a concept that was originally endorsed by Mitterrand. For its part France's preferences were a bit unclear, with Mitterrand publicly endorsing the idea behind unification in early November

---

[17] Zelikow and Rice 1995, 137.
[18] Bush and Scowcroft 1998, 192.     [19] Grachev 2008.     [20] Sarotte 2009, 61.
[21] Sarotte 2009, 61.     [22] Baker and DeFrank 1995, 235.
[23] Sarotte 2009, 7.     [24] Savranskaya 2010, 33.
[25] Savranskaya 2010, 34. See also Savranskaya et al. 2010, Doc. 96.

(before the wall fell) but privately expressing concerns that any process would have to include France, given the shared borders and historical relationship. Mitterrand, who was also president of the European Community (EC) due to rotating presidency, believed in the importance of a European solution to Germany. And, as Sarotte argues, Mitterrand held the keys to a powerful European bloc that could slow, or stop, the unification process if it wanted to.[26] In sum, Gorbachev, Thatcher, and Mitterrand each conveyed to Bush that German unification, not to mention NATO integration, was not on the agenda.[27] Thus it is perhaps a bit of an understatement when Dennis Ross notes that the "the obstacles [to reunification] were formidable,"[28] given the competing perspectives on how order should be restored.

### Plan and Intention Competition

From the US perspective overcoming the practical obstacles to German unification while satisfying the needs of the major "Two Plus Four" players (the "two": Federal Republic of Germany, the German Democratic Republic; plus the "four" powers: France, USSR, UK, and US) required a strategy of reassuring each party that their concerns would be accounted for and instilling the sincere intention of the US to not simply try to steamroll a solution over Europe. This perspective was reflected in the very initial "lackluster" response to the events of November 9. As Lesley Stahl, anchor of the *CBS Evening News* put it to Bush, "You don't seem elated and I'm wondering if you're thinking of the problems." Bush responded, "I'm not an emotional guy, but I'm very pleased." Zelikow and Rice interpreted this as inattention to ceremony,[29] while Bush himself later reflected that he did not want to produce a backlash, an indication that he was at least partially worried about how an exuberant President would be viewed from a lack of empathy perspective. While Bush was attempting to downplay the triumphalism of the moment, Secretary of State James Baker was similarly providing boilerplate responses, but with hints of the US intentions to come. Speaking to Chris Wallace of *ABC* that same evening, Baker said, "it has been the policy of the NATO Alliance and it has been the policy of the United States of America to support reunification for over forty years," hinting at the important role the US believed NATO should play in what was to come. Wallace responded that the policy sounded like boilerplate, to which Baker noted, "That is our policy."[30] As Sarotte argues, establishing this policy would be of the highest priority in both

[26] Sarotte 2009, 56.    [27] Naftali 2007, 86.    [28] Ross 2008, 37.
[29] Zelikow and Rice 1995, 105.    [30] Sarotte 2009, 55.

Washington and Bonn, while reacting to it strategically the most pressing for both France and the USSR.[31]

Early in the process, each individual decision-maker had their own ideas about how unification should proceed (if at all) and each entered the negotiations with different identities. For instance, Gorbachev on November 10 proposed his restoration model to London, Paris, and Washington. Baker, working with his counterparts in Bonn was able to quell the idea in the short-term, but the proposal showed just how far apart the US and USSR models were. Thatcher reiterated a position close to Gorbachev's at Camp David on November 24, telling Bush that "reunification was not just a matter of self-determination: the Four Powers had certain responsibilities," noting the danger of Gorbachev being "toppled" and the "larger vision of democracy in Eastern Europe [vanishing]." In public she echoed similar concerns noting in a speech in London that, "We must remember that times of great change are times of great uncertainty and even danger."[32] Mitterrand agreed. In a phone conversation with Gorbachev on November 14, Mitterrand reportedly relayed "the French position [as follows]: We would like to avoid any kind of disruption...I do not think that the issue of changing borders can realistically be raised now – at least up until a certain time."[33]

Despite this pessimism, Helmut Kohl pushed the unification process forward, an initiative undertaken partially as a result of an important face-to-face encounter with Nikolai Portugalov, an advisor to the Central Committee of the Soviet Communist Party, on November 21. While little is known of the specifics of this meeting, it appears that Former West German security advisor Horst Teltschik relied on Portugalov for an independent reading of what was occurring in Moscow.[34] Portugalov entered Teltschik's office and handed over handwritten pages intended for Kohl. The contents were staggering. "West and East Germany [should be freed] from the relics of the past." And, just as importantly, "the Soviet Union was already thinking about all possible alternatives with regard to the German question, even the unthinkable." The notes suggested that the Soviet Union would be willing to negotiate "German confederation" in exchange for a guarantee that Germany would not possess a nuclear weapon. This language existed on the "Unofficial Position" of the communiqué; the "Official Position" that existed on a separate page was less striking, but did call for an "all-European order of peace." Alongside the note Portugalov told Teltschik, "As you can see, we are thinking about all possible alternatives for the German question,

---

[31] Sarotte 2009, 55–56.    [32] Sarotte 2009, 67.
[33] Sarotte 2009, 68.    [34] Sarotte 2009, 70–71.

even things that were practically unthinkable."[35] Teltschik was "electri-fied" by this new information, reading from Portugalov that the Sovi-ets could go much further than had previously been viewed as possible. This encounter would serve as the basis for a speech that Kohl would make days later, laying out his "Ten-Point-Program" for the future of Germany.[36] As Andrei Grachev argues based on interviews with par-ticipants, "[t]his probably unique exercise in personal diplomacy by a Secretary of the Central Committee without the knowledge of the Gen-eral Secretary (not to speak of the Minister of Foreign Affairs) was the inspiration behind rather sensational subsequent developments."[37] As analysts of this episode, including Zelikow and Rice, have suggested, it is difficult to know how accurately this new information reflected actual intentions. They note that Telschik may have "selectively" heard what he wanted to,[38] though Teltschik maintains to Sarotte that he understood Portugalov perfectly.[39] Further, as Sarotte notes, the signal "fit well with a message that Bonn had received from Shevardnadze, suggesting that peaceful change was welcome."[40] While Kohl and Teltschik had no way of independently verifying the accuracy of these Soviet intentions, there were reasons for Teltschik to take what he learned from Portugalov, in other words, at face value.

Kohl's model, which he would present in front of the Bundestag on Tuesday, November 28, reflected older ideas adapted for current geopo-litical realities. For example, it "borrowed traditional Ostpolitik rhetoric about the 'all-European process' and the sacred 'peace order' while actually completing the subversion of old Ostpolitik and returning to 'change through strength.'" As Zelikow and Rice argue, it was brilliantly constructed both because it connected abstract unification ideas with concrete ways to accomplish it while also mollifying concerns through vague phrases.[41] The aim of the plan was to provide relatively short-term (though both Kohl and Teltschik conceded that achieving the goals of the plan would likely take at least a decade) aid to the East German economy while stemming the tide of refugees, all while placing the con-federation firmly within the principles of both the EC and Conference on Security and Cooperation in Europe (CSCE).[42] As the plan stated, "The future architecture of Germany must fit in the future pan-European architecture." The construction of the plan itself was only one part of the broader political process. The next salient decision would be who to tell about the plan before unveiling it to the public. Ultimately Kohl chose a strategy that reflected both confidence, likely fueled by his

---

[35] Zelikow and Rice 1995, 118.    [36] Savranskaya 2010, 36.
[37] Grachev 2008.    [38] Zelikow and Rice 1995, 118.    [39] Sarotte 2009, 71.
[40] Sarotte 2009, 72.    [41] Zelikow and Rice 1995, 120–21.    [42] Sarotte 2009, 73.

meeting with Portugalov, and a desire to "[ask] for forgiveness rather than permission,"[43] resolving to tell only Washington of his plans. In the end, however, the message sent to Bush was received only as Kohl's speech was being delivered; it was actively being translated as Kohl began to speak.[44]

The reaction to Kohl's speech was swift. During the speech itself there was an outburst from a Green Party member regarding political prisoners in East Germany.[45] After the speech Moscow relayed frustration through foreign minister Hans-Dietrich Genscher. Gorbachev reportedly labeled Kohl's speech as "crude," while violating East German sovereignty. Shevardnadze noted that "even Hitler did not allow himself anything like that," while Gorbachev further noted that Bonn had "prepared a funeral for the European processes."[46] For his part, Mitterrand was dismayed to have not been notified of the speech beforehand (particularly since they had spoken the day before), though he expressed support publicly.[47] Britain was still relatively unimpressed.

Nevertheless, Kohl had decided on a plan and broadcasted it to the world. The next step would be to work out how the confederation structures in Germany would operate while simultaneously managing the relationships of the United States, Soviet Union, France, and Britain. Kohl's bold plan was a starting point, but it was not clear in late November 1989 that the plan would be adopted by the major players.

### The US Strategy: A Flurry of Face-to-Face

From the US perspective there were two main hurdles that needed to be cleared. First, US leaders needed to understand if the Soviets did indeed have an intention to pursue unification, as the Portugalov meeting suggested. Second, if unification was to move forward, either through the Kohl plan or through other means, intention understanding regarding process specifics would have to be created between the major leaders. As Ross notes in his memoir, achieving both of these required significant efforts in personal diplomacy:

The president and the secretary of state conducted a highly personal diplomacy that involved an extraordinary number of face-to-face meetings with other leaders. Certainly phone calls were made, especially in the interim between meetings or to brief other leaders on the meetings that had just taken place with their fellow leaders . . . Though these calls, and meetings at lower levels, were an essential part of the diplomacy, *there can be no doubt that the face-to-face meetings at the president's and secretary's level were the heart of the effort.*[48]

---

[43] Sarotte 2009, 73.    [44] Savranskaya et al. 2010, Doc. 109.
[45] Sarotte 2009, 75.    [46] Sarotte 2009, 76.    [47] Sarotte 2009, 76.
[48] Ross 2008, 39. My emphasis.

Gates told me that Bush was a big believer in the "feel" one received from meeting face-to-face and was willing to trust his intuitions that were gained from the personal interactions. Both the intensity of the meetings themselves and sheer number of disparate interactions were staggering. Ross notes that Bush met Kohl in either a bilateral or "on the margins of broader multilateral events" nine times in the span of one year.[49] For his part Kohl undertook a "blitzkrieg diplomatic campaign" aimed at "lavish[ing] assurances about Germany's peaceful intentions."[50] Genscher met Shevardnadze thirteen times in 1990 alone.[51] Bush met with Thatcher eight times in total, three of which were strictly bi-lateral. He met with President Mitterrand eight times, twice exclusively, in that same one-year time span. James Baker exercised even greater use of the face-to-face meeting. Ross counts close to thirty different encounters with his German, British, French, and Soviet counterparts over the same year-long period. Indeed it is difficult to recall as short a period of time with such intensity of face-to-face diplomacy.

One of the most important considerations for the US diplomacy team was understanding if the Soviets actually had a true specific intention of moving forward with a unified Germany, as was communicated in the Portugalov memo. Baker notes that, "[The Soviets] were saying the right things, but it was important that we match action with words."[52] Cheap talk was not enough – in order to make a determination about intentions, Baker sought a series of face-to-face meetings, beginning according to Baker, in May of 1989, with his Soviet counterpart, Edward Shevardnadze. Baker notes that the meetings were critical in order to "test their intentions" and determine that the Soviets could be pushed toward unification. By this point there was growing recognition in the administration that, according to Chollet and Goldgeier, the administration "now saw uncertainty as more, not less reason to work with the Soviets to implement lasting change."[53] Baker was able to get a sense that Shevardnadze "was a serious [man]" and specifically with respect to intentions regarding moving forward, they provided "a determination in my own mind that it was time to move forward."[54] Crucially, Baker understood from Shevardnadze that "[t]hese were not the words of a government minister reading off a prepared briefing paper," but rather, "[t]hey were the words

[49] Ross 2008, 39.    [50] Kort 2014, 392.
[51] Schmidt and Ritter 2012, 199.
[52] 1997 James Baker Interview, George Washington University National Security Archive. Available: http://nsarchive.gwu.edu/coldwar/interviews/episode-23/baker1.html.
[53] Chollet and Goldgeier 2003, 164.
[54] 1997 James Baker Interview, George Washington University National Security Archive. Available: http://nsarchive.gwu.edu/coldwar/interviews/episode-23/baker1.html.

of a man involved in a historic struggle."[55] Baker ultimately would recall that the intention understanding that developed through their face-to-face encounters was critical;[56] it was, in other words, through this type of interaction that Baker was able to see through public rhetoric and understand that the Soviets could be amenable to some structured unification, confirming in his own mind the Portugalov communication. This determination would also set the stage for two salient meetings in early December: the Malta face-to-face interaction between Bush and Gorbachev, and a meeting between Bush and Kohl the day after.

Before turning to the interactions themselves it is important to note that these face-to-face interactions were not costless. Indeed some in Bush's close circle advised that the costs would be too high. President Richard Nixon, for example, conveyed to Bush that he needed to exercise caution in interacting with the Soviet leadership, noting that it had been "a mistake for Reagan to put his arm around Gorbachev physically and rhetorically in Red Square" earlier. With respect to a meeting that Bush had planned for December 2–3 with Gorbachev in Malta, Nixon noted, "For you to leave a similar impression after your meetings in Malta would only add credence to the mistaken idea so emotionally being propounded by the prestigious Beltway media that because the wall is coming down, we have no differences with Gorbachev that can't be settled by a few friendly meetings and warm handshakes."[57] Nixon's bottom line was thus simple and clear: "I would strongly urge that you indicate that you are *not* going to negotiate German reunification or the future of NATO with Gorbachev."[58] Brent Scowcroft echoed similar ideas. He feared a face-to-face interaction would put undue pressure and expectations on both sides to reach a monumental agreement. Worse, "the Soviets might grandstand and force [the United States] into agreements that would ultimately not be good [for us]."[59] There is some evidence that Bush took this "interesting thinking" to heart, as he asked that it be included in his team's preparations for Malta,[60] but ultimately, as Gates told me, Bush believed in the face-to-face meeting.

The aim for the Malta Summit, from the James Baker's perspective, was to "gain a clearer understanding" of Gorbachev and "probe" his thinking on "the transformations underway in Eastern Europe" specifically.[61] The important interactions that were used to achieve this,

---

[55] Chollet and Goldgeier 2003, 161.
[56] Baker and DeFrank 1995, 135, 38, 52. See also Chollet and Goldgeier 2003, 163; Ekedahl and Goodman 2010, 119–21.
[57] Sarotte 2009, 77.      [58] Sarotte 2009, 77.
[59] Sarotte 2009, 77.      [60] Sarotte 2009, 77.
[61] Document 79, in Savranskaya and Blanton 2017, 523–27.

aboard the Soviet cruise liner *Maxim Gorkii*, were hindered by stormy seas; indeed many of the planned events had to be cancelled. Nevertheless, Bush and Gorbachev were able to meet face-to-face for the first time since the fall of the wall. Bush knew that Gorbachev and Soviet military leaders such as Akhromeyev were skeptical of US intentions and believed that Bush "did not support perestroika."[62] The intentional "pause" had been picked up on a year earlier on Governors Island and Bush understood that it was important to convey his sincere intentions. Bush therefore decided to open the interaction with a lengthy general discussion about the need for more US–Soviet economic cooperation and more arms control on both sides. He also attempted to put Gorbachev at ease by highlighting that the US had not responded to the Berlin Wall coming down by "[jumping] up and down", even though his administration had encouraged him to do so. Importantly, this information was not new: the US had communicated to Gorbachev and the Soviets immediately following the events that led to the fall of the wall that their response would be subdued,[63] which was reflected in communications to the Soviets as well as the initial reactions on television documented above. What was new was the modality of the interaction, the face-to-face encounter, which allowed Gorbachev to decide for himself if Bush was being sincere.

Among the substantive give and take of the interaction, both sides made clear what their concerns and specific intentions were moving forward.[64] Bush emphasized that the United States could not be asked to disapprove of German unification. Gorbachev offered a veiled, but optimistic, reading of the situation: "You can tremble and some panic, but if you look at it philosophically – things fall into place. We are dealing with fundamental processes if nations and people are involved in the developments – one can't expect it to be smooth."[65] Gorbachev asks Bush, assuming unification were to happen, "[w]ould a unified Germany be neutral, not a member of any military-political alliances, or would it be a member of NATO? I believe we should let everyone understand that it is still too early to discuss either of these options."[66] Put simply, on unification Gorbachev was not pushing back,[67] even entertaining the notion of a unified Germany in NATO. Bush was vague in response to this, noting that the US was trying to act "with a certain reserve." The two agreed that democratic values are universal and not simply "Western," as Bush and his officials had intimated in earlier letter correspondences and that both leaders had the same vision for self-determination of political, cultural, or economic systems moving forward.[68] Gorbachev also wanted

---

[62] Zelikow and Rice 1995, 127.    [63] Bush and Scowcroft 1998, 190.
[64] Savranskaya et al. 2010, Doc. 110.    [65] Zelikow and Rice 1995, 129.
[66] Zelikow and Rice 1995, 129.    [67] Sarotte 2009, 78.
[68] Zelikow and Rice 1995: 129

to reassure Bush of Soviet intentions regarding war and the image it held of the United States: "First and foremost, the new U.S. president must know that the Soviet Union will not under any circumstances initiate a war. This is so important that I wanted to repeat the announcement to you personally. Moreover, the USSR is prepared to cease considering the U.S. as an enemy and announce this openly."[69] As Chernyaev would note in his diary, the result of the meeting was "that the USSR and US are no longer enemies. This is the most important thing."[70] Bush reflected this back to Gorbachev, noting that the administration would "avoid doing anything that would damage your position in the world."[71]

The press conference following the personal interaction exhibited similar non-confrontational tones. The two leaders spoke together and noted that both sides would show restraint. The US would not demonstrate "on top of the Berlin Wall to show how happy we are about the change, [but] we are happy about the change."[72] For Gorbachev's part, he intimated that the German question was "the decision of history" and "history itself decides the processes and fates on the European continent and also the fates of those two states."[73]

For the US contingent, the change in tone and demeanor at the Malta interaction from earlier interactions was striking. Gorbachev had previously given the impression, publicly *and* privately, of being uneasy about the specific developments in Germany. Indeed just one week earlier Gorbachev expressed great concern about German unification to Canadian prime minister Brian Mulroney (who later told his American counterparts about the interaction), noting to Mulroney: "people have died from eating unripened fruit," an allegory to the problem of hastily uniting the two Germanys.[74] And of course just days before the Malta meeting Moscow had reacted harshly to Kohl's plan. Gorbachev himself noted to Bush at the very beginning of their face-to-face interaction that Kohl had not acted "seriously and responsibly" and there was concern that "the topic of reunification may be exploited for electoral gain."[75] Similar unease was conveyed in correspondences between the Soviet leadership and their US counterparts.

[69] Transcript of the Malta Meeting, December 2–3, 1989. Source: Gorbachev Foundation, Fond 1, Opis 1. Document 10, p. 21. Available: http://nsarchive.gwu.edu/NSAEBB/NSAEBB298.

[70] Excerpt from Anatoly S. Chernyaev's Diary, January 2, 1990. Available: http://nsarchive.gwu.edu/NSAEBB/NSAEBB298/Document%2013.pdf.

[71] Savranskaya et al. 2010, Doc. 110.      [72] Zelikow and Rice 1995, 129.

[73] Zelikow and Rice 1995, 130.      [74] Zelikow and Rice 1995, 124.

[75] GWU National Security Archive, "Document No. 3 Excerpts from the Soviet Transcript of the Malta Summit: December 2–3, 1989." Available: www.gwu.edu/~nsarchiv/NSAEBB/NSAEBB296/doc03.pdf.

It was thus surprising that the uneasy and anti-unification Gorbachev was replaced by a more open and philosophical Gorbachev. As Zelikow and Rice note, "Gorbachev's relaxed demeanor convinced the Americans that the Soviet leader was malleable on the German question."[76] Chollet and Goldgeier pick up on this as well, noting that it was the tone, as much as the content of the meeting, that was crucial.[77] Akhromeyev, for his part, later reflected that Gorbachev had made a crucial error in this soft demeanor and failure to give a "concrete answer" to the German question opened the door for the West to move ahead with their vision, albeit softly and strategically.[78] The lack of a strong stance by Gorbachev in the face-to-face interaction with Bush meant that Bush would not face strong opposition on the German question. As Akhromeyev reflects on the meeting, "Bush realized that had a position like this been formed, it would have been expressed by M. Gorbachev in Malta... It is hard to doubt that Bush informed Kohl about this."[79] Bush referred to Gorbachev's new disposition as one of openness to the German question, if there was "a formulation which doesn't scare him."[80]

Gorbachev went into Malta having just expressed considerable public disdain for the idea of a unified Germany and left the Malta interaction having impressed upon Bush that progress on unification was possible. Literally in hours "positions" had changed. The face-to-face interactions allowed Bush to read Gorbachev's intentions with respect to progress moving forward on; his easy demeanor and relaxed nature were a stark contrast to the rhetoric exhibited earlier. The words being said publicly were attempts to shield what Gorbachev evidently internally believed and was shared by Portugalov days earlier: the German question was ready to be answered and unification could be part of the answer. Had it not been for the face-to-face interactions with Gorbachev, Bush would have only had the stark public discourse for intention understanding and opinions of his advisors (both in Washington and those communicating with their Soviet counterpart in person) and likely reached different conclusions. As Akhromeyev notes, ultimately these face-to-face interactions likely resulted in an outcome that many in the USSR did not want. While he was encouraged to convey a hard-lined position to Bush in their meeting, he was able to do this in rhetoric only. Gorbachev had "given away the store," not in what he said but in what Bush was able to read from his face in the face-to-face encounter. Crucially, there were strong incentives

---

[76] Zelikow and Rice 1995, 130.      [77] Chollet and Goldgeier 2003, 165.
[78] Zelikow and Rice 1995, 130.      [79] Zelikow and Rice 1995, 131.
[80] Zelikow and Rice 1995, 131.

for Gorbachev to dissemble here. By projecting a position of strength, by demonstrating that the USSR intends *not* to allow Germany to be unified, Gorbachev potentially could have engendered a more favorable outcome. That is, Akhromoyev's intuition that Gorbachev did not need to convey that the USSR was intending Germany to be unified, even if this was their sincere intention, is likely correct. By being "malleable" on the Germany question Gorbachev ultimately likely obtained a sub-optimal outcome. I will return to this important point in the final section of the chapter, but for present purposes it is worth noting that the incentives to dissemble for Gorbachev in Malta were significant.

While it is often difficult to discern precisely what a politician's intentions are, we do know that as of December 1989 the Soviets had noted that unification was inevitable. As Pavel Palazhchenko, Gorbachev's translator, recounts:

No one was happy in Moscow either. Men as different as Shevardnadze and Ligachev said the same thing at the Central committee plenum in January 1990: the pace of Germany's unification was alarming, and its membership in NATO would be dangerous. But even in December 1989, on the plane to Brussels, one thing clearly emerged from our heated discussion: we were dealing with a national issue and a national drive; unification was inevitable; we could perhaps slow it down but we could not stop it.[81]

It is of course difficult to know precisely when these views were set, be it in November as Portugalov suggested, or literally on the plane in December, but the timing from both accounts suggests that by December the Soviets did not possess an intention to uphold unification.[82]

---

[81] Palazhchenko 1997, 159.

[82] In the 1996 oral history conference at Princeton, Chernyaev stated that it is difficult to set a specific date on which Gorbachev agreed to unification, though by the summer of 1989 "inevitability" was setting in. "The answer is that there is no such date. There was a certain evolution of his views. Almost from the start – as early as 1987 – he said that it was the will of history that there are now two German states and history will eventually decide what is going to happen, and we will see – it may take a hundred years for it to decide, it may take ten years. We don't know. Let's wait and see. That was his initial formula. He said that to President Weiszacker of Germany in 1987, and this was his position to which he was sticking. Of course, that position was innovative in a way, compared to the position of our foreign policy in the pre-Gorbachev period. That is to say, even then in principle he did not rule out the possibility of German unification. In private discussions among close friends even then he was saying that to force a great nation to remain indefinitely divided is wrong and we are not going to have a common European house while that situation persists. The decisive moment that really persuaded him of the inevitability of that process was his visit to Germany in the summer of 1989. He saw a different country. He saw a new country. He shed the stereotypes that at the time still persisted among our leaders and also among our people with respect to Germany..." (52). Later Chernyaev notes, "the fact that [Gorbachev] understood the inevitability of unification is attested by a phrase that he uttered in

Palazhchenko further recounts that Gorbachev subsequently told him in conversation that "at no point in the process was the use of force to prevent unification proposed as a possible course of action either by himself, by other members of the Soviet leadership, or by the military."[83] It is *this* understanding that unification was inevitable, that the Soviets intended to pursue unification, that Bush ultimately gains in Malta through interpersonal face-to-face interaction with Gorbachev.

Finally, it is important to note that Bush was risking quite a bit on this intention understanding derived through the face-to-face meeting. As he notes:

I took a great deal of flak in the press, from leaders in the US Baltic communities, and from 'experts,' that I was too accommodating, accepting Gorbachev's 'new thinking' and reforms at *face value*. I was acutely aware of the dangers, but my experience with Gorbachev at Malta, and Baker's excellent relationship with Shevardnadze, made me confident that Gorbachev was sincere in his efforts to match his words with actions.[84]

Put simply, the consequences of being wrong about the intentions and misreading the seemingly cooperative demeanor and tone of Gorbachev would be significant for Bush. Similarly, the notion that one could read intentions from others was not one that made for a particularly easy sell; political opponents happily attacked the notion. Bush was placing a large bet that his reading of Gorbachev and Baker's reading of Shevardnadze were correct.

For his part, Gorbachev also read Bush correctly. In a conversation between Gorbachev and Mitterrand three days after the summit, Gorbachev admits to not being entirely satisfied with the outcome of the Malta summit. He notes to Mitterrand, "I have a feeling that the US is not completely open about their position [regarding German unification], that they are not presenting it fully." Mitterrand concurs, telling Gorbachev, "That is true . . . The Americans are not telling the complete truth, including on the German issue."[85] As mentioned earlier, the US intention was that a reunified Germany should be in NATO. By being purposefully vague with Gorbachev on the issue of NATO he hoped to quell uncertainty regarding Germany's future. Gorbachev is able to read between the lines, however, and pick up from Bush that he is shielding

a conversation with President Bush at Malta in early December 1989. He said that that time, as though in passing, 'Maybe a united Germany should be neutral.' When you discuss whether a united Germany should be neutral, that means that you accept the possibility of a united Germany, and that was very early on" (54–55). The formal communication was made to Gorbachev's inner circle days later in January (55).

[83] Palazhechenko 2007, *xviii*.     [84] Bush and Scowcroft 1998, 207; italics added.
[85] Savranskaya et al. 2010, Doc. 114.

his intentions. Similarly, in a conversation with Genscher on December 5, Gorbachev suggests that "Maybe it is Bush who is heating the situation up?" with respect to Kohl's perceived "ultimatum" that Gorbachev perceives in the 10-point plan. This is an indication that Gorbachev is not particularly trusting of Bush when it comes to the latter's pledge to simply not oppose unification.[86] This has important implications for the notion that trust developed between Bush and Gorbachev at Malta, which will be discussed later in this chapter.

Based on this new understanding of Gorbachev, Bush went directly to meet Kohl in Laeken, outside of Brussels ahead of a NATO session that was to begin the next day. Bush and Kohl met face-to-face over dinner, with Kohl unsure of how the interaction would go. After all, Kohl had days earlier put forth a plan for Europe without first consulting the United States. Perhaps even worse, Bush had to meet with European leaders as well as Gorbachev himself without a chance to discuss the plan directly with Kohl. As Sarotte argues, "Being required to discuss an unfamiliar proposal on short notice – one that he knew nothing about before it appeared, and had no role in creating – might be common tasking for a Washington subordinate, but not for the president. It clearly showed that the initiative came from Bonn, not Washington."[87] As such Kohl landed in Laekan ready to defend himself. In a telephone conversation between Kohl and Scowcroft the day after Kohl's speech he pledged that he was not going alone and that his plan should not be viewed as an alternative to the United States' strategy. The face-to-face encounter in Laeken solidified this position.

Kohl repeated in the meeting to Bush his commitment to the United States plan: "We are part of Europe and continue as part of the EC. Ten points is *not* an alternative to what we are doing in the West."[88] Bush responded in the strongest terms, essentially backing Kohl with tremendous support.[89] "I think the answer is self-determination, and then let things work."[90] As Scowcroft notes, this face-to-face meeting marked a turning point from the perspective of both sides: "There seemed a perfect conjunction of the minds on reunification, and the atmosphere of comradeship in a great venture was palpable to me. The easygoing discussion seemed to give Kohl confidence, almost visible to me at the time, that he had the President behind him. Kohl, in his memoir of reunification, also points to this meeting as an important moment."[91] While the same information had been conveyed days earlier through both

[86] Savranskaya et al. 2010, Doc. 113.    [87] Sarotte 2009, 78.
[88] Bush and Scowcroft 1998, 198.    [89] Savranskaya et al. 2010, Doc. 111.
[90] Savranskaya et al. 2010, Doc. 111.    [91] Bush and Scowcroft 1998, 199–200.

letters and telephone calls, there was something about the face-to-face encounter that brought comfort to Kohl that the previous interactions could not. It also brought comfort to Bush. As Sarotte reports, Zelikow recalls that Bush was "a deeply emotional man who trusted his instincts. In Laeken, those instincts were telling him that Kohl was right."[92] The plan for German unification would go forward with Kohl leading the initiative in Europe.

Before turning to the final negotiations regarding unification and sub-sequent NATO integration, it is important to remember that personal diplomacy involves dyads. The Soviet side appeared to use a similar sin-cerity assessment strategy as the US, utilizing face-to-face interactions as a way to gain a sense of US sincerity. Sergey Akhromeyev, Chief of the General Staff of the Soviet Armed Forces under Gorbachev and key negotiator with US Joint Chiefs stated in an interview that before 1988 he was very skeptical and distrustful of US intentions. This would quickly change after a series of interpersonal meetings. John Hines sum-marizes Akhromeyev's perspective based on his interview: "The first and several subsequent meetings reassured him that the joint chiefs were thoughtful and responsible people. The mutual understanding that came from face-to-face discussions helped to create a fairly stable situation in Europe. The intentions ascribed for many years by each side to the other were incorrect."[93]

Former chairman of the Joint Chiefs of Staff, Adm. William J. Crowe Jr., Akhromeyev's counterpart and interlocutor, echoed similar senti-ments. He notes that Akhromeyev told him that prior to 1988 he had believed that the United States would attack the Soviet Union, a posi-tion that changed only after visiting personally with his US counter-parts, beginning in late 1988.[94] Crowe writes in his memoir, "Sitting opposite each other with our interpreters, we had the time and pri-vacy for exchanges that eventually gave both of us a better perspec-tive on the US-Soviet relationship and where both sides were com-ing from as we made our way past the rocks and shoals of the Cold War."[95] The substance of the meetings regarded US and Soviet inten-tions. Crowe notes that what he wanted to talk about were Soviet inten-tions: "[Akhromeyev] had come prepared to convince me that the Soviet military was not the threatening offensive machine we considered it to

---

[92] Sarotte 2009, 79.
[93] Summary of interview by John Hines, February 8, 1991, George Washington Univer-sity National Security Archive. Available: http://nsarchive.gwu.edu/nukevault/ebb285/vol%20II%20Akhromeev.pdf
[94] Jackson 1991.    [95] Crowe and Chanoff 2001, 281.

be."[96] For his part Crowe had similar aims, noting that his goal was to convey to Akhromeyev the American psychology, or "deep background against which a more understanding approach to our nations' geopolitical concerns might be achieved."[97] Both sides were communicating their intentions to each other in a face-to-face context. Ultimately Crowe believed, as Akhromeyev did, that these encounters allowed both to understand each other and "break through a legacy of fear and misunderstanding."[98] This is important because it illustrates the utility of face-to-face diplomacy not only at the head of state level, but lower levels of engagement as well. As Gates told me, these interactions, particularly between Baker and Shevardnadze, were critical.

On the other hand, Gorbachev presented a more cautious approach to face-to-face meetings. Perhaps after perceived disappointment by giving up too much in expressive behavior in Malta, Gorbachev essentially curtailed his personal diplomacy with Western leaders in early 1990. There are many reasons for this as Sarotte notes, such as pressing economic concerns in the USSR, rising secessionist pressures in territories such as Lithuania, and perhaps a "lack of clarity" on how to proceed.[99] Gorbachev having sent signals to the US team through private meetings that unification would occur was also still trying to maintain the prospects for the restoration model that emerged early in the process, to no avail. Indeed from mid-December 1989 through early 1990 Kohl had been trying to arrange a face-to-face meeting with Gorbachev directly. Kohl wanted to reassure Gorbachev that his emphasis was on maintaining stability, that unification would occur through "all-European structures" (presumably this was to reassure Gorbachev that it was not the United States pulling the puppet strings behind the scenes), and finally, that Kohl recognized the Soviet Unions' legitimate security concerns about reunification. The response Kohl received was, as Zelikow and Rice put it "cold."[100] Gorbachev pledged to "neutralize" any intervention in the GDR's affairs and that East Germany was fundamentally a partner of the Soviet Union and the two Germanys was a "historic fact." Clearly traditional diplomatic channels of the written word were not engendering the type of persuasion or understanding that Kohl was seeking. Kohl's intuition that if he could meet face-to-face with Gorbachev in order to reassure him that it was Europe that was in control of unification, and not the United States, was likely correct, but Gorbachev, still feeling

[96] Crowe and Chanoff 2001, 281
[97] Crowe and Chanoff 2001, 281
[98] Crowe and Chanoff 2001, 281
[99] Sarotte 2009, 101.
[100] Zelikow and Rice 1995, 147.

the negative effects of his face-to-face encounter with Bush in Malta, demurred.

Nevertheless after meeting with his advisors at the end of January 1990, Gorbachev decided that the unification process should be prolonged, the Soviets should pursue a "strategy" of playing on the fears of West Europeans regarding the influx of East Germans into Western economies.[101] If unification was to occur the Soviets needed to be part of the process. Two salient face-to-face meetings were set, first with Baker on February 7–9, 1990 and then with Kohl on February 10. Meanwhile Akhromeyev was charged with putting together a plan for Soviet troop withdrawal from East Germany.[102] At this point the strategy was about "buying more time and brooking no NATO membership for Germany."[103]

### The NATO Controversy

Just as Gorbachev and his team were crafting a strategy with how to proceed with unification in a way that maintained Soviet oversight, the US team was also emerging with a plan that would provide a forum for the two Germanys, plus the four powers ("2 + 4" with the two Germanys representing the most important states at the table), to negotiate the technicalities of unification. As the US State Department assessment of Soviet intentions noted, "beneath it all is an increasingly plaintive insistence that they must be given some new, enduring role."[104] In a face-to-face private meeting between Baker and Genscher on February 2 this plan was agreed to, and in a joint press conference Genscher revealed that he and Baker both agreed that "there was no interest to extend NATO to the East."[105]

NATO was a thorny problem on a number of levels. First, West Germany was already integrated into NATO. A unified Germany where NATO boundaries did not extend into the eastern regions of the unified state was difficult to envision. Second, the Soviet Union maintained over 350,000 troops in East Germany, a legal right provided to them in 1945 after German surrender at the end of the Second World War. East German territory integrated into NATO would theoretically mean that Soviet troops would stay in NATO territory or they would have to be removed and the Soviet Union would need to renounce its legal claims as part of the bargain. Lastly, Gorbachev, coming to the realization that the restoration model that had failed a month earlier

---

[101] Sarotte 2009, 102.    [102] Savranskaya et al. 2010, Doc 118.
[103] Savranskaya 2010, 37.    [104] Quoted in Sarotte 2009: 107
[105] Sarotte 2009, 105.

would no longer serve as the vision for Europe, would rather see brand new pan-European institutions replace both NATO and the Warsaw Pact moving forward.[106]

Baker's arrival in Moscow in early February was with regard to the NATO issue. After lengthy discussions regarding arms control, the discussion turned to unification, the details of which are important to understanding later controversies. Baker relayed the notion of the "2 + 4" framework as a way of satisfying German concerns while also maintaining an important role for the USSR and Western powers. They also discussed NATO. In Baker's notes, transcribed by Sarotte, he wrote: "End result: Unified Ger. Anchored in a *changed (polit.) NATO-whose juris. Would not move *eastward!"[107] Baker reportedly asked Mr. Gorbachev, "Would you prefer to see a unified Germany outside of NATO, independent and with no U.S. forces or would you prefer a unified Germany to be tied to NATO, with assurances that NATO's jurisdiction would not shift one inch eastward from its present position?" and Gorbachev, in return, emphasized "Certainly any extension of the zone of NATO would be acceptable"; Baker responded that "we agree with that."[108] And thus an important ambiguity was created: what was the specific zone of NATO that was being discussed? As Sarotte notes, this was a moment that was very significant to Gorbachev, who would recall that that meeting "cleared the way for a compromise" on Germany.[109] Importantly, no documents were signed on that day, with only notes and recollections available to piece together what was conveyed. For his part Gorbachev was likely unwilling to commit formally to unification at that point in time, preferring to prolong the negotiations, as noted above.

The significance of this meeting is difficult to overstate. Future NATO expansion years later would mean that the Soviet Union would have little recourse in protesting enlargement to the East. Russian presidents would later lament that the US had given an assurance that NATO would not expand, while the US would retort that the conversation was a simple one in a series of negotiations. Angela Stent goes further, noting that "The record showed that no explicit promises on NATO expansion were made, but what was implied during the negotiations ultimately lies in the eyes of the beholder."[110] Importantly, Kohl was not present at the meeting, arriving in Moscow the next day. In order to prepare Kohl for his discussions with Gorbachev, Baker had a secret letter drafted by Dennis Ross which would be left behind and given to Kohl when he arrived in Moscow. The letter that Baker approved

---

[106] Sarotte 2009, 105.  [107] Sarotte 2009, 110.  [108] Sarotte 2009, 110–11.
[109] Sarotte 2009, 110–11.  [110] Stent 2000, 140–41.

noted that Gorbachev seemed interested in the "2 + 4" mechanism and that Baker had explained to Gorbachev that a united Germany would stay in NATO. Baker quoted the question he posed to Gorbachev cited above and Gorbachev's response. Baker ends by noting that he believed that Gorbachev was "not locked-in" and looked "forward to comparing notes with [Kohl] after [his] meeting."[111] Publicly there would be much ambiguity regarding the pledge. As Baker remarked in a press conference after his talks on the 9th, he noted that the United States favored a unified Germany with "continued membership in, *or association with*, NATO."[112]

Members of the National Security Council in Washington were concerned about the Baker formulation. In response the NSC drafted a letter from Bush that was sent to Kohl the same day. Rather than speaking in general terms about NATO, Bush's letter used very specific language, such as agreeing to "special military status for what is now the territory of the GDR."[113] Zelikow noted to Sarotte that it was clear that the White House preferred a different approach to Baker's, attempting essentially to change the conversation by assuming that a letter from the President would "trump" a letter from the Secretary of State.[114] Before talking to Gorbachev, Kohl had the opportunity to read both letters and ultimately chose to echo the works of Baker rather than Bush. Kohl assured Gorbachev that "naturally NATO could not expand its territory to the current territory of the GDR" and emphasized a European solution to unification. For his part Genscher told Shevardnadze that, "for us, it stands firm: NATO will not expand itself to the East."[115]

Unlike the Baker–Gorbachev interaction from the day before, the Kohl–Gorbachev meeting ended with a deal. Gorbachev agreed that Germany could unify and Kohl wasted no time in publicizing the agreement that same night at 10 pm. Kohl noted in his press conference that Gorbachev had agreed that it was the "sole right of the German people" to decide their own future and that "Gorbachev has promised me clearly that the Soviet Union will respect the decision of Germans to live in one state, and that it will be a matter for Germans themselves to decide the path to, and timing of, their unification."[116] Kohl returned home the next day to begin working on unification logistics.

The controversy of these two face-to-face meetings would continue to linger and in some respects continues into the present. Baker, as reported

---

[111] Sarotte 2009, 111.
[112] Adomeit 2006, 6. See also Thomas L. Friedman, "Gorbachev Accepts Deep Cuts in Europe," *New York Times*, February 10, 1990 (italics mine).
[113] Sarotte 2009, 112.    [114] Sarotte 2009, 112
[115] "Enlarging NATO, Expanding Confusion." *New York Times*, November 29, 2009.
[116] Sarotte 2009, 113.

in the Zelikow and Rice narrative, said to Kohl that he had discussed with Gorbachev that a unified Germany, tied to NATO "with assurances that NATO's jurisdiction would not shift one inch eastward from its present position." What this referred to, in Baker's view, was East Germany and not other countries in the Warsaw Pact; NATO's jurisdiction would not move east in a unified Germany.[117] Importantly, however, regardless of Baker's views on the topic, Gorbachev had made a deal with Kohl, who could not speak for NATO or the United States. In addition, by not obtaining a commitment in writing, Gorbachev would be left with little to work with in subsequent negotiations. Finally, Gorbachev did not pick up on clues that were sent almost immediately after the Wall fell in 1989, such as the public statements regarding NATO that Baker had made on television. Gorbachev would later argue that he felt that he had been trapped by Kohl in the meeting.

Reviewing the available evidence, Sarotte argues that at the time of the discussions there was "no evidence that the thinking about NATO's future went beyond East Germany, although such ideas would emerge within the year." In the second half of 1990 speculation would emerge regarding the expansion of NATO to the East, but at the time of the meetings the US did not have the intention to enlarge NATO by offering membership to former members of the Warsaw Pact. As such, Gorbachev likely read Baker correctly with respect to US intentions at the time. These intentions would later change and without a legally binding agreement, Russia would have little leverage. Gorbachev, during a time of quickly moving pieces and much uncertainty, relied on his personal intuitions regarding what Baker was conveying regarding NATO. And while those intuitions were likely correct at the time, the diachronic problem remains. Russia would ultimately in September 1990 sign accords that would allow NATO to extend into East Germany, a move that Zelikow would argue shows that "Western leaders recognized that a Russian leader they valued and wanted to help was genuinely worried about the image of NATO forces moving closer to the borders of the USSR. They took his concerns seriously. They came up with creative ideas for addressing them."[118]

*Assessing Face-to-Face Diplomacy at the End of the Cold War*

In addressing the counterfactual raised at the beginning of the chapter, of the many striking features of the process, timing, and outcome of the end of the Cold War, particularly Germany's unification and membership in

---

[117] Sarotte 2009, 207.
[118] "NATO Expansion Wasn't Ruled Out," *New York Times*, August 10, 1995.

NATO, the distinct phases of activities and strategies – engagement and pause – stand out. Between 1985 and 1991 the US and USSR underwent significant variation in their interactions, both US–Soviet and interpersonal. Most broadly, the first phase between Reagan and Gorbachev in 1985–1989, as cataloged in the previous chapter, is characterized by intense high-level summits of face-to-face interpersonal interactions that gradually clarified intentions among the leaders and was crucial. The second phase is characterized by a stark reversal in the form of interaction. The "Bush Pause" of 1989–1990, including the fall of the Wall is a period characterized by a stark *lack* of face-to-face interaction. In essence the Bush administration's early strategy was a repudiation of the intensive interactions that had convinced Reagan of Gorbachev's intentions of peacefully ending the Cold War. Finally, the German unification negotiations of 1990–1991 represent a significant change in this strategy and is characterized by a flurry of face-to-face interactions as US leaders attempted to derive the intentions of Soviet and European leadership regarding specific aspects of unification. This broad correlation of intensity of face-to-face engagement provides a striking observation: the times of greatest misunderstanding correlate with a lack of face-to-face diplomacy. Understanding why requires looking at the interactions in detail.

It is of course too simplistic to argue that face-to-face interactions, or the lack thereof, explain the ebb and flow of the US–USSR relationship completely. Soviet economic decline and changing ideational structures certainly played a role in changing strategic intentions. The aim of this chapter has been to show that *communicating* those intentions was made possible not through sending costly signals, where the evidence suggests that they were routinely discounted by many in US defense and foreign agencies, as I suggest below, but through face-to-face encounters. The German unification talks took place at multiple levels of engagement, but it is clear that the heart of the effort involved interpersonal meetings at higher levels, including head of state and other executive levels. In particular, meetings between Bush and Gorbachev at Malta, and also Bush and Kohl after Malta, were integral to the process of unification on both sides, because they helped to clarify specific intentions. Further, high level meetings between Akhromeyev, Baker, Crowe, and Shevardnadze helped to supplement the understanding engendered at the highest levels of interaction.

One of the striking aspects of the process was that those who harbored the most negative beliefs regarding Soviet or European intentions were often elites who had very little interaction with those leaders directly. Caspar Weinberger, Reagan's Secretary of Defense from 1981 to 1987, for example, had little interaction with Gorbachev, Shevard-nadze, etc. yet maintained some of the most stringent views of him.[119] As late as 2002, Weinberger had maintained that "Gorbachev to this day is a committed Communist and still believes that what is necessary is to strengthen communism."[120] This is in sharp contrast to those who had significant face-to-face interactions with counterparts, such as Shultz, who maintained that interactions with Shevardnadze allowed him to know that "[Shevardnadze] would not deliberately mislead me." There are of course many reasons why these beliefs differed; coming from dif-ferent backgrounds and representing different aspects of the administra-tion clearly had some effect. Yet it is striking that continually through the period individuals who engaged in face-to-face interaction better under-stood their counterparts than those who eschewed the interactions.

One of the other key aspects of these meetings was the latent infor-mation scarcity and ambiguity, which led to more reliance on personal impressions of intentions. As Rice makes explicit, the conditions under which the talks took place were fluid and information was coming in from a variety of sources. Faced with this type of environment, the leaders attempted to cut through the information malaise in interpersonal con-tact in order to simplify matters. Chernyaev argues that a similar type of information overload was occurring on the Soviet side as well, as advisors struggled to keep up with the "dramatic moments," such as German uni-fication, which "took up only five or six percent of the considerations of Gorbachev and the Politburo."[121] Further, at key moments of interaction there is reason to believe that the information presented between time $t_1$ and $t_2$ in two different interactions, such as letters/phone calls and then face-to-face interaction, such as in the interaction between Kohl and Bush, was the same. This helps to control for the notion that it was new or changed information that affected the sincerity reading and not the interpersonal interaction itself. Perhaps most importantly, the diplomats and leaders involved in the negotiations spoke specifically of the ambi-guity of the situation in creating the need for face-to-face interactions. As Baker notes, "they were saying the right things" but their intentions needed to be tested; put another way, there was some ambiguity with respect to how much trust should be assumed. Or, as Michael Sodara puts it, before the face-to-face interactions, "ambiguities and reserva-tions abounded."[122] This is important because it supports the notion that decision-makers will not only seek out face-to-face interactions, but

---

[119] On this point in particular see Yarhi-Milo 2014.
[120] Quoted in Yarhi-Milo 2014, 214.
[121] Savranskaya et al. 2010, 146.      [122] Zelikow and Rice 1995, 33

rely on intuitions particularly in times of crisis, where latent uncertainty, cognitive overload, and ambiguous information are abundant.

Importantly, the evidence suggests that ambiguities abounded even with new information presented in the form of letters, cable wires, and telephone calls. The Portugalov memo was made less ambiguous because of the personal interaction Portugalov had with Teltschik. The new information presented to Bush by Gorbachev in Malta was not substantive in the sense of new proposals or positions, as much as it was about the intuition that Bush received about Gorbachev's intentions. Similarly, the encounter between Kohl and Bush the next day was not about an exchange of positions but an exchange of intuitions regarding intentions with respect to how to move forward with unification. One of the recurring themes in these encounters was that the information on positions and ideas presented at time $t_1$ and time $t_2$ remains relatively constant; what changes is new information presented about intentions which is intuitional and empathy-based in nature.

While it is impossible to rerun the tape of history in order to definitively assess the counterfactual, there is significant reason to believe that the personal sincerity assessment had a significant effect on the timing and outcome of unification. It is important to recall that for negotiators on both sides intention reading and understanding were hindered early on in the process precisely by a lack of face-to-face interpersonal interaction. As Akhromeyev admits in his memoirs and interviews, it was through the interactions with US counterparts that he came to understand that his reading of the intentions was incorrect. Nevertheless, German unification has been analyzed from a variety of theoretical perspectives, some of which would problematize the notion that face-to-face interactions made any difference at all. It is to those explanations that I will now turn.

## Alternative Explanations: Rivals or Complements?

### Costly Signals

As argued in the theory chapter, costly signals represent one way that states assess the intentions of other states. The logic is straightforward: insincere states will attempt to project sincerity as long as it is relatively cheap to do so; on the other hand, sincere states are more willing to pay a cost to reveal their type. In evaluating the moves that states make, states are able to approximate the intentions of others by assessing the costs that had to be paid to convey that intention. For example, Andrew Kydd has written extensively on the application of signaling games to the end of the Cold War and argues that costly signals changed the way that the US viewed Soviet intentions because with each costly signal the US was forced to reevaluate their approximations of the Soviet's willingness to reciprocate cooperation.[123] An arms control agreement that limited offensive capabilities, for example, is costly to a state that is actually aggressive, and therefore can be taken as signal that they are, in fact, security-seeking. Applied to the Cold War this argument is compelling. Clearly the Soviet Union's series of concessions were made, in part, to convey to the US that they were serious in their stated aims. It is not my argument that these moves did not matter. However, as the last two chapters have shown, costly signals are not always received by the target in the way that the sender intends them to be received. Rather than a costly signal serving as an objective measuring stick of sincerity, policymakers often do not see the signal as being costly, instead preferring to see them as a trap.[124] Further, the costly signal is not the only basis for judging intentions; rather, policymakers want to see for themselves what other leaders intend.

In addition, the timeline for when costly signals are sent in the Cold War case suggests a more complex picture of how states infer intentions. Many of the costly signals that Gorbachev sent, such as those in the lead-up to Reykjavik, *followed* the face-to-face interactions that led to Gorbachev understanding Reagan's sincere intentions in Geneva. Put simply, Gorbachev believed that the US had defensive intentions once they had been clarified and based on this understanding had more agency in making the significant cuts that formed the costly signal. This should make us question how costly the signals actually were. As Chernyaev wrote, Gorbachev was "taking this gamble because [he believed that] nobody is going to attack us even if we disarm completely."[125] If Chernyaev's reading of the situation is correct, then Gorbachev couldn't send signals without first believing that the US had benign intentions.[126] Or, put another way, the costly signal already presupposed some intention understanding of the other side. Further, as Hall and Yarhi-Milo point out, Reagan continued to put much stock in the personal impressions he derived from Gorbachev *after* the INF Treaty was signed during the Washington summit. Reagan was

---

[123] Kydd 2005, 187.
[124] Also see Wheeler 2018 for a strong critique of the costly signaling literature.
[125] Quoted by English 2000, 206; also quoted in Booth and Wheeler 2008, 169.
[126] Also see Lebow 2003, 319 on the size of the peace movement in the United States which implied to Moscow that they had room to maneuver without the United States attacking.

attempting to read Gorbachev's intentions through face-to-face interaction well after the costly signals had been sent.

Second, while the Gorbachev concessions were viewed favorably by
Reagan, Shultz, and Matlock, many others in the administration were
either slow to revise their beliefs or doubled down on their priors. In
both the Reagan and Bush administrations there was continued and
widespread disagreement over the *meaning* of the signals that Gorbachev
was sending. Put another way, there is significant observable variation in
how individual policymakers responded to Gorbachev's actions. Shultz
never seemed to believe that Gorbachev harbored aggressive intentions
toward the United States. Reagan does initially but updates his beliefs
around 1987. Weinberger was far more hawkish. As late as 1990 Weinberger had written that "Not only did Gorbachev give up all of the Soviet
'non-negotiable' demands [such as the INF treaty], but he gave us precisely the kind of treaty that the President had sought for seven years.
That act of course does not mean – any more than does the Soviet withdrawal from Afghanistan – that the USSR has given up its long-term
aggressive designs."[127] The explanation for this divergence of intention
belief, in my view, is that lacking the intensity of face-to-face interactions
with the Soviet leadership that Reagan, Shultz, and Matlock had, Weinberger and other hawks such as Gates, were unable to read sincere intentions. For the costly signaling explanation to work we would expect to see
much less variation in the way that the signals were received. This is not
to argue that the costly signals and actions taken by Gorbachev were
irrelevant. Indeed they likely did reinforce the beliefs that Shultz and
Reagan engendered, but the empirical record suggests that one cannot
explain the peaceful end of the Cold War through costly signals alone.

In addition, it is striking that policy-makers in Washington tended to
discount many of the costly signals that Moscow was sending even as
events were quickly transforming the situation on the ground. For example, one explanation for the end of the Bush "pause" may be the various
revolutions in Communist regimes in Eastern Europe in 1989. Moscow
responded to these through restraint, not using Soviet forces to put the
revolutions down, arguably a form of costly signal since by doing so the
USSR was slowly slipping away.[128] Despite this, policymakers in the US
attached little significance to this and instead emphasized the personal
interactions among the important players on both the US and Soviet
sides.[129] These findings are consistent with Wheeler, who argues that

---

[127] Weinberger 1990, 348–49.
[128] Booth and Wheeler 2008, 157 highlight this as a potential counter-explanation.
[129] Chollet and Goldgeier 2003, 167–71.

costly signals are fundamentally difficult to assess and interpret correctly without the development of interpersonal trust.[130]

*Power and Structure*

Additionally, there is another salient counter-argument to the one presented here, namely that power and structural constraints explain the outcome.[131] The argument made so far, that the extraordinary events leading up to German unification, specifically the Soviet Union's change in position over the course of less than a year, would not have been possible without significant interpersonal interaction, is essentially about statecraft. The United States successfully lobbied the Soviets not through displays of power or major concessions, but rather through intention understanding engendered in one-on-one meetings at multiple levels of diplomatic structure. This is a controversial argument. To argue that statecraft helps to make sense of the end of the Cold War suggests that material or structural explanations leave something out. For instance, the realist explanation for the end of the Cold War is straightforward: the Soviet Union was suffering relative power decline during the late 1980s and by early 1990 the Soviet Union was suffering from a major economic crisis. It is not inconceivable, and perhaps probable, that Gorbachev felt that he had little choice in dealing with the West, given that he was dependent on Western aid at the time. Thus by the time that the Two plus Four talks were starting, the USSR would have had no choice but to capitulate on the German question with respect to unification and NATO membership.

A number of points are important here. First, as Zelikow and Rice point out, Moscow did have an alternate choice when it came to negotiating with the United States and Germany: it could have offered a choice between unification and NATO membership. This would have allowed Gorbachev to "[channel] the surging tide for unity against the supporters of the alliance," thereby creating a structure where Germans had to choose.[132] As Risse points out, elections in East Germany were coming up in March and West German elections followed later in the year. If pressured for a choice by Gorbachev, Kohl likely would have had a difficult time supporting a unified Germany *and* a Germany in NATO. "What if the Soviet Union had continued much longer than until the summer of 1990 to present the Germanys with a

[130] Wheeler 2018.
[131] See Wohlforth 2011 on a recent retrospective on the ability for realist theory to stand the test of time with respect to end of Cold War explanations.
[132] Zelikow and Rice 1995, 196.

choice between unification and NATO membership? How would this have affected the German domestic debate on unification? And what if the Social Democrats had won elections in the German Democratic Republic in March 1990?"[133] These domestic politics questions, while representing counterfactuals, are useful for conceptualizing the choices Gorbachev had at the time. As Robert Zoellick notes, if Gorbachev was the one who had given the United States the choice, Gorbachev likely would have put Bush in a difficult position. For instance, Gorbachev could have insisted that Germany was part of NATO, but not part of the integrated military command, or it could be part of NATO without nuclear weapons. These conditions may have put pressure on German–US relations, which in turn would have strengthened the Soviet position. While structural accounts tend to view Gorbachev as having no choice in the matter, counterfactuals problematize this view.

Second, and most simply, there was an additional option on the table for Gorbachev that involved asserting legal rights to East Germany and declaring Germany, as a whole, as an Allied Power.[134] This is indeed what the Bush administration originally believed the Soviets would attempt to do and needed to clarify in their interactions. The option was discussed and debated by Soviet leadership in the lead-up to the Two plus Four talks.[135] While the USSR did not want to use military force to prevent German unification, it could have theoretically tried to use legal force. The counterfactual here is straightforward: if Gorbachev had confronted the United States and asserted a legal right to Germany, what would have happened? An international crisis was not in the United States', Germany's, or NATO's interest. It is conceivable that a strong stance on Germany by the Soviets would have been met with capitulation. If nothing else, it certainly does not seem to be the case that the outcome is preordained. As Risse points out, the Soviets had 300,000 troops deployed in East Germany to help make their case. If there had been no Two plus Four agreement, would the troops "have remained there until today?"[136] As Risse alludes to, it is possible to construct a scenario that does not dismiss the structural constraints whereby Gorbachev chooses precisely the opposite path of the one taken. In sum, as Forsberg has persuasively argued, Gorbachev had agency in this process and it was not material that explains Gorbachev's choices, but rather changes of identity that occurred through the period.[137]

---

[133] Risse 1997, 164.    [134] Zelikow and Rice 1995, 196–97.
[135] Risse 1997, 164.    [136] Risse 1997, 164.
[137] Forsberg 1999. For a specific application, see Bleiker 2000 on the value changes that occurred through slow dissent throughout the 1980s in East Germany. Subtle resistance arguably had very strong effects in the lead-up to 1989.

Most importantly, it is clear that US policymakers overestimated Soviet power during this crucial period of the late 1980s.[138] US officials "estimated that the Soviet Union's military power was growing; that the Soviets were modernizing their strategic force comprehensively; and that the Warsaw Pact had a strong advantage over NATO in almost all categories of force as a result of its continuing weapons production."[139] It appears that perceptions regarding the balance of power did not change until late 1989.[140] Therefore the potent argument that the decline of Soviet power led US officials such as Reagan and Shultz to gain more favorable outcomes in the negotiation is belied by the intelligence reports, reports that were provided to Reagan, which claim just the opposite. Ultimately it appears that such estimates did not matter much to Reagan, who preferred to assess intentions personally. As Jack Matlock argued recently, "They [referring to Reagan and Shultz] are very experienced people and experienced politicians and it means much more to them what they were experiencing."[141]

But perhaps the structural account is not supposed to predict foreign policy decisions at all. Structural realists have long argued that material structure creates a set of conditions that constrain the choices of states, but they do not necessarily tell us what precise decision a state will make.[142] In this case structural accounts help us to understand the legitimate choices that Gorbachev had in front of him, but they do not help us to understand why he chose the path that he did. A structural account leaves us with the same puzzle we started with: why did Soviet leadership change their preferences with respect to German unification in such a short amount of time? As Spohr asks, "[w]hat ultimately really made Gorbachev change his mind on the German unification question from a hardline position to consent? Was it a shift in the Soviet leader's outlook on European politics and part of his 'new thinking' or was it the result of successful US-Soviet summits?"[143] The preceding analysis suggests that the German unification process was a personal one. Personal communication, especially face-to-face interactions, allowed key policymakers to communicate and clarify their intentions, which in turn had a causal effect on political decisions. We cannot fully understand changes in Gorbachev's position, as well as the changes in US and European positions, without understanding the role not only of the summits that occurred in 1989–1990 but the intensive personal diplomacy, at various levels of government, that complemented those initiatives. As Chollet and Goldgeier have argued, the shifting US–USSR relations between

---

[138] Yarhi-Milo 2013, 29.      [139] Yarhi-Milo 2013, 29.      [140] Yarhi-Milo 2013, 29.
[141] Quoted in Yarhi-Milo 2013, 38.      [142] Waltz 1979.      [143] Spohr 2000, 888.

1988 and 1989, where we see cooperation under Reagan to competition under Bush to cooperation under Bush coupled with relatively constant (if not even more conciliatory) Soviet behavior, are difficult to explain through structure alone. As they note, "[s]omething else had to be at work."[144]

### Trust

The answer they privilege is the growing trust that stemmed from the personal diplomacy at the highest levels of government, particularly the interactions between Baker and Shevardnadze. The argument I have presented here shares much in common with their perspective, but looks at the critical step in the causal pathway that they do not emphasize or theorize: the intention beliefs required for trust. As Chollet and Goldgeier argue, "[t]he evidence reveals that as personal relations developed, the U.S. policymakers perceptions of Soviet intentions changed for the better, thus enabling them to pursue a strategy based on cooperation and conciliation."[145] I have suggested that while it is certainly likely that trust developed among many of the policymakers involved, it is the intention understanding that comes through face-to-face interactions that is a necessary, though not sufficient, condition for trust-building. As such, individuals can gain a sense of each other's intentions without requiring trust to develop.

Unpacking the face-to-face interactions in this way helps to explain important puzzles of the period, such as why the Malta meeting between Bush and Gorbachev was so important despite little substantive new information being shared and the fact that it was the first meeting between Bush and Gorbachev in a year. As Savranskaya and Blanton argue, "Malta's most significant outcome was simply the reassurance it provided to the two leaders through a face-to-face meeting."[146] Indeed throughout much of 1989 Bush remained skeptical of Gorbachev, only proposing a summit in July after visiting Eastern Europe and witnessing the destabilizing potential of revolts and the effect that it might have on US–USSR relations. The initial plan for Malta was not based on trust but pragmatism: Bush could not put off a summit any longer. The trust-building that Chollet and Goldgeier point out between Baker and Shevardnadze occurred largely after this invitation, with meetings in Paris and Jackson Hole in the summer and fall preceding the Malta summit. Trust-building takes successive and iterative personal interactions,

---

[144] Chollet and Goldgeier 2003, 168.     [145] Chollet and Goldgeier 2003, 144.
[146] Savranskaya and Blanton 2017, 488.

so it would be difficult to argue that trust was created between Bush and Gorbachev in Malta. Further, there is evidence that Gorbachev did not trust Bush at Malta, reflected in his discussion with Mitterrand where he reveals that he believes Bush is hiding his true intentions. This reading was of course correct, as it had been the intention of the US delegation to include a unified Germany in NATO.

Rather, as I have suggested, the key to Malta was Bush's reading of Gorbachev's intentions, a reading that gave him confidence that Gorbachev did intend the unification of Germany (even if he felt that he had been pushed to it by circumstances surrounding him) and therefore could be significantly malleable on the issue. This confidence is then displayed in Bush's meeting with Kohl in Laeken, a meeting which reinforced for Kohl Bush's intentions of providing Kohl with the autonomy and agency to push for unification on his own terms. Thus a recurring theme of this chapter has been the development of intention beliefs without *necessarily* requiring trust to develop, though it often does.

Yet, intentions and trust are very closely linked, a point that I pick up in the concluding chapter of the book. It is important to note here, as in the previous chapter, empirically it is often difficult to separate the two. This is particularly true in instances where intention understanding precedes the creation of trust and the historical record may not be detailed enough in order to parse out the differences between the two. For this reason it is important to look at cases where we explicitly have intention understanding but an overt lack of trust, which will serve as the basis for the next chapter, the Camp David Accords of 1978.

### Conclusion

While many have connected the events of 1989–1990, particularly the ambiguity regarding NATO and its expansion Eastward, with Russian views of betrayal and broken promises that potentially are affecting current politics, including the recent crisis in Ukraine, annexation of Crimea, and strained Obama–Putin relations, the peaceful transition of two states into one in many ways illustrates the importance, and value in world politics, of face-to-face diplomacy. This chapter has argued that intentions were conveyed in a way that would not have been possible through other means and has provided much support for the propositions outlined earlier. The evidence in this chapter suggests that face-to-face interactions were not only important to this intention understanding but also served as a causal factor in the crucial decisions of elites that managed this peaceful transition. Importantly, while US and Soviet leaders were integral to the process, many of the salient interactions occurred between other European leaders, particularly German elites. At key moments of contingency German leaders were playing an active role in attempting to understand the intentions of both Soviet and US leaders.

It is difficult to explain certain aspects of German unification, particularly the *process* and *timing* with which it occurred, without taking into account face-to-face interactions. I agree with Philip Zelikow's recent remark that "[t]he timing of unification is crucial." As Jack Matlock points out in retrospect, "there was nothing inevitable about the timing, the shape, or the form of the settlements that reunited Germany."[147] Akhromeyev, reflecting back on those crucial hours in Malta, laments that the timing and process of unification ultimately seemed to hinge on that one interaction sitting where Gorbachev sat face-to-face with Bush and failed to convey that unification was off the table, even if he knew that it was not. As Akhromeyev indicates, in that one meeting Bush gained what he needed to know from Gorbachev, that there would be no pushback on unification, and that he could go directly to Kohl, from Malta, to convey this understanding. And, as we now know, this is precisely what happened. While it would be unwise to claim that any single meeting affects the course of history, particularly in as complex an environment as the end of the Cold War, it is difficult to overstate the importance, shared by both sides, that the Malta interaction played in conveying intentions. If we reran the tape of history and removed the Malta face-to-face diplomacy with Gorbachev and the subsequent face-to-face meeting with Kohl, it is quite likely that both the timing and form of unification, particularly with Germany in NATO, would have looked vastly different. Indeed, not believing that Gorbachev intended unification would have likely led to one of the other reunifications models identified by Sarotte to be pursued, as it was Bush's meeting with Kohl, where Kohl's model was given support, that occurred precisely because of the understanding of Gorbachev engendered in Malta.

The previous chapter began with an oft-asked question: who won the Cold War? In that chapter I contend that both Reagan and Gorbachev share that honor as it was a series of face-to-face interactions in summitry that allowed each side to better understand the other and ultimately resulted, in my view, with reassurance that neither side intended aggression toward the other. But the story of German unification suggests that the interactions between Bush and Gorbachev were no less important from a distributive perspective. In many ways Reagan and Gorbachev laid the foundation such that Bush and Gorbachev could happen. While it is true that Bush's "pause" slowed progress in ending the Cold War,

---

[147] Matlock 1996, 386–87.

ultimately, in my view, it was the reassurance gained through the summits of the late 1980s that made possible the interactions that would solve the Germany problem. It is hard to imagine, for example, questions of distribution being solved without first solving the questions of reassurance. Most importantly, this chapter has also identified the importance of the European leaders, particularly Kohl, in structuring, and pushing for, particular models of German unification. The end of the Cold War story cannot be told without highlighting the protagonists found not only in the US and USSR, but Europe as well.

I now turn to a case that more explicitly deals with these issues of reassurance and distribution, as well as the issue of intention understanding despite a lack of trust. Or, in the case of Egyptian–Israeli relations in the 1970s, intention understanding embedded in long-held intractable conflict and emotional hatred, two characteristics that make it a particularly hard case for successful intention understanding to occur.

# 5    Overcoming Distrust at Camp David

## Intractable Conflict and Face-to-Face Diplomacy

The previous chapter on German unification demonstrated that the unfolding events at the end of the Cold War, from reassurance between Gorbachev and Reagan to the final negotiations regarding NATO expansion between Gorbachev, Baker, and Bush, cannot be understood, and explained, without intention understanding engendered through face-to-face diplomacy. For both reassurance (exemplified by the Gorbachev–Reagan interactions) and distributive reasons (exemplified by Gorbachev–Bush), the consequences of no agreement would create an unstable international system. In this chapter I turn to a very different type of case, one where there is reason to believe that neither side was particularly anxious to cooperate.[1] The type of conflict investigated here is one characterized by its long-standing nature, its strong emotional component, and critically, a lack of trust between the parties. It may be that for collaborative problem-solving missions, such as the German unification process, face-to-face adds value because it helps the various parties understand the intentions of each other. But it is intuitively difficult to understand how face-to-face can be of value when two actors have, at best, a personality conflict and do not get along, or, at worst, mistrust or hatred for each other. This is where reassurance is needed most and is least likely to be found.

Experts in conflict resolution have long recognized that some disputes are so highly emotional and involve so many complexities that they are seemingly *intractable*.[2] Intractable conflicts not only tend to exhibit a lack of understanding of the other's intentions, but there is a lack of trust involved that makes each part intransigent.[3] In these conflicts it is not clear that simply placing two individuals in a room together will produce

---

[1] There are other, of course, important interpretations of this that I will discuss in detail below, most notably declining Egyptian power which may have pushed Sadat toward agreement.
[2] See, for example, Bar-Tal 1998.    [3] Holsti 1962; Kelman 2005.

a desirable outcome. Indeed, that strategy may serve to make the conflict worse; instead, incremental progress is thought to require relatively small steps.[4] When state policymakers view each other through mindsets where the other is stereotyped as the adversary, overcoming bad-faith models may require unilateral conciliatory moves in order to build trust between the parties. Importantly, this does not require reciprocation to work; rather, incremental progress, over a relatively long time horizon, can help to overcome bad images of the other.

I demonstrate that this was largely *not* the case in the lead-up to the Camp David Summit. There were moments of important conciliatory gestures, such as Anwar Sadat's courageous trip to Jerusalem, but most analysts, including those who took part in the negotiations such as William Quandt, agree that there was a severe lack of trust among the main protagonists. Jimmy Carter's experience at Camp David mediating negotiation between Israeli and Egyptian leadership is therefore often told as a story of the *failure* of face-to-face to overcome intractable conflict and lack of trust. The case is often remembered for Carter having to separate Menachem Begin, Prime Minister of Israel, and Anwar Sadat, President of Egypt, as the two could not get beyond emotional outburst and argumentation when meeting face-to-face. A key question therefore emerges: to what extent can face-to-face diplomacy play a role, either positive or negative, in understanding intentions in the most intractable and emotional negotiations where mistrust is rampant?

I illustrate in this chapter that viewing Camp David as a failure of face-to-face misunderstands the reason why face-to-face has value in diplomacy and misconstrues the events of the case. As I will demonstrate, Sadat and Begin's face-to-face interactions, the ones that failed, were not focused on specific intentions but rather historical wrongs and disagreements about the past. They never reached the point of being able to discern the specific intentions of each other because the discussion never moved to specific intentions. We should not expect such types of interaction to lead to intention understanding. Carter's decision to separate Begin and Sadat and work with them face-to-face individually, over very specific intentions, and convey that intention understanding to the other party, is ultimately what saved the summit. Face-to-face failed early at Camp David because of the content of the discussions, as the theory would predict, but it succeeded masterfully late, once the content of those discussions changed from history and emotion to specific intentional acts. I investigate this variation in outcome by focusing on three distinct phases of the summit process where intentions were conveyed

---

[4] Osgood 1962. See also Wheeler 2018.

in face-to-face interactions. These include the presummit assessments that Carter engaged in in order to determine that a Camp David summit could be successful in the first place; the iterative Sadat-Carter and Begin-Carter interactions where Carter intuited *specific intentions* such as Begin's "back stage" position on settlements, and the strategy of Carter not only conveying this understanding of intentions to the other but also the ability to see a zone of possible agreement that others could not. In each case the aim is to address the counterfactual inherent to assessing whether intention understanding could have obtained without the face-to-face interactions.

The Camp David Accords of 1978 between Israel and Egypt have received substantial attention but remain puzzling. After decades of conflict and four devastating wars, Egypt and Israel came together amid great hostility and seemingly intractable positions to sign a historic peace agreement. From a bargaining perspective, both sides exhibited perplexing behavior. Egypt, for instance, ended up shifting its long-held historical pattern of behavior of backing the Pan-Arabist movement, at tremendous risk of isolating itself from the rest of the Arab world. Similarly, Israel made concessions regarding the Sinai Peninsula that were deemed not only unlikely prior to the negotiations but provided as *red lines* by the principals involved. Both sides crossed their red lines and therefore the distributive deal that was struck would have been difficult to predict based on previously held positions and interests. Positions, and ultimately intentions, changed at Camp David. Understanding how this happened requires understanding how face-to-face interactions led to intention understanding on both sides and how intention dynamism fundamentally changed the dynamics of the conflict.

### The Summit That Almost Did Not Happen

The Camp David summit was an attempt, initiated and pursued by Jimmy Carter, to settle conflict in the Middle East that had been present, in modern form, since the founding of the state of Israel in 1948. The Arab–Israeli war of 1948–1949 resulted in over six hundred thousand Palestinians fleeing Israel and taking residence in refugee camps in Jordan and the Gaza Strip. This twenty-eight mile strip of land would, over the next decades, serve as one of the roots of Palestinian resentment and discontent. Further, surrounding Israel were Arab states that rejected Israel's right to exist: Egypt, Jordan, and Syria all would become more-or-less permanent enemies of the state of Israel. In addition to the latent political questions of recognition and border disputes, the Levant, or large area to the east of the Mediterranean Sea represents the Holy

Land, with significant religious importance for Judaism, Christianity, Islam, and Bahá'í faiths. Dispute over who should occupy and control portions of the Holy Land resulted in conflict in the 1960s and 1970s, shaping Carter's perspective on the need for a lasting peace plan.

A devout Southern Baptist, and well-read in Biblical and other religious documents including Hebrew scripture, Carter viewed the Holy Land in both political and personal terms. Carter recounts in his memoirs a memorable trip to Israel in May 1973 where he first saw the River Jordan, which instilled in him a sense of closeness of the Holy Land to his own homeland in rural Georgia, as well as sympathy for the Zionist movement and cause.[5] Zbigniew Brzezinski, Carter's national security advisor, observed that Carter had strong feelings regarding Israel: "On the one hand, he felt that Israel was being intransigent; on the other, he had a genuine attachment to the country as 'the Land of the Bible' [and] he explicitly disassociated himself from the more critical anti-Israeli view."[6] As William Quandt, a member of the National Security Council at the time and an active member of the peace process negotiations, told me, "Carter... had a personal investment in peace in the Holy Land... This was a mission for him."[7] Specifically, Carter understood the need to make progress in the Middle East before midterm elections in 1978 and second-term campaigning took hold. Therefore what would become known as the Camp David process was the continuation of an initiative that began as a fledgling idea before Carter's inauguration and gained political steam shortly after Carter's inauguration.

Beginning in 1977 and aimed at creating a framework and general settlement for the Middle East, the effort envisioned the US and USSR facilitating negotiations that were to culminate in a conference in Geneva (the "Geneva Process"), as had previously occurred in December 1973. President Carter, a believer in the importance of personality, individual psychologies, and the personal meeting, pursued a series of face-to-face interactions in order to assess the prospects for peace. One of the first occurred with Israeli Prime Minister Yitzhak Rabin on March 7, 1977. Before the meeting with Rabin, Carter received reports about Rabin portraying him as someone who possessed "great intelligence and personal courage."[8] His received base-line led Carter to think "that among the Israeli leaders he [Rabin] would be the one most committed to exploring new ideas and discussing the prospects for progress with me."[9] Nevertheless, Carter decided to test the wisdom of these beliefs against

---

[5] Carter 2009, 13.    [6] Brzezinski 1985, 97.
[7] Personal interview with William Quandt, November 5, 2014.
[8] Carter 1995, 287.    [9] Carter 1995, 287.

his impressions from interactions with Rabin, which he describes as "a particularly unpleasant surprise." Carter's diary and memoir portray a rather frigid first meeting with Rabin:

Prime Minister Rabin came over from Israel...I found him very timid, very stubborn, and also somewhat ill at ease...When he went upstairs with me, just the two of us, I asked him to tell me what Israel wanted to do when I met with the Arab leaders and if there were something specific, for instance, that I could propose to Sadat. He didn't unbend at all, nor did he respond. It seems to me that the Israelis, at least Rabin, don't trust our government or any of their neighbors. I guess there's some justification for this distrust. I've never met any of the Arab leaders but am looking forward to seeing if they are more flexible than Rabin.[10]

Subsequently, Carter described the interaction with Rabin as if "talking to a dead fish."[11]

It is not hyperbole to note that this meeting had a profound effect on Carter. In his memoirs he notes that "[Rabin's] strange reticence caused me to think again about whether we should launch another major effort for peace."[12] Carter came to quickly realize that the issue of stubbornness and an unwillingness to look for creative solutions was going to be a problem. He intuited from Rabin an intention *not* to negotiate, which would be detrimental to any plans for a peace process. One of the reasons why Rabin was likely displaying reticence at this meeting is that the Israeli side believed that "Geneva was...a giant trap to be avoided. The Israelis feared that the Americans and Soviets would gang up on them and try to impose a pro-Arab compromise."[13] Therefore there is evidence that at this point Rabin was expressing an intention not to get caught up in a peace process that would ultimately result in an agreement unfavorable to Israel, hence the hesitancy in this initial meeting. Carter intuited this, which caused reflection and rethinking the strategy of launching a major peace initiative.

For his part, Sadat was privately put-off by some of Carter's pro-Israel comments during the election, though the meeting between the two leaders stood in stark contrast to Rabin's meeting and the two hit it off almost immediately.[14] Sadat began his conversation on the peace process by noting, "we need to develop mutual understanding and friendship between our two countries and at the level of the Presidents."[15] Carter

---

[10] Carter 1995, 287.    [11] Quoted in Wright 2014, 8.    [12] Quoted in Wright 2014, 8.
[13] Morris 2001, 445.    [14] Rosenbaum and Ugrinsky 1994.
[15] *Foreign Relations of the United States*, 1977–1980, Volume VIII. Arab-Israeli Dispute, January 1977–August 1978, ed. Adam M. Howard (Washington: Government Printing Office, 2013), Document 25, page 168.

indicated that "[there] was an easy and natural friendship between us from the first moment... It soon became apparent that he was charming and frank, and also a very strong and courageous leader... extraordinarily inclined toward boldness."[16] Sadat later in his life would remark that Jimmy Carter "is my very best friend on earth"[17] and their first meeting remained in Sadat's consciousness as a positive experience. As David Reynolds points out, however, it would be a mistake to take Sadat's display of affection toward Carter too far, as he was prone to similar displays of affection with other leaders. In January 1974, for instance, Sadat kissed Henry Kissinger and declared: "You are not only my friend, you are my brother."[18] Nevertheless, the positive personal connection between Sadat and Carter stood in contrast to that of Carter and Rabin. Just as Israel's leadership saw Geneva as a trap, Egypt's leadership saw it as an opportunity, both of which were reflected in these early meetings with Carter.

The significance of these face-to-face encounters is that they convinced Carter that the potential for Middle East peace was real. Although Carter found hesitancy with respect to Rabin, he was able to understand it based on Israel's prior experiences and the desire to avoid a settlement that was pushed upon them. And Carter was undoubtedly encouraged by the frank and collaborative approach of Sadat. Reflecting on their initial meeting, Carter notes that he was able to push "him hard on [Carter's] ultimate goals: Israeli use of the Suez Canal, his diplomatic recognition of Israel, and exchange of ambassadors – and he finally agreed that these goals might be possible 'after five years of peace.'"[19] Carter reflects that the day he met Sadat was, up to that point, his "best day as president" as it provided an impetus for attempting a peace settlement.[20] Carter intuited from Sadat that he *did* intend to negotiate for peace.

This enthusiasm would be short-lived, however. Shortly after Sadat's visit to Washington the dramatis personae of the peace process changed markedly. Rabin announced that he would be leaving office by not seeking reelection. In addition, to the surprise of many analysts, the *Likud* (Unity) party, gained control from the Labour Party, which had been in office since the country's political inception in 1948. This *Mahapakh*, or "upheaval," placed the head of the party, Menachem Begin, into power. Begin, the former leader of the militant Zionist organization *Irgun*, whose mandate was a form of revisionist Zionism based on the writings of Ze'ev Jabotinsky, maintained conservative views with respect to the Holy Land.

---

[16] Carter 1995, 289.     [17] Reynolds 2009, 291.     [18] Hirst and Beeson 1981, 51.
[19] Carter 2009, 29.     [20] Carter 2009, 30.

Writing in his autobiography, Begin argues, "... if you love Freedom, you must hate Slavery; if you love your people, you cannot but hate the enemies that compass their destruction; if you love your country, you cannot but hate those who seek to annex it."[21]

Carter's reaction to the election was similar to many in the United States. "Israeli citizens, the American Jewish community, and I were shocked. None of us knew what to expect."[22] The problem for Carter and the United States was that while Rabin was not the most forthcoming with respect to concessions or ideas for the peace process, nor was he particularly amenable to Carter from a personality or trust perspective, Begin was known mostly as "a radical firebrand," who was best known perhaps for "previously [being] named by the British as one of the most notorious terrorists in the region after a bombing by his organization in 1946 killed almost a hundred people in the King David Hotel in Jerusalem."[23] Perhaps most important, Begin was an outspoken critic of the idea of Israel giving up any gains it had made in the 1967 war. "In short, he rejected the principle of trading 'land for peace' on which both UN Security Council Resolution 242 and Carter's diplomacy were based."[24] This introduction of a new leader worried Carter and introduced pessimism that a framework for peace could be constructed. Others agreed. Cyrus Vance, Secretary of State at the time, cautioned against his unpredictability, noting that he was "a combination of Old Testament prophet and courtly European. He can be harsh and acerbic at one moment and warm and gracious the next."[25] Ultimately, Carter was nervous. As Quandt told me, the view of the administration at that time was that "Begin was a problem; we were not sure what to make of all this ideological verbiage."

In order to understand what to make of Begin's words and in preparation for his first meeting with the Israeli leader, Carter requested a personality assessment from psychologists at the Central Intelligence Agency (CIA). Recently declassified intelligence reports suggest a more nuanced reading of Begin than what Carter was able to gather through public reputation alone, particularly when it comes to negotiating and importance of interpersonal meetings. The personality assessment, dated July 7, 1977, twelve days before the first meeting between Carter and Begin, indicated that while known as a "hardliner," "highly principled," with "strong beliefs," Begin also had the ability to understand the positions of others, particularly in face-to-face contexts:

[21] Begin 1977, *xxvi.*    [22] Carter 1995, 292.    [23] Carter 2009, 30.
[24] Reynolds 2009, 292.    [25] Vance 1983, 181.

Begin believes that face-to-face meetings with world leaders can bring about changes in their approaches to complex and seemingly intractable international problems. In line with this belief, he says that the United States and Israel can come to an understanding on the Arab question and continue their long history of good relations, a fundamental objective of Israeli foreign policy.[26]

Despite these positive aspects of Begin's personality, particularly the belief in the importance of personal diplomacy, Carter was concerned. As he noted in his diary, "[i]t was frightening to watch his adamant position on issues that must be resolved if a Middle Eastern settlement is going to be realized."[27]

The meeting itself went much better than expected. The Prime Minister's personal visit to Washington belied the tough public exterior he projected. From his diary notes, Carter penned, "There have been dire predictions that he and I would not get along, but I found him to be quite congenial, dedicated, sincere, deeply religious...I think Begin is a very good man and, although it will be difficult for him to change his position, the public-opinion polls that we have from Israel show that the people are quite flexible...and genuinely want peace."[28] This did not mean that Begin would be easy to cajole. While "[h]is IQ is probably as high as anybody I've ever met," Carter recalls, he made it clear that "he wasn't going to do a damn thing."[29] His final diary note on the subject suggested more optimism, however: "My own *guess* is that if we give Begin support, he will prove to be a strong leader, quite different from Rabin."[30] Begin also told Carter that he had planned to meet with Sadat and made promises to "try to accommodate" the United States on a freeze on new settlements.[31] It is safe to say that for Carter and his administration, Begin represented something of a complex puzzle that would have to be solved if peace were to be achieved, yet he had seen enough to be assured that continuing the process was a worthwhile endeavor; he did not intuit from either Sadat or Begin an intention *not* to try and with Begin he intuited at least the *possibility* of flexibility. Carter needed the interpersonal perceptual assurance that both Sadat and Begin would be accommodating of a peace process. After all, Carter's received belief with respect to Israeli intentions, particularly those he intuited from Rabin, had been negative with regard to an accelerated peace process. Further, Begin's public words belied an intention to negotiate and make concessions.[32] Receiving assurance that Begin would negotiate, and would even be willing to be pushed and be flexible on some issues,

[26] CIA Document CR M 77–13279, July 7, 1977.
[27] Carter 1995, 284.    [28] Carter 1995, 297.    [29] Quoted in Wright 2014, 30.
[30] Carter 1995, 295, my italics.    [31] Carter 1995, 291; Quandt 1986a, 82–83.
[32] Personal interview with William Quandt, November 5, 2014.

obtained largely through reading the other during interpersonal diplomacy, provided confidence for Carter that Begin and Sadat could work together.

### Laying Groundwork

Much work was still required. Vance traveled to the Middle East in August where Sadat presented him with a draft peace plan and asked Vance to gather comparable plans from Israel, Syria, and Jordan such that the process of bridging differences could begin. Sadat also indicated to Vance that he sought a meeting with Begin and asked Vance to convey this information when they were to meet in Jerusalem.[33] The subsequent meeting between Vance and Begin did not go as well as that between Begin and Carter. "In Jerusalem, Vance encountered a truculent Begin, who compared American willingness to deal with the PLO to Chamberlain's readiness to appease Hitler. He made it clear that he had no intention of withdrawing from the West Bank and Gaza, though the Arabs in these territories could be granted 'cultural autonomy.'"[34] It was not the meeting that Vance was hoping for and the subsequent written plan that Sadat had requested made no mention of significant territorial concessions. Additionally a letter sent later to Vance from Moshe Dayan, Begin's foreign minister, indicated that Israel intended to retain the Gaza Strip, Sharm Ash-Sheikh, and a part of eastern Sinai.[35]

While the American initiative was stalling, a secret process was underway to increase Israeli–Egyptian dialogue through the mediation of Romanian president Nicolae Ceausescu. Begin traveled to Romania in August and asked Ceausescu to organize a meeting with Sadat. In Morocco, Dayan met with Hassan Tuhami, the Egyptian deputy minister, who indicated to Dayan that Sadat was "deadly serious in his quest for peace," but that it would have to be one that included withdrawal from the occupied territories, including East Jerusalem.[36] Sadat apparently was not willing to sign a separate peace and would only meet with Begin if Israel first agreed on the conditions.[37]

Dayan's initial impressions of Tuhami suggested rigidity and confidence, with a tone that verged on being aggressive.[38] This was softened

---

[33] Quandt 1986a, 108.    [34] Morris 2001, 446.

[35] It is difficult to know precisely what Israeli intentions were at this time, though it seems likely that Vance's disappointment represented sincere intentions, since a willingness to negotiate regarding settlements was only communicated to Begin, and then eventually to Carter, much later in the process – specifically the final days of the Camp David summit, as discussed below.

[36] Morris 2001, 447.    [37] Morris 2001, 447.    [38] Dayan 1981, 44.

later in the interaction, particularly over dinner when the two were left alone to discuss matters. Dayan observes that "[t]he impression grew on me as the talks proceeded that Tuhami was definitely interested in securing peace...He was guided by one overriding principle: peace in exchange for our complete withdrawal from the territories we had occupied since the Six Day War. Arab sovereignty should be absolute and the Arab flag should fly in all these territories, including East Jerusalem."[39] The importance of secrecy was not lost on Tuhami, who noted that only Sadat and Vice-President Hosni Mubarak knew about the discussion; not even the Americans could be told.[40] Dayan argued that leadership from the two countries should meet in order to discuss their differences. Begin would later inform Cairo that Israel was not willing to make concessions on territory in exchange for a meeting with Sadat.[41]

Subsequent discussion of this interaction suggests that Dayan may have committed more than previously thought. David Kimche, ex-Mossad executive, indicates that Dayan handed Tuhami "a three-line, hand-written message...for Sadat's eyes only," which suggested an exchange of the entirety of Sinai for peace.[42] Dayan denies this charge. Morris, in reviewing the evidence, suggests that Dayan likely did not make a clear commitment, but nevertheless "gave Tuhami good cause to believe that Israel would agree to full withdrawal from Sinai in exchange for peace."[43]

Sadat through this period was growing impatient. In March of that year, Carter dealt with fallout from a speech where he highlighted at least two prerequisites of lasting peace: recognition of Israel's right to exist and "a homeland provided for the Palestinian refugees who had suffered for many, many years."[44] Carter was the first American president to make a commitment to a Palestinian state and the response from Jewish-Americans and Israelis was strong. In a memo written by Hamilton Jordan, one of Carter's assistants, Hamilton warned that such statements regarding a Palestinian state were difficult because there was "no political counterforce" to the political pressure that the American Israel Public Affairs Committee (AIPAC) could mount. Indeed as Reynolds points out, in 1977 AIPAC represented "an effective veto in the upper house," given the number of seats it has influence over in the Senate. As Morris argues, Sadat was very much influenced by a U.S.–Soviet communiqué in October 1977 that had argued for the "withdrawal of Israeli

---

[39] Dayan 1981, 45.    [40] Dayan 1981, 45.    [41] Morris 2001, 447.
[42] Quoted in Morris 2001, 447.    [43] Morris 2001, 447.
[44] Carter Speech in Clinton, MA: March 16, 1977. Available: www.jewishvirtuallibrary.org/jsource/Peace/carteronME.html.

armed forces from territories occupied in the 1967 conflict" and resolution of the Palestinian question.[45] Sadat perceived Carter as backtracking from this, first with a speech to the UN General Assembly where he said the United States would not try to impose a peace settlement and then a US–Israel joint communiqué of their own which argued that acceptance of the previous US–Soviet communiqué was not a precondition for revival of the peace process. Put simply, Carter appeared to be backing down from his previous movement toward the Arab position. Sadat and others believed that Carter had been affected by domestic American Jewish pressure and would not be able to deliver an agreement. If progress was to be made Sadat would have to work directly with the Israelis, most notably in the extraordinary face-to-face encounter that occurred in Jerusalem in November 1977.

### Sadat's Visit to Jerusalem

Sadat's visit reflected his flair for the dramatic. As Sadat's Foreign Minister Mohamed Kamel noted, Sadat believed that the trip to Jerusalem would help to "remove suspicions and psychological barriers."[46] One such barrier, according to a memo from Zbigniew Brzezinski, was Sadat's perception of Begin's reputation for inflexibility and lack of imagination. A dramatic trip, a theatrical moment, would help to overcome that barrier.[47]

The proximate cause for the trip came in the form of a letter. Sensing that the prospects for a summit were dwindling quickly, Carter used his friendship with Sadat for personal appeal. On October 21 Carter sent Sadat a handwritten note with "a very personal appeal for [his] support,"[48] referencing the need to remove obstacles in the path to Geneva. While Sadat did not respond immediately in a way favorable to the United States (he recommended an unrealistic meeting of UN Security Council leadership in Jerusalem on the recommendation of his Foreign Minister, Fahmy), he did promise in a handwritten note on October 31, a "bold step." Sadat had evidently been thinking about a move at least since President Ceausescu indicated that Begin wanted to have a face-to-face meeting, having essentially given up on the prospects for peace in Geneva. Sadat may also have been motivated by a sense that time was running out. As Morris argues, "If peace was not achieved soon, a new war would erupt. And for him – aged fifty-seven – personally,

---

[45] Morris 2001, 447–48; Quandt 1986a, 122–23.    [46] Kamel 1986, 282.
[47] Morris 2001, 448.    [48] Quandt 1986a, 139–45.

it was now or never. He had suffered two heart attacks; how long did he have left to fulfill his historic mission?"[49]

A few days after promising a bold step, Sadat told his National Security Council that he was going to Jerusalem to give a speech in front of the Knesset in order to "save the blood of my sons."[50] By stating that Sadat would travel to Israel to talk about peace, it signaled a credible commitment to progress. This commitment was credible because it was politically costly for Sadat to make such statements that stood in stark contrast to public opinion vastly throughout the Arab world.[51] The idea that an Egyptian leader should travel to Israel to speak in front of the Knesset was an unpopular one. Sadat's advisors were horrified.[52] Even Washington, which had just asked Sadat for help, was not pleased. The American idea for progress involved continuation of the Geneva process; this trip to Jerusalem would leave Sadat "isolated and exposed" in the Arab world.[53] Sadat was taking on significant vulnerability by traveling to Jerusalem.

If policymakers in Washington were surprised by Sadat's initiative, policymakers in Jerusalem were shocked. Experts in government had warned that Egypt might renew hostilities as early as October, believing that there was little change among Egyptian policymakers.[54] As Morris points out, one of the reasons for this surprise was that the IDF and Weizman were unaware of the Tuhami–Dayan meeting and other Israeli–Egyptian exchanges that had occurred in the previous months. Begin did not inform them of the meetings until the day before Sadat's arrival.[55] The director of military intelligence was similarly concerned, arguing that Sadat's trip amounted to a "well-laid trap."

The day before Sadat's departure to Jerusalem, Carter told Sadat via telephone, "I will watch you on TV, as will the whole world." King Hassan told Sadat that he admired his courage.[56] Others were not as enthusiastic. Crowds protested in Baghdad. Syria declared an official day of mourning. And members of Sadat's own government, including Fahmy and his deputy Riad, resigned.[57]

Sadat's arrival on November 19 was a momentous and dramatic event. "People were stunned," Sadat would later remark.[58] After arriving at the King David Hotel, Sadat had an impromptu unscheduled face-to-face meeting with Begin. Sadat conveyed that he had come to Jerusalem to speak on behalf of the Palestinians and not to try to reach an Israeli–Egyptian bilateral deal. Begin indicated that Israel would give back Sinai

[49] Morris 2001, 449.      [50] Fahmy 1983, 266.      [51] Quandt 1986a, 146.
[52] Morris 2001, 449.      [53] Vance 1983, 191, 94.      [54] Weizman 1981, 19.
[55] Morris 2001, 450.      [56] Quoted in Morris 2001, 451.      [57] Fahmy 1983, 277–79.
[58] Sadat 1978, 309.

in exchange for peace and Sadat replied that he would not move his army east, "implying a demilitarization of the bulk of the peninsula after it was restored to Egyptian sovereignty."[59] Sadat reportedly said, "[w]hatever happens, we shall remain friends." Begin states that "[t]here is a real bond between us. We exchanged jokes."[60]

The next day Sadat delivered his speech in the Knesset. In his address Sadat noted the mutual distrust and suspicion that kept Israel and the Arab world apart:

> Yet, there remained another wall. This wall constitutes a psychological barrier between us. A barrier of suspicion. A barrier of rejection. A barrier of fear of deception. A barrier of hallucinations around any action, deed or decision. A barrier of cautious and erroneous interpretations of all and every event or statement. It is this psychological barrier which I described in official statements as representing 70 percent of the whole problem.[61]

Sadat was making a clear argument. Suspicion, "fruitless discussions," and a "lack of confidence" were stalling peace. While part of the barricade between Israel and Egypt was based on political positions, another significant barricade was psychological. Suspicion, mistrust, fear, etc. would need to be overcome in order to obtain lasting peace. Resolving political differences would only be effective, according to Sadat, if each side could trust that the other would follow through and were acting in good faith. It is important to note that this was not simply a case of framing the issue; as Sadat's Foreign Minister Mohamed Kamel noted, Sadat really believed that the trip to Jerusalem and eventually the Camp David summit would help to "remove suspicions and psychological barriers."[62] Sadat laid out his logic and his terms:

> ... we really and truly welcome you to live among us in peace and security... [But Israel must] give up once and for all the dreams of conquest and give up the belief that force is the best method for dealing with the Arabs... Expansion does not pay... There are Arab territories that Israel has occupied and still occupies by force. We insist on complete withdrawal from these territories, including Arab Jerusalem... Any talk about peace based on justice... would become meaningless while you occupy Arab territories by force of arms... There can be no peace without the Palestinians... It is no use to refrain from recognizing the Palestinian people and their right to statehood.

[59] Morris 2001, 452.    [60] Morris 2001, 452.
[61] Sadat speech in Jerusalem, November 29, 1977. Full text available at: www.mfa.gov
.il/mfa/foreignpolicy/mfadocuments/yearbook3/pages/73%20statement%20to%20the
%20knesset%20by%20president%20sadat-%2020.aspx.
[62] Kamel 1986, 282.

He also appealed directly to the Israeli people: "Encourage your leadership to struggle for peace."[63] The speech was immediately received coolly by the Israelis. Begin said: "This is an ultimatum." Weizman wrote, "The words surprised me by their intransigence. There was a menacing undertone I didn't like." Weizman passed a note to Dayan that stated, "We have to prepare for war."[64] Dayan reflected that Sadat's speech was a long list of "Noes," or the "things he and Egypt would not do."[65] Despite this, Dayan notes that there was something about the speech that conveyed intentions. "He radiated sincerity, and was at one with his audience, as though speaking personally to each individual from the heart ... Even after hearing his extreme demands, I judged that there was a chance of coming to an understanding with him."[66]

Begin, in response to Sadat's speech, was diplomatic. "We have a different position regarding the final borders between us and our neighbors ... I suggest that everything will be open to negotiation." This left the door open to further dialogue, though there were large differences in positions that would need to be worked out. As Weizman famously reflects back on the period: "Both desired peace. But whereas Sadat wanted to take it by storm ... Begin preferred to creep forward inch by inch. He took the dream of peace and ground it down into the fine, dry powder of details, legal clauses, and quotes from international law."[67] The Egyptians were disappointed by this, having expected more flexibility given the momentous occasion. In the words of Vance, the speech had failed "to produce the basic shifts in Israeli ... positions that [Sadat] was seeking."[68] Breaking down the barrier of mistrust, suspicion, deception, and distortion would prove difficult. Sadat was attempting to send a signal with his trip, but the reception was frigid. Later that night at dinner the mood was unpleasant; Weizman likened it to having just returned from a funeral.[69]

Nevertheless, Sadat left Jerusalem with two important notions of progress. First, while vague and without detail, there was the backbone of agreement taking shape. Israel's withdrawal from Sinai and subsequent demilitarization of the peninsula, in exchange for peace, represented an important beginning of what could be an eventual agreement. Second, by going to Jerusalem and paying a heavy cost to do so, Sadat was able to project leadership from the Arab world that he wanted peace enough that he was willing to take on those costs. This ramification, the reception of the trip in the Arab world, was perhaps even more important than

---

[63] Quandt 1986a, 345–55.  [64] Weizman 1981, 32–33.  [65] Dayan 1981, 81.
[66] Dayan 1981, 82.  [67] Weizman 1981, 136–37.
[68] Vance 1983, 195.  [69] Weizman 1981, 56.

the reception in Israel. As the Israeli historian Benny Morris argues, the importance of an Arab leader coming to Jerusalem in order to make concessions is difficult to overstate. "Through Israel's history . . . the government had successfully hidden from the public the fact that there were Arab leaders who were willing to make peace and to make concessions to achieve it. But now there was obviously 'someone to talk to' out there, someone ready to make a deal."[70] This was the public sentiment at the time. In the minds of Israeli leadership, however, there was still opacity. Neither Begin nor Weizman really understands if they should be expecting peace or war in the days and months to come.

### The Post Jerusalem-Trip Process

A further indication that the Sadat trip was not a particularly transformative catalyst was that three months after the visit there had been little political movement. The Begin–Sadat relationship was deteriorating as both sides retrenched into familiar positions with no compromise. Further, neither side was living up to commitments they had made earlier. "The Israelis were not honoring the commitment Dayan had given me about their settlement policy, but were building up those enclaves in the occupied territories as rapidly as possible."[71] Similarly Sadat was threatening to "renounce the talks with Israel because of his growing embarrassment and frustration" with the entire process.[72] Dayan concluded about the negotiations, "unless the Americans could . . . throw their weight behind the negotiations, the wheels of peace would remain at a standstill."[73]

Jerusalem had opened a window of opportunity, but the United States needed to act. Central to the US strategy, in a parallel to the early efforts to engage European leaders on the issue of German unification, were "endless numbers of [face-to-face] meetings," at multiple levels of the administration, from ambassadors to the executive level, aimed at better understanding what lay behind the positions of each leader. Quandt and others in the administration produced position reports for Carter to read, which outlined the geopolitical issues and stances of each of the parties. Carter was unsatisfied with these and pushed for more. He was focused on personalities. For example, according to Quandt, Sadat was saying the right things in Jerusalem, but the Carter administration still needed to figure out what he really wanted: would a separate bi-lateral

---

[70] Morris 2001, 455.    [71] Carter 1995, 312.
[72] Carter 1995, 313.    [73] Dayan 1981, 97.

peace deal with Israel suffice or "does he need something more?"[74] As Quandt indicated to me, in the aggregate the administration spent a year in "attempt[ing] to get inside his head . . . we realized he had agency, he could say yes or no to the various proposals that came to him; we tried to find out what he really cared about."[75] Empathizing with Sadat, particularly through face-to-face meetings, in order to obtain his true positions and interests, was deemed crucial to Carter and his team.

Carter also understood that the key regarding how to move forward was on solving the puzzle of Begin: "Is Begin simply too intransigent to deal at all with these issues?" According to Quandt, the administration was essentially "trying to get inside [Begin's] head" in order to understand if his wants and strategies were something "that we could work with."[76] Through these face-to-face meetings, the Carter administration ended up gaining glimpses into the "back stage" of the Israeli thought process. "We had seen little hints of a side of Begin that was a little bit more pragmatic. Even though his typical stance was to be shrill and rhetorical," there was a sense that he did really want agreement.[77] As Quandt notes, the interpersonal meetings helped to "[break]-through the political drama that [Begin] was very good at creating and we saw a different side of [the] man."[78] Therefore, while the political obstacles to agreement were substantial, and the personalities involved perhaps even more daunting, face-to-face meetings with both Sadat and Begin gave Carter a certain confidence that he could bring the two together to work productively toward peace. By seeing their intentions, and separating them from the public rhetoric, Carter's team was able to begin crafting a strategy.

Before the United States would get heavily involved in the actual negotiations, a series of meetings occurred over the next several months that would set the stage. In December, Weizman traveled to Ismailia, Egypt in preparation for a further Begin–Sadat meeting to take place later that month. It was Begin's first trip to Egypt and very little progress was made. Sadat was hoping that Begin would reciprocate his visit to Jerusalem with something monumental, but instead both sides simply rehashed their positions. As Gamasy, Egyptian Defense Minister, noted: "It was one of the worst conference I have ever attended . . . a complete failure."[79] Later Sadat would tell the American delegation that he had

[74] Personal interview with William Quandt, November 5, 2014.
[75] Personal interview with William Quandt, November 5, 2014.
[76] Personal interview with William Quandt, November 5, 2014.
[77] Personal interview with William Quandt, November 5, 2014.
[78] Personal interview with William Quandt, November 5, 2014.
[79] Morris 2001, 458.

been outraged at Begin; according to Brzezinski "Sadat was especially outraged by the arrogant attitude which Begin had adopted with him," and threatened to break off all Egypt–Israel talks.[80] Interestingly, however, Brzezinski recorded that while Sadat's comments were concerning, Brzezinski had "a sneaking suspicion that this was a bluff designed to elicit some sort of U.S. commitment."[81] Things would not get much better the following month in Jerusalem as meetings continued and both sides dug in their heels. On the third day of the conference Sadat ordered his delegation home. This apparently was the final signal that the United States must take a larger role. What is important in this interaction is the intuition that Brzezinski retains regarding Sadat's ploy. We know from future interactions that Sadat believed at this time that US involvement was critical to progressing the peace process. Brzezinski is therefore correct in his reading of Sadat at this time and is an important moment where the US administration is able to get inside Sadat's head, which was their aim, in order to understand his intentions.

In order to save what remained of good spirit following Sadat's visit, Carter proposed to Brzezinski, two days after Egypt withdrew from the talks in Jerusalem, to bring Sadat and Begin together in order to induce agreement.[82] Carter envisioned crafting a rough "American plan" that was as comprehensive as possible and used face-to-face meetings in order to find compromise between the two individuals based on the American framework.[83] Ideally, the psychological barrier of mistrust would be broken with Carter playing a mediator role. In addition, Carter believed that bringing Sadat and Begin together to meet face-to-face would have a positive effect on the two understanding each other's intentions.[84]

The plan was not particularly popular. "My advisers feared that such a meeting would fail, with dire consequences for the United States and the Middle East."[85] While Henry Kissinger agreed with Carter's analysis and approach of face-to-face talks, he "cautioned against coming back from Camp David with any indication of substantial agreement between Sadat and [Carter], because that would put the Israelis on the defensive."[86] Advisors warned that if the meeting took place and progress was not made, the consequences might be worse than not having the meeting at all. This was particularly true given Carter's weak favorability ratings. At the time Carter had a sixty one percent negative rating in the Harris Polls, while his strong approval rating was limited to eleven percent.[87]

[80] Brzezinski 1985, 243.    [81] Brzezinski 1985, 243.    [82] Carter 1995, 205.
[83] Carter 2009, 34.    [84] Rosenbaum and Ugrinsky 1994.    [85] Carter 2009, 34.
[86] Carter 1995, 313.    [87] Glad 1980, 443.

In addition, there was considerable skepticism among the Carter contingent about the focusing on psychological aspects of trust and intention understanding. William Quandt notes that upon hearing Carter's plan for bringing the two individuals together to work out differences, he had a negative reaction. "Oh my goodness. We're here for group therapy. What are we doing?"[88] While the group therapy idea might make for a good speech in front of the Knesset, clearly not everyone agreed that it was practical, achievable, or worth trying at all.

Finally, after a significant period of little progress in the region in late 1977 and early 1978, war was beginning to look likely. In March 1978, Israeli soldiers crossed the Lebanese border in Operation Litani, aimed at eradicating what Israeli Defense Minister Ezer Weizman referred to as "terrorist concentrations in Southern Lebanon." Perhaps as a consequence, another movement was occurring in Israel simultaneous to discussions in the United States about the viability, and desirability, of bringing Sadat and Begin together at Camp David. The "Peace Now" movement emerged in early 1978 and caused Begin to "feel the weight of large-scale domestic dissent."[89] A total of 348 IDF officers and soldiers, including colonels, majors, and war heroes, signed and circulated an "Officer's Letter" to Begin that called for better relations with Israel's neighbors.[90] Thousands added their names to petitions and rallies ensued in Jerusalem and Tel Aviv, with an event gathering 40,000 people, making it one of Israel's largest political demonstrations.[91] The movement was particularly popular in universities and kibbutzim and, as Morris argues, was harder to dismiss as it grew and signaled to ministers that the "will to peace" was shared by large segments of the population, beyond liberal students.[92]

By the end of July, Sadat had grown frustrated by the continued lack of progress, but Carter was ready to make a decision. He announced the idea for Camp David, an idea that originated with his wife Rosalynn, who noted that it would be difficult to "still carry a grudge" in such a beautiful setting like Camp David, to his advisors on July 30. Carter was ready to take a chance, a chance that he would later write was admittedly slim,[93] and would serve as his last major effort for peace. As Carter later told his advisors before the conference began, the emphasis would have to be resolving trust issues and misunderstandings. And the timeline would have to be relatively quick. "Let me tell you what's going to happen at Camp David. I've invited Sadat and Begin here to overcome

---

[88] Rosenbaum and Ugrinsky 1994, 162; Quandt 1986a, 206.
[89] Morris 2001, 461.    [90] Quoted in Morris 2001, 461.    [91] Morris 2001, 461.
[92] Morris 2001, 461.    [93] Carter 1995, 316.

a real problem, and that is the fact they don't *trust* one another, and they don't see the good point in each other's position . . . I think I can bring them to understand each other's positions better. My intention is to meet with them for a couple of days, try to work through the misunderstanding, and within a very few days – two or three at the most, we will reach agreement on broad principles."[94]

## Begin, Carter, and Sadat Face-to-Face

### The Early Dynamics and Discussions

There are a number of characteristics of Camp David itself and the summit design that are noteworthy as they had a material effect on the face-to-face interactions. First, in order to ensure that neither the Egyptians nor Israelis were speaking for a broader audience or grandstanding instead of focusing on each other, Carter decided to minimize access for the press. This largely removed the "public" element from the negotiations, theoretically allowing Sadat and Begin the opportunity to focus on each other rather than the "front stage" of the awaiting public. In addition, Carter sought to ensure that the meetings were kept informal. Unlike some other summits, Camp David would be bereft of protocols for speaking, meetings, seating at meals, and especially dress. President Carter led by example in this regard by donning blue jeans. Moshe Dayan reciprocated with khaki pants ("Since I was neither a President nor an American, I possessed no jeans"),[95] though the Egyptian delegation remained relatively formal.[96] Carter viewed his role "as a bridge between the other two camps and tried to ease tensions and make everyone feel at home."[97]

Finally, the cabins that each of the leaders stayed in were chosen on a proximity basis, such that informal meetings and face-to-face interactions would be relatively easy. Many of the salient interactions that occurred at Camp David resulted from ad-hoc moments where Carter visited a neighboring cabin to discuss issues. As Betty Glad argues, the camp arrangement allowed for individual meetings as required. Rather than having to deliver messages through formal means that would have harmed the negotiations process, the leaders were able to meet with each other informally to talk.[98]

The aim of the meetings, at least from the perspective of the Carter administration, echoed this relaxed approach to atmosphere. While a

---

[94] Rosenbaum and Ugrinsky 1994, 162 (my emphasis).    [95] Dayan 1981, 155.
[96] Carter 1995, 330–39.    [97] Carter 1995, 339.    [98] Glad 2009, 146.

comprehensive peace plan would be ideal, transcending the psychological barrier would be most important. Cyrus Vance noted in a memo to the President: "Our main objective at Camp David is to break the present impasse at the highest political level so that ministerial-level negotiations can proceed towards detailed agreements. Our objective is not to achieve a detailed agreement." Carter had more ambitious goals. "We had already risked the possibility of total failure and great embarrassment. We could not lose much more by aiming at success."[99]

Prior to the summit Carter again requested the CIA to provide psychological briefings of the leaders in an attempt to get "steeped in the personalities of Begin and Sadat,"[100] and their reputations as "derived from a detailed scrutiny of events, public statements, writings, known medical histories, and interviews with personal acquaintances of the leaders under study."[101] Jerrold Post, a trained psychologist, prepared three reports: "[Begin's], which called attention to the increasing tread of oppositionism and rigidity in his personality; [Sadat's], which stressed his increasing preoccupation with his role in history and the leverage that could provide in negotiations; and a paper that discussed the implications for negotiations of the contrasting intellectual styles of Begin and Sadat."[102] Carter also understood that his own reputation would be important for both leaders, and therefore wanted to know "attitudes toward me and the United States" in addition to their views of the other.[103] Carter intensely studied the materials, which he later claimed to "pay rich dividends."[104]

In terms of positions, Israel leadership was united. "No withdrawal of settlers or soldiers from the West Bank and Gaza, and no Palestinian self-determination; and both of the air bases in eastern Sinai must remain in Israeli hands, as must all or most of the settlements."[105] Sadat was similarly clear in his aims. "No settlements and no Israeli troops or air bases must remain in Sinai." Sadat varied on his level of insistence on how much Israel must withdraw from the West Bank and Gaza, but on Sinai he was adamant.[106] While both Sadat and Begin quickly accepted Carter's invitation, Begin was more skeptical and worried that he might be headed into a trap. Morris, in reviewing the evidence, indicates that Begin wanted peace but he also was in a difficult position with the peace rallies; to not accept the invitation would mean he would have a difficult domestic problem at home.[107]

---

[99] Carter 1995, 320–21; see also Quandt 1986a, 218.     [100] Cited in Post 2004, 266.
[101] Carter 1995, 327.     [102] Post 2004, 267.
[103] Carter 1995.     [104] Carter 1995, 327.     [105] Morris 2001, 463.
[106] Quandt 1986a, 215.     [107] Morris 2001, 463.

The summit began on Tuesday, September 5, 1978 with Sadat's delegation arriving first. Almost immediately upon arrival Sadat and Carter began substantive discussions. "[Sadat] emphasized that he was eager to conclude a total settlement of the issues, and not merely establish procedures for future negotiations. He was convinced that Begin did not want an agreement and would try to delay progress as much as possible."[108] Sadat further noted that he was prepared to be flexible on all issues except for land and sovereignty. His bottom line was quite clear: the Israelis must be prepared to leave Egyptian territories and any agreement must have provisions for the Palestinians and West Bank. Carter delayed proposing anything substantive until he had a chance to speak with Begin, but expressed positivity and hope for the negotiations that were to ensue.

Menachem Begin and his delegation arrived two hours later. Unlike the previous interaction with Sadat, Carter noted that he and Begin were "somewhat ill at ease."[109] Contributing to this perhaps was Begin's emphasis on formality and procedural issues.[110] Begin also had other more personal concerns. He was put off by the repeated hugs exchanged between Sadat and Carter which seemed to go beyond the protocol required.[111] In a move that further demonstrated Begin's concerns about walking into a trap, the Israeli delegation was instructed to not use the phones in their rooms, fearing they were bugged (Brzezinski had suggested that the rooms be bugged in order to gain an information edge).[112]

Later the evening of the first night Carter met with Begin again and made a plea for giving Sadat a chance in a more intimate and informal face-to-face setting. "I spelled out to Begin the advantages of a good rapport between him and Sadat during the days ahead. I believed that as they got to know each other, it would be easier for them to exchange ideas without rancor or distrust."[113] Begin eventually agreed to consider the proposition of direct talks, but with great hesitancy, which suggests that the costly signal Sadat had sent by traveling to Jerusalem did not sufficiently eliminate Begin's uncertainty about Sadat's intentions to negotiate in good faith.

---

[108] Carter 1995, 336.    [109] Carter 1995, 336.
[110] Carter 1995, 337.    [111] Morris 2001, 463.
[112] Brzezinski 1985, 254. There were other problems as well. As Brzezinski notes, "A diplomatic incident was at the last second averted by the Secret Service as [Brzezinski's daughter Mika] was about to ram Prime Minister Begin with a golf cart in which she and Amy [Carter] were driving."
[113] Carter 1995, 340.

Carter's optimism for a good rapport between Sadat and Begin was dealt a significant blow on the second day prior to the first tripartite meeting between leaders. Carter visited Sadat to set the stage for the meeting and Sadat relayed the position he would bring to Begin. While "[Sadat] promised to go to extremes in being flexible," he also noted that "if our efforts at Camp David should be unsuccessful, then when the equitable Egyptian proposal were made known, they would bring the condemnation of the world on the Israeli leader."[114] The proposal that Sadat had formulated was one of extreme positions and shocking to Carter. Dismantling of settlements, banning nuclear weapons, transferring authority in the West Bank and Gaza to Jordan and Egypt, were all included in the demands. No one in the room would believe that this was a serious proposal aimed at specific actions to be taken. Rather, it read more as an airing of grievances.

If this proposal were to be presented to Begin as written, it would clearly set back discussion rather than propel them forward. As Quandt put it, "Carter realized that Begin would violently reject almost all of the Egyptian document."[115] Nevertheless, Sadat assured Carter of his flexibility and supported the strategy by providing Carter with a three-page list of concessions that Sadat was willing to make. Put simply, Sadat was "showing his cards" *before* the discussions with Begin had even begun. Sadat's strategy seemed to be to confront Begin with extreme demands all the while using the United States as a broker for compromise. Extreme demands would hopefully result in a favorable compromise for Egypt. Sadat's strategy exposed the disjuncture in aims between Sadat and Carter. Whereas Carter hoped to build trust and overcome misunderstanding, Sadat was focused on political positions and negotiating strategy.

The first meeting between the three parties took place on day two in the afternoon. Begin arrived first and Carter immediately warned that Sadat would propose an aggressive proposal and asked Begin not to overreact. Interestingly, it was Sadat who expressed signs of discomfort as he read aloud his proposed framework. From Carter's notes, "I noted that Sadat was strangely ill at ease, uncharacteristically fumbling for words and repeating himself several times."[116] We know from Sadat's discussions with Carter that Sadat was being deceptive about Egypt's intentions. These positions did not represent realistic groundwork to build from, but rather represented a negotiating strategy. Begin left the meeting unclear about Sadat's intentions, though he had picked up on something from Sadat's demeanor that implied deception. Sadat had read his

[114] Carter 1995, 346.     [115] Quandt 1986a, 222.     [116] Carter 1995, 352.

positions from a piece of paper, but Begin was not convinced that these were his true intentions. As Moshe Dayan notes after speaking to Begin following the meeting:

We broke up our meeting with Begin without being certain of Egyptian intention. Was their proposal really submitted as material for negotiation, in the knowledge that they would have to climb down later and change most of its clauses? Or were they intending to make it public in order to show the Arab rejectionist States that Egypt had herself taken the very aggressive and extreme position they themselves held.[117]

It is possible that Sadat's fumbling and repetition belied his true intentions. Or, alternately, perhaps the positions were so extreme that no one would assume that they were legitimate. In either case, the Israelis were left somewhat confused. If the goal of the talks had been to *reduce* misunderstanding, the initial meeting had not been a productive one.

From the very first meetings each side used the face-to-face interaction to read the specific intentions of the others. In addition to Carter's interpretation of Sadat's fumbling for words and being at unease, Moshe Dayan notes that Begin similarly paid attention to facial expressions and clues regarding intentions. "While arguing with Sadat ... [Begin] took careful note of the remarks – and facial expression – of Carter to try to discern which points he supported and which he opposed."[118] Begin would later use this data to, in Dayan's words, "detect [Carter's] pattern of thinking on some of the subjects."[119] The most significant subject for Begin was Carter's claim that if Begin proposed a Knesset motion to remove Israeli settlements in Sinai then it would be passed. Dayan notes that even though Begin analytically disagreed with Carter, it did worry him.[120] Brzezinski intuited from both Dayan and Weizman a flexibility and open-mindedness that he believed that he could work with.[121]

The second meeting the following day was far less collegial. Having had time to review Sadat's proposal in detail, Begin was, as Carter recounts, "irate."[122] In a breakfast meeting between Begin and Carter, Begin responded to Sadat's proposal: "This smacks of a victorious state dictating peace to the defeated! This document is not a proper basis for negotiations."[123] With this serving as the emotional background, Carter chose to have Sadat and Begin converse with minimal interruptions. Carter situated the two leaders directly across from each other, facing each other across Carter's desk. Begin began his rebuttal of

[117] Dayan 1981, 162.     [118] Dayan 1981, 163.
[119] Dayan 1981, 163–64.     [120] Dayan 1981, 164.
[121] Brzezinski 1985, 255.     [122] Carter 1995, 354.     [123] Carter 1995, 354.

Sadat's proposal from the day before and the atmosphere was collegial until Begin derided the notion of Israel's "paying reparations for the use of the occupied lands."[124] Begin even refused to use contemporary names, preferring to call the West Bank by its Biblical names of Judea and Samaria.[125] Sadat became incensed and the two began arguing over which state had conquered whom. Carter diffused the situation by convincing both that neither were defeated nations and negotiations should continue. When questions of territory were raised, heated arguments resumed. Sadat at one point leaned forward and pointed directly at Begin, shouting: "Premier Begin, you want land!" The argument that ensued moved on to the West Bank and Lebanon. Eventually, later in the session, Sadat summed up his point of view succinctly: "Minimum confidence does not exist anymore since Premier Begin has acted in bad faith."[126] Sadat presumably referring here to his trip to Jerusalem, was insinuating that previous progress on confidence building and breaking down the psychological barrier has been materially affected. And it all occurred as Sadat and Begin were looking each other in the eye. "I did not know where to go from there," Carter would later confess in his memoirs.[127] The idea of bringing Sadat and Begin together face-to-face in order to transcend psychological barriers had clearly not worked as he had hoped. While there had been moments of inspiration and signs of the potential for progress, the talks were going extremely poorly and both sides were moving toward the exit, both figuratively and literally. Toward the end of a negotiating session on Day 3, it looked as if the talks would come to an end:

[Begin and Sadat] were moving toward the door, but I got in front of them to partially block the way. I urged them not to break off their talks, to give me another chance to use my influence and analysis, to have confidence in me. Begin agreed readily. I looked straight at Sadat; finally, he nodded his head. They left without speaking to each other.[128]

While neither side knew it at the time, this would be the last time the two leaders would meet each other for a substantive face-to-face meeting during the summit itself.

Face-to-face diplomacy was failing to produce Carter's desired outcome. But Carter had an intuition: face-to-face could still clarify intentions, but in order to do so the form of the negotiations would have to change. Begin and Sadat were unable to get past differences of historical interpretation and strong emotions to get to specific intentions with one another. Carter believed that he could overcome this by working with

[124] Carter 1995, 354.   [125] Wright 2014, 62.   [126] Carter 1995, 360.
[127] Carter 1995, 363.   [128] Carter 1995, 367.

each protagonist directly. This would represent a significant change in strategy but one that, arguably, reflected an accurate read of the situation.

### From Direct Talks to Shuttle Diplomacy

The result of this breakdown was a change in strategy. With word leaking that the talks were on the brink of failure and both Sadat and Begin ready to leave, Carter switched gears by placing himself in the center of the negotiations. The Americans would put together a draft document and Carter would pursue mediated "shuttle" or "proxy" negotiations, serving as the intermediary, using a "single document" strategy. This would involve Carter interacting with Begin and Sadat independently and conveying to each other the ideas and intentions of the other. Face-to-face talks would continue, but the actors involved in the interactions would change. Rather than Sadat and Begin interacting face-to-face, Carter–Begin and Carter–Sadat would interact. Once an understanding was reached, it would be reflected in the document and reviewed by the other protagonist.

This changed the dynamics in several ways. First, while Sadat and Begin would be integral to the process, shuttling between camps allowed Carter some flexibility in who he dealt with and when. On the Egyptian side, for instance, Carter found that dealing with Sadat directly was often easier than involving his aides. With Israel, the opposite held true; Carter would bring in Moshe Dayan and Ezer Weizman as a way of balancing Begin's rigidity with flexibility. Brzezinski notes in his memoirs that Begin "clearly did not trust his Foreign Minister [Dayan]." The reason was that Dayan found it difficult to shield his "contempt for Begin." Begin, for his part, conveyed "the impression that the Defense Minister [Weizman] was not to be taken seriously." Dayan further suggested in private moments that Weizman was a superficial person. All of these personality characteristics and ability to derive feelings and perspectives in personal meetings helped the United States to craft its strategy. Brzezinski would seek one-on-one meetings with Dayan and Weizman separately in order to triangulate intentions. Brzezinski notes in his journal that on the crucial question of settlements, for example, "Dayan and Weizman separately have sent us word that they think that Begin is too rigid on the settlements. Weizman tried to move him, but to no avail."[129] These types of insights were invaluable to deriving an understanding of where, and on what issues, the Israeli team could be pushed. Brzezinski was

[129] Brzezinski 1985, 258.

also very attuned to tone. "[I]t was interesting to note that Weizman first and then Dayan would speak to Begin in Hebrew, and judging from the tone of their remarks, they were inclined either to tone Begin's obduracy down or to actually argue with him. Later on they began to do so also in English."[130]

Second, and as importantly, shuttle diplomacy allowed Carter to set a very specific agenda with each meeting he had with the various leaders. Rather than a spiraling argument that would encompass everything from territory to disagreements about history, Carter could seek agreement on smaller, specific issues as a way of building momentum, and hopefully, consensus on a shared plan for peace. Negotiations would occur line-by-line, specific proposal after specific proposal. For instance, Carter worked with each side on the specific issue of settlements. On September 11, a week into the summit, Carter and Sadat discussed Egypt's intentions with respect to Israeli settlements in eastern Sinai. Sadat conveyed that Jews would be allowed to live in "Cairo or in Aswan," but not in Sinai. Carter retorted that this was an illogical position and Sadat countered that "Some things in the Middle East are not logical or reasonable. For Egypt, this is one of them." Nevertheless after negotiating on this specific intention Carter was able to convince Sadat to accept an extended deadline for IDF withdrawal from Sinai. All told these types of specific proposals and counter-proposals resulted in twenty-three draft proposals from the United States.[131]

Over the next few days Carter had multiple meetings with the two delegations as well as face-to-face meetings with Sadat and Begin separately. Each team worked with Carter on finding flexibility in positions and areas for potential agreement, though the challenges were formidable. Carter needed to build an understanding of the protagonists' intentions among each other, since they were unable to do so themselves. Building this type of understanding required Carter conveying to each side his sincere assessment of the other protagonist. This occurred at both cognitive and affective levels: "[i]t was clear that we had a long way to go . . . Over the next eleven days, I was to spend much of my time defending each of the leaders to the other."[132] For example, to Sadat, Carter explained "the imperatives of political life for Begin in a democracy." To Begin he explained "the sensitive role Sadat was having to play in representing, without their expressed approval, the interests of other Arabs."[133] Similarly, he stressed to Begin "Sadat's courage and his personal sacrifice in making the peace initiative," signaling Sadat's intention to negotiate in

---

[130] Brzezinski 1985, 261.     [131] Morris 2001, 467–68.
[132] Carter 1995, 347.     [133] Carter 1995, 347.

good faith. A recently declassified briefing memo suggests that conveying understanding was precisely the strategy: "Begin should understand that you [Carter], without taking sides on the specific issues at hand, can understand why Sadat, from his perspective, believes that his act has not yet been reciprocated," referencing Sadat's trip to Jerusalem.[134]

Carter also went to great lengths to convey to Begin that Sadat was flexible when it came to finding the ultimate arrangement that would bring about peace, despite what he was saying publicly. Carter indicated to Begin that there "were some things the Egyptians could not propose as their own preference," but may nevertheless be willing to accept.[135] As the same briefing memo suggests, "convey[ing] to [Begin] our understanding of Sadat's reluctance to [normalize relations] in the absence of something he can use in the wider Arab context," was critical.[136] Carter is essentially attempting to instill in Begin his own reading of Sadat's intentions and those intentions suggest that a deal can be made. One of Begin's biographers, Daniel Gordis, argues that Begin "intuited" such a deal with Sadat, where the latter would gain peace and the Sinai, which would satisfy the wider Arab context.[137] In any case, Carter's strategy was to ensure that Begin understood where he was coming from and to convey Sadat's willingness to find compromise, despite the blustery language and acrimonious debates over the first few days.

For his part, Sadat crucially saw in Carter a man who could empathize with his position. While it is difficult to discern with precision when this occurred, Sadat comments on it directly during a field trip off Camp David to Gettysburg. Nevertheless, viewing the likelihood of agreement on the contentious issues as quite low, Sadat's Foreign Minister Kamel urged Sadat to leave Camp David and suspend the summit. Kamel argued that if agreement could not be reached with Israel on these major issues, they would be better off negotiating with other Arab states instead. Kamel's idea was to bring King Hussein and the Saudis into the discussions and possibly form a unified allied block. After a particularly heated argument with Dayan, Sadat's delegation requested a helicopter and Sadat began packing his things.[138] Carter's advisors had seemingly been correct. The threat of no agreement was beginning to look worse than not having the summit at all. While Carter momentarily did want

[134] *Foreign Relations of the United States*, 1977–1980, Vol IX, Arab-Israeli Dispute, August 1978–December 1980, ed. Alexander R. Wieland (Washington: Government Printing Office, 2013), Document 7, page 23.

[135] Carter 1995, 373.

[136] *Foreign Relations of the United States*, 1977–1980, Vol IX, Arab-Israeli Dispute, August 1978–December 1980, ed. Alexander R. Wieland (Washington: Government Printing Office, 2013, Document 7, page 23.

[137] Gordis 2014, 172.    [138] Carter 1995, 401.

to give up and simply announce that the talks had failed, he resorted to one last face-to-face encounter with Sadat in an attempt to change his mind.

Carter approached Sadat, who was standing on the porch of his cabin. Sadat explained to Carter that Dayan had said that Israel would not sign any agreement and this infuriated him. Carter listened closely and then laid out the possible repercussions of walking away at the present, including harm to both the state and interpersonal relationship. Whether it was because Sadat viewed Carter's words as a political threat or a personal appeal (see below), he agreed to stay on one condition: if the Americans and Egyptians made agreement, any Egyptian concessions could not be then used for Israel's benefit as the basis for future negotiations. The Egyptian team was concerned that the Israeli team would not sign any agreement and if negotiations were to resume in the future, the Israelis could use what was discussed at Camp David as a new starting point. "The Egyptians have already agreed to all these points. Now we will use what they have signed as the original basis for future negotiations."[139] Sadat intuited from Carter, and later noted in his memoir, that he believed Carter intended not to use Egypt's concessions against them. This, after all, was a major concern for Sadat: if Egypt's bottom line was simply pocketed and not reciprocated, Egypt would be in a much worse negotiating position in the future, representing a significant trust problem in negotiations.[140] Sadat's reply to Carter renewed the process with hope: "If you give me this statement, I will stick with you to the end."[141] While Carter's attempt to convince Sadat to stay at Camp David could be interpreted as a political threat, or the exercise of American power, there are reasons to think that Sadat's reading of Carter's abilities to empathize with his position was most critical to the outcome. Carter did not strong-arm Sadat with a "sign or else" exercise of power, but rather asked Sadat to "stick with [him]." Indeed, as Sadat told his aides, Carter is "a great man" who had "solved the problem with the greatest of ease ... I shall sign anything proposed by President Carter without reading it."[142]

The face-to-face encounter between Carter and Sadat had saved the day for three reasons. First, Sadat clearly cared about Egypt's relationship with the United States. Arguably this was Sadat's *main* interest, ensuring a good relationship with Carter was perhaps even more important than arriving at a peace agreement with Begin. Second, it is clear that Sadat valued Carter's personal friendship and did not want to let

---

[139] Carter 1995, 402.     [140] Thanks to Brian Rathbun for pointing this out to me.
[141] Carter 1995, 402.     [142] Quoted in Safty 1992, 83.

him down. Third, the face-to-face personal appeal by Carter was ultimately successful because Sadat intuited Carter's intention of not holding Egypt to what was said at Camp David in the event of a breakdown in
negotiations. These reasons for Sadat staying are not mutually exclusive
and may reinforce each other. At the end of this particular day, standing in front of Sadat's campaign, however, Sadat and Carter looked each
other in the eye and understood one another's very specific intentions.

### "Breakthrough!"

Having listened carefully to what both sides said and did not say during
the negotiations, and crucially attempted to convey that understanding
to both sides, Carter realized what issues were vital in order to reach
an agreement between Israel and Egypt, and what issues were not. This
led Carter to pursue a different strategy toward the end of the summit, a change crucial to the outcome of the summit. It also reflected
his ability to understand which issues he could push the two leaders
on, and which issues required limitations or constraints. In the words
of Vance, "Carter told the political team of his concern that in our preoccupation with the West Bank-Gaza complex of issues ... we had overlooked a chance to negotiate an Israeli – Egyptian peace treaty ... not
only did the differences on the Israeli-Egyptian bilateral issues seem less
profound in this area, but also that the presence of Sadat and Begin provided a unique opportunity to negotiate a framework for a peace treaty
between two of our closest and most dependable friends in the Middle
East."[143] Not all members of Carter's team shared this assessment. Most
of the State Department specialists, as well as Brzezinski and Quandt
from the National Security Council, had "fundamentally different judgment[s] ... on what Sadat needed as political cover." They believed that
Sadat would insist on a resolution of the Palestinian problem in order
to demonstrate "that he was not abandoning his Arab brothers."[144] But
having listened to both sides, Carter believed that only a minimal degree
of linkage to the West Bank and Gaza issues was necessary and that
such a linkage would not obstruct the search for a bilateral agreement.
As Quandt explains, it was not that Carter did not care about the Palestinian issue; rather, he realized that for domestic political and ideological
reasons, Begin would not agree to give up claims to future sovereignty of
all of the West Bank and Gaza.[145] Carter could, however, push Begin on
dismantling settlements in Sinai even if Begin had previously said that

---

[143] Vance 1983, 223.    [144] Vance 1983, 223.
[145] Personal interview with William Quandt, November 5, 2014.

he would not do it. As Quandt argues, part of arriving at this strategy involved trying to disaggregate Begin's "core position" from his "negotiating style." That is, the Americans were beginning to understand that part of Begin's strategy was the creation of "political drama," cultivated through distracting exercises in diction, the placement of commas, and so forth. Once they saw through this negotiating style, through face-to-face interactions with the man himself, and recognized Begin's "other side," that he *did* want agreement with Egypt at the end of the day, the path to cooperation became clearer.[146] Carter understood that the core interest of Begin was an Egyptian peace agreement, but that his intention was not to make a deal on Palestine. At the same time, Carter also understood what Sadat could and could not accept. Carter believed that he could get Sadat to accept his trade-off proposal: dropping reference to withdrawal from the West Bank and Gaza in exchange for Israeli willingness to leave the Sinai completely, which was what Sadat most wanted.

Put differently, Carter's ability to take the perspectives of the two sides allowed him to recognize a zone of possible agreement that other members of his team did not. This strategy required, however, exerting more pressure on Begin to commit to dismantle the Sinai settlements, which he was not yet willing to do. As Begin pledged at one point: "My right eye will fall out, my right hand will fall off before I ever agree to the dismantling of a single Jewish settlement."[147] Carter was able to see through this. As Quandt notes, Begin was suggesting that "this is my real position and there is no other position. We had to really work to see if there just might possibly be."[148] Carter's strategy to push Begin on Sinai but not on the final status of the West Bank and Gaza paid off, and a breakthrough occurred when Begin agreed to have the Knesset vote on removing the Sinai settlements, contingent upon settling all other Sinai issues. There were a number of reasons for this change, but perhaps most importantly, Carter emphasized to Begin that this was a deal breaker. Despite pledging back home that he would "pack his bags and go back home" before dismantling settlements, Begin capitulated.[149] What Carter and his team did not know at the time, but would be revealed only later, is that the Israeli delegation had been authorized to concede the Sinai settlement issue on September 14:

---

[146] Personal interview with William Quandt, November 5, 2014.
[147] Quandt 1986a, 240.
[148] Personal interview with William Quandt, November 5, 2014.
[149] Morris 2001, 470.

Unbeknownst to the Americans, members of the Israeli team had arranged to have the hawkish minister of agriculture, Ariel Sharon, telephone Begin to say he would agree to give up the settlements if that was the price for peace with Egypt.[150]

This was a game changer and perhaps for this reason Begin's position seemingly changed overnight – Carter was intuiting a sincere intention.

On September 16, Saturday, Carter was engaged with Begin and Dayan in a final attempt to gain agreement on the American draft that had been reviewed and discussed for days. Carter's hope was that by going through the entire document it would make clear to the Israelis that they agreed with the Egyptians on more than they thought and what separated the two was a small number of issues. Begin pushed for an agreement on Sinai in which the parties would continue negotiating for a peace treaty for three months. If, after that time, they were successful he would address the Knesset about withdrawing settlements. This is a position that Begin had refused to accept since the beginning. After much discussion and negotiation, including a commitment by the United States to provide loans to Israel to build modern air bases, Begin finally agreed to turn the question over to the Knesset for a vote over removing the Sinai settlements. This offer was contingent upon settling all other Sinai issues, such as airfields in the region. Begin essentially had conceded on the issue and with that laid the groundwork for agreement. What had seemed impossible only days earlier was now becoming a concrete reality. As Carter noted in his diary: "Breakthrough!"[151]

The next day proved to be the final day of the summit. It began with Carter reviewing with Sadat the agreement he had worked out with the Israelis the night before. While Sadat was happy with the settlement issue, a new problem emerged with respect to the exchange of letters each side would send to each other. Reading the US letter that stated that East Jerusalem was a "conquered territory," Begin was furious, and instructed his delegation to "pack our bags and go home without another word."[152] The American delegation changed the letter to remove this specific language, but before delivering it to Begin, Carter's team had an idea that produced an important emotional shift that served as a final turning point: autographing photographs of the three leaders together.[153] Carter said to Begin, "I wanted to be able to say, 'This is when your grandfather and I brought peace to the Middle East.'"[154] As Carter argued, this change in emotional state laid the foundation for the ultimate deal that was reached. Begin reportedly told Carter, with tears

---

[150] Quandt 1986a, 241.    [151] Carter 1982, 405.    [152] Glad 2009, 151–52.
[153] Carter and Richardson 1998, 160–61.    [154] Quoted in Wright 2014, 259.

running down his cheeks, "Why don't we try one more time?"[155] After seeing Begin's tears, Carter also cried.[156] What the experience signaled to both Carter and Begin was the solidification of an empathic relationship: they were both experiencing the same emotions and understood what the other felt. Or, as Anderson puts it, "[b]y reaching into the affective, relational reality of the human heart, breaking it open to an empathic awareness of self and other," Carter and Begin "opened an empathic horizon for dialogue across intransigent differences."[157] While it is hard to disentangle Carter's touching gesture from the face-to-face aspect of their encounter, it is difficult to imagine the gesture having such a profound impact in another interaction modality. Carter and Begin understood each other in this moment and what they understood was that both sides intended agreement.

Begin agreed with the new formulation in the letter and after another round of discussion, agreement was finally reached. Put into negotiation terms, after this moment of affective empathy, Carter was able to find a wording of the letter acceptable to Begin, who was able to creatively problem-solve the settlements issues in Sinai, linking the return of Sinai to Egypt with the creation of a large demilitarized zone, essentially enlarging the pie such that both sides could attain beneficial outcomes – more security for Israel and the return of territory for Egypt.

Not everyone was pleased with the agreement. Egypt's Foreign Minister, Muhammad Ibrahim Kamel did not attend the signing ceremony as he had previously urged Sadat not to sign the accords. Kamel argued privately with Sadat that any agreement with Israel that did not include a commitment to withdraw from the West Bank would be viewed unfavorably by Egypt's Arab neighbors. Kamel therefore urged Sadat to not sign the agreement and return home to consult with Arab state allies.[158] Nevertheless, Sadat's goal that he espoused in Jerusalem, tearing down psychological barriers of mistrust and fear had, at least for the moment, seemingly been achieved. For the moment, the three heads of government were able to take refuge in the notion that they had accomplished what many previously had viewed as, at best unlikely, and at worst, impossible. In the end the documents did not constitute full peace treaties but rather frameworks that were to serve as the basis for an Israel–Egypt peace treaty. Such a treaty was signed six months later in March 1979. The Camp David frameworks had provided an important step toward peace.

---

[155] Carter 1998.  [156] Carter and Laue 1991, 287; Carter 1995, 408.
[157] Anderson 2013, 114.  [158] Kamel 1986, 364–65.

## Assessing the Face-to-Face Interactions at Camp David

Ultimately, I have argued in this chapter that Carter was able to understand which issues he could press Sadat and Begin hard on and where to let go in order to reach an agreement. While Sadat and Begin were unable to empathize with each other, Carter provided a substitution for the lack of empathy between the two, developing intention understanding with each individually. The agreement signed at Camp David was by no means perfect: Sadat was disappointed that Carter did not press Begin to agree to an eventual withdrawal from the West Bank and Gaza, but he trusted Carter's assurances that he would continue to work with him to see that Israel fulfilled both framework agreements.[159] On his part, Begin was not thrilled that he had to go back on his pledge not to dismantle settlements in the Sinai, and recognize in writing that the Palestinians had "legitimate rights" and would be given "full autonomy." But, as Quandt puts it, "Carter was very much the architect of the Camp David Accords. He had played the role of the draftsman, strategist, therapist, friend, adversary, and mediator. He deserved much of the credit for the success and he bore the blame for some of the shortcomings."[160] Carter was able to reach agreement that both men accepted, though did not necessarily love. This reflects the potential for intention dynamism through face-to-face diplomacy, particularly in the case of Begin, who entered his interactions with Carter with a specific intention not to touch the Sinai settlements.

In sum, the events and interactions leading up to and during the Camp David negotiations suggest a strong role for Carter's ability to demonstrate a keen understanding of the perspectives and affective states of Sadat and Begin, and in particular their ability to eventually understand each other's distributive intentions even if those intentions seemed deadlocked. The counterfactual is compelling. It is difficult to see how agreement between Israel and Egypt would have obtained were it not for the face-to-face interactions between Carter and Sadat/Begin which clarified intentions. Particularly crucial here was Carter's ability to convey to Sadat and Begin the other's intentions, filling in for the lack of empathy between the two interlocutors. This is particularly true given the various structural constraints discussed above that made agreement, of any kind, unlikely.

---

[159] Vance 1983, 226

[160] Quandt 1986a, 258. One key shortcoming was that Carter did not go back to Begin on the last day of the summit to ask him to confirm in writing his promise for a prolonged freeze on settlements in the West Bank and Gaza.

One could argue that this outcome can be explained by Carter's particular personality characteristics. There was something about the *man* that was willing to take risks of bringing two warring heads of state together, when nearly everyone in his team was skeptical of the idea, and did not back down in the face of impending failure. And, of course, Carter's ability to mediate and find a zone of agreement where others were unable to, suggests a particular capacity that may be unique to him. Indeed Bill Clinton, in similar circumstances decades later, was unable to engender a similar outcome through mediation.[161] All of these personality characteristics are important and likely necessary for the agreement at Camp David, but are not sufficient to explain the outcome. In what follows I make the case that it was precisely the face-to-face interactions and intention intuitions Carter formed that were necessary for the positive outcome at Camp David.

### Form or Content?

The Camp David negotiations exhibit two distinct structures of face-to-face interaction over the course of the fortnight. First, during the early discussions, Carter brought the three heads of state together in hopes that through the tripartite format he could help to facilitate understanding and transcend the psychological barrier that Sadat noted in Jerusalem. When these talks began to break down, dissolving into emotional outbursts and arguments over history, and were not as fruitful as Carter had hoped, he switched strategies and separated the leaders. While Sadat and Begin did not meet each other again for substantive face-to-face discussions until the very end of the summit (though they did meet during the excursion to Gettysburg), they would have iterative face-to-face interactions with Carter who served as the intermediary. Therefore in assessing the effect of face-to-face at Camp David there is within case variation that needs to be explained: why did face-to-face interaction in the tripartite fail to produce cooperation but mediated proximity talks were successful? A number of points stand out.

One way scholars have attempted to explain this puzzle of "failure early, success late" is through timing. Put simply, assuming both parties want to find agreement (that is, their alternative to a negotiated agreement is less desirable than an agreement would be), the closer a negotiation comes to stalemate the more amenable each party often becomes to proposals. William Zartman has coined the term "ripeness" to refer to this effect.[162] From this perspective early disputes are explained by the

---

[161] Holmes and Yarhi-Milo 2017.        [162] Zartman 1985.

lack of a compelling need to find agreement. It could be argued that this is what occurred at Camp David: the failure early and success later were a function of each party not feeling the pressure to find agreement until significant time had elapsed. In the early days of the summit, with many days of negotiation ahead of them, each party could take hard-line positions in order to see what they would be able to get away with. As the summit progressed and the shadow of the future became significantly shortened, each side was pressed to make an agreement or walk away empty-handed.

One problem with this explanation of timing is that it is not clear that both sides *did* prefer an agreement to no-agreement. With respect to Egypt, for instance, Sadat was ready to leave Camp David with nothing and threatened to do so when it appeared that the negotiations were headed toward stalemate. His own Foreign Minister advised leaving with no deal, feeling that Sadat was signing a bad deal that heavily favored the Israelis by not committing Israel to a withdrawal from the West Bank.[163] It is not at all clear that Sadat would have suffered politically if the Camp David process had failed. After all, a lack of agreement on the West Bank would be a justifiable reason to break off talks, particularly in the Arab world. Egypt's best alternative to negotiated agreement (BATNA), therefore, was preferable to a bad agreement. Moshe Dayan similarly reflects on Begin's position as being one of caution. A peace agreement would be beneficial, but not at the cost of giving up significant concessions. Perhaps the only leader involved who sensed impending catastrophe if no agreement was reached was Carter. Carter, on the other hand, the organizer and leader of the meetings, had much to gain from a peace agreement but also much to lose if cooperation did not develop.

Instead, what was crucial for agreement was not that each side needed one necessarily, but rather the content of the negotiation changed. Concomitant with separating Sadat and Begin from each other was a shift in strategy where Carter began to focus on the *specific intentional actions* that could be understood and agreed to by both parties. What explains the change in outcome in the early face-to-face interactions versus the mediated interactions is not just the change in the negotiations structure but the level of specificity of the discussion. What is striking about the early tripartite discussions is that there *was no* particular specific act to form an intention belief about. As Carter notes in his memoirs regarding that first face-to-face encounter, Sadat did not dwell on details; "he spelled

---

[163] Kamel 1986, 364–65.

out his positions in broad terms."[164] They fought about history and emotional reactions and broad principles rather than specific intentions and proposals. Carter had brought Sadat and Begin together explicitly in an informal setting with minimal guidance for how the talks were to proceed. Carter preferred to allow the two to explore differences and hopefully gain some trust by interacting with each other. This did not work. Sadat arrived with concerns about the past and Begin arrived with his, with little or no area of agreement between the two.

This is significantly different from what occurred in the later discussions. Carter, realizing that the tripartite talks were not working, shifted to proximity talks while at the same time changing the focus of the discussions. Small steps and specific proposals and intentions, often line-item by line-item, of action replaced the grand discussion that had dominated the early negotiating sections. This focused both the Egyptian and Israeli delegations on *focal points* that carried with them specific actions to be taken. For instance, after the second face-to-face meeting between Begin and Sadat, Carter crafted a document that included all of the remaining issues that would need to be worked out. These included demilitarization of the Sinai, Israeli settlements in the West Bank, Gaza, and Sinai, etc. Once Carter gained Sadat and Begin's agreement that the list was more or less complete, he worked with his team to develop a negotiating strategy for each particular issue and decided to tackle the larger negotiation piece by piece. Thus, on Day 3, Carter focused on discussions of Sinai with Sadat and his delegation. The specific intentions Carter sought from Sadat revolved around how long Sadat was willing to allow Israel to phase out settlements in Sinai. Once Carter was satisfied that he had Sadat's intentions of a timeframe on settlements, he moved on to Israel's desire to have a United States airbase near Yamit in Sinai.[165] The discussions continued in this vein until after midnight. Carter essentially developed larger agreement by working piecemeal building specific intentions upon specific intentions. He worked with each protagonist face-to-face in order to gain an understanding of intentions of each and then conveyed that understanding to the other.

---

[164] Carter 1995, 345. This frustrated the Israeli delegation which wished to "[break] down the principle of withdrawal into its component parts and [discuss] how to implement it on the West Bank and so forth ... Dayan then underscored this point by saying they wished to go into the question of what withdrawal would actually look like in all its specifics rather than argue over abstract formulations." *Foreign Relations of the United States*, 1977–1980, Vol IX, Arab-Israeli Dispute, August 1978–December 1980, ed. Alexander R. Wieland (Washington: Government Printing Office, 2013), Document 3, page 114.

[165] Carter 1995, 368–72.

Importantly, this move seemingly belies much of the advice that is typically given with respect to negotiations, which tends to suggest starting with broad principles and working on specifics later, so as to not get bogged down.[166] This is misleading however because by the time Sadat and Begin have arrived at Camp David, Carter has intuited from both of them an intention to negotiate in good faith and find an agreement. He has, in effect, already established the broad principles with each side directly and is therefore able to switch to specific intentions after the first two days of the Summit. Put another way, Carter's strategy is consistent with insights from negotiation theory that suggest focusing on interests before positions and specific intentions is a worthwhile endeavor.

In the end the proximity talks allowed Carter to advance the negotiations by breaking the larger negotiation into focal points and then working with each side face-to-face *in order to ascertain each individual's specific intentions regarding that point.* In the case of extreme emotional distance between individuals, face-to-face may serve to produce no normatively positive effect at all or possibly a negative effect. Put another way, simply placing two individuals into a room to work together in hopes that they will develop a bond and begin trusting each other is unlikely. The Camp David example illustrates specific conditions under which face-to-face can fuel emotional distance or aid in cooperation and intention understanding. Ultimately, understanding these conditions helps to explain the within case variation at Camp David: unstructured emotional talks were replaced with highly specific talks about intentions and face-to-face aided cooperation by helping to clarify the latter.

In light of the argument made above, we can assess Carter's strategy of bringing leaders together face-to-face. It is a strategy that has been criticized from three different perspectives. First, Quandt and others were critical of the initial strategy because of its "group therapy" overtones; it seemed, at the time, a bit naive and foolish to try to build understanding between leaders of warring nations. Thus from the outset many were skeptical. Second, some have argued that it was the mediation "shuttle" aspect of the negotiations that ultimately led to success; the strong mediator (and good timing) of Carter could overcome the need for direct interaction.[167] Others have questioned whether Carter may have given up on face-to-face too early in the process. Tom Princen, citing Herbert Kelman's work in simulations between Israelis and Palestinians,

---

[166] See, for example, Fisher and Ury 1983. Princen (1991) takes this perspective and argues, even with the benefit of post-hoc hindsight, that Carter probably gave up on the strategy of allowing Sadat and Begin to work out their differences face-to-face too quickly.

[167] cf. Bercovitch 1986.

argues that the decision to change the structure of the talks after the first few negative interactions between Sadat and Begin may have been a mistake.[168] If the two had been given more time to flesh out their differences in a face-to-face fashion, it may be that they would have come to agreement more quickly or perhaps even found greater agreement than that which occurred through the mediated talks.

The evidence presented in this chapter suggests that this claim misses what the change in negotiation structure was actually about. The initial negative meetings were unproductive not because of the mode of interaction, but because of the substance of that interaction. As argued above, Sadat and Begin attacked each other about a variety of topics, all regarding grand historical narratives and questions of fairness and inequity. It was not until Carter broke the negotiations into smaller pieces that progress was made. Second, and more importantly, the evidence presented suggests that face-to-face is most likely to aid in cooperation when the question at hand is one of specific intentions. In the initial face-to-face meetings, the question of intentions, let alone their specific nature, never had a chance to come up. Indeed specific intentions only entered the conversation once Carter began working with Sadat and Begin individually. This was not about group therapy but rather detailed and specific negotiations over particular intentional acts. Understanding those intentions was integral to the success of the summit because it allowed both sides, Sadat and Begin, to understand where their interests aligned and where there was room for agreement.

Finally, as was the case with German unification, interactions among officials at levels below head of state were crucial to the timing and process of agreement. Dayan's meetings with Tuhami, where a Portugalov memo-like communication is provided, both in a hand-written note and confirmed through the face-to-face interaction, provided an early assessment of Israeli and Egyptian intentions.

## Alternate Explanations: Signaling, Trust, Power

What role did face-to-face diplomacy play in the Camp David case relative to other compelling explanations? For instance, some have suggested that Camp David was bound to succeed since the ultimate agreement between Israel and Egypt did not involve sensitive issues such as a freeze on settlements in the West Bank or the status of Jerusalem. Further, the decline of the Soviet Union, together with Sadat's search for an alliance outside the Arab world, meant that he was more inclined to cooperate

---

[168] Princen 1991.

with the United States and thus concede more. Others point out that Sadat's unilateral gestures and declarations during his visit to Jerusalem, as well as the secret contacts between the two delegations prior to the summit revealed too much of his bargaining position, allowing Israel to exploit him. All of this is to say that the positive outcome of Camp David arguably would have obtained regardless of the intention understanding engendered through face-to-face interactions amongst the three leaders. As with the end of the Cold War, the success of the Camp David process is attributable to many different causal factors, though the evidence presented in this chapter allows us to assess each of these explanations in order to determine how large of a role they likely played in the outcome.

First, the empirical record suggests that there was significant concern in the Carter administration about the likelihood of the summit's success. As Carter notes in his diary, "I asked Mondale, Vance, Brown, Brzezinski, and Jordan to come to Camp David [ . . . ] none of us thought we had much chance of success, but we could not think of a better alternative."[169] Once word of the planned summit got out, Carter was "deluged with warnings from my closest advisers and friends."[170] The problem was that few could identify what a successful summit might look like. "No one, including me, could think of a specific route to success, but everyone could describe a dozen logical scenarios for failure – and all were eager to do so."[171] Further, Congress was concerned about organizing a peace summit because of the damage it might cause the US–Israel relationship.[172] This belies the notion that policymakers perceived Egypt's movement toward the US and Israel reciprocating as inevitable due to shifting power dynamics. If anything, many in the administration were cautious of such arguments. As Quandt notes, there was a realization "how slim the chances for peace really were," which is why Assistant Secretary Harold Saunders "asked his staff to prepare a paper on the consequences of failure in the current negotiations."[173]

Perhaps even more importantly, face-to-face meetings that took place *before* anyone arrived at Camp David helped to determine whether there would be a summit at all. First, Carter's first meeting with Rabin in Washington allowed Carter to gain an understanding that Rabin had the specific intention *not* to bend on important questions that would require bending if the negotiations were to be successful. This caused Carter to doubt whether even attempting a negotiation was a good idea. Carter changes his mind about the prospects for negotiation only after

---

[169] Carter 1995, 316–17.    [170] Carter 1995, 324.    [171] Carter 1995, 325.
[172] Kleiboer 1998.    [173] Quandt 1986a, 201–02.

meeting Sadat face-to-face and reading his intentions of bold new thinking and interacting face-to-face with Rabin's replacement, Begin. Thus
there is evidence to suggest that without face-to-face interaction the idea
for Camp David itself may have never germinated, providing important
insight into the "dogs that don't bark problem," as well as evidence
for our counterfactual; were it not for face-to-face diplomacy it seems
unlikely the summit would have occurred at all. In Carter's case he did
not like what he saw in the face of Begin and therefore if a decision
had been made at that point in time, a summit may never have occurred.
Face-to-face, in other words, was not epiphenomenal in this case; rather,
it provided crucial input into decisions to pursue further negotiations.

In addition, the dynamics between Sadat and Begin on the first two
days of the summit suggest that they were not close in their ability to
negotiate and compromise. If power dynamics were paving the road to
agreement, the road was very rocky in the early days of the summit.
Finally, if presummit negotiations and unilateral conciliatory gestures
revealed preferences in such a way that agreement could be reached,
then it is difficult to explain why the early negotiations between Sadat
and Begin were particularly unproductive and Carter needed to separate the two parties. Carter observed that the "atmosphere between
the two [leaders] is not conducive to any agreement;"[174] "the chemistry was so unworkable that each meeting became less and less promising, and more and more explosive."[175] The protocols of Camp David
thus suggest that contrary to conventional wisdom, the costly signaling
of Sadat's Jerusalem trip, or the decline of Soviet power, do not ade-
quately explain the outcome of the summit.[176] I have suggested in this
chapter that Sadat's trip to Jerusalem was an important step, but it was
not received by the Israelis in the way that Sadat intended, as a costly
signal of his credible commitment. Indeed the evidence suggests that the
Israelis were skeptical of the trip initially, dismayed by the words used in
the Knesset speech, though it was through tone and body language that
they read sincerity in Sadat's behavior. Most importantly, events after
the Jerusalem trip stalled progress. If the trip was a sufficient and/or necessary condition for peace, it is not clear why the process should have
been so difficult in the months following the trip. Sadat may have felt

---

[174] Carter 1995, 367.       [175] Rosenbaum and Ugrinsky 1994, 155.
[176] On Sadat's visit as a costly signal, see, for example, Morrow 1999. Mitchell theorizes
the trip differently, not as a costly signal but as a "conciliatory gesture" that ultimately
helped to transform the relationship between Egypt and Israel. The authoritative take
on Camp David 1 bargaining through the lens of power and structural considerations
is Telhami's 1992 excellent account.

that his trip would be enough to change the psychological dynamics of the conflict, but the Israelis did not see it that way.[177]

As Robert Strong has argued, "[t]he conventional wisdom among experienced foreign policy experts is that important meetings between heads of state are most useful when no agreements are expected... or when major agreements have already been negotiated and the national leaders can merely go through the motions of ironing out a few remaining details and then share credit for the success." Neither of these were true of Camp David. Carter brought Begin and Sadat together when the chances of agreement were relatively slim and little had been prearranged. Indeed, in this instance, "Carter defied the conventional wisdom."[178]

All of this suggests that while changing power dynamics might have been an enabling condition for creating an opportunity for peace, there was nothing deterministic about that opportunity; indeed the evidence suggests that the opportunity was almost missed several times, both before the summit took place in the form of empathy litmus tests, and during the summit itself. Or, as Kurtzer et al. put it, "Carter did not wait for a 'window of opportunity' to open but instead worked to create opportunities for forward movement."[179] Put into methodological terms, it is difficult to see this particular episode of diplomacy as being endogenous to other concerns since its occurrence was unlikely in the first place and the initial negotiations were so tense. If power and structure had paved the way for agreement it was not reflected in the negotiations. Nor is it reflected in the anxiety experienced by Carter and his advisors prior to the summit. As Brzezinski records, "on the eve of the summit, Carter confided to me for the first time his sense of uneasiness about the prospects for success."[180]

Relatedly, one of the most intriguing moments of the summit occurs early in the process, when Sadat, feeling that he could trust Carter, revealed his negotiation positions (and potential concessions) to Carter. The basis for this trust was the shared understanding that developed

---

[177] Weizmann was particularly concerned about Sadat's trip being understood as more monumental than it was. In a recently declassified memorandum of conversation Weizmann apparently "spoke at some length about the problem of getting Sadat to understand that his visit to Jerusalem, important as it had been, could not wipe out all previous history of conflict and remove overnight the reasons why the Israeli people still feel terribly insecure about their borders. Weizmann said he had tried to get this across himself to Sadat but without success." *Foreign Relations of the United States*, 1977–1980, Vol IX, Arab-Israeli Dispute, August 1978–December 1980, ed. Alexander R. Wieland (Washington: Government Printing Office, 2013), Document 3, page 116.

[178] Strong 2000, 207.    [179] Kurtzer et al. 2012, 6.

[180] Brzezinski 1985, 254.

between the two; they "shared some important personal qualities," enabling each to understand the other and develop powerful feelings of empathy. "Both were deeply religious men who had an essentially optimistic world view. Both were strong-willed, capable of long-range planning, and willing to take genuine political risks in their quest for major accomplishments."[181] Sadat's empathy enabled him to place significant trust in Carter; he once declared he would "sign anything proposed by President Carter without reading it."[182] The Egyptian leader sought to "coordinate his plan with Carter [and] to put virtually all his cards face up on the table before the president."[183] Sadat gave Carter "in advance a series of concessions to be used at the appropriate moments in the negotiations," thereby providing Carter with valuable information to be used in his private conferences with the more obstinate Begin.[184] Sadat's belief that Carter could empathize with him was therefore vital to the success of the summit. "Sadat had all along placed greater faith in President Carter than in his own Ministers and advisors,"[185] observes Adel Safty, leading to concerns within the Egyptian delegation that "the relationship between President Carter and President Sadat had become so close that Sadat was willing to make the kinds of concessions that [harmed] Egyptian interests." Because "Sadat often failed to distinguish between personal (social) and state (professional) relations[...], his personal relation with Carter also seemed to obscure relevant professional considerations. 'Sadat seemed to trust me too much,' remarked Carter,"[186] as he had previously provided him with a list of concessions he would accept.[187] Therefore the success of Camp David may be read as a story of personality and trust. It was, in this view, Sadat's trust in Carter, and Carter's in Sadat, that paved the way to agreement.

While this explanation helps to make sense of the Sadat and Carter relationship, one of the intriguing aspects of the case was a *lack* of trust between not only the Egyptian and Israeli sides, but also between the US and Israeli delegations. Begin's team displays a lack of trust upon arrival at Camp David, not using the phones because they believe that they may be tapped and interpreting Carter's hugs with Sadat as indicative of a special relationship between the two that made Begin suspicious. For his part, according to Quandt, Carter "never quite trusted Begin, feeing that he had been misled by him early on and that Begin did not negotiate in good faith." Part of this may have been related to the frequency of meetings that took place with Sadat relative to the number of interactions

[181] Strong 2000, 204.    [182] Finklestone 1996, 248.
[183] Quandt 1986a, 208.    [184] Quandt 1986a, 222.
[185] Safty 1991, 477.    [186] Telhami 1990, 164.    [187] Carter 1995, 340.

with Begin. Nevertheless, while Carter might not have trusted Begin, he did see in him strong leadership and someone "he would have to work with."[188] Therefore the Camp David case is an important one because it establishes that the face-to-face diplomacy mechanism of intention understanding, a form of empathy, can occur even in the absence of trust.

Further, if Camp David succeeded primarily because of trust between Carter and Sadat, the role of face-to-face interactions in engendering the empathy that developed into trust should not be overlooked. I have focused my attention on intention understanding, but as noted in Chapter 2, intention understanding and empathy are required for trust. Therefore a trust explanation that does not provide a mechanism for its development misses a crucial part of the story. I will return to this point in the concluding chapter of the book. If trust developed between Sadat and Carter then it was largely because of the face-to-face interactions where intention understanding was engendered that provides the underlying mechanism.

In addition the Camp David process was remarkable for another reason, namely there was little arm-twisting or political threats on part of the US. There is little evidence of overt use of power by Carter to bring either Sadat or Begin in line. Simply put, proclaimed Carter, "no outsider could impose peace."[189] Because "Washington was never in a position to impose terms of settlement on either Egypt or Israel [ . . . ] the United States did not resort to heavy-handed pressure on either side." Since the Americans lacked "clear preferences"[190] on most issues, they simply sought a mutually agreeable settlement. Carter had "an aversion to hard bargaining," notes Tom Princen, as well as "posturing for the crowd back home, making extreme offers, [and] exaggerating the significance of concessions."[191] Perhaps more importantly, however, the scrutiny of Carter's actions due to domestic political opposition and immense public pressure placed the American president in a comparatively delicate position. "A success – almost any success – was needed," to prevent overwhelming public consternation with Carter's leadership, reminisces Quandt.[192] As the Egyptians and Israelis were well aware, "Carter had already spent considerable political capital on this [peace] effort [ . . . ] and the US presidential election was not far off. To walk away with perfunctory statements about good will and the desire for peace would have devastated the Carter presidency." He was in no

---

[188] Undated Quandt interview available at: http://91581084.weebly.com/william-quandt .html (Accessed September 15, 2014).
[189] Quandt 1986a, 78.    [190] Quandt 1986b, 360.
[191] Princen 1991, 60.    [192] Quandt 1986a, 205.

position to impose American wishes on either Middle Eastern nation. Conversely, "it seems that it was Begin who was able to use threats against Carter," by recognizing the fragility of Carter's rule and claiming to consider withdrawing from the talks.[193] When Begin or Sadat threatened to leave, Carter appealed largely to friendship and empathy, rather than power. Carter did not strong-arm Sadat with a "sign or else" exercise of power, but rather asked Sadat to "stick with [him]."

Another way of analyzing both the process and outcome at Camp David is through the lens of structural power. Specifically, Camp David presents a puzzle for scholars because Egypt signed a bilateral agreement seemingly at the expense of Egypt's relations with its Arab neighbors. Viewed from a power perspective, it risked upsetting key allies in the balance against Israel. Put simply, Sadat arguably had no choice but to follow the United States' desires for peace with Israel and sign the agreement. The focus of this particular argument lay in the distribution of economic and military power over time.[194] Specifically, Shibley Telhami argues that realist theory explains Egypt's move to reach an agreement with Israel because of changing dynamics between the two superpowers during the Cold War. Telhami notes that the United States and Soviet Union became directly involved in the Middle East in the late 1960s and 1970s more than any time since World War II. As the superpowers both gained strategic parity through the 1960s, Egypt came to understand that it needed a close and formal alliance with one of the superpowers in order to advance its own objectives. Sadat and his advisors originally sought alliance with the Soviet Union but "economic disparity between the superpowers limited Soviet capacity and willingness to aid Egypt."[195] In addition, the Soviet Union in pursuing détente with the West, privileged the technological transfer from the West and subordinated its relationship with Egypt.[196] The result of these key realist variables changing for Telhami is that it provided a strong incentive for Sadat to look to the West, and specifically the United States, for a partnership.

Further, at a regional level Egypt's relative power was in decline due to the rise of oil-producing neighbors. As Neil Kressel points out, Arabism and anti-Zionism were no longer enough to maintain leadership in the region.[197] In this sense the Camp David process for Egypt was as much about Egypt's relationship with the United States as it was between Egypt and Israel. As Telhami argues based on interviews with Sadat's aides, "Sadat himself was apparently willing to live with a failure to reach an agreement with Israel as long as closer American-Egyptian relations at

---

[193] Safty 1992, 475.    [194] Telhami 1992.    [195] Telhami 1992, 47.
[196] Telhami 1992, Chapter 3, fn. 6.    [197] Kressel 1992, 806.

the expense of Israel's relations with the United States did result."[198] Lastly, while the ultimate framework for peace side-stepped sensitive issues such as the West Bank and Jerusalem in large part, the negotiations themselves did not. These were both sources of friction from the beginning and arguably integral to the hostility that was felt between Begin and Sadat.

Ultimately, the process by which the Camp David accords occurred suggests an important role for the individuals involved and the face-to-face interactions they engaged in. Structural changes may have provided an opportunity for peace, but it was an opportunity that needed to be taken. Once taken, it was an opportunity that needed to be fleshed out in great detail where questions regarding specific intentions loomed very large. Ultimately, this chapter has argued that face-to-face interactions were critical to agreement at Camp David because they allowed Carter to understand Sadat and Begin's intentions. It was this understanding that made agreement possible and, I have argued, without it there would likely not be a peace treaty. By being able to discern the intentions of the main protagonists, Carter, as a mediator, was able to envision a zone of possible agreement and craft an agreement that others were unable to see. Face-to-face diplomacy therefore helps make sense of both the process and outcome of Camp David.

In the final case study to follow, I turn to an even more difficult case for face-to-face diplomacy than intractable conflict: overt deception.

[198] Telhami 1992, 631.

# 6     "Munich"

Neville, you must remember that you don't know anything about foreign affairs.
— Austen Chamberlain, Neville's brother, over dinner in 1936[1]

## Concealing and Revealing Deception Face-to-Face

While the previous chapters have shown the largely salutary effects of face-to-face diplomacy, this chapter turns to the ostensibly negative side of interpersonal meetings: deception. As I argued in the introduction, high profile cases of failed face-to-face diplomacy, such as Yalta, loom large and have lasting effects, both for theorists of international politics and the practitioners charged with making decisions about whether to engage in diplomacy or not.

In this chapter I explore one of these cases, perhaps the most infamous of all, Neville Chamberlain's face-to-face diplomacy with Hitler in the run-up to the Second World War leading to the so-called "Munich agreement."[2] This case is chosen for a number of reasons. First, while in retrospect the intentions of Nazi Germany do not seem to have been well-guarded secrets – particularly after the publishing of Hitler's *Mein Kampf* – in the 1930s there was significant debate in Britain regarding Hitler's intentions. Not able to derive Hitler's intentions through approximation and theorizing from London, face-to-face diplomacy was chosen by the leadership as the preferred method of assessing Germany's aims. This decision to pursue diplomacy with Hitler, while much maligned as

---

[1] Self 2006, 235.

[2] As Stacie Goddard (2015, 95) has argued, "Few grand strategies have been more scrutinized than Britain's decision to appease Nazi Germany," and "[t]he literature on appeasement is too voluminous to cite in its entirety." I agree. Goddard divides the schools of historiography into three camps: "a 'traditionalist' school, which largely condemns appeasement as irrational; a 'revisionist' school, which sees appeasement as, if not completely effective, a generally rational response to Germany given strategic constraints; and a 'post-revisionist' school, which questions the rationality of appeasement."

foolhardy appeasement by many scholars in retrospect (and indeed some policymakers at the time), was one that, the empirical record suggests, was made carefully and not the product of naiveté. Understanding that decision-making process is important to understanding why policymakers often decide to engage in face-to-face diplomacy.

Second, as was the case in the previous chapters, meetings at the highest level were complemented by many prior face-to-face interactions at lower levels of government. While "Munich" is remembered largely for the interaction between Chamberlain and Hitler, an important part of the story involves the ambassadors, foreign officers, and diplomats who engaged directly with Hitler in the years prior to the fateful meeting in Berchtesgaden. Additionally, there is significant within-case variation in the modalities that these policymakers interacted with German officials, creating an opportunity to investigate what role face-to-face diplomacy played in their understanding of German intentions.

Most importantly, the case is also chosen because it is a crucially difficult one for an argument that suggests intentions can be understood through face-to-face encounters. Not only are there many competing theoretical interpretations that suggest the outcome was structurally predetermined, the facts of the case, as it were, could not be worse for the theory presented in this book. The prevailing wisdom is that, in this case, face-to-face *aided deception* rather than understanding true sincere intentions. Indeed "Munich" may be the hardest case in the twentieth century for the positive effects of personal diplomacy.

In the narrative of the case that follows, I seek to make several points that should refine this received wisdom and address our main counterfactual: would Britain's understanding of Hitler's intentions have been different were it not for face-to-face interactions? First, while the eventual outcome of the meeting between Chamberlain and Hitler was one of disappointment for Chamberlain, as Yalta would eventually be for Roosevelt, there are important clues left behind from the interaction to suggest that Chamberlain may not have been as naïve, and overtly duped, as many historians and political scientists assume. Rather, there is evidence that Chamberlain picked up on the behaviors, tone, words, and so forth that deception detection experts claim are critical clues to picking up on lies. In addition, in their first face-to-face encounter Chamberlain *does* successfully understand Hitler's intentions, before Hitler revises them in the conversation. The transcripts of the meeting suggest that Chamberlain in fact read Hitler quite well in their encounter, only to be eventually persuaded of different intentions subsequently. This is not to say that Hitler's intentions were crystal clear in the face-to-face encounter; they were indeed murky. Yet this does belie the notion that

Chamberlain was merely duped and gained no correct, and actionable, insight from his encounter with Hitler.

Further, while Chamberlain provides only passing evidence of what he picked up on, others in his government, particularly the ambassadors stationed in Berlin and foreign officers who made multiple trips to see Hitler, are much more explicit in the lies that they are able to detect and the ultimate deception that Hitler tries to get away with in those encounters. There are of course many potential explanations for the variation in why the diplomats read Hitler correctly while Chamberlain did not; I will argue that Chamberlain's narcissism is an important personality characteristic that likely played a significant role. As I will demonstrate, Chamberlain's personality, stemming from well before the Munich episode, understood through his discourse and actions, exhibits high levels of narcissism and hubris, which, as argued in Chapter 2, worked against successful deception detection.

Ultimately, a similar pattern emerges in the Munich case as with the other cases: by and large the individuals who ultimately understood Hitler the best were the ones who interacted with him face-to-face the most. And, the opposite is also true. As the historian Abraham Ascher has argued, the tragedy of Munich is that by and large ambassadors in Berlin, who had regular access to Hitler face-to-face, were predicting, with precise detail, what would happen with his leadership and the rise of the Nazi party. Yet, those warnings were not heeded by many in London; policymakers preferred to theorize about Germany's intentions from afar and were therefore quite late in understanding the danger Hitler presented.

Hitler was a very good liar, a master at invoking a social setting that aided his deceptive capabilities and he possessed a very keen skill of saying the right things based on the individual personality that he was dealing with. Some have suggested that he was a psychopath and possessed a great ability to read others for deceptive purposes. Therefore anyone interacting with him face-to-face faced an uphill battle in sorting truth from fiction, sincere intention from deception. And yet, as the experiences of Rumbold, Phipps, and even to a certain extent Chamberlain himself, all who caught aspects of Hitler's deception suggest, even skilled deceivers provide clues to their deception. Thus we find qualified support for the counterfactual that has driven all of the empirical cases in this book: were it not for face-to-face interactions, it is unlikely that many British leaders and decision-makers would have so clearly understood Hitler's intentions. Though, as alluded to in previous chapters and will be addressed more fully in the next, understanding intentions, unfortunately, is not always a guarantee of a peaceful outcome.

In what follows I will begin with the "early" diplomacy of the foreign office and ambassadors, after Hitler's rise to power, compare their analysis to that which was conducted from afar in London, and then focus on the critical face-to-face encounter between Chamberlain and Hitler where the two discussed Hitler's intentions with respect to Czechoslovakia.

*Early Interactions: Rumbold and Phipps*

The international community initially responded to the Nazi ascent to power and Germany's aggression with worry, protestation, and veiled threats. A November 26, 1931 British "Report to Cabinet" warned of the importance of the Nazi party gaining power and signaled that the course of world history may indeed be at stake. In May 1933 the Foreign Office warned that Germany was pursuing "a point of preparation, a jumping off point from which she can reach solid ground before her adversaries can interfere." The memo predicted that there would be "a European war in four or five years' time," noting that public speeches left little doubt of Germany's dissatisfaction.[3] While Germany would require time to rebuild, the prediction was clear. As Simon, the foreign secretary, saw things, "[An Anschluss] would be her first move in a general policy of the reassertion by force, if necessary, of her international position – a policy of which German rearmament, Germany domination of Central Europe, and the eventual recovery of the Polish Corridor are the other principal objectives."[4]

Dispatches from Berlin echoed a similar concern. Sir Horace Rumbold, the British Ambassador beginning in August 1928 was particularly prescient. Only three months after Hitler took power, Rumbold sent a widely read memo to the Foreign Office, a memo that, as Ascher argues, "reads like an analytical assessment of the Nazi regime that one might expect from a mature, insightful historian after the collapse of the Nazi state, when the relevant sources were available."[5] The memo became known as the "*Mein Kampf* dispatch," as it so clearly articulated Hitler's aims and ambitions. In it Rumbold warns of Germany's intention to expand into Russia and the Baltic states by force, the desire to lull enemies "into such a state of coma that they will allow themselves to be engaged one by one," and that Germany has been suffering from a nationalism complex that comes from "patriotism by inferiority

---

[3] "The Foreign Policy of the Present German Government," May 16, 1933, The National Archives: The Cabinet Office Papers (hereafter CAB) 24/241.
[4] Memo by John Simon, "Austria," January 22, 1934, CAB 24/247.
[5] Ascher 2012, 26.

complex." While Hitler was able to overcome the inferiority complex, he did so by "burdening Europe with a new outbreak of nationalism."[6] Perhaps most importantly Rumbold foreshadows the difficulties of trying to convince Hitler to moderate his aims. "Hitler's own record goes on to show that he is a man of extraordinary obstinacy. His success in fighting difficulty after difficulty during the fourteen years of his political struggle is a proof of his indomitable character. He boasts of his obstinacy."[7] Two weeks after sending the memo Rumbold meets with Hitler face-to-face for the first time in order to, among other goals, test his reading of Hitler's intentions.

The meeting lasted for approximately an hour, though it was long enough for Rumbold to size Hitler up.[8] Hitler began by telling a number of perceived lies, which Rumbold noted but did not respond to. For example, Hitler claimed that his rise to power was unique due to the "minimum of violence and bloodshed... not even a pane of glass had been broken," a dubious claim given reports of violence in Berlin during the ascendancy. Rumbold brought up the Jewish question, at which point Hitler worked himself "into a state of great excitement: 'I will never agree,' he shouted as if he were addressing an open-air meeting, 'to the existence of two kinds of law for German nationals. There is an immense amount of unemployment in Germany, and I have, for instance, to turn away youths of pure German stock from the high schools. There are not enough posts for pure-bred Germans, and the Jews must suffer with the rest. If the Jews engineer a boycott from abroad, I will take care that this hits the Jews in Germany.' These were remarks delivered with great ferocity." Hitler's reaction to questions about the treatment of Jews helped to instill in Rumbold the notion of Hitler's personal fanaticism and "extraordinary obstinacy." The face-to-face encounter allowed Rumbold to confirm his priors and presuppositions regarding Hitler's intentions.

Summing up his position in June 1933 Rumbold warns, "I have the impression that the persons directing the policy of the Hitler Government are not normal. Many of us, indeed, have a feeling that we are living in a country where fanatics, hooligans and eccentrics have got the upper hand, and there is certainly an element of hysteria in the policy and the actions of the Hitler regime."[9] Rumbold emphasizes that these impressions, garnered through his interaction with Hitler and observations made while living in Berlin, were shared among his colleagues.

---

[6] Documents on British Foreign Policy (hereafter DBFP), Series F, vol. 44, 143.
[7] DBFP, Series F, vol. 44, 139.     [8] Ascher 2012, 28.
[9] DBFP 1919–1939, vol. 2–5, 389. Horace Rumbold, June 30, 1933.

Rumbold was "struck by the unanimity of their views on the present situation. They are bewildered by the whirlwind development of Hitler's internal policy, and view the future with great uneasiness and apprehension." Germany's withdrawal from the conference of the League of Nations a few months later in early October of 1933 only served to cultivate a period of intense speculation regarding Germany's ultimate intentions.

Sir Eric Phipps assumes the role of ambassadorship in the summer of 1933, taking over for Rumbold, and almost immediately seeks to gain his own impressions of Hitler. Phipps was an experienced diplomat and brother-in-law of Vansittart, Permanent Under-Secretary for Foreign Affairs, who recommended him for the position, partially perhaps because of their agreement on the threat that Germany posed.[10] Therefore it is clear that Phipps had priors as well. In Phipps' first meeting with the Chancellor on October 24, 1933, the two discuss a number of topics, including remarkably, German expansion to the East. As Phipps recounts the meeting in his diary, he notes a number of passionate outbursts by Hitler, including the security threat from Russia and the need for security by expanding Eastward. Hitler was, in this encounter, making his intentions regarding security through expansion to the East quite clear. "Hitler then proceeded, after a long disquisition on Russia and the danger which that country presented to Germany from an industrial, economic and agricultural point of view owing to the lower standard of living existing there, to remark rather vaguely that he sought certain possibilities of expansion in eastern Europe: he disclaimed, however a wish to rectify the 'absurd and unfair corridor question' by force."[11] Phipps' impressions are that Hitler is a very emotional person, prone to torrential downpours of words and excitement. "I could see him as he spoke, advancing, unarmed and Mahdi-like,[12] clutching his swastika flag to meet death from a French machine gun. A trace of healthy, human fear of death would have reassured me more. Once or twice I felt inclined to smile at Herr Hitler's shouting crescendo, but the seriousness, not to say tragedy, of the situation prevented the inclination from developing. It is disquieting to feel such power in the hands of so unbalanced a being. I fancy it is to the emotion of Germany's dictator rather than to his reason that we must suddenly appeal on any vital issue."[13]

On substance Hitler made reference to very specific intentions, including that Germany only demanded defensive weapons in its armament, rather than offensive ones; that he was willing to give a security

[10] Ascher 2012, 30.    [11] Phipps and Johnson 2004.
[12] Phipps here is making fun of Hitler.    [13] Phipps and Johnson 2004, 27–28.

guarantee to France; and, when the subject turned toward the military, "an eloquent torrent of protestation" followed. Phipps even laughed, in jest, on occasion due to the ways in which the Chancellor referred to some of his military installations. With respect to the *Sturmabteilung* and *Schutzstaffel* (paramilitary organizations under the Nazi party) Hitler compared them "to the Salvation Army...here I regret to say that I laughed."[14] In sum Hitler spoke more than Phipps, where the latter's "several interpolations could only be made when the Fuhrer paused for breath in the torrent of his eloquence."[15]

Phipps ultimately found Hitler and the other Nazi leaders, during this period, to be something of a conundrum, concluding in July of 1934 that "one thing only is *certain* and that is the *general* uncertainty."[16] Nevertheless, despite espousing uncertainty, Phipps "demonstrated an understanding of Hitler's psychological makeup that was shrewd as well as penetrating. His portrait of Hitler the man, sprinkled with humorous aside, still stands up as thoroughly convincing...such a portrait of his psychology was potentially very useful to the officials in London who shaped Britain's foreign policy."[17] Phipps thus picks up on a number of aspects of Hitler that are relevant. First, his expressive behavior reads like a veritable checklist of the expressive clues to deception, as identified in Chapter 2. Second, Phipps' reading of Hitler's intentions regarding security through Eastward expansion is correct – Hitler is revealing his ultimate intentions in a clear way. And, finally, Phipps understands Hitler's emotional constitution, realizing that it must be taken into account when dealing directly with him.

A year after the first meeting the Foreign Office continued to be concerned about rapid rearmament in Germany and asked Phipps to again meet with Hitler in November 1934 to impress upon him the seriousness of Germany's actions and to again derive his intentions. While the Nazis had continued to claim that the rearmament was only for defense, Phipps believed that Hitler's goal was strategic; "the fact remains that the psychological reaction on others is to inspire suspicion of an offensive purpose." When Phipps voiced this to Hitler he went into a rage and warned Phipps that "Germany cannot consent any longer to allow other States to wipe their boots on her." Hitler further declared with certainty that Russia and France had formed an alliance. As Phipps notes, the Führer was not in a good mood, which "[did not] increase his charm or attractiveness. Whilst I spoke he eyed me hungrily like a tiger. I derived the distinct impression that had my nationality and status been different,

---

[14] Ascher 2012, 32.     [15] Phipps and Johnson 2004.
[16] Ascher 2012, 31.     [17] Ascher 2012, 31.

I should have formed part of his evening meal."[18] Phipps met Hitler again a year later in December 1935 and suffered through another similar bout of odd behavior. Hitler called the Russians "noxious microbes who should be politically isolated," noting his "supreme contempt" for them. Phipps notes the occasional physical stomping of feet; "At times he ground the floor with his heel, as though crushing a worm."[19] Ultimately Phipps comes away from the meeting with the same impression that he had in his first meeting in October of 1933.

The result of the Phipps face-to-face encounters with Hitler is a prescient warning to London. Phipps understands, remarkably well, Hitler's psychology and strategy of using the security dilemma to his advantage. He sees through the torrent of words and outrageous expressive behavior to derive that Hitler cannot be trusted with what he says, particularly when it comes to his stated defensive intentions, not to pursue the "Corridor Question" by force. Hitler is not bluffing when it comes to Germany's security. He warns his superiors in the Foreign Office that returning land to Germany "would not only act as a stimulating *hors d'oeuvre* to the German gormandizer, it would enormously increase Hitler's prestige and power." While Phipps argues that the situation "was not yet desperate," since Germany was not ready for war in his view, there should not be, under any circumstances, aid given to Germany to help her along with that process. Phipps, after moving to Paris to become ambassador in April 1937 confided to his American counterpart, William Bullitt, that "[Hitler was] a fanatic who would be satisfied with nothing less than the domination of Europe," that he could not "see the faintest possibility of coming to any kind of agreement with Hitler," and "[the] only thing that would impress the Germans today was military force."[20] Rumbold and Phipps were on the same page regarding Hitler's intentions, engendered through their personal interactions with the Führer.

There was therefore remarkable consistency in the ways in which the two British ambassadors in Berlin, Rumbold and Phipps, understood Hitler in the early years of Hitler's rise to power. As Ascher notes, "During the five years that Rumbold and Phipps served as ambassadors in Nazi Germany, remarkably little division of opinion could be found within the British diplomatic corps in Berlin and other German cities with regard to the new regime."[21] Face-to-face interactions with Hitler had provided a nuanced understanding of Hitler's deceptive intentions:

---

[18] BDFP, Series F, vol. 46, 395–98.    [19] BDFP Series F, vol. 46, 395–98.
[20] Quoted in Johnson 2013, 256. Thanks to Adam Richardson, University of Leeds, for bringing this quote from Phipps to my attention.
[21] Ascher 2012, 48.

in short, his claims of defensive intentions were not sincere. This understanding was not always congruent with the views of foreign secretaries and others in the Foreign Office, however.

### Eden's Two Visits

Anthony Eden was appointed Lord Privy Seal and Minister for the League of Nations under Stanley Baldwin's Government in 1934. Eden had foreign policy expertise and had developed a fairly strong anti-war philosophy, preferring to work through international institutions such as the League of Nations than force in order to settle disputes. In February 1934 Eden was dispatched to meet with Hitler in an attempt to "discover whether the German demands are in truth exorbitant, as I anticipate, or reasonable." Eden's intuition was that, "If the former, the sooner British public opinion wakes up to the fact the better. If the latter we shall then have something definite upon which to work." Eden notes in his memoirs that at the outset Hitler appeared "smaller and slighter than I had expected from his photographs," though "he was restrained and friendly." Eden describes how Hitler would go on "talking at some length...once he got going," though "he was always quite ready to accept questions or interruptions." On this day Hitler was quiet, "I was told that he was quieter than usual...There were neither fidgets nor exclamations." When Eden spoke Hitler paid intense attention. "As I spoke he fixed me quietly with his pale, glaucous eyes, which protruded slightly, a feature often associated with an overactive thyroid." The initial impression Eden received was generally favorable, "Hitler impressed me during these discussions as much more than a demagogue. He knew what he was speaking about and, as the long interviews proceeded, showed himself completely master of his subject. He never once had need to refer either to von Neurath or to any official of the Wilhelmstrasse." Eden later told his wife, "Dare I confess it? I rather liked him."

Substantively Hitler "declared that Germany had no interest in aggression," and "had no desire for offensive weapons and was prepared to renounce all military aviation if other nations would do the same." Hitler was even accommodating on a number of negotiation points. Eden was able to gain a concession from Hitler on the idea for a verification system for arms reductions, assuming an agreement could be reached. As Eden reflected back on the interaction, "For all I then knew, these sentiments might be sincere."[22] The next day the two dined at the British

---

[22] Eden 1962, 68–71.

Embassy and developed more of a rapport. Eden quotes from his diary, "We talked freely enough with the help of an interpreter and my limited German. Hitler thawed materially, especially when we discussed the war, which he likes to recall like most Germans . . . We also spoke of Bavaria, and he begged me to come and stay with him in his cottage on the Austrian frontier. He warmed up as he described its scenery." Eden goes on to write in his memoir that, "This was the first time I heard the name Berchtesgaden."[23] It would certainly not be the last, though at this point there is little that Eden reads from Hitler that would support the notion of inevitable war. "I find it very hard to believe that the man himself wants war. My impression is much more that this country has plenty to do internally to be thus preoccupied for five years to come." Interestingly, however, with the ability of hindsight, Eden writes that though the Embassy at that time "held the opinion in these early days that the Nazi doctrine was not chauvinist; there was much suspicion on my part, but as yet no certainty."[24] As Thorpe, Eden's biographer notes, "Hitler knew how to turn on the charm when needed, and he played all the cards with Eden, a tacit acknowledgement that Eden would be an important witness back home in Britain."[25] It is difficult to know why Eden derived such a different understanding from Hitler in this interaction than that of Phipps and Rumbold in similar interactions in Berlin, though as the theory predicts, repeated exposure should make deception detection easier; initial interactions, on the other hand, present a challenge in sincerity assessment.

Back home in Britain, assessments of Germany's intentions from afar were indeed taking place. The meaning of the announcement of Germany's nonaggression pact with Poland in January 1934 was debated heavily and the Defence Requirements Committee (DRC) concluded the next month that Germany represented an increasing danger. The words of individual policymakers in Britain echoed similar themes. Simon, for example, believed that Germany's aim was "to create abroad an impression of the peaceful nature of German foreign policy and thereby, if possible, further to divide the remnants of the war coalition."[26] Vansittart was even clearer: "There is no doubt whatever of the ultimate intentions of Germany . . . In the place of the men of Weimar, there are now men whose ultimate aims are much of the same, but whose radically different methods may at some future

---

[23] Eden 1962, 68–71.    [24] Eden 1962, 78–79.    [25] Thorpe 2011.
[26] Memo by John Simon, "Germany's Illegal Rearmament and Its Effect on British Policy," March 21, 1934, CAB 24 (247).

date precipitate an international conflict."[27] Vansittart believed that Germany's policies, and level of aggression, would likely come in stages, first defined by internal reform, followed by expansion. Thus when Vansittart concludes that there was no "immediate danger," the future was much less certain; "the Germans are too competent, and matters are now moving too fast, to make a long estimate a safe one."[28] Others, such as cabinet member Samuel Hoare, thought the threat was exaggerated and debate continued.[29] With little consensus on how Britain should proceed, Eden and Simon traveled to Germany once again to assess Hitler's willingness "to participate in a series of multilateral security pacts."[30] Unlike the first visit, this time Eden came away with a very different impression.

Eden's second visit in March 1935 was characterized by an overtly negative feeling. In his diary, Eden notes that the "future looked ominous." The discussions "were bad ... whole tone and temper very different to a year ago, rearmed and rearming with the old Prussian spirit very much in evidence. Russia is now the bogey." Hitler's suggestions were "ridiculous," echoing the view of both Phipps and Rumbold from their earlier encounters. Further Hitler was "more sure of himself than a year ago." On the specific topic of paramilitaries, Hitler once again "poo-poohed their significance." One of the more intriguing discussions occurred when Hitler likened the paramilitaries to teaching children to use rifles in school; Hitler specifically mentioned the school that Eden attended which caused Eden to laugh, noting that the training was "not taken so seriously. For many boys they were the occasion for smoking on field days." Hitler "shook his head, completely unconvinced." Hitler went on to suggest that these schools were producing paramilitaries and that Germany should have the same right. Eden's "protests were disregarded as patriotic deception." Eden quickly realized that the optimism engendered from his previous encounter was misplaced.[31] Now it appeared that "an agreement [with Hitler] is impossible."[32]

### Chamberlain and the Theory of Appeasement

After the German invasion of Austria in 1938 it was becoming clearer what Hitler's political agenda looked like. In a letter to his sister, the

[27] Memo by Robert Vansittart, "The Future of Germany," April 9, 1934, CAB 24 (248), 251.
[28] Memo by Robert Vansittart, "The Future of Germany," April 9, 1934, CAB 24 (248) 256.
[29] Yarhi-Milo 2014, 61.      [30] Yarhi-Milo 2014, 62.      [31] Ascher 2012, 61.
[32] Eden 1962, 156–59. See also Weinberg 2013, 161–62.

newly appointed Prime Minister Neville Chamberlain noted it is "evident now that force is the only argument Germany understands and that 'collective security' cannot offer any prospect of preventing such events it can show a visible force of overwhelming strength backed by the determination to use it . . . Heaven knows I don't want to get back to alliances but if Germany continues to behave as she has done lately she may drive us to it."[33] One of Hitler's next aims was to provide civic rights to Sudeten Germans,[34] first by "demanding devolution for the Sudetenland" and eventually through attempts to "undermine the Czechoslovak state."[35] Nevertheless war would be costly and it was unclear whether Germany's economy could sustain itself during a conflict with France and Britain.[36]

In May 1938 rumors of German aggression toward Czechoslovakia began to circulate and it appeared as if Hitler's "Case Green," the plan for quick annexation, was in the process of being implemented. Henderson prepared for evacuation of the Embassy in Berlin, for fear that war may be imminent.[37] Germany did not invade and the inaction was attributed to Czech and British deterrence, a conclusion drawn by the press which infuriated Hitler and prompted instructions on May 30 to his generals: "It is my unalterable decision to smash Czechoslovakia by military action in the near future."[38] Britain's response, upon notification of this position, was that it "could not guarantee that they would not be forced by circumstances to become involved also."[39]

For its part Britain was very concerned about the Czechoslovakian problem. As Reynolds notes, on a continent where dictatorships were on the rise, Czechoslovakia was a functioning democratic holdout.[40] At the same time, Germany's strong airpower capacities posed a direct threat to Britain. Even before taking office as Prime Minister, Neville Chamberlain was cognizant of the fact that there existed a "yawning gulf . . . between Britain's vast imperial commitments and its limited military capabilities."[41] There was also recognition among many that the current post-Versailles order was no longer sufficient; Germany could no longer be denied great power status. On the other hand, Czechoslovakia's alliance with the Soviet Union worried many policymakers. At root, however, was a key question regarding the stability of Europe. "Was Hitler simply trying to right the wrongs of Versailles? Or was he another Napoleon in the making, who should be nipped in the bud?"[42]

Chamberlain, at the age of sixty-eight was forced to confront these questions immediately. Chamberlain understood that the small nation

---

[33] Self 2006, 304.    [34] Bendersky 2000.    [35] Reynolds 2009, 38.
[36] Tooze 2008, 268–74.    [37] Thanks to Adam Richardson for pointing this out.
[38] Reynolds 2009, 40.    [39] Reynolds 2009, 274; Woodward and Butler 1949.
[40] Reynolds 2009, 41.    [41] Self 2006, 236.    [42] Reynolds 2009, 42.

of forty-seven million people was in a position of needing to defend imperial installments encompassing a quarter of the world's land and population. Worse, it was forced to do so with what Robert Self, one of Chamberlain's biographers, has termed "dismally depleted military resources of a third-rate Power."[43] This was coupled with the realization that Japan, Germany, and Italy all provide significant potential challengers to Europe generally, and Britain in particular, should they want to revise the status quo in the system. The relative power situation, in other words, was bleak. As Kennedy notes, "the fighting strength of the British Empire was weaker in relation to its potential enemies than at any time since 1779."[44] Faced with this grim reality, Chamberlain and his government faced a fundamental problem of how to best protect a nation with relatively limited resources.

Chamberlain continually struggled with the compromise required to "strike an appropriate balance, to achieve the maximum of effective deterrence for the minimum outlay of non-productive (and possibly unnecessary) expenditure."[45] One of the ways Chamberlain found to strike this balance was to argue for the importance of active diplomacy. Chamberlain was realistic about what Britain could hope to achieve through armament and what it could not. As such, Chamberlain argued that the country must obtain security that it could afford and use diplomacy to appease challengers. Chamberlain viewed Japan and Italy as secondary challengers with the main security focus remaining on Germany as the principle historical threat. Chamberlain further believed that if Britain could successfully help to settle Germany's legitimate Versailles Treaty grievances, it could remove Germany as a potential threat, thereby reducing the danger from Japan and Italy.

After the threat of war in May, the growing concerns over Germany's intentions, and warning from government officials that the pace of rearmament would not be sufficient to protect the country from challenges from Germany, Chamberlain hoped to be able to secure an agreement with Germany that would trade territory in Europe for restricted German military growth.[46] This appeasement of Germany sought the pacification of Europe through non-violent diplomacy, with Britain serving as mediator. By seeking a strategy of appeasement Chamberlain was hoping to satiate desires of challengers in the short term. As Robert Paul Shay puts it, "Conciliation was the only course they could see by which it was possible to save the nation from the threat posed from without by too few arms and from within by too many."[47] While there is disagreement

---

[43] Self 2006, 236.     [44] Kennedy 1989, 99–100.     [45] Self 2006, 236.
[46] Reynolds 2009, 43.     [47] Shay 1977, 175.

about what Chamberlain's ultimate precise strategy was, avoiding short-term crisis with Germany is documented in the Cabinet notes and was clearly an aim.[48] Less clear is whether Chamberlain believed in the "buying time" strategy such that Britain could prepare for the long-term possibility of war with one of its main challengers. There is significant, and unresolved, debate regarding Chamberlain's long-term vision. On the one hand, as noted earlier, there is evidence to suggest that his appeasement theory was not simply about idealistically satiating desire of land for long-term peace, but rather was based on the realistic assessment of Britain's capabilities and its prospects of fighting a short-term war with Germany. On the other hand, Chamberlain is particularly slow and reluctant to admit that appeasement had ultimately failed, suggesting a strong ideational pull, and relatively sticky belief, in its ability to deter war.

Concurrent with implementation of the appeasement strategy, uncertainty regarding Germany's intentions increased. Additional evidence, such as that offered by Sir Nevile Henderson, British ambassador in Berlin, suggested that Germany wanted to avoid war and, in particular, a conflict with Britain. Henderson was a well-known appeaser, though not of the same type as Chamberlain, preferring to see both the good and bad sides to Nazism.[49] Though an appeaser, even Henderson experienced reservation during his face-to-face interactions with the Chancellor. For instance, based on meetings in 1938 Henderson confessed that Hitler "left me with a feeling of profound disappointment," because of his unwillingness to answer questions regarding his specific intentions vis-à-vis Austria and Czechoslovakia. He also noted that he could not find a "common basis for reasonable discussion. Hitler's sense of values is so abnormal that argument seems powerless. The ordinary rules of the game seem to have no meaning for him and some of the statements which he makes and which, to give him his due, I am sure he believes to be true, leave one aghast." Henderson concluded, "His capacity for self-deception and his incapacity to see any point which does not meet his own case are fantastic, and no perversion of the truth seems too great for him to accept as the gospel of Hitler and of Germany." In September

---

[48] For example, Ripsman and Levy (2007) argue that Britain's strategy during this time was to buy time in order to allow Britain to complete a rearmament program before the need to fight Germany. Layne (2008), in contrast, suggests that Chamberlain's ultimate goal was avoiding war with Germany and therefore chose a strategy of diplomacy. As Layne argues, "The primacy of war avoidance in British strategy meant that one of Britain's most important objectives was to reserve in its own hands the ability to decide when, and for what reasons, it would fight" (413). Layne 2008; Ripsman and Levy 2007.

[49] Ascher 2012, 67.

1938 Henderson went further, arguing that Hitler was "driven by mega-lomania inspired by military force which he has built up..., he may have crossed the border-line of insanity." He was unable to gain insight into Hitler's intentions because "everything depends on the psychology of one abnormal individual." As Ascher argues, Henderson was in a dif-ficult place. As an ideological appeaser Henderson felt a certain affin-ity for the Nazi program, believing that it was not fueled by an *animus dominandi*. He seemed to believe that Hitler was capable of doing good, and indeed would also lavish praise on Hitler from time to time.[50] It is therefore striking that Henderson's prior beliefs, and experiences in the face-to-face encounters with Hitler, were completely contradictory. Henderson was also known for contradictory information sent in reports; indeed Ascher notes that Henderson "made contradiction into a fine art," often displaying a frustrating inconsistency that left readers of his dispatches puzzled.[51] For instance, despite the amazing portrait of Hitler possessing an abnormal psychology where normal rules do not apply, Henderson cautioned that London should not discount his posi-tive qualities.[52] As Neville argues, it is easy to underestimate the strain the ambassadors in Berlin were under, trying to make sense of a compli-cated time and environment.[53]

Reviewing the intelligence, Chamberlain believed that Hitler had not yet made up his mind to take Sudetenland by force. Rather than issue a threat of war as a deterrent, Chamberlain argued that no democratic state "ought to make a threat of war unless it was both ready to carry it out and prepared to do so."[54] This was something that Britain was not able to credibly do, as Chamberlain realized quite well.[55] Rather, Cham-berlain and his Cabinet preferred to "try to keep Germany guessing" regarding Britain's intentions.[56] This policy of keeping Germany guess-ing was predictably not satisfactory to everyone in Chamberlain's Cab-inet. In particular, Duff Cooper, first lord of the admiralty, expressed the belief that Britain should stand firm through deterrence, perhaps through acceleration of naval maneuvers.[57] The argument that Cooper and other dissidents made was that a show of force, rather than diplo-macy, would be required to prevent war.[58] As Reynolds documents, in order to gain support for his position "Cooper began leaking accounts of Cabinet discussions to parliamentary critics such as Churchill."[59] As a result Chamberlain shifted strategies, forming a small inner group of four (himself, Halifax, and Sir John Simon (chancellor) and Sir Samuel

[50] Ascher 2012, 73.     [51] Ascher 2012, 80.     [52] Ascher 2012, 73.
[53] Neville 2007, 110.     [54] Reynolds 2009, 45.     [55] Reynolds 2009, 45.
[56] CAB 23 (94), 316.     [57] CAB 23 (94), 305–11.     [58] Norwich 2007.
[59] Reynolds 2009, 46.

Hoare (home secretary)) that would keep plans for dealing with the German question secret from the rest of the Cabinet. "[W]ith the crisis mounting, the prime minister shifted decision-making into channels that he felt confident that he could control."[60]

### The Secret: "Plan Z"

Chamberlain's secret inner circle, as well as the rest of the world, witnessed a remarkable speech by Hitler in Nuremberg on September 12 that accelerated the need for action. In the speech Hitler made it clear that his words would be backed by action: "the Reich would not tolerate any further oppression of these three and a half million Germans."[61] While Hitler did not declare war in the speech, he made it clear to the international community that he reserved the right to deal with the Sudetenland problem himself, demanding justice and self-determination for the region. The political response was swift, with Sudeten Germans rioting and martial law instituted by the government in Prague. Chamberlain decided the next day to implement a plan that had been in the works since August, "Plan Z."

The idea behind Plan Z was simple: if it seemed that war was inevitable, and "zero hour" had arrived, Chamberlain would involve himself directly in the negotiations with Germany by flying to meet personally with Hitler. In the words of Horace Wilson, one of Chamberlain's senior advisors, "The success of the plan, if it is to be put into operation, depends upon its being a complete surprise, and it is vital that nothing should be said about it."[62] Meeting personally was a crucial part of the plan for Chamberlain: "you could say more to a man face-to-face than you could put in a letter."[63] Chamberlain also believed that the face-to-face interaction would help Hitler to better understand Britain's intentions: "doubts about the British attitude would be better removed by discussion than by other means."[64] Chamberlain was also of the belief that the dramatic nature of the visit would be important. Rather than have Hitler visit London, he thought the unprecedented nature of the visit to Germany would have a productive effect.[65]

While the plan was only to be implemented as a last resort, this should not belie the confidence Chamberlain possessed in his ability to bring about peace. A year earlier Chamberlain wrote privately of "the far-reaching plans which I have in mind for the appeasement of Europe

---

[60] Reynolds 2009, 47.    [61] Faber 2009, 263–66.
[62] Prime Minister's Files at The National Archives (hereafter PREM) 1/266A/363, Wilson memorandum, August 30, 1938.
[63] Reynolds 2009, 49.    [64] Reynolds 2009, 49.    [65] Reynolds 2009, 48.

& Asia and for the ultimate check to the mad armaments race."[66] With respect to the fate of the Czechs, Chamberlain remarked, "I am sure that some day the Czechs will see what we did was to save them for a happier future. And I sincerely believe that we have at last opened the way to that general appeasement which alone can save the world from chaos."[67] Similarly he told his sister in August of 1937, "I could hardly have moved a pebble: now I have only to raise a finger & the whole face of Europe is changed."[68] In March 1938, noting the publication of a new book chronicling the history of Europe, "At the present moment I am too busy trying to make the history of Europe to read about it."[69]

It should be noted that Chamberlain's aspirations and strong beliefs in his abilities did not end in Czechoslovakia; indeed Chamberlain told his sisters, "It *would* be another strange chapter in our family history if it fell to me to 'settle the Irish question' after the long repeated efforts made by Father and Austen."[70] As Reynolds argues, this remark "takes us into the deepest recesses of Chamberlain's character,"[71] illustrating Chamberlain's confidence, narcissism, and strong belief in his abilities to bring about peace. Chamberlain also had a significant family reputation to live up to and this was an important part of Neville's psychology, as the references to his father attest. His father, Joseph, and older half-brother, Austen, recipient of the Nobel Peace Prize, were both successful politicians and statesmen. As Austen wrote to Neville when he took up the post of Chancellor some six years earlier, "You will be the Chancellor to complete the building for which I laid the first brick in 1919. Father's great work will be completed in his children ... Don't think me absurd or pretentious if I say that I feel something of your success of what Father thought of mine. It is something more than a brotherly interest, it is an immense love and a possessive pride."[72] Therefore in addition to the pressure of facing Nazi Germany and what a failed strategy might mean for Britain, Chamberlain also was faced with what failure might mean personally and for his family name.

Importantly, the plan was kept a secret not only from the press and greater public, but from the majority of Chamberlain's own government. Indeed, initially Chamberlain sought to keep the plan secret from the Germans themselves, until he was in the air on his way, but was warned that if Hitler did not receive him, or felt that he was being forced to meet, that the consequences might be negative,[73] or as Wilson dryly noted, "this would be very awkward."[74] As such, Chamberlain asked

[66] Goldstein 2012, 276–77.     [67] Goldstein 2012, 277.     [68] Goldstein 2012, 278.
[69] Goldstein 2012, 278.     [70] Reynolds 2009, 49.     [71] Reynolds 2009, 49.
[72] Self 2006, 163.     [73] Reynolds 2009, 50.
[74] PREM 1/266A/359–60, Wilson to Henderson, September 9, 1938.

Hitler about meeting personally but did not tell his own Cabinet. The few individuals who did know of the plans were explicitly instructed not to tell others, "either in or out of the Cabinet," of the secret trip.[75] The reasons for keeping the trip secret were straightforward. First, Chamberlain was concerned about criticism regarding the plan. Indeed, one of the individuals who was aware of the plan noted that "it was like [the Emperor] Henry IV going to Canossa [all] over again,"[76] in order to humiliate himself in front of Pope Gregory VII and request revocation of his excommunication. Indeed Chamberlain seemed to possess the intuition that while face-to-face diplomacy would be helpful with Hitler, many would likely disagree. Second, the "Foreign Office much preferred to 'keep Hitler guessing' about British intentions."[77] Implicitly the Foreign Office seemed to realize that by sending Chamberlain to Hitler the British would be providing Hitler with an opportunity to assess what British intentions toward Germany were at the time.

On September 13, Chamberlain received word from his secret service that all German embassies had been told that Czechoslovakia would be invaded in less than two weeks, on the 25th of September. With this knowledge, combined with the threatening speech made the day earlier, Chamberlain activated the plan and sent a message to Hitler indicating that he was willing to fly to Germany in order to negotiate directly.[78] Chamberlain did not inform his Cabinet of the trip until after sending the message to Hitler at which point the Cabinet approved the trip.[79] Hitler accepted and the following morning Chamberlain flew to Munich in order to meet Hitler at his retreat outside of town at Berchtesgaden. While some historians believe the trip had modest goals, Chamberlain's own letter to the King George of England informing him of the trip suggests that he had loftier goals for the session: "I have been considering the possibility of a sudden and dramatic step which might change the whole situation."[80] The aim "was to convince Hitler of [Britain's] sincerity & to ascertain what objectives he had in mind."[81] Chamberlain needed to understand, for himself, what Hitler's specific intentions were for Czechoslovakia and what it would take to negotiate a settlement.[82]

For his part, Hitler had previously declared that he would not receive a visit from any British Prime Minister, partially because he believed Britain was only buying time.[83] But in this case Hitler seemed to be reassessing the situation and believed that Chamberlain may be coming to Munich with the intention of telling Hitler that Britain was ready

[75] Reynolds 2009, 50.    [76] Reynolds 2009, 50.    [77] McDonough 2011, 194.
[78] DBFP 3/2, doc. 862.    [79] Reynolds 2009, 50.    [80] Faber 2009, 277.
[81] Quoted in Goldstein 2012, 287.
[82] Adams 1993, 105.    [83] Reynolds 2009, 51.

for war. According to Josef Lipski, Polish diplomat and Ambassador to Berlin, Hitler thought "Chamberlain was coming to make a solemn declaration that Great Britain was ready to march."[84] German policymakers were uncertain of what to make of Chamberlain's visit, with Josef Goebbels arguing that "the crafty English" were attempting to lay blame at Germany's feet should the crisis come to war.[85] After all, an exercise in personal diplomacy may be viewed as an exercise in taking the moral high-ground, or as Goebbels put it, it provided the British with "a moralistic alibi."[86] von Weizsacker, State Secretary of the Foreign Office, argued that the meeting had much greater salience, seemingly beyond alibis, and indeed would determine inevitable "war or peace."[87]

After the meeting details had been set, the press was notified at 9 p.m. on the 14th. The excitement, from both political sides, was palpable. The *News Chronicle*, a liberal newspaper that had been critical of the government's policies, noted in its editorial page that "Britain's Prime Minister wins credit today for one of the boldest and most dramatic strokes in modern diplomatic history. In whatever guise, the name of Neville Chamberlain is now assured of a place in history."[88] As Reynolds argues, the excitement and emotional rollercoaster of the next two weeks would help to sear the trip deeply into popular memory.[89]

### Chamberlain's Meeting with Hitler Face-to-Face

After landing in Munich, Chamberlain traveled by train to Berchtesgaden.[90] Chamberlain "felt quite fresh and was delighted with the enthusiastic welcome of the crowds who were waiting in the rain, and who gave me the Nazi salute and shouted 'heil' at the tops of their voices all the way to the station."[91] Upon arrival the first meeting lasted three hours and laid the groundwork for agreement. He wrote to his sister his impressions upon seeing Hitler face-to-face at his estate: "You would never notice him in a crowd and would take him for the house painter he once was."[92] Later Chamberlain remarked to his Cabinet that Hitler seemed to be "the commonest little dog he had ever seen," but "it was impossible not to be impressed with the power

---

[84] Jedrzejewicz 1968, 408.      [85] Reynolds 2009, 52.
[86] Reynolds 2009, 52.      [87] Schmidt 1951, 90.
[88] *News Chronicle*, September 15, 1938, 1.      [89] Reynolds 2009, 54.
[90] There are two documents that record the Berchtesgaden interactions that I am aware of, both of which are included in the *Documents of British Foreign Policy*. Chamberlain's account is written after the event, from memory. The other is from Dr. Paul Schmidt, the German translator for Hitler, who began interpreting for the Foreign Office in 1924.
[91] Taylor 1979, 738.      [92] Self 2006, 346.

of the man."[93] After a half hour of platitudes over tea, Hitler jumped abruptly into substantive discussions and suggested that Chamberlain and he proceed in private, with only the interpreter present for the actual negotiation.[94] This move had been negotiated in advance by Henderson and Weizsacker.[95] One consequence of this decision was that the only account made during the meeting was Schmidt's, the interpreter, though Chamberlain later that evening dictated a "bare record" of the conversation.[96]

Chamberlain began by attempting to frame the discussion around the creation of new understanding between the two states, attempting to move the conversation naturally from the general to the specific, to specific intentions.[97] He aimed to spend the afternoon seeking "a clarification of each other's point of view so that each might know exactly what the other had in his mind."[98] Hitler abruptly pointed out that the situation involving Sudeten Germans was "very urgent and could not wait."[99] Chamberlain acquiesced, "All right . . . Go ahead." Reports were circulating that day that 300 Sudeten Germans had been killed and Hitler wanted an immediate solution. Hitler launched into a rather lengthy speech, or what Faber would term a "tirade,"[100] arguing that he had a political mandate from a public that had suffered many wrongs, including the Treaty of Versailles and the League of Nations, and had achieved much on behalf of the German public.

Chamberlain later reflected on Hitler's style: "For the most part H. spoke quietly and in low tones. I did not see any trace of insanity but occasionally he became very excited and poured out his indignation against the Czechs in a torrent of words so that several times I had to stop him and ask that I might have a chance to hear what he was talking about."[101] Chamberlain nevertheless listened quietly to most of what Hitler presented, interjecting for clarification when needed. As he had told his Cabinet earlier, his goal in the trip primarily was to better understand Hitler's goals and intentions. For Hitler's part, Schmidt took note that "nothing in [Chamberlain's] clear-cut, typically English features with their bushy eyebrows, pointed nose and strong mouth, betrayed what went on behind his high forehead."[102] In general, from Schmidt's perspective, "[t]he protagonists, it was clear, were taking each

---

[93] CAB 23 (95). Reynolds 2009, 57. See also NC 18/11/1069 Neville Chamberlain to Ida Chamberlain, September 19, 1938 and Norwich 2007, 260.
[94] Faber 2009, 289.
[95] For more on the Berchtesgaden meeting, see Weinberg 2013, 613.
[96] Taylor 1979.    [97] Reynolds 2009, 58.    [98] Reynolds 2009, 58.
[99] Reynolds 2009, 58.    [100] Faber 2009, 291.    [101] Self 2006, 312.
[102] Schmidt 1951, 92.

other's measure for the ensuing conversation, at which the issue would be war or peace."[103] The intention reading attempts evidently were occurring on both sides of the interaction.

The culmination of Hitler's monologue was an emotional outburst regarding the fate of Sudetens. He angrily suggested to Chamberlain that he would make it his mission to answer the call of the three million Sudeten Germans just as he had answered the call of the seven million Germans in Austria. Further, he noted that he would do it at any cost: "I am ready to face a world war. I am forty-nine years old, and I want still to be young enough to lead my people to victory,"[104] he shouted. Chamberlain interjected and moved straight to the heart of the logic of the appeasement strategy:

Hold on a minute; there is one point on which I want to be clear and I will explain why: you say that the three million Sudeten Germans must be included in the Reich; would you be satisfied with that and is there nothing more you want? I ask because there are many people who think that is not all; that you wish to dismember Czechoslovakia.[105]

Hitler responded in a rambling manner[106] and the impression Chamberlain was left with was that it was "impossible that Czechoslovakia should remain like a spearhead in Germany's side [but] he did not want a lot of Czechs, all he wanted was Sudeten Germans." Chamberlain, "looking Hitler full in the face,"[107] replied by noting that he would be prepared to consider solutions to Germany's interests as long as the use of force was ruled out. The exchange was remarkable for it revealed specific intentions and the quick reversal of those intentions:

HITLER: "Force! Who speaks of force? Herr Benes applies force against my countrymen in the Sudetenland... I shall not put up with this any longer. *I shall settle this question in one way or another. I shall take matters into my own hands.*"[108]

CHAMBERLAIN: "If I have understood you aright [sic], you are determined to proceed against Czecho-Slovakia in any case... If that is so, why did you let me come to Berchtesgaden? Under the circumstances it is best for me to return at once. Anything else is now pointless."

HITLER: "If, in considering the Sudeten question, you are prepared to recognise the principle of the right of peoples to self-determination, then we can continue the discussion in order to see how that principle can be applied in practice."[109]

---

[103] Schmidt 1951, 92.     [104] Dalton 1957, 178.     [105] DBFP 3(2), 350–51.
[106] Faber 2009, 292.     [107] Schmidt 1951, 92.
[108] My emphasis. As Schmidt notes, "This was the first time, in a discussion with a foreign statesman, that the phrase 'in one way or another' had been used – a phrase which I observed then and later to be an extreme danger signal" (1951, 92).
[109] Schmidt 1951, 92.

As Schmidt notes, "At that moment the question of peace or war was really poised on a razor's edge. But the astonishing happened: Hitler recoiled."[110] At the very moment where war could have been chosen, Hitler had backed down from what seemed to be a relatively straightforward claim regarding his intentions, to settle the question "one way or another... [taking] matters into my own hands." Hitler denies the intention to use force and this is the one that Chamberlain ultimately accepts. Chamberlain notes to Hitler that he would have to consult his cabinet, but understood that he had Hitler's agreement to not take military action in the meantime. The meeting ended with a "win" for Chamberlain: Sudetenland would be allowed self-determination, but that would be an end of expansion and force. As he wrote to his sister later that evening, Chamberlain "didn't care two hoots whether the Sudetens were in the Reich or out of it."[111]

After the meeting, Hitler escorted Chamberlain to his car and Chamberlain was driven back to his hotel. The joint press communiqué noted that the meeting was a "comprehensive and frank exchange of views" and that "in the course of a few days a further conversation will take place."[112] Hitler offered to show Chamberlain around a bit more "when all this is over."[113]

### The Public Declarations

Curiously, immediately following the meeting the British diplomatic party was refused a copy of interpreter Schmidt's transcript of the interaction. As Ian Kershaw points out, this was a tremendous "breach of diplomatic courtesy" that had come from Hitler himself.[114] "He evidently wanted his bargaining position to be kept as open as possible, and to avoid being bound by particular verbal formulations."[115] While Hitler did not share the transcript of the interaction with Chamberlain, he did share his admiration for him through back-channel communications. Joachim von Ribbentrop had his personal secretary confide to Horace Wilson that Hitler "felt he was speaking to a man."[116] As Self argues, this calculated flattery was quite successful in playing into

---

[110] Schmidt 1951, 93.

[111] NC 18/1/1069, Neville Chamberlain to Ida Chamberlain, September 19, 1938.

[112] *Daily Express*, September 16, 1938, 1.

[113] NC 18/1/1069, Neville Chamberlain to Ida Chamberlain, September 19, 1938.

[114] Kershaw 2000, 111. Schmidt argues that the move was made as "a pure act of spite by Ribbentrop, who wanted to have his revenge for being excluded from the conversation with Chamberlain" (Schmidt 1951, 95).

[115] Kershaw 2000, 111.    [116] Self 2006, 314.

Chamberlain's vanity and providing him with the sense that he had won the negotiation.[117]

Externally, Chamberlain conveyed a strong confidence upon arriving home to Britain. He noted to both his inner circle of advisors as well as the full Cabinet that it had been clear upon arrival in Germany that the situation was "one of desperate urgency. If he had not gone he thought that hostilities would have started by now. The atmosphere had been electric." Chamberlain knew, however, that the crucial question remained regarding future intentions. Was Sudetenland "the end" or "only a beginning"? According to meeting minutes, Chamberlain noted:

> Herr Hitler had a narrow mind and was violently prejudiced on certain subjects; but he would not deliberately deceive a man whom he respected and with whom he had been in negotiation, and he [Chamberlain] was sure that Herr Hitler now felt some respect for him. When Herr Hitler announced that he meant to do something it was certain that he would do it... The crucial question was whether Herr Hitler was speaking the truth when he said that he regarded the Sudeten question as a racial question which must be settled, and that the object of his policy was racial unity and not domination of Europe. Much depends on the answer to that question. The Prime Minister believed that Herr Hitler was speaking the truth. Herr Hitler had also said that, once the present question had been settled, he had no more territorial ambitions in Europe. He had also said that if the present question could be settled peaceably, it might be a turning-point in Anglo-German relations.[118]

Chamberlain's justification for believing Hitler rested on the personal relationship he had cultivated with the man and the empathy that he had apparently believed he engendered with Hitler that led him to believe that the leader could be trusted to honor his word. Importantly, Chamberlain pointed to changes in Hitler's behavior as an indication of his true intentions. Cabinet notes suggest that "Herr Hitler's manner was definitely different when they left his study; he [Hitler] had stopped halfway down the stairs and lamented the fact that the bad weather made it impossible for him to take the Prime Minister to see the view from the top of the mountain. Herr Hitler had said that he had hoped this might be possible on some other occasion."[119] Chamberlain further insinuated to the Cabinet that the Führer had been "most favorably impressed" and that this was "of the utmost importance, since the future conduct of these negotiations depended mainly upon personal contacts."[120] He told the Cabinet there was "great importance to the dramatic side of the visit."[121] And, as Reynolds argues, Chamberlain "saw himself as pioneering a diplomatic revolution."[122]

---

[117] Self 2006, 314.     [118] CAB 23 (95), 179.     [119] CAB 23 (95), 80.
[120] Reynolds 2009, 63.     [121] CAB 23 (90), fos. 70, 80.     [122] Reynolds 2009, 63.

The Admiralty was not as confident as Chamberlain that Hitler's intentions derived through personal contact could be trusted. The First Lord of the Admiralty, for instance, noted "he was certain that Herr Hitler would not stop at any frontier which might result from the proposed settlement."[123] Rather than wait and see whether Hitler would keep his word, what the First Lord suggested "was to order general mobilization forthwith. This would make [Britain's] position clear to the German Government and might yet result in deterring them from war."[124] Duff Cooper's recorded impressions were harsher and importantly picked up on some of the contradictions inherent to Chamberlain's account and Hitler's appeal to narcissism:

Although [Chamberlain] said that at first sight Hitler struck him as "the commonest little dog" he had ever seen, without one sign of distinction, nevertheless he was obviously pleased at the reports he had subsequently received of the good impression that he himself had made. He told us with obvious satisfaction how Hitler had said to someone that he had felt that he, Chamberlain, was "a man."[125]

Thomas Inskip, Minister for Coordination of Defence, had a similar understanding. "The impression made by the P.M.'s story was a little painful... The P.M. said more than once to us he was just in time. It was plain that H. had made all the running: he had in fact blackmailed the P.M."[126] Thus, while Chamberlain was portraying confidence from his face-to-face encounter with Hitler, his Cabinet and related policymakers back in London remained unconvinced. Chamberlain's confidence in Hitler's intentions was not winning over many of the politicians.

To the public, on a live radio broadcast on BBC, Chamberlain proudly announced the mutual understanding he and Herr Hitler had arrived at:

Yesterday afternoon I had a long talk with Herr Hitler. It was a frank talk, but it was a friendly one, and I feel satisfied now that each of us fully understands what is in the mind of the other.[127]

The BBC reports that the crowds gathered responded with applause and joy. This, in turn, affected Chamberlain and increased his confidence that he had succeeded in preventing war.

---

[123] CAB 23 (95), 184.     [124] CAB 23 (95), 184.
[125] Taylor 1979, 749.     [126] Taylor 1979, 749.
[127] BBC Written Archives, R34/325.

*The Private Doubt*

While this was occurring publicly in front of his Cabinet and the nation, there is an indication not only that privately Chamberlain had at least a passing moment of doubt of his success, but of Hitler's sincerity as well. In a letter to his sister written shortly after his meeting with Hitler, Chamberlain notes " . . . in spite of the *hardness and ruthlessness* I thought I saw in his face, I got the impression that here was a man who could be relied upon when he had given his word."[128] Just months earlier he had further written that he was convinced of Germany's fundamental "untrustworthiness." Throughout the crisis he also noted on several occasions in letters to his sister that he believed Hitler was "half mad" and a "lunatic." Finally, as noted above, Chamberlain also famously proffered to his Cabinet that "force is the only argument that Germany understands." Thus, while Chamberlain was publicly conveying a level of confidence, it is not immediately clear that this confidence was mirrored on the inside as well. One should not make too much of single words or sentences written in letters, but the disjuncture between Chamberlain's words to the Cabinet (strong, confident) and the words he uses with his sister (questioning, conjecture) is striking. It is noteworthy that Chamberlain did not express to the Cabinet that he thought he saw *ruthlessness* on Hitler's face. In addition, as Faber argues, Chamberlain was fond of repeating what had been told to him by Hitler's associates regarding negotiating with a "man," and also that Chamberlain had heard from a trusted source that he was "the most popular man in Germany."[129]

Also noteworthy is the impression that Ambassador Kennedy received when speaking with the Prime Minister in private shortly after the Hitler meeting. Kennedy's account, much more than others, highlights Chamberlain's severe distaste of Hitler's personality. Kennedy notes, "Chamberlain came away with an intense dislike . . . he is cruel, overbearing, has a hard look and . . . would be completely ruthless in any of his aims and methods." Chamberlain believed that the Czechs would "talk big but probably accede," and if an agreement with Hitler was reached according to "the principle of self determination," Chamberlain would push for it to be based on "orderly elections and protection of peace and order while the plans are being worked out." While it is difficult to know why Kennedy's reading of Chamberlain's account is markedly different from other reports, it does help to convey that there was at

---

[128] NC 18/1/1069, Neville Chamberlain to Ida Chamberlain, September 19, 1938.
[129] NC 18/1/1069, Neville Chamberlain to Ida Chamberlain, September 19, 1938.

least some doubt in Chamberlain's mind about Hitler's personality and, importantly, his ruthlessness.

Nevertheless, shortly after meeting with Hitler in Berchtesgaden, the agreement was formalized in Munich early in the morning of September 30. At Chamberlain's request Hitler signed a peace treaty between the United Kingdom and Germany, ostensibly ensuring the two countries would never be at war in the future. Chamberlain returned to Britain with a piece of paper that promised Britain "peace for our time" and received a hero's welcome. A few months later Nazi expansion continued out of Sudetenland and into the rest of Czechoslovakia, betraying the agreement that Chamberlain and Hitler had reached some months earlier. This ultimately served as a significant causal factor in the outbreak of the Second World War.

There is some evidence to suggest that Neville Chamberlain never saw Hitler's deception coming. Indeed, this is the way the history is normally told. As Groth notes, for instance, "a very short personal exposure was sufficient to create, or at least strongly confirm, a misinterpretation of Hitler's policy."[130] Chamberlain's biographer similarly concludes that Chamberlain's reliance on his "personal touch" was a "tragic misapprehension."[131] This seemingly empirical "fact" that Chamberlain was duped has had consequences for his historical image. As Robert Beck has noted, the orthodox characterization of Chamberlain is of a "wishful-thinking bumbler," an "umbrella-toting utopian," or "self-deluded Lear."[132] It is therefore relatively easy to construct a narrative of blind deception: Chamberlain naively visited Hitler believing in the ability for personal encounters to transcend political reality and could not see that Hitler was lying through his teeth.

### The Successful Deception Check-List

This orthodox story has, over the last few decades, been challenged on a number of fronts. First, with respect to personality and personal characteristics, even critics of Chamberlain note that the characterization of a blindly following naïve utopian is unfair. As one critic puts it, "the truth was that Chamberlain's diagnosis of Nazi Germany and its intentions was not constant and consistent; that behind his policy lay not a single, simple motive, but several interwoven motives, partly idealistic, partly expedient, partly inspired by hope and partly by fear; and sometimes one element and sometimes another came to the fore."[133] Other historians

---

[130] Groth 1964, 836.    [131] Self 2006, 314.    [132] Beck 1989, 167–69.
[133] Barnett 1972, 514.

highlight that while Chamberlain may have suffered from momentary doubt, he was highly intelligent and once he had reached a decision he had a profound ability, much to his detriment, to steadfastly believe he was right, perhaps as a form of cognitive closure:[134]

Chamberlain was a strong-willed, intelligent and clear-sighted political tactician, who followed a foreign policy he was convinced was not only the right one but vastly superior to any of the alternatives. He sometimes wrestled with private doubts and uncertainties, but it was a confident, even obstinate, belief he was right which determined his actions.[135]

This characteristic of firmly believing in a given course of action meant that Chamberlain ultimately was able to ward off criticism in the knowledge that he was making the right decision.

Yet, if Chamberlain was often realistic in his assessment of Hitler and understood his ruthlessness and untrustworthiness, how did he not see the deception coming? The narrative described in his letters suggests that there *were* the type of clues that detection-deception experts, such as Ekman, identify as crucial indicators for deception detection as discussed in Chapter 2: high emotions (Hitler's "emotional outburst"), merciless demeanor (reading an expression of "ruthlessness" on the face of Hitler), tirades ("indignation against the Czechs in a torrent of words"), and so forth. Chamberlain's letters can be read as a checklist of facial clues to deception detection.[136] Put another way, Chamberlain did pick up on clues that hinted at Hitler's concealed intentions, but did not privilege those clues in the final analysis. Before turning to why Chamberlain did not act on the clues that Hitler was providing it is useful to return to the experiences of the Berlin ambassadors and diplomats who also interacted with Hitler and reported similar types of expressive behaviors.

The early interactions between the Berlin ambassadors and diplomats display a similar checklist of deception clues. Rumbold noted the excitement and ferocity with which Hitler spoke, his obstinacy, the obvious lies he was telling, and the overarching impression that Hitler was "not normal." Phipps through his various encounters catalogs the passionate outbursts, long disquisitions, shouting crescendos, tempestuous flow of words, torrent of eloquence, and so forth that all combines to create a portrait of a very emotional unbalanced man that Phipps has trouble taking seriously and also indicates that he believes Hitler to be lying. Eden's experiences were a bit more nuanced, finding a very different Hitler disposition in meeting one versus meeting two, but in the aggregate Eden finds that Hitler is very hard to take seriously, holding back laughter in

---

[134] Thanks to Brian Rathbun for pointing this out.
[135] McDonough 1998, 46.    [136] Holmes 2013.

the second meeting. As predicted, repeated exposure allowed Eden to gain a better sense of Hitler's lies over time. Henderson, perhaps more than any of them, picks up on Hitler's self-deception and his abnormal personality, where normal rules of personal engagement do not apply, reading megalomania and, potentially, insanity in his face. It is striking that during these face-to-face visits they picked up on many of the very same clues that Chamberlain wrote down, though they came away with a psychological portrait that suggested that Hitler could not be trusted, whereas Chamberlain reached the opposite conclusion. Why did they get it right while Chamberlain was so wrong?

First, there is reason to believe that Chamberlain very strongly *wanted to believe* Hitler had very limited aims. Chamberlain potentially colluded in Hitler's deception because the alternative, recognizing he had been lied to and that the strategy of appeasement that he personally had a great stake in (not to mention the nation) had failed, would be difficult to deal with psychologically and practically.[137] The future of Europe, as Chamberlain makes clear in his letters to his sister, is in his hands. As Ekman argues, our psychologies often push us toward postponing that which is very unpleasant, derived from both cognitive closure and confirmation bias. As a condition for understanding the true intentions of another, wanting to believe that one is being told the truth may serve as a strong motivating factor for collusion. The other diplomats and ambassadors were largely interacting with Hitler at a time when choices could be made and Britain had time on her side. As they often referenced, the situation was not yet desperate. Similarly the ambassadors and diplomats had far less to lose personally by being wrong; Chamberlain through his dramatic Plan Z had staked his reputation on averting war through face-to-face diplomacy. Put another way, by the time that Chamberlain arrived in Berchtesgaden the situation *was* desperate. Indeed the entire premise of Plan Z was that it would be a strategy of last resort. By colluding in Hitler's deception Chamberlain disregarded the data points that were not congruent with his preferred outcome, such as the ruthlessness on his face and the fact that Hitler, in the very same interaction, made his intentions clear. It may well be that when the priors are strong enough, the possibilities for intention dynamism are at their lowest.[138] I return to this point in the following chapter.

Second, Chamberlain, unlike the ambassadors who eventually would read Hitler correctly by interpreting his expressive behaviors, had *very little data to work with*. In retrospect there were a number of data points in the case that the face-to-face information could have informed, including

---

[137] Ekman 2009.    [138] Thanks to Nicholas Wheeler for pointing this out.

Hitler not providing a transcript of the interaction immediately following it. If Chamberlain had coupled what he thought he saw in Hitler's
eyes regarding ruthlessness and anger with other available data, this may
have bolstered the notion that Hitler was planning on reneging on his
words. One of the reasons why the ambassadors in Berlin got Hitler
right was that they were combining data points derived from being in
Berlin and witnessing the rise of Nazism and Hitlerism firsthand *with*
the data they received in the face-to-face interactions. As the deception detection experts from the CIA point out, deception detection is
best accomplished when viewed as a clustering activity. The intuitions
derived through face-to-face encounters form data which then may serve
as the basis of creating actionable beliefs. If Chamberlain had combined
his intuitions with other available data, the beliefs that were created may
well have been different. The experience of Eden is fruitful here. Eden
got Hitler wrong in their first face-to-face encounter, but he did not get
him wrong subsequently.

Third, as is often the case in international political negotiations, Hitler
was *able to construct a social setting that made deception easier.* Recall from
Chamberlain's own account of arriving in Germany that Hitler made
use of flattery to bring the two individuals together. This undoubtedly
had an effect on Chamberlain's psychology as he returned home and
reported to the Cabinet that Hitler could be trusted. As mentioned in
Chapter 2, psychology research has long recognized the importance of
"liking": bringing two individuals closer together as friends or acquaintances can have an effect on the ability to persuade. Successful salesmen
are, first and foremost, effective empathizers. Creating a social structure where Chamberlain believed that Hitler liked him, respected him,
empathized with him, and trusted him, made deception easier. Hitler
playing to Chamberlain's sensibilities potentially aided the concealment
a great deal. Some have suggested that Hitler, in addition to potentially
possessing psychopathic tendencies (see below), certainly possessed high
levels of Machiavellianism, in which individuals tend toward the use of
manipulation for personal gain, typically against their self-interest.[139]
Creating a strategic setting for deception would therefore be expected.

This social setting perhaps explains why Chamberlain was quick to
believe Hitler when his Cabinet, Admiralty, and diplomats stationed in
Berlin were not. Chamberlain attempted to read Hitler's intentions from
within the social structure of flattery, self-importance, confidence, etc.
as noted above. The Admiralty, working in London hundreds of miles
away, was not subject to this same structure. The diplomats stationed in

[139] Wilson et al. 1996, 285.

Berlin did not have the same fanfare with their routine visits nor did they experience the grandeur of Hitler's country retreat. Their more careful approach signifies that the social structure Chamberlain found himself embedded in may have had an effect. However, what London did not have that Chamberlain did was the potential to read Hitler correctly. It was this data, that which was gained through the face-to-face encounter, that was potentially quite relevant and helpful, and only available through face-to-face.

This social setting worked particularly well because of a variety of personality characteristics that may have affected the outcome. First, Hitler *utilized personal power to his advantage*. As Chamberlain's letters suggest, while Chamberlain publicly downplayed Hitler's personal power, calling him a common dog, Chamberlain was indeed greatly impressed and intimidated by Hitler's stature. Hitler was able to utilize this by playing to Chamberlain's *ego*, suggesting to Chamberlain that he was glad to be negotiating with "a man" and showering praise upon him. According to Self, this had a significant effect on Chamberlain as Hitler became more approachable and likable. I will return to this notion of interpersonal power in the following chapter.

Most importantly, this tactic worked with Chamberlain largely because it likely stoked his own narcissism. While personality assessments, particularly of historical figures, are difficult and traditionally have been fraught with problems, such as the inability to be falsified, such efforts have improved in recent years, partially due to more sophisticated measurement of personality variables and new methods in textual analysis to reveal personality characteristics.[140] Using these new methods, there is evidence to suggest that Chamberlain possessed both clinical narcissism and hubris syndrome, which may have contributed to beliefs regarding his ability to read others and the formation of intention beliefs. An analysis of Chamberlain's public words finds that he possessed hubris syndrome and Chamberlain's own private words to his sister and others about his transformative capabilities as a leader suggest a high degree of egoistic admiration.[141] As noted earlier, Chamberlain also had a family name to live up to. His father was one of the more important British politicians in the late nineteenth and early twentieth centuries, serving as leader of the opposition.

---

[140] See, for example, Garrard et al. 2014.
[141] Owen and Davidson 2009. The method that Owen and Davidson employ involves looking for evidence of fourteen symptoms of hubris syndrome, which correspond in many cases to personality disorders in DSM-IV such as anti-social personality disorder, histrionic personality disorder, and narcissistic personality disorder.

These characteristics likely had an effect on his decision to engage with Hitler. As Ascher notes, Chamberlain "had no doubt about his ability to handle the dictator. Throughout the 1930s, Chamberlain never spoke of Hitler as an unstable person whose policies were unfathomable." As the studies on deception detection from Chapter 2 suggest, it is precisely high levels of narcissism that cloud detection. Interestingly, the same study conducted of Chamberlain finds less support for hubris syndrome in Eden, though Eden does display "hubristic traits,"[142] potentially explaining why Eden picked up on Hitler's personality a bit better than Chamberlain, though it took the second meeting in order to do so.[143]

Narcissism also has effects with respect to confirmation bias, the tendency of individuals to favor information that is congruent with their prior-held beliefs. As Chamberlain's biographers point out, while Chamberlain occasionally suffered from doubt, once he had made a decision he stuck with it unfailingly. As appeasement had been in the works for the better part of a decade, it is relatively easy to see how the "decision" regarding how to approach Germany generally and Hitler specifically would have been formed from early on in the conflict. It is also important to note that these personality characteristics are gathered throughout Chamberlain's career, not just during the Munich crisis. This is critical since Chamberlain's difficulties with Hitler and the failure of appeasement undoubtedly have affected the ways historians have interpreted his comments. "A more balanced evaluation of the man and his broader career" is still somewhat hindered "by the fact that Chamberlain's name has become synonymous with the ambivalent and rapidly changing emotions generated by 'Munich' and the disastrous drift into total war."[144]

Similarly, studies conducted from available materials of Hitler's personality suggest characteristics that may be relevant as well.[145] In 1918 after suffering from a gas attack during the First World War, Adolf Hitler was diagnosed by neuropsychologist and medical officer Dr. Edmund Forster as "a psychopath with hysterical symptoms." Psychopathy is a disorder normally characterized by a *lack* of empathy and a shallowness of affect.[146] Importantly, however, psychopaths also possess a strong ability to manipulate others. Reviewing recent studies suggests that not

---

[142] Owen and Davidson 2009, 1396–406. It is important to note, however, that Eden's profile was constructed largely from sources drawn from when he was Prime Minister, from 1955 to 1957. It is conceivable that his personality earlier in life showed different characteristics.

[143] Owen and Davidson 2009, 1399.        [144] Self 2006, 3.

[145] Hyland, Boduszek, and Kielkiewicz 2011; Coolidge, Davis, and Segal 2007; Murray 1943.

[146] Hare 2003; Lockwood et al. 2013.

only do psychopaths often not have cognitive perspective-taking empathy deficits, they may have superior perspective-taking abilities.[147] Indeed new models suggest that cognitive-perspective taking is not impaired in psychopathy, though affective empathy may well be impaired. Arguably this ability to understand others, including their beliefs and desires, aided Hitler in his ultimate deception of Chamberlain at Berchtesgaden and subsequent Munich agreement. Empathy, and the ability to express it, in other words, is as much a part of successful egoistic manipulation required for deception as it is required for trust and cooperative outcomes.

### Conclusion: The Tragedy of "Munich"

Thus the tragedy of "Munich" was set in motion well before any documents were signed in 1938. For the five years prior to the agreement British officials had warned, often in great detail, of the dangers of Hitler and the lies that he told. These warnings, cultivated from face-to-face diplomacy with the Chancellor himself, did not translate to policy for a number of reasons that included Britain's material concerns. But just as importantly Chamberlain's own "faith in the essential rationality of all human beings, his abhorrence of war, and his supreme confidence in his own judgment had prevented him from realizing sooner that the riddle of Hitler had in fact been solved three months after the Nazis assumed power." While counterfactuals are difficult in world politics, Ascher makes the compelling case that "Had the leading officials in Britain (including Chamberlain) heeded the advice of their ambassadors in Berlin in the first years of Hitler's rule, they would have reined in the Fuhrer while Germany was still militarily weak."[148]

Chamberlain's complicated experience with Hitler outside of Munich is a difficult one for a theory of intention understanding through diplomacy, though it does provide support for many of the propositions regarding face-to-face diplomacy. First, Chamberlain's visit was a very calculated one that was aimed explicitly at attempting to derive concealed information about Hitler's intentions. Chamberlain believed that the best way to gain this understanding of Hitler's secrets was through face-to-face interaction. He also understood that keeping the trip concealed from the public and his own government was prudent, not just because it would increase the drama of the event (which it did), but also because it prevented debate and criticism within his own cabinet that could have stalled, or prevented, the initiative. Chamberlain was taking

---

[147] See Lockwood et al. 2013.    [148] Ascher 2012, 90–91.

a calculated risk with the trip. By going to Munich to read Hitler he was also giving Hitler the ability to read Chamberlain's intentions which, prior to implementation of Plan Z, had been left intentionally vague. Hitler received Chamberlain for similar reasons. Britain had purpose-fully tried to keep Hitler guessing. As McDonough argues, the British Foreign office realized that a "personal meeting would inevitably show that Britain did not want to fight a war on account of Czechoslovakia or for that matter on behalf of any small state in Eastern Europe."[149] The implication was clear: if Chamberlain traveled to meet Hitler it would provide Hitler with an opportunity to read Chamberlain's intentions. The plan to keep Hitler guessing worked. Hitler assumed that Cham-berlain was coming with a strong message of deterrence, and agreed to the face-to-face interaction, in part, in order to confirm these intentions personally with his counterpart in order to reduce uncertainty.

While the evidence is spotty, there is an indication of the type of intu-itional thinking and belief-formation occurring in Chamberlain's assess-ment of Hitler. First, Hitler did reveal his specific intentions to settle the Czech Crisis, even by force if necessary, which Chamberlain calls him on, forcing a retreat from Hitler. In this moment Chamberlain is reading Hitler correctly. Second, Chamberlain *did* pick up on concealed information that Hitler was providing, after the reversal, most notably a ruthless nature that Chamberlain was not sure he could trust. This intu-ition was quickly replaced with other beliefs, beliefs that would become much stronger over the following days when he would justify his trip in front of the public and proclaim that he was sure that Hitler was telling the truth with respect to Czechoslovakia. Thus while not privileging the quick System-1 intuitional information he received in the interpersonal interaction, there is evidence to suggest that Hitler's secret deception was not kept perfectly to the vest; clues to Hitler's concealed intentions were provided. However, Chamberlain's own personality characteristics, most notably narcissism, served as a driver of the ultimate belief that was formed upon reflection in System-2. It is striking to note that other indi-viduals interacting with Hitler face-to-face who may not have shared the same narcissistic tendencies, reached different conclusions. As such, it is reasonable to deduce that were it not for the face-to-face encounters, British officials would have been unable to arrive at the same conclusions regarding Hitler's intentions.

Ultimately, however, Munich is remembered for what went wrong. Chamberlain traveled to Hitler and read him incorrectly, with disaster to follow. One underappreciated aspect of this story, however, is how many

[149] McDonough 2011, 194.

got it right. In particular the diplomats and ambassadors stationed in Berlin, who had the ability to meet with Hitler when they needed to in order to gauge his intentions, paint a portrait of a man who stands up to history and everything that we now know in retrospect. In this way face-to-face diplomacy *was* ultimately successful in conveying Hitler's intentions, remarkably successful given the strong incentives that Hitler had to keep his plans secret, and therefore should not necessarily be remembered so much as a failure of face-to-face but rather a failure to act on the information that face-to-face provided.

As with the other case studies, competing explanations exist. As noted above, one of the ubiquitous explanations for the Munich agreement was simply that Chamberlain put too much trust in Hitler. "The man who trusted Hitler," as the *New York Times* put it,[150] erred, according to this logic, by believing what Hitler said with respect to his intentions. There is much support for such a reading, most particularly Chamberlain's own words on the subject matter, both to his Cabinet as well as to his sister, as documented above. On the other hand, Chamberlain enters the inter-action with Hitler having expressed, just months earlier, "how utterly untrustworthy and dishonest" the government in Berlin actually was.

Perhaps most importantly, it is difficult to see how Chamberlain could have engendered anything more than a modicum of interpersonal trust given the lack of interaction with Hitler from a temporal perspective. As Adler and Barnett point out, "Trust does not develop overnight but rather is accomplished after a lifetime of common experiences and through sustained interactions and reciprocal exchanges, leaps of faith that are braced by the verification offered by organizations, trial-and-error, and a historical legacy of actions and encounters that deposit an environment of certitude not withstanding the uncertainty that accompanies social life."[151] While an argument could be made that this is what occurred in the Reagan–Gorbachev interactions from Chapter 3, for example, it is difficult to see the same type of development of trust occurring in the Chamberlain–Hitler relationship, given the paucity of their meetings. How did Hitler make himself vulnerable to Chamberlain in their encounter? If anything, Hitler congratulated himself on his ability to control that "silly old man . . . with his umbrella."[152] And, just as importantly, the interactions of Rumbold/Phipps/Eden with Hitler do not convey much trust in Hitler at all.

Power and signaling provide other mechanisms by which the British government, and policymakers in the Foreign Office, attempted to

---

[150] "The Man Who Trusted Hitler," *New York Times*, February 17, 1985.
[151] Quoted in Booth and Wheeler 2008, 243–44.
[152] Kirkpatrick 1959, 135.

approximate German intentions. Some scholars, such as James Morrow, have typically interpreted the events in the late 1930s as "a concrete example of signaling."[153] By occupying Czechoslovakia, Hitler's Germany was signaling that its aims were not simply to unify ethnic Germans into a single state, as they could have accomplished this without occupying the non-German parts of Czechoslovakia, but instead possessed aims that transcended a unified ethnic Germany.[154] Morrow argues that Hitler's behavior in the earlier part of the decade serves to signal "deliberately... [that] he sought limited revisions in the status quo to conceal his true long-term objectives."[155] And, according to the argument, this worked quite well as it prevented Britain and France from taking "a stronger stand against him at that time."[156] Crucially, however, when looking at the balance and power and moves that Hitler made in 1935–1937, a more complicated picture of signaling emerges.

Recalling the discussion above, Britain found itself in a bleak relative power situation for much of the 1930s. As Yarhi-Milo chronicles, perceptions of an increasing German air force (the *Luftwaffe*), buildup in the German army, and changes in the European balance of power all contributed to significant concerns among British policymakers that the balance of power had changed toward Germany's favor by 1936.[157] This was true vis-à-vis Britain as well as Western Europe. "Germany will have an advantage in respect to prewar preparedness. Our naval forces will be greatly superior to those of the Germans... [but] the German army will be numerically superior to the combined British and French armies. Germany seems likely to possess a marked advantage over the allies in air striking power."[158] Further, the Germans sent a number of costly signals, indicating their offensive intentions, throughout the period, including the remilitarization of the Rhineland in 1936, "which was the first time Germany used its military force outside the Reich." While Germany did send signals of reassurance, such as signing a Naval Agreement with Britain in 1935, Yarhi-Milo concludes that "the majority of Germany's actions [during this period] were hostile, not reassuring." From a costly signaling perspective, combined with the buildup in air force and armaments, the intentions of Hitler's Germany should have been relatively clear. Yet, the intention approximation from London was continually hampered by debate and uncertainty, leading ultimately to Chamberlain's attempt to clarify Hitler's intentions by meeting with him face-to-face. Therefore Morrow is right to point out that Hitler sent a costly signal with the invasion and occupation of Czechoslovakia in 1939, and

---

[153] Morrow 1999, 86.    [154] Morrow 1999, 86–87.    [155] Morrow 1999, 87.
[156] Morrow 1999, 87.    [157] Yarhi-Milo 2014, Chapter 2.
[158] Quoted in Yarhi-Milo 2014, 57.

he did send some signals of reassurance in the years preceding this, but crucially the signals were mixed with the bulk existing on the offensive side of the scale. As such, the costly signaling method of interpreting and approximating intentions remains something of a mixed bag in this case. Policymakers in Britain did not quite know how to interpret the mixed signals they received.

Somewhat relatedly, it is also important to note that this case illustrates the importance of prior-held beliefs. As noted in Chapter 2, prior beliefs can be "sticky" in their resistance to updating and revision. In this case we see variation in the role that these beliefs play. For example, Rumbold and Phipps both enter their initial interactions with Hitler *already possessing* negative beliefs regarding Hitler's intentions. Indeed Rumbold had "written the book" on German aims before his interaction with Hitler. The face-to-face encounters only serve to reaffirm existing beliefs. Eden is a more complicated case. Eden enters his initial interaction with Hitler with more positive priors regarding Hitler's aims, and in his first encounter these priors are confirmed and strengthened. Yet, in the second encounter with Hitler the strengthened prior beliefs are eventually revised based on the intuitions engendered in the interaction. Henderson enters his interaction with Hitler with relatively positive priors, indeed even finding positives in the Nazi regime, but is ultimately disappointed by the face-to-face encounter and revises his beliefs. This variation in priors, and the subsequent strengthening or revision of them, as a result of the face-to-face interaction implies that it is not necessarily the priors that dictate what one gleans from a face-to-face encounter. Indeed in this case there are ample examples of face-to-face interactions providing intuitional information that leads to the abandonment of firmly held prior beliefs.

In the following chapter I conclude the book by returning to international relations theory and taking stock of what we can learn from these four case studies. In particular I argue that face-to-face diplomacy ultimately allows individuals to escape the security dilemma at the interpersonal level. I also attempt to create a framework that will be beneficial for others in conducting the type of neuroscience and psychology-oriented research in International Relations scholarship I have utilized in this book.

# 7    Escaping Uncertainty

[I]t all gets down to the conduct of foreign policy being personal. . . . I think it's vitally important that not only you know and have as hard of a read as you can get on the foreign leader with whom you're dealing, friend or foe, but that leaders know that what you say, what you do, what you propose is real . . .

– Former US Vice President Joe Biden[1]

## Dealing with "Unresolvable Uncertainty"

*Reassessing the Face-to-Face Diplomacy Puzzle*

In Roosevelt's aforementioned 1945 inauguration speech before his trip to Yalta, the President spoke of the need to find a lasting peace in the world by transcending fear and mistrust. If the world was to stabilize, escaping the uncertainty of the near future would be critical. The United States was engaged in war on two fronts, and victory was very much uncertain. "In the days and in the years that are to come we shall work for a just and honorable peace, a durable peace, as today we work and fight for total victory in war," he declared. "We can and we will achieve such a peace." His strategy was clear. "We have learned the simple truth, as Emerson said, that 'The only way to have a friend is to be one.' We can gain no lasting peace if we approach it with suspicion and mistrust or with fear. We can gain it only if we proceed with the understanding, the confidence, and the courage which flow from conviction."[2]

After the ceremony, Roosevelt prepared for travel. He went over his will with his son James and told him where funeral instructions and other important family documents were kept. He asked James to wear the family ring in case anything happened to him. A few days later Roosevelt

---

[1] "The Geopolitical Therapist," *The Atlantic.* Available: www.theatlantic.com/international/archive/2016/08/joe-biden-interview/497633/
[2] Full text of the inauguration speech is available at: http://avalon.law.yale.edu/20th_century/froos4.asp

embarked on the long voyage. Roosevelt's first destination was Newport News, Virginia, where he boarded the *USS Quincy* to travel to Malta. Security concerns aboard the *Quincy* abounded. The security team was very concerned about leaks to the press. "Loose lips sink ships" was not only a popular saying at the time, but a serious security directive. In addition to information concerns, there were also concerns about German submarines mining the Atlantic. Precautions were taken, with destroyers and cruisers protecting the *Quincy*. The ships sailed at night with no lights. Cables were sent by other boats to avoid detection. Planes from US bases in North Africa and aircraft carriers provided air cover.

Upon reaching Malta, concerns regarding Roosevelt's health began to mount. The President had suffered from a cold through most of the voyage across the Atlantic and many who met him in Malta found him to be "gravely ill." As the British foreign secretary, Anthony Eden put it, Roosevelt gave "the impression of failing powers." Indeed, members of his delegation were reportedly shocked by his graven appearance. Despite concerns over Roosevelt's failing health, the meetings with Prime Minister Winston Churchill went well, though the two differed on the extent to which they desired a firm plan and strategy for the upcoming summit in Yalta. Churchill wanted to get down to business; Roosevelt demurred, preferring an informal encounter to the formal business that typically characterizes meetings between heads of state. This worried Eden in particular, with him noting that "we were going into a decisive conference and had so far neither agreed what we would discuss nor how to handle matters with a Bear who would certainly know his mind."[3]

While the idea for a tripartite meeting between the three leaders, Roosevelt, Churchill, and Stalin, came from Roosevelt, Churchill was also a believer in face-to-face diplomacy. Churchill believed strongly that sitting down with friends and adversaries in peacetime and crisis, in order to hash out agreements and find cooperative outcomes, was crucial. As Churchill's biographer Klaus Larres documents, there was perhaps no firmer believer in this type of diplomacy than the Prime Minister.[4] In a speech at McGill University in Montreal, Churchill argued, "What an ineffectual method of conveying human thought correspondence is – telegraphed with all its rapidity, all the facilities of our – of modern intercommunication . . . They are simply dead, black walls compared to personal – personal contact." While Neville Chamberlain is largely credited with pioneering modern summitry, Churchill "made it almost routine."[5] The personal face-to-face meeting was a cornerstone of Churchill's foreign policy.

[3] Reynolds 2009, 119.    [4] Larres 2002.    [5] Reynolds 2009, 104.

After the planning meeting, Roosevelt and Churchill departed for Crimea. Roosevelt's plane, called the "Sacred Cow" because of its heavily guarded nature, took off under the cover of darkness. The plane took a circuitous route to avoid hostile fire from the ground. Upon reaching the Saki air base, FDR's doctor was very concerned. "The President looked old and thin and drawn... he sat looking straight ahead with his mouth open, as if he were not taking things in." The Soviet doctors at the air base concurred, noting FDR's poor health and exhausted nature. An hour after landing, the heads of state boarded armored Soviet limousines and left Saki for Yalta. Most of the six-hour trip was along a route guarded by Soviet troops. Churchill, in particular, found the ride to be unpleasant. "Christ! Five more hours of this," he noted to his daughter. Both delegations arrived after nightfall, weary from the trip and ready to rest before conducting negotiations with Stalin in the days ahead.

The conference at Yalta took place over seven days and ultimately was integral to the postwar reorganization of Europe. While the ultimate agreement is still debated by historians, Roosevelt and Churchill believed they had reached consensus with Stalin on a number of fronts, including the partitioning of Germany, inclusion of the Soviet Union in the United Nations Organization, Soviet involvement in the Asian front of the war, and future of Poland, which was to be decided by Poles, "on a broader democratic basis."[6] Roosevelt returned to Washington confident that Stalin would be a cooperative partner in the building of postwar peace and democracy. "I come from the Crimea Conference with a firm belief that we have made a good start on the road to a world of peace."[7]

Shortly thereafter, Roosevelt realized he was mistaken. A month after the summit, Roosevelt's USSR Ambassador, Averell Harriman, who had the opportunity to meet face-to-face with Soviet leadership on a regular basis, notified the President that the optimistic assessment of Stalin garnered at Yalta could no longer be supported. "[W]e must come clearly to realize that the Soviet program is the establishment of totalitarianism, ending personal liberty and democracy as we know it."[8] Roosevelt came to the realization that "Averell is right," shortly thereafter.[9] Stalin, in the words of Roosevelt, "has broken every one of the promises he made at Yalta."[10] Thus the reward for a trip where Roosevelt effectively put his own life on the line would be tremendous disappointment.

[6] For text of the Yalta agreement see: http://avalon.law.yale.edu/wwii/yalta.asp
[7] Roosevelt 1950, 571.    [8] FRUS, 1945, V, April 4, 1945, p. 819.
[9] Gaddis 1991, 249.    [10] Gaddis 1991, 249.

As mentioned at the beginning of this book, this received wisdom has been reexamined. Plokhy suggests, for example, that what the prevailing view tends to miss is both the poor negotiating position of the West as well as attributing agreement on key issues where there was not agreement. With respect to the former, as Anthony Eden, Secretary of State for Foreign Affairs at that point, summed up, "[W]e had not very much to offer them, but . . . we required a great deal *from them*."[11] Securing Soviet support in Japan and a pledge to join the United Nations Organization were significant positive outcomes for Roosevelt. On the critical question of Poland, the Soviet Union wanted the country, one with a long shared border with the USSR, to remain in their sphere of influence for security reasons. It was a red line for the Soviet Leadership; as Molotov reportedly said: "We cannot lose Poland. If this line is crossed they will grab us too."[12] As Plokhy argues, the only way to ensure that Poland was under Soviet influence and responsible to Stalin was to install a puppet government, maintained by the Red Army, and thus antithetical to any type of legitimate democratic governance or elections. The United States could not ideologically support such a structure and therefore disagreements over Poland were rooted in "a clash of geopolitical vision, ideology, and culture."[13] These disagreements were not resolvable in a week-long conference. And, as Plokhy points out, that was not the intention. Yalta was not a postwar conference but rather a mid-war summit and therefore Churchill and Roosevelt did not see a lack of guarantee regarding Poland's democracy to be a devastating failure.

Most importantly, the Soviet record suggests that at the time of the conference, "Stalin had not yet decided what to do with Eastern Europe."[14] Indeed as late as May 1946 Stalin told leaders in the Polish government that "Lenin never said there was no path to socialism other than the dictatorship of the proletariat; he admitted that it was possible to arrive at the path to socialism utilizing the foundations of the bourgeois democratic system such as Parliament."[15] It appears that there were no specific intentions about Poland communicated at the time, partially because, as the evidence suggests, Stalin's intentions were not yet well-formed. In the end, while Roosevelt was ultimately unable to reassure Stalin, and thus not able to escape the uncertainty that would fuel the Cold War, he did read Stalin correctly on many issues and engendered significant cooperation from the interaction, cooperation that likely would have been difficult, if not impossible, to obtain in other ways. As Plokhy puts it, both states ultimately did misjudge

---

[11] Plokhy 2010, 393. My emphasis.    [12] Plokhy 2010, 394.
[13] Plokhy 2010, 394.    [14] Plokhy 2010, 399.    [15] Plokhy 2010, 399.

intentions going forward, and mistrust would follow, but the Cold War "came later, as a result of decisions made by individuals many of whom, at least on the Western side, never set foot on Crimean soil."[16] As so often has been the case in this book, those assessing intentions from afar contributed to the uncertainty, rather than reduced it.

As Khong has forcefully argued, one often need do little more than to say a word, such as "Munich" or "Yalta" in order to evoke powerful imagery and a strategic analogy of the dangers of personal face-to-face diplomacy.[17] Why do leaders continue to pursue such a dangerous activity? Why has face-to-face diplomacy been largely ignored by scholars of international politics, yet deemed essential by practitioners? As I have argued in this book, face-to-face diplomacy is undoubtedly one of the most prevalent forms of international political practice, a practice that diplomats and leaders take very seriously, and indeed intuitively understand as being critical to the conduct of international politics, yet it has largely been dismissed or ignored by theories of international relations in large part because of its perceived "cheap talk" nature. This view of face-to-face diplomacy as cheap talk is rooted in an important assumption about the nature of human interaction, an assumption derived from folk psychology theories about how individuals understand each other, namely that we cannot gain access to the private information that exists in the minds of other people and therefore need to theorize about what they might be intending. If this assumption is wrong, and there are times when we have sophisticated, precise, and reliable access to the minds of others, then this severely undercuts the problem of intentions that is at the heart of the cheap talk argument, and more broadly, the security dilemma itself.

I have argued that rather than approximating or theorizing the intentions of others through folk theories of behavior interpretation and observations from the outside, which is the dominant perspective taken by other approaches to the intentions problem in IR theory, face-to-face diplomacy provides a mechanism by which individuals can understand each other's intentions from the inside. I have drawn on the growing body of work at the intersection of psychology, philosophy of mind, and social neuroscience that shows how, through the mirroring system in the brain, individuals are able to actively simulate the mental and emotional states of others, and replicate for themselves what is occurring in the other's brain. Even though we are not able to subject this specific claim to testing in the context of actual face-to-face diplomacy, my argument is that this unobservable casual mechanism provides an important

---

[16] Plokhy 2010, *xxxvi*.    [17] Khong 1992.

explanation of why face-to-face diplomacy is such an effective way of reading the minds of one's diplomatic interlocutors. The accuracy and effectiveness of this process are mediated by a number of important factors, including prior-held beliefs, such as those that might exist in intractable conflict, and personality characteristics, such as high levels of narcissism. Ultimately these brain and bodily mechanisms suggest that diplomats and leaders are able to transmit information to each other, even when they have strong incentives not to do so and do not intend to, such as in crisis diplomacy or peace summits. They thus suggest new reasons why face-to-face diplomacy should be taken seriously: while not foolproof, signaling of intentions is not as difficult in diplomatic settings as IR theories have suggested.

These insights imply important points about the study of IR. First, this book contributes to a renewed emphasis on both the role individual decision-makers and leaders play in international politics as well as the interpersonal realm of interaction in which they do it. I suggest that the activities of individual diplomats and leaders, and in particular the inter- action methods in which they engage with each other, help to explain outcomes. What matters is not just material structure, though diplomacy can never be divorced from these factors, but rather diplomats and lead- ers have agency in diplomacy: the activities they engage in matter a great deal as well. For example, understanding the relationship development "pause" during the Cold War in transitioning between the Reagan and Bush administrations is difficult when investigating structure, material, costly signals, and so forth alone. Indeed scholars have been baffled by such a pause when looking at those factors for some time. By bringing the individual back in, in particular individual differences in the decision to pursue face-to-face interactions with Gorbachev, as well as the inter- personal interactions they engaged in, we are able to transcend structural perspectives and better understand the importance of face-to-face inter- personal meetings among individuals in the international system.

Second, I suggest that the problem of intentions in IR theory need not be as thorny as scholars often make it out to be. Rather than need- ing telepathy to understand the political intentions of friends and adver- saries, we may just need mirroring, specific intentions, and a lack of nar- cissism when it comes to believing that we have understood the other. This resonates with our experiences in day-to-day life where we directly experience the intentions of others by rote. We use a sophisticated brain apparatus to read the minds of others on a daily basis and we normally do so quite well. But just because we do so in daily life does not mean that leaders do not do so in high-stakes environments as well. Menachem Begin and his team found it quite natural to attempt to read the facial

expressions of Jimmy Carter in the meetings at Camp David precisely
because it was something they had grown accustomed to doing over time.
They made a concerted effort to pay attention to such details because it
paid dividends, even in a case where the long-term security of Israel was
on the line. We read each other daily in making very important decisions,
even in matters of life and death.[18]

Third, the development of an intuition or belief regarding the intentions of another implies important ramifications not only for the development of trust, which I will discuss below, but also the ways in which we
think about the latent nature of the international system. The "default
switch" in the international system, at least since Thucydides, has been
one of uncertainty. The evidence presented in this book suggests, however, that individual leaders are often much more certain in their assessments of others than the uncertainty switch should allow. It may be
worthwhile to think through what would happen if we were to flip
the default switch of uncertainty characterizing the international system
under anarchy from constantly being uncertain about the intentions of
others to believing that we are more certain than previously believed.
It appears that arguments privileging paths to war and peace based on
certainty rather than uncertainty may have material-level support.[19] If
individuals are actually relatively certain about the intentions of others,
even in a system characterized by anarchy, then a core principle shared
by IR theories must be reevaluated. This would have profound effects on
theory construction because the latent uncertainty that drives much of
state action, such as self-help, would be more difficult to explain. This
would not be a problem just for realists, but indeed each of the paradigms
of IR theory that embrace uncertainty, albeit in different forms.[20]

The security dilemma, for example, exists because states are fundamentally uncertain about the intentions of others. As Booth and Wheeler
have argued, *unresolvable uncertainty* under anarchy combined with a
concern for security, results in states finding themselves in a state of
"Hobbesian fear" (Butterfield's term) where "kill or perish" (Herz's
term) begins to dictate state actions. Because of the problem of intentions, states live in a state of mutual incomprehension, an "irreducible
dilemma" stemming from a lack of understanding. According to Booth
and Wheeler, the best we can hope for is to *transcend* the security
dilemma while never escaping the unresolvable uncertainty latent in the
problem. Yet, as we have seen, practitioners of international politics not

---

[18] See, for example, Gunnell and Ceci 2010 on jurors reading faces in determining guilt
and sentencing.
[19] Mitzen and Schweller 2011.      [20] Rathbun 2007; Holmes 2011.

only often display tremendous confidence that they know the intentions of others and sometimes are certain of it, but they are often quite correct in their assessments. Put another way, if there is fundamental uncertainty in the international system which leads to a problem of intention under-standing, practitioners often belie that uncertainty and *act as if* they are certain about the other.[21] Critically, as I have suggested in the empirical case studies, leaders often, as in the case of Reagan and Gorbachev, use this knowledge to actively empathize with the other, thereby exercising security dilemma sensibility.[22]

The ultimate upshot of the findings in this book is that the security dilemma is less of a problem than IR theory takes it to be. I largely agree with Booth and Wheeler's formulation of this point that "the security dilemma cannot ultimately be escaped, but it can be transcended,"[23] though for different reasons than they do and go one step further. Booth and Wheeler argue that "unresolvable uncertainty will be a persistent characteristic in world politics," though it should not "be the end of the story." I have suggested in this book that there are moments in time when uncertainty *is* resolved, where individuals *are* aware of the inten-tions of others, they have certainty in that feeling, *and there is good reason for them to be certain*: because they are right. Put another way, the syn-chronic security dilemma at the interpersonal level *can be* escaped. This is not the last word on the security dilemma, however. The security dilemma between states and the diachronic problem, however, may still be present. Typically state decision-making involves not just individuals, but groups, organizations, and a variety of other entities that can intro-duce considerable uncertainty into the equation. Leaders themselves change, sometimes surprisingly so. And, as realists are correct to point out, intentions can change, not least because the individuals involved may change. Though, as I have argued, escaping the security dilemma in the present is a critical ability for leaders who find themselves in a crisis environment.

This analysis has significant policy implications. If my theory is cor-rect, then we can begin to outline when personal face-to-face diplomacy should be sought and when it should be avoided. On the signaling end,

---

[21] Somewhat relatedly, Mitzen and Schweller (2011) have theorized the notion of "mis-placed certainty," instances "where decision makers are confident that they know each other's capabilities, intentions, or both; but their confidence is unwarranted yet persists even in the face of disconfirming evidence." The theory and evidence in this book sug-gests that there are often good reasons for states to be more certain about the intentions of others than our theories of international relations would admit, but this understand-ing should only apply in the special type of face-to-face diplomacy I have outlined.

[22] Booth and Wheeler 2008.    [23] Booth and Wheeler 2008.

there are times when leaders will want to be as forthcoming with intentions as possible and therefore seek strategies that aid in intention understanding, such as in reassurance situations. Cases of nuclear competition are particularly amenable to such intervention. As Matias Spektor, Nicholas Wheeler, and Dani Nedal have argued, it was a series of face-to-face interactions at the highest levels between Brazilian and Argentinian leaders in the 1980s that served to reassure each side of their benign intentions.[24] There are also times when leaders will want to be able to keep intentions close to the vest, yet still participate in diplomatic visits, such as in distributive bargaining sessions. This calculation must be balanced with the salutary effects of receiving intentions via face-to-face signaling. After all, the political calculus of face-to-face diplomacy is that while it allows one to read others, it also allows for the ability to be *read*. The decision to engage in face-to-face diplomacy is thus a strategic one, since intention understanding may not necessarily be in the interest of all leaders all the time. This is a logic that leaders seem to intuit. Mikhail Gorbachev sought face-to-face interactions with Ronald Reagan partially because he wanted to convey his intentions; he wanted to be read. George H.W. Bush avoided face-to-face encounters with Gorbachev early in his presidency arguably for the exact opposite reason, preferring to keep US intentions regarding the Soviet Union close to the vest.[25]

Previous efforts to look at these types of practical dynamics of diplomacy, where scholars privilege the "taken for granted" nature of the work of practitioners, have argued that the intuitions of policymakers are important. When Ronald Reagan had the intuition in the mid-1980s that he needed to sit down with Soviet leadership and convey US intentions, he was employing a practical sense of what needed to be done in that particular situation. The recent "practice turn" in IR theory has begun to theorize these moments, turning focus away from the traditional agent/structure dichotomy and focusing, instead, on the everyday activities that populate the lives of policymakers in international politics.[26] The difficulty with these attempts at understanding the

---

[24] Spektor, Wheeler and Nedal 2015, 20.

[25] There are of course many other reasons why leaders may wish to pursue, or not pursue, face-to-face interactions, many of which have been discussed in previous chapters. Personal beliefs about the efficacy or inefficiency of the personal meeting, a social value orientation toward proself rather than prosocial, a reputation for being productive or unproductive in face-to-face meetings, and so forth are all part of the prior puzzle of why we sometimes see face-to-face diplomacy when other times we do not.

[26] See, for example, Pouliot 2010; Adler and Pouliot 2011a; Adler and Pouliot 2011b; Pouliot and Cornut 2015; Sending, Pouliot, and Neumann 2015; Pouliot 2016. Also McCourt 2016 for a recent review on this literature.

day-to-day practices of policymakers is that, as Erik Ringmar has force-fully argued, there are definitional and under-specific *mechanism* prob-lems that plague the practice turn research. On the definitional side, different activities and concepts are lumped together under the practice label.[27]

Perhaps more importantly, the underlying mechanism through which individuals come to gain practical sense is underspecified. As Ring-mar points out, many of the practice theory approaches derive from Bourdieu's theory of practice, where practices are formed by the *habitus* of society: the dispositions that tell us what is "accept-able . . . possible . . . normal . . . and expected."[28] What is critical for Bour-dieu is that he has a materialist ontology: *habitus* "reflects the class divi-sions of society, engendered by the capitalist mode of production, but it simultaneously also makes sense of, and perpetuates, those divisions."[29] In applying Bourdieu to IR, scholars have tended to lose this socio-economic backdrop to the theory, which not only removes the materi-alism, but removes the ways in which practical sense is sustained and maintained. "Scholars of international relations pick the cherries from Bourdieu's theoretical pudding, and one feature they characteristically shy away from is his rump-Marxism . . . [i]n this way Bourdieu's contri-bution differs little from what a traditional rational choice theorist might supply."[30] How practices become practices, in other words, remains mystifying without an identifiable mechanism.

The aim here is not to argue that practice theory is unintelligible or a problematic research agenda, indeed the perspective of this book shares many similarities with a practice theory perspective, but rather to high-light the difficulties in picking up on what it is *precisely* that individuals are doing when they gain a practical sense, or intuition, for what should be done. This has been the aim of the book. By concentrating on one particular form of interaction, two particular mental states in intention intuitions and intention beliefs, a set of neurons, and the mechanism by which those neurons turn observation into understanding, we can both conceptualize a particular form of international practice, face-to-face diplomacy, and highlight what it does with a high degree of specificity and prediction. Thus rather than defining practices and their mecha-nisms broadly and vaguely, I have attempted to go the other direction, defining one practice as specifically as possible and supporting it with a very discrete plausible material mechanism. Therefore, Pouliot is quite right to point out that the "practice of diplomacy rests on some forms

---

[27] Ringmar 2014, 6.    [28] Ringmar 2014, 9.    [29] Ringmar 2014, 9.
[30] Ringmar 2014, 9–10.

of inarticulate knowledge from which strategic, reflexive, and intentional action becomes possible."[31] This book has attempted to shed light on one specific way that inarticulate knowledge is created.

Having summarized the main arguments of the book, in the remainder of this concluding chapter I wish to accomplish several tasks. First, a couple of ancillary, but important, threads have weaved through the empirical chapters and as of yet have not been resolved. The most notable of these is the issue of trust. In what follows I provide a view of trust from an intention intuition and intention belief perspective, thereby wading into an important debate within IR theory. A second issue relates to the limits of face-to-face interaction in reaching breakthroughs despite understanding one another. Put simply, what happens when you understand that the other wants war, or at the very least does not want peace? Third, I look ahead to the future of psychological and neuroscience integration with international relations, with specific emphasis on how the disciplines may be bridged in future research by focusing on the identification of theoretical causal mechanisms and further engagement with an emotional logic of politics. Finally, I identify some additional questions for future research that have come out of the argument, including the power of the interpersonal domain in international politics.

## The Relationship between Intentions and Trust

In each of the case studies, trust served as an important counter-explanation. This is logical since intentions and trust are closely related. Indeed if empathy is ultimately about understanding the intentions of others, then as Booth and Wheeler argue, "trust requires empathy," because "a capacity to empathize with the fear and suffering of one's adversaries is a critical precondition for building trust."[32] Put into the terms used in this book, trust requires the ability to understand what the other is feeling. Clearly, however, empathy may be a necessary condition for trust but it is not sufficient. Empathy may also lead to deception and attempts to strategically "destroy" the enemy.[33] Nevertheless, empathy, even the thin version, and trust clearly go hand in hand. Yet, what is trust and how does it work? Surprisingly an agreed-upon definition continues to elude and disagreements abound. Or, as Martin Hollis put it, "although trust is an obvious fact of life, it is an exasperating one. Like the flight of the bumblebee it works in practice but not in theory."[34]

[31] Pouliot 2011, 545. See also Sending, Pouliot, and Neumann 2015.
[32] Booth and Wheeler 2008, 237.      [33] Booth and Wheeler 2008, 237.
[34] Hollis 1998, 1.

Two important aspects of trust conceptualization are relevant here: the type of mental state trust *is* in the body, and to what extent trust is the product of rational calculation or interpersonal bonding. First, scholars disagree on the extent to which trust is a mental state and what type of mental state it might be. Rathbun argues that "[t]rust is the *belief* that one will not be harmed when his or her fate is placed in the hands of others . . . trust is the *belief* that others will cooperate when one cooperates, that they will not exploit one's vulnerability but rather respond in kind."[35] Hoffman argues that "*trust* refers to an *attitude* involving a willingness to place the fate of one's interests under the control of others. This willingness is based on a *belief* . . . that potential trustees will avoid using their discretion to harm the interests of the first."[36] Wheeler similarly argues that trust is a "psychological belief that another person can be trusted."[37] In Wheeler's case, interpersonal interaction allows leaders to build bonds of trust with one another. Key to the development of trust is belief-formation, but Wheeler goes one step further in theorizing the development of an additional mental state he terms "suspension," which enables individuals to make decisions without risk calculation. The end result is transcendence from risk calculation, though it is bounded by a particular issue area or domain. These approaches, which I group together as "trust as belief," privilege a cognitive approach to understanding what trust is: trust is something we think about consciously and is represented by a discrete mental state. It might develop from interpersonal interaction, and other mental states such as suspension might precede it, but trust exists as a belief. And, in Wheeler's case, the belief can eventually itself be transcended to a different mental state altogether.[38]

This group of conceptualizations can be contrasted by work that does not necessarily require cognition for trust to exist in one individual toward another. For example, Hopf's "logic of habit" proposes the possibility that trust may be habitual in nature, something that occurs not because we consciously think about it but because it has become hard-wired in the brain as a habit.[39] Similarly the practice approaches discussed above allow day-to-day diplomacy to result in trust without individuals necessarily consciously thinking about it.[40] Pouliot makes the

---

[35] Rathbun 2012, 10, emphasis added.
[36] Hoffman 2006, 17, some of the emphasis added.    [37] Wheeler 2018.
[38] In this way Wheeler's conceptualization bridges, in a sense, the two forms of trust I identify here. Trust as belief, which occurs through interpersonal bonding and maintains forms of probabilistic thinking, and trust as suspension, also created through interpersonal bonding and escapes probabilistic thinking, are both accounted for in his model.
[39] Hopf 2010.    [40] Pouliot 2008.

distinction between representational knowledge ("knowing-that") and practical knowledge ("knowing-how") where the former is conscious and verbalizable while the latter is tacit and inarticulate and automatic.[41] Elsewhere I have suggested that trust might be akin to something that philosophers of mind call an *alief*, an affective emotional intuition that sits alongside, and often contradicts, our beliefs.[42] What this second group of conceptualizations, which I group together as "trust as intuition," suggests is that trust need not necessarily be conscious and inculcated in beliefs in order to affect the development of trust between individuals. Trust may be a habit, practice, suspension, or alief as much as it is a belief.

The second area of disagreement concerns what trust is fundamentally about. Some scholars in the rationalist tradition have suggested that trust obtains from rational calculation of the preferences of actors. Kydd, for example, conceptualizes trust in game-theoretic terms, highlighting that trust is "a belief that the other side prefers mutual cooperation to exploiting one's own cooperation."[43] Trust for Kydd is probabilistic, it is an assessment of the likelihood that the other has a particular preference in a given situation. In contrast, Ruzicka and Wheeler argue that it is possible "that actors might develop trusting relationships which they value independently of the pay-off structure."[44] From this perspective trust is about "more than predicting the behavior of others. It includes trustors' perceptions that their trustees have a *responsibility* to fulfill the trust placed in them even if it means sacrificing some of their own benefits."[45] Trust then is "based on beliefs about the honesty and integrity of potential partners,"[46] which can be cultivated in interpersonal interactions.[47] One of the critical aspects of this interpersonal approach is the inclusion of an emotional component, which sits

---

[41] Pouliot 2010, 29.

[42] The logic of the alief is captured in the following anecdote drawn from Gendler 2008, 634–35. "In 2007, the Hualapai Tribe opened a skywalk over the Grand Canyon. The skywalk is a glass structure that is suspended over the canyon, 4,000 feet above the ground. As the New York Times reported, visitors often feel a sense of dread when walking out on to the glass and feel a strong intuition to retreat ... [T]his is a case where the individuals experiencing the feeling of dread do not believe that they are unsafe. After all, who would willingly walk out onto a glass structure that they believe to be unsafe? The emotional response here invokes irrational behavior. The emotion of fear undermines, rather than enhances, rationality. Instead of strengthening a belief of insecurity, it creates some other type of belief-like mental state; and if we look for beliefs to explain relevant behavior, we would come up empty. The belief of security and action representing insecurity conflict with one another; emotion serves to create an intuition that we should get off the skywalk as soon as possible. In this case, feeling is definitely not believing" (Holmes 2015).

[43] Kydd 2005, 6.    [44] Ruzicka and Wheeler 2010, 73.
[45] Hoffman 2006, 20.    [46] Rathbun 2009, 351.    [47] Wheeler 2018.

alongside the behavioral and cognitive dimensions of trust. As Mercer has argued, without an emotional component trust becomes redundant. "Rationalists drain the psychology from trust by turning it into a consequence of incentives. Emphasizing incentives as the basis for trust eliminates both the need for trust and the opportunity to trust."[48] Or, as Wheeler puts it, "[t]rust will remain elusive if we fail to grasp its emotional basis."[49] For Booth and Wheeler, the emotional basis comes, critically, from the "human factor," which gives trust a very subjective and personal quality.[50] Emotion ultimately "gives meaning and value to the ways people feel."[51]

These disagreements on two critical aspects of the ontological status of trust are important and have rescued trust from a particularly thin rationalist conceptualization, which strikes many as inadequate.[52] However, problems remain. As Michel argues, what exactly this human factor is, and what it does, "is far from clear."[53] It has been described as feelings, attachments, empathy, emotion, and so on. Put simply, how does the human factor work and what is going on within it to create trust? Extending the framework and theory presented in this book, in a provisional way, can help to further this debate.

First, trust, like intentions, can be intuitions or beliefs. The theory in this book suggests that face-to-face diplomacy leads to intention intuitions which then may turn into intention beliefs upon reflection. The same is true of trust and this helps to account for the wide array of ways that trust, as a particular mental state, is discussed in the literature. Trust often is constituted by a well-formed belief. If Wheeler is correct that Reagan and Gorbachev did eventually come to trust each other at an interpersonal level, then this involved both individuals interacting with each other over time and reflecting back on those interactions to form trust beliefs. Yet, crucially, in each of their personal interactions, they were gaining insight into the other and deriving intuitions about whether they could trust each other. And, as Wheeler argues, intuitions played a large role, as did the eventual development of the suspension mental state, one that is different from a cognitive belief. Put another way, in some instances disagreement about whether trust is constituted by beliefs or intuitions may be instances of scholars agreeing more than they disagree.

Second, the framework in this book also provides a way of thinking about what the "human factor" or "emotional bonding" actually

[48] Mercer 2005, 95.    [49] Wheeler 2007, 6.
[50] Booth and Wheeler 2008, 234.    [51] Hutchison 2016, 106.
[52] Michel 2012.    [53] Michel 2012. 4.

is. Face-to-face interactions *provide* the human factor in a very specific way: the mirroring of intentions, emotions, and other expressive behaviors *constitutes* the human factor.[54] In face-to-face interactions individuals are actively simulating what is occurring in the mind of the other – there is a bond that is created precisely through this process of interaction. In a recent study in the field of computational modeling, researchers attempted to create a computer program that could predict, above human accuracy, the extent to which individuals would trust others in a social interaction. They were able to do this by programming the computer to observe "trust-related nonverbal cues expressed in . . . social interaction."[55] The idea is simple: individuals engaged in interpersonal interaction convey trust and trustworthiness not just through what they say, but what they express on their faces and in their body language. Individuals interpret this behavior and gain intuitions about the other: "when people have access to the nonverbal cues of their partner, they are more accurate in their assessment of their partner's trustworthiness."[56] Put into rationalist terms, if trust is probabilistic, then face-to-face interaction *helps individuals to derive the probabilities*. Therefore face-to-face interaction is not only key to intention understanding, but may also be, crucially, one route to interpersonal trust development.

Understanding the value of face-to-face interactions therefore helps to resolve thorny puzzles in the trust literature. First, trust may be constituted by intuitions or beliefs, and there are precise and specific ways to model how the former becomes the latter. Second, the face-to-face interactions are the human factor and emotional bonding that allow trust to develop. Specifically it is through the conveyance of expressive, rather than verbal, behaviors that this occurs. More work is required in this area, specifically in delineating the precise roles of rationality, strategy, and emotion (to the extent that they are separable) in developing interpersonal trust, but incorporating existing work in psychology and

---

[54] The resultant human bonding through face-to-face interaction implies a specific role for face-to-face encounters in reconciliation processes in addition to trust-building. As Hutchison and Bleiker (2008) point out, reconstituting identity after trauma requires what they term "emotional reconciliation," a type of emotional healing where salient social interactions play a large role. While they do not explicitly invoke the importance of face-to-face encounters, future research on face-to-face and emotional bonding may help to delineate precisely when such interactions aid, or hinder, reconciliation. As a survivor of the Rwandan genocide of the community-run *gacaca* courts put it, "The reason I came to gacaca today is because I want to speak to the killers . . . Talking to them face to face is important for our reconciliation. How can I live with them again unless I can talk to them first?" Quoted in Clark 2010, 314.

[55] Lee et al. 2013, 893. Also see Holmes and Yarhi-Milo 2017 on the role of body language and expressive behaviors in conveying capacities such as empathy.

[56] Lee et al. 2013.

computational modeling into IR frameworks and theories demonstrates the value of bridge-building between IR and other disciplines, specifically psychology.[57] I deal with this point more explicitly below.

A crucial question that emerges from this analysis is why some dyadic relationships between leaders result in the type of bond of trust Wheeler discusses, while other relationships never seem to get off the ground from a trust-perspective. Consider the difference between Reagan and Gorbachev's interactions in the second half of the 1980s compared with those of Barack Obama and Vladimir Putin's over the first half of the 2010s. Whereas the former relationship was characterized by many positive aspects of the human factor – chemistry, social bonding and so on – it would appear the latter lacked any meaningful development of those qualities. The changing dramatis personæ evidently matter quite a bit. Material structural conditions certainly play a role, as diplomacy can never be divorced from overarching structural enablers and constraints, but the variation in diplomatic dyadic interpersonal relationships vis-à-vis bonds of trust is striking: some dyads seem to "hit it off" while others do not. Can it be explained? If so, what explains it?

### The Limits of Face-to-Face Interaction and Deviant Cases

The preceding discussion and its culminating questions suggest something very important about face-to-face diplomacy: there are limits to what can be accomplished. The argument in this book is that face-to-face interaction provides a mechanism for intention understanding. This does not imply or guarantee, however, that intention understanding results in normatively desirable outcomes, preference change, or intention dynamism. Consider the infamous 1961 encounter between John F. Kennedy and Nikita Khrushchev in Vienna. Kennedy traveled to Vienna to meet with the First Secretary of the Communist Party, a meeting that some argue laid the foundation for both the Cuban Missile Crisis and Vietnam War.[58] The summit is largely known for Kennedy's poor performance and Khrushchev's overbearing style, facilitated perhaps by, among other things, Khrushchev not taking Kennedy seriously, dismissing him as "very inexperienced, even immature."[59] Kennedy's words immediately following the summit got to the heart of the matter: "[Khrushchev] just beat the hell out of me. So I've got a terrible

---

[57] See Wheeler 2018 on how to incorporate psychological and rationalist/economic-based conceptualizations of trust into a useful theory and framework.
[58] Reynolds 2009, 163.    [59] Quoted in Reynolds 2009, 206.

problem. If he thinks I'm inexperienced and have no guts, until we remove those ideas we won't get anywhere with him." Kennedy's concern was arguably validated the following year, when an emboldened Khrushchev, perhaps buoyed by Kennedy's appearance of weakness and lack of resolve, sent missiles to Cuba, beginning what would become a crisis in short order.[60]

Going into the summit, the US State Department had a number of goals. One of those was "to gain a clearer understanding of Khrushchev as a man and of Soviet policy and intentions," a theme that resonates with the other cases in this book. In terms of this objective, there is reason to be confident that Kennedy and Khrushchev *did* gain a better understanding of where each other stood on crucial specific questions, such as the fate of Berlin. Khrushchev conveyed that he was adamant regarding his intentions to sign a separate peace treaty with Berlin; Kennedy conveyed that his intention was not "to accept arrangements totally inimical to U.S interests," which is how he interpreted the effects of a separate peace treaty. In sum what both sides ultimately learned was that the intentions of the other were not yet in a zone of possible agreement; indeed significant distance separated the two and their priors may have been too strong to prevent intention dynamism.[61] As Kennedy put it after the meeting, "Our views contrasted sharply but at least we knew better at the end where we both stood . . ."[62] The first goal of intention understanding had arguably been satisfied.[63]

One of the other main objectives identified by the State Department, however, was to "improve the prospects of finding an acceptable and workable basis for improving relations with the Soviet Union."[64] For

---

[60] See Hall and Yarhi-Milo 2012, 571 for a review of this literature.
[61] See Reynolds 2009, 163–221 for detailed analysis of the summit.
[62] Speech transcript: www.presidency.ucsb.edu/ws/?pid=8180.
[63] It should be noted, however, that the evidence here is a bit murky, partially because of the difficulty in assessing Khrushchev's sincere intentions vis-à-vis Berlin going into the summit. Reynolds (2007, 198) for example interprets Khrushchev's intentions regarding Berlin as one of leveraging the West into a favorable deal regarding Germany. Zubok and Pleshakov (1996, 247) similarly suggest that Khrushchev was bluffing when it came to discussion of potential war over Berlin. In any case, one point that seems clear is that Khrushchev's specific intentions toward Berlin at this point in time was the pursuit of a separate peace deal unless the United States capitulated. It is this understanding that Kennedy reads in the meeting and relays to Congress after the encounter. Kennedy also suggests that Khrushchev "probably had a knife in himself a little on [Berlin]," suggesting to Congress that Khrushchev did not have all the "advantages on his side," despite his rhetoric in Vienna. See also *Foreign Relations of the United States*, 1961–1963, Vol V, Soviet Union, eds. Charles S Sampson and John Michael Joyce (United States Government Printing Office, Washington, 1998), Document 91.
[64] *Foreign Relations of the United States*, 1961–1963, Vol V, Soviet Union, eds. Charles S Sampson and John Michael Joyce (United States Government Printing Office, Washington, 1998), Document 72.

his part, Khrushchev had a similar goal in mind: "I attach a lot of significance to the meeting with Kennedy, because we are approaching
the moment when we must solve the German question."[65] Solving the
German question would mean finding an acceptable and workable solution that could improve Cold War conditions between the two superpowers. With this latter goal, the summit produced far less success. Unable
to find much common ground, particularly on divisive issues such as
Berlin, where the possibility of war was raised by Khrushchev, Kennedy
closed the summit by remarking that "it will be a cold winter." Kennedy
similarly told the American public that the meetings with Khrushchev
had occurred over "a very sober two days." He would go on, "We have
wholly different views of right and wrong... We have wholly different
concepts of where the world is and where it is going."[66] Put simply,
Kennedy and Khrushchev might have read the intentions of one another
accurately, but that intention understanding did not result in any type of
intention dynamism that would allow both sides to reassure the other.

The Vienna summit illustrates the difficulties of finding agreement
even if intentions are understood. One way to interpret the Vienna interaction is through the paradigm of negotiation strategy: both Khrushchev
and Kennedy arrived at the interaction in a value-claiming mindset.
The former sought a separate peace deal that would be beneficial to
the USSR, the latter did not as it was not perceived to be beneficial to
the United States, and neither were in a position, or had the inclination,
to work toward value-creation. Or, as Reynolds puts it, "[T]actically,
however, neither man was properly prepared for their encounter in
Vienna."[67] As such, coercive bargaining ensued with no bargain reached.
Another reading suggests that the two never possessed security dilemma
sensibility in the same way that others in this book, such as Reagan
and Gorbachev, did and thus were unable to transcend, as Wheeler
puts it, "the ideological fundamentalism" that characterized each side's
approach to the interaction.[68] Additionally it may be that in 1961 the
situation was not "ripe" for agreement; Kennedy had just entered office
and, as Jervis argues, "[i]t takes any administration at least a year to
find its legs, and this period is almost always rocky," with Kennedy's
performance in Vienna an "obvious [example]."[69] Ultimately, understanding that the other possesses a particular intention might be useful
in understanding where they are coming from and crafting strategy moving forward, but the Vienna case suggests that merely understanding the

---

[65] Reynolds 2009, 195.
[66] Speech transcript: www.presidency.ucsb.edu/ws/?pid=8180.
[67] Reynolds 2009, 219.    [68] Wheeler 2013, 488.    [69] Jervis 2013.

intentions of another is not always enough to reassure or resolve conflict; after all, one's intentions might be to harm the other. When intentions clash, changing them can be difficult. What does it take to change intentions if the actors involved have apathetic, at best, and malign, at worst, intentions toward one another?

As Jervis alludes, these salient moments in history raise a fascinating counterfactual: would a different dyad of leaders have produced a similar outcome? Jervis, while not focusing on the summit per se, wonders if "it could be argued that the Cuban Missile Crisis might have ended in war had Nixon been president...because he was more headstrong than Kennedy." We can ask similar questions about the interaction in Vienna as well. If the negotiation strategy were an issue, then replacing the leaders who employed different styles, such as value-claiming approaches, may have resulted in a different outcome.[70] More generally, Vienna and cases like it highlight the need to better understand why it is that some dyads of leaders are able to "hit it off," bond, produce chemistry, and crucially convince one another to change their intentions, while others are not and cannot. Jervis, Rathbun, and others, are likely right that dispositions matter a great deal. Experience, personal history, and other characteristics matter as well.[71] But it also may be that the interpersonal dynamics *between* individuals matter as much as the disposition of the individuals engaged in the interaction. Put another way, interpersonal interaction, particularly face-to-face interaction, is salient not just because of its mechanism for intention understanding, but because of the social bonding that often emerges from it. Recent work in microsociology suggests that these emergent properties, such as a bond, are not reducible to either of the particular individuals in an interaction. As such, interpersonal interaction itself, rather than the individuals involved, may provide clues to explaining and predicting when dyadic interaction between leaders and diplomats will result in social bonding and, in turn, potentially intention dynamism as well. I take up this question in the final section below.

## Bridging Psychology and IR: Where do we go from here?

The discussion of trust and the limits of face-to-face interaction in terms of intention dynamism serve as a useful transition to a broader discussion on building bridges between psychology and IR. As I suggested

---

[70] See, for example, Rathbun 2014 on proself vs. prosocial dispositions and their links to negotiation strategies.
[71] See, for example, Saunders 2011; Horowitz, Stam, and Ellis 2015; Saunders 2017.

in the theoretical chapter, at first blush the distance between psychology/neuroscience and IR seems vast. While scholars in recent years have shown how psychological variables such as fear and hatred are, in many instances, the cornerstone of IR theories,[72] systemic or macro-level theories of IR have tended to discount the role of individuals, and the substance of the theories tends to have little focus on psychological variables or models. The epistemologies and methods of psychology/neuroscience and IR are also seemingly quite different, with the two disciplines in disagreement about how to approach the object of study. Yet, as discussed in previous chapters, many of the core claims from systemic theories, such as the problem of intentions, have their roots in implicit psychological assumptions. If those assumptions turn out to be incorrect, as I have argued is the case with the intentions problem, then the consequences need to be studied and evaluated. Yet, studying psychology is not only useful for problematizing assumptions, it also helps IR scholars to build theories, clarify their concepts, and specify scope conditions for theories. Kahneman and Tversky's work in prospect theory, appropriated to IR by Rose McDermott, provides a nice illustration of this, highlighting not only the limits of rational decision-making but indeed informing what it means to be rational in the first place. What it means to be "rational" is a central question that continues to be debated, with refined answers coming from insights in psychology and neuroscience. Therefore the link between psychology and IR has arguably always been present and always will be.

Perhaps the most promise in psychology and neuroscience is offered by the ability to identify the microfoundations and causal mechanisms of social behavior. In the last few decades, across the social sciences, there has been a push to look inside the "black box" of causality in order to break down complex phenomena into their core individual components.[73] This, as referenced in Chapter 1, is sometimes referred to as the "reductionist" move or connected to the strategy of "methodological individualism." Elster provides an illustrative reason why such a reductionist strategy is necessary:

...suppose somebody asserted that unemployment causes wars of aggression and adduced evidence for a strong correlation between the two phenomena. We would hardly accept this as a lawlike generalization that could be used in explaining specific wars unless we were provided with a glimpse inside the black box and

---

[72] Goldgeier and Tetlock 2001; Bleiker and Hutchison 2008. Though, see Ross 2014. See Hutchison and Bleiker 2014; Hutchison 2016 for excellent reviews of the emotions literature.

[73] See, for example, Elster 1983; Hedström and Swedberg 1996; Elster 1998; Lebow 2014; Kertzer 2016.

told *how* unemployment causes wars. Is it because unemployment induces political leaders to seek for new markets through wars? Or because they believe that unemployment creates social unrest that must be directed toward an external enemy, to prevent revolutionary movements at home?...Although many such stories are conceivable, some kind of story must be told for the explanation to be convincing, whereby "story" I mean "lawlike generalization *at a lower level of aggregation.*"[74]

Elster, and others, have essentially called for the black box to be opened. At the systemic or state level, this is a relatively straightforward proposition as the analyst needs to simply change the unit of analysis of inquiry in an attempt to link lower level microfoundations with higher-level outcomes. In social interaction, however, the problem has largely been one of access. Behavioral experiments allow researchers to identify average causal *effects*, but in order to truly open the black box in order to determine mechanisms, to see what is causing those effects, lower levels of aggregation need to be accessible. Lower levels of aggregation are difficult to access in human beings since they exist in the body and brain. Neuroscience undercuts this problem significantly by allowing for the observation and measurement of the operation of neural mechanisms. While we are still in the relative infancy of behavioral neuroscience experimentation, it is becoming increasingly possible to directly manipulate a hypothesized neural mechanism in the brain, such as a neuron, in order to link stimulus with a particular behavioral response.[75] This means that the accessibility issue of opening the black box of the human being is severely undercut. This has significant ramifications for not only the substantive study of political and social behaviors, but our overarching positions on the philosophy of science as well. Consider the scientific realist position discussed in earlier chapters. On this view the analyst is essentially playing a "wager" that an observed effect has a particular cause, despite that cause remaining unobservable. By investigating face-to-face interactions in both behavioral and neuroscientific environments, IR and psychology together can systematically investigate, and perhaps even observe, the causal mechanism in action, paying off the scientific realist wager.

Significant and important problems remain, however. One of the central problems confronting a scholar who wishes to bring cutting-edge psychology and neuroscience studies into our understanding of international politics is the inevitable "experimental lag" that occurs between

---

[74] Elster 1998, 47–48, emphasis added.

[75] See, for example, Imai, Tingley, and Yamamoto 2013 for a review of such studies in the context of political science. More generally, see McDermott 2004a and 2004b; Frith and Wolpert 2004.

insights derived from political and neuroscientific experiments and real world politics. Consider the aforementioned debate regarding the mirroring system in the human brain. Studying the mirroring system in a relatively simple laboratory environment is hard enough; studying the system in complex environments and in a messy social world is difficult, if not impossible. Constructing experiments that definitively show a strong role for mirroring in actual interactions among leaders, or even experiment participants, is not easy with current technology. Further, even with better technology, disaggregating mirroring of specific political intentions, for example an intention to permit without strong pushback the unification of Germany, from other types of mirroring, such as facial expressions, emotions, and so forth, is a particularly challenging proposition. These difficulties are paralleled in any discipline where simple experimental designs are utilized to gain insights into more complicated behavior, which is the backbone of social psychology epistemology, though the introduction of brain and biological systems complicates the matter further. Importantly this is not simply a debate about internal *versus* external validity, but rather whether we can gain sufficient internal validity *for a theory about international politics* at all with neuroscientific evidence.

Therefore in interpreting brain and other biological evidence one must decide for oneself how comfortable one is extrapolating from simple designs to more complex environments. I have argued in this book that while the extrapolation from simple designs to more complicated interaction may not be perfect, and perhaps often is messy, it is a justifiable jump as it represents the core method that neuroscience, and *any other science* including the social, uses to make predictions about complex interactions. Theory building requires the very type of simplified models that neuroscience, and other reductionist approaches, provide. Indeed the folk psychological theory that suggests intentions *are inaccessible* is similarly built upon a simplified model of social interaction and the problem of other minds. Put another way, if we want to understand what is occurring at higher levels of analysis we need to posit mechanisms at lower levels. Nevertheless the "bets" or wagers we make about assumptions, be they ontological assumptions about how the world works, epistemological assumptions about what we can know, or methodological assumptions about how we can know it, are crucial to any theory and not everyone will make the same bets.[76] Assumptions based in psychology and neuroscience may be bets that some are not willing to make; it is therefore crucial that the hypotheses and propositions that are derived from such theories are investigable and in the real world.

[76] Wendt 2005; Wendt 2015.

I have attempted in this book to create a theory that does not *rely* on one accepting the causal mechanism bets that I have made in order to accept the value of face-to-face diplomacy, which has been demonstrated empirically.

After all, the important part of using neuroscience is that it tells us something about the substantive topic we are interested in, namely the messy social and political world. Phil Tetlock has made a similar argument, suggesting that the value of psychology is ultimately in combining its insights with "independent evidence that the hypothesized psychological processes are indeed operating in the political world."[77] Insights from brain systems, such as the mirroring system, not only are useful for identifying potential mechanisms that underlie behavior and may problematize latent assumptions, but also provide useful behavioral hypotheses about social behavior that are then testable in actual politics.

In progressing from where we are, there is good reason to be optimistic about the ability of new technologies to tell us a great deal more about the inner-workings of social and political interactions in the future, which should be able to clarify many of the bets that political psychologists are forced to make. Emerging fMRI technology now allows for "multiple-perspective" or two-person testing. Many social neuroscientists have identified face-to-face interaction as an ideal-type with respect to brain imaging because it allows the researcher to look at, in real-time, variation in response between the two individuals:

Face-to-face conversation as a dyadic interaction could be a good model system for future brain imaging of social interaction, especially when combined with eye tracking... Given the great importance of dyadic interaction in human behavior, it is important to study brain functions of two interacting subjects at the same time.[78]

By conducting a dyadic interaction experiment while monitoring the responses in the brain of each participant, researchers will be able to create an index of responses to particular stimuli, including facial expressions and the simulation of more complex intentions, which allows for providing physical evidence, either confirming or falsifying, theories of mirroring, and simulating complex intentions. All of this suggests that while we are far from understanding all of the intricacies of social interaction, turning to neuroscience has not only already contributed important new understanding of the complex processes involved, but the future is particularly exciting as well.[79]

---

[77] Tetlock 1998, 870.    [78] Hari and Kujala 2009.
[79] Put another, slightly more abstract way, psychology has long been interested in a topic of great interest to theorists of international politics, the relationship between the

One benefit of attempting to tackle these difficult problems before everything is figured out is that it increases the dialogue between political science and neuroscience. Rose McDermott has argued, quite rightly, that political science need not merely be a consumer of neuroscientific insight but a producer of knowledge as well.[80] Neuroscientists have similarly called for greater engagement between their work in the lab and scholars who utilize neuroscientific insights in other fields, largely because they can benefit as well. Both fields can benefit, she argues, through increased research synchronization. This is particularly true in the case of intentions, which political scientists and neuroscientists alike have found puzzling. Neuroscientists want to know how political scientists conceive of intentions, which at root is a philosophical rather than scientific concept, and scholars of IR can benefit from thinking about the ways in which neuroscientists conceive of intentional action and the relationship between present intentions and future intentions, as discussed in previous chapters. Ultimately this type of discussion helps to bridge the seemingly large gap between international relations and psychology that exists not just because of a level of analysis problem but because of different conceptualizations of key concepts that may hinder usefully importing insights from one discipline into the other.

## Raising New Questions

As is often the case, this book has raised many more questions than it can answer. As social neuroscience as a field is relatively new, and its integration into IR even newer, any application of findings poses additional questions that will likely drive future research for some time to come. I will conclude the book with six areas that are likely to be important in the future as IR considers more neuroscientific evidence: individual power and optical threat perception, emotional intelligence and other individual differences, explaining and predicting interpersonal chemistry in face-to-face interactions, emotional contagion and group emotion, new communication technologies, and the mind/brain relationship.

One of the inarguable truisms in IR is that power matters, though to what extent, what counts as power, how it operates, and so forth continue to be debated. An under-theorized source of variation in power

---

material and ideational. Social neuroscience, for example, has focused on the interaction and interplay between the micro material level (neurons, chemical reactions) and the macro social level (behavior, thoughts), providing material microfoundations for social outcomes. This parallels debates in IR regarding the dualist interplay between material and ideational factors.

[80] McDermott 2009.

is at the individual level; just as states enjoy different levels of perceived power, individuals possess different levels of perceived interpersonal power.[81] This is a point not lost on leaders. As Donald Regan, White House Chief of Staff at the time documents, on the first day of the Geneva Summit as Gorbachev was arriving to the summit, Reagan greeted him outside, in the cold weather without a coat, providing an optical juxtaposition to Gorbachev who was bundled in winter clothing. Reagan, the older of the two men, then placed his arm around Gorbachev and gently helped him up the stairs of the chateau where the meeting was to take place. The optics of interpersonal power, in that moment, were clear. As Sergei Tarasenko, one of the Soviet delegates reflects on that opening move, perhaps, a half-joking manner: "We lost the game . . . in this first movement. You can compare it to a chess game and we lost it in the first move."[82] Just as power affects dynamics at the state level, there is preliminary evidence to suggest it might affect interpersonal interactions, and potentially intention understanding, as well. For instance, individuals with higher power tend to be more expressive than individuals with lower levels of power.[83] Individuals with higher levels of power are also more likely to mimic the emotions of others they are engaged with, and accurately recognize emotions, in face-to-face interactions. Mimicry, in general, is more likely to occur with individuals possessing higher levels of power.[84] These findings suggest that individual level power may play a significant role in both engaging the mirroring system and also reading the minds of others. Further experiments are required to better understand how these dynamics work, but the initial results suggest that IR theory may need to incorporate individual-level power into its conceptualization of state power.

With respect to optics and the visuality element of mirroring more generally, recent experimental evidence suggests that individuals make very quick judgments regarding the level of threat and trustworthiness of other individuals. Within milliseconds of seeing a human face, we make automatic and implicit judgments that are, in many cases, long-lasting, vivid, and have been shown to affect decision-making in a variety of diverse domains, from voting behavior to university teaching evaluations.[85] This suggests that the "individual first encounter" and subsequent impressions made within seconds of face-to-face meeting might matter a great deal in terms of setting a baseline of threat/trustworthiness. For example, returning to the example

[81] Hsee et al. 1990; Snodgrass, Hecht, and Ploutz-Snyder 1998.
[82] Kenneth Adelman speech, May 8, 2014, Heritage Foundation.
[83] Schmid Mast, Jonas, and Hall 2009.     [84] Bombari et al. 2013.
[85] See Holmes 2016 for a review of literature.

above of the Khrushchev and Kennedy infamous interaction in Vienna, the first meeting between the two was actually not in Vienna in 1961, but rather two years earlier, in September 1959 in the United States. Kennedy was a junior senator at the time and had a brief face-to-face encounter with Khrushchev after the latter's speech to the Senate Foreign Relations Committee. Kennedy noted Khrushchev's appearance: "Tan suit – French cuffs – short, stocky, two red ribbons, two stars."[86] Khrushchev told Kennedy that he looked too young to be a senator. As Reynolds has argued, "this was the comment that stayed with Kennedy, always sensitive to hints that he lacked gravitas and experience."[87] Years later, Khrushchev recalled that he "[remembered] liking his face, which was sometimes stern but which often broke into a good-natured smile."[88] For his part, Kennedy saw in Khrushchev someone slightly more formidable: "a tough-minded, articulate, hard-reasoning spokesman for an ideology in which he was thoroughly versed and in which he thoroughly believed."[89] While it is impossible to know whether the reason Khrushchev treated Kennedy in "such a hostile way" two years later was related to his first impressions of Kennedy as a young and inexperienced senator, it seems clear that Khrushchev quickly formed a nonthreatening intuition regarding Kennedy. This likely made the idea of a summit negotiation more palatable to Khrushchev than it otherwise would have been, an idea he pushed for immediately following Kennedy's inauguration. Both leaders seemed to gain intuitions regarding the other and, at least in the case of Khrushchev, his intuition increased the likelihood of further diplomatic engagement with Kennedy. How these automatic intuitions are formed, how long they last, and how the first impressions regarding trustworthiness and threat affect the further development of the relationship as well as subsequent face-to-face encounters, are questions that require further research and may pay significant dividends in further extrapolating, with precision, what is occurring in face-to-face interpersonal interactions.

In addition to power and the visuality of faces, another source of individual-level variation is in emotional and social intelligence. In the previous chapters I investigated one personality characteristic that is often linked to emotional intelligence, narcissism, but there are other characteristics that may be relevant as well. Emotional intelligence refers to the ability to understand one's own, and others', emotional states and the capacity to successfully navigate social relationships. As O'Sullivan argues, it is likely that emotional intelligence, for example, is distributed

---

[86] Beschloss 1991, 15.    [87] Reynolds 2009, 178.    [88] Beschloss 1991, 15.
[89] Kennedy 1960, 9.

in a similar way to general intelligence: most individuals are average, but at either side of the distribution we see very strong, or very poor, detection capabilities. Critically, studies suggest that the individuals that perform best at detecting deception are those that score highly on emotional intelligence measures and consequently are able to interpret nonverbal cues accurately. "In sum, the expert lie detectors are extraordinarily emotionally intelligent people . . . they listen and watch people in order to understand them and then, having understood them, they are able to accurately determine their truthfulness."[90] We therefore expect individuals with higher emotional intelligence to be better at picking up on nonverbal cues and deception, while individuals with lower emotional intelligence to be worse at both activities. It may be, in fact, that successful leaders are those that, all else being equal, possess high levels of emotional intelligence.[91] Some have suggested that the success of particular US Presidents may be partly attributable to emotional intelligence.[92] All of this suggests that there is further variation in the ability to pick up on intentions through expressive behavior and detect deception in face-to-face diplomacy that can be explored empirically.

It is not just differences that exist at the individual level, however, that are relevant. One of the striking conclusions drawn from the cases examined in this book is that there is great variation in the interpersonal dynamics that occur when individual leaders and diplomats engage in interpersonal face-to-face interaction. While the focus here has been on intention understanding, there are broader questions about interpersonal chemistry and social bonding we can ask that likely have an effect on outcomes, such as the ability to change intentions. As alluded to earlier, if Khrushchev and Kennedy had better personal chemistry, would they have found it easier to come to agreement on Berlin in 1961? While microsociologists and psychologists cannot answer this particular question, they have been able to identify many of the determinants of successful interpersonal bonding and have investigated the predictability of dyadic face-to-face interactions resulting in social bonds. Randall Collins, for example, argues that interaction with others brings the promise of an emotional payoff. When interactions go well, an emotional bond is created, positive emotions are felt, and "emotional energy" emerges from the interaction itself. For Collins, emotional energy is "a feeling of confidence, elation, strength, enthusiasm, and initiative in taking action."[93] Emotional energy is an emergent property of the interaction. Crucially, the determinants of whether emotional energy is created

---

[90] O'Sullivan 2005, 248.    [91] Goleman 2005; Goleman et al. 2002.
[92] Greenstein 2009.    [93] Collins 2004, 49.

has less to do with the individuals involved per se, in terms of their dispositions and characteristics, but rather on the characteristics, and dynamics, of the interaction *itself*. Specifically, Collins identifies four broad conditions required for the development of positive emotional energy: physical co-presence, mutual focus of attention, common emotional mood, and a boundary to outsiders.

Physical co-presence is defined by Collins as "two or more people are physically assembled in the same place, so that they affect each other by their bodily presence, whether it is in the foreground of their conscious attention or not."[94] The physical nature of the co-presence is important; mediated interactions, such as through the telephone or even those that occur through information rich mediums such as video conferencing, do not provide the same physical and emotional connection. Mutual focus on attention refers to "a common object or activity" where individuals in a dyad or larger group "become mutually aware of each other's focus of attention."[95] Meandering conversations without a clear focus, or where there is a lack of attention paid to a common theme or question, will be less likely to result in positive experiences. While in this face-to-face interaction individuals must also "share common mood or emotional experience."[96] Common affect, for example, seems to be crucial. Lastly, barriers to outsiders ensure "that participants have a sense of who is taking part and who is excluded,"[97] in the interaction itself. When interaction rituals succeed, they produce a number of important outcomes that can constitute a social bond. Group solidarity, even among dyads, allows participants in the interaction to have a feeling of membership. The strength of this membership depends on the amount of positive emotional energy created. When these conditions are not met, "there is low level of collective effervescence, the lack of momentary buzz, no shared entertainment at all or disappointingly little." Emotional energy is not created, solidarity is low, and the social bond is weak or non-existent. In short, the face-to-face interaction falls flat from a chemistry and bonding perspective.

While it is the case that dyadic face-to-face encounters at the highest levels of international politics are highly idiosyncratic, with topics and themes ranging from encounter to encounter, the works by Collins and others suggest that we can gain insight into the vexing question of why some interactions are able to engender normatively desirable outcomes while others fall flat. Further, since emotional energy is a shared property, it may be that the microsociological lens provides a

[94] Collins 2004, 48.    [95] Collins 2004, 48.    [96] Collins 2004, 48.
[97] Collins 2004, 48.

new way of understanding how Alter and Ego come together, creating a shared space of sorts, where Alter's intentions, through self-reflection, are capable of changing in relation to Ego's intentions, providing more insight into the plausible mechanism of intention dynamism. Material and ideational structural constraints clearly play a significant role, but the wager of applying microsociological insight to face-to-face diplomacy is that, *ceteris paribus*, there is variation that can be explained, and potentially predicted, by analysis that includes the conditions that Collins and others have identified.

Finally, the microsociological perspective provides promise in bridging symbolic interactionist perspectives, those that put significant emphasis on bodily expressive behaviors, and linguistic perspectives that privilege the role of language in world politics. While this book has focused its attention on a mechanism of intention understanding that resonates with the former, there is no question that the latter identifies an important role for language in social interaction. Consider the discussion above regarding Kennedy and Khrushchev in Vienna. Language constitutes a significant portion of the social interaction itself; both leaders are attempting to understand one another as well as to convince (or compel) the other through particular speech acts. The face-to-face interactions provide value in intention understanding, I have argued, but cannot be separated from the cultural context, including language itself, in which it takes place. Neuroscientists have attacked this problem experimentally by measuring neural synchronization in interactions when individuals are face-to-face and back-to-back, while reading from the same linguistic script, as noted in Chapter 2. Yet, neural synchronization is not the same as interpersonal chemistry or bonding, and leads to important questions about the necessity of language in dyadic interactions. More broadly, as Fierke has argued, understanding language games is crucial to identifying how "the individual becomes a part of the social context, both constrained by its rules and capable of agency within it."[98] Can individuals who do not share a language engender emotional energy and form a bond with one another? Or is common language one of the crucial enabling factors of bonding? More specifically related to world politics, does the existence of a third-party interpreter affect the dynamics of bond formation and, if so, can we elaborate how? This book has suggested that there is a force to the face-to-face aspect of interpersonal interaction; future research, particularly incorporating microsociological perspectives, can help to identify how that force interacts with another force: power of shared, or unshared, language.

[98] Fierke 2003, 68.

Lastly, combining a microsociological approach with recent work at the intersection of emotions in IR may well yield insights and answers to important questions revolving around the logic of emotions in world politics. In particular, recent debates have centered on both the nature and operation of collective emotions, be it at the group or state level.[99] How precisely group emotions emerge, are shared, and move between communities and collectivities has remained both a thorny theoretical puzzle and empirical challenge. While the mirroring system provides one plausible mechanism by which emotions can be shared among individuals, such as contagion through processes of mimicry and simulation, the microsociological approach provides a potential antecedent: emotion as an emergent property of interpersonal interaction. This interaction may be dyadic or, conceivably, have little upper limit in terms of the number of individuals involved. The key, rather, is the *physical* co-presence of individuals who can engage, creating the emotional energy, which may then be transferable to other individuals through processes of simulation and mirroring, providing a mechanism by which a collective emotion may come into existence and propagate among individuals. At a higher level of abstraction, such processes may also be integral to the development of the superorganism of the state, the controversial claim that the state can be usefully understood as a form of life with collective consciousness and emotion.[100]

With the advent of new communication technologies, further research will also be required to better understand the consequences of new media on the types of intention understanding discussed in this book. One of the areas of significant promise, attention, and excitement among theorists and practitioners alike is the development of digital or "e-" diplomacy defined broadly as the use of the digital tools to manage change in the international system.[101] The idea behind digital diplomacy is that there are functions, such as large-scale data accumulation and analysis and public information dissemination, that digital tools and social media can aid states in accomplishing. Twitter, for example, allows states, and state leaders, to communicate to, and hear from, publics around the world, constituting something of a dialogical relationship. The Trump administration, for example, has been labeled a "Twitter Presidency," with some analysts and pundits asking to what extent Trump's tweets may reveal sincere intentions. Similarly, virtual collaboration technologies allow diplomats and leaders to work together

[99] See, for example, Sasley 2011; Jeffery 2014; Mercer 2014; McDermott 2014; Hutchison 2016.
[100] See Hutchison 2016, 280–83 for an excellent discussion.
[101] Bjola and Holmes 2015.

on data-gathering and problem-solving tasks. Each of these tools provides ways for individuals to manage the small daily incremental changes occurring in the international system, and diplomats report doing so quite effectively. While human beings are quite bad at assessing and managing large amounts of information, computers excel at the task.

What these new tools lack, however, is the information richness, visuality, and optics of face-to-face interactions that allow for intention understanding and deception detection. In a networked world, where states are making assessments of intentions based on analysis of data gathered in the field, the findings in this book suggest that we should be skeptical regarding what states can actually learn about the intentions of others with the data that is available to them. As Edward R. Murrow put it in 1963, referencing public diplomacy and the limitations of technology, "It has always seemed to me that the real art in this business is not so much moving information or guidance or policy five or 10,000 miles. That is an electronic problem. The real art is to move it the last three feet in face-to-face conversation."[102] The findings of this book suggest that when it comes to high-level intentions, where knowing what other high-level decision-makers are likely to do, and how likely they are to be telling the truth, there is no better replacement for the face-to-face meeting. There may be, however, other domains where immense amounts of data, analyzed through sophisticated digital tools, can lead to important insights. Not all diplomatic activities require being attuned to deception. Not all diplomatic activities are similar to the types of negotiations that are discussed in this book. As such, elucidating the precise role for digital technologies in particular types of cases will be a worthwhile endeavor.

As knowledge of the brain increases, and more sophisticated technologies allow us to better understand the intimate details of brain functioning in social and political interactions, IR will be better equipped to grapple with important questions regarding the relationship between the mind and the brain.[103] Recent findings in neuroplasticity have caused philosophers of mind to reconsider the causal pathway between brain and mind, throwing doubt to the notion that the brain is prior, and causal, of the mind. Neuroplasticity suggests that the brain can be rewired through reflective processes.[104] In one study, for example, two groups of volunteers, none of whom knew how to play piano, were taught the same sequence of notes, providing instructions on which fingers

---

[102] Edward R. Murrow on ABC's "Issues and Answers," August 4, 1963.
[103] See Holmes and Traven 2015 for a review of this literature.
[104] Schwartz and Begley 2003; Doidge 2007

should be used for each note. One of the groups was placed in front of an electric piano for two hours a day for five days and asked to imagine playing the sequence and hearing it played. The second group actually played the music for the same amount of time. Both groups had their brain mapped both before, during, and after each day's piano "playing" and each group was asked to play the sequence while a computer monitored their accuracy. Remarkably, *both* groups learned to play the sequence and both groups showed similar brain changes. The mental practice of imagination and consciously controlled simulation produced the same physical changes as actually playing the piano.

As with the mirroring system in the brain, it would be a mistake to assume that this only applies to motor actions. Jeffrey Schwartz in a series of pioneering studies has shown that conscious thought regarding abstract concepts results in brain changes. Schwartz studied individuals who suffered from obsessive-compulsive disorder and asked them to consciously think about the obsessive thoughts they were experiencing when they manifested. Patients with this disorder often have an intuition that something is wrong, a "mistake feeling," or "nagging sense" that prompts particular behaviors.[105] Instead of giving into the thought, Schwartz instructed patients to confront the thought by meditating on the notion that the basis of the thought was a "faulty circuit." After several weeks, this therapy not only had a significant number of the patients improved with the intuitions, but brain scans demonstrated significant changes in the area of the brain where OCD behaviors manifest, the orbital frontal cortex. Similarly, studies of psychotherapy have shown that the practice of therapy itself results in detectable changes in the brain.[106] These studies suggest that individuals can change the intuitions they experience, in cases of trauma and unpleasant memories the negative thinking associated with those episodes, through conscious reflection and the attendant changes in the brain that occur. By opening the black box of the brain, researchers were able to demonstrate the precise mechanisms by which intuitions are created and changed.[107]

These studies prompt important questions for the study of diplomacy and international politics. What are the neuroplastic changes that occur among high-level officials when engaged in iterative diplomatic interactions with another? Can diplomacy, like piano, be learned, practiced,

---

[105] Doidge 2007, 169.    [106] Etkin et al. 2005; Doidge 2007.

[107] See, for example, Holmes 2014, where I argue that neuroplasticity and the interaction between the social and material, where ideas in the mind affect and alter the underlying material basis in the brain, may suggest a "new materialism" in IR, one that transcends the traditional material-ideational divide.

and trained? For that matter, do other types of activities, such as trusting or empathizing, evoke the same types of neural circuitry changes that playing piano does? Can diplomats be taught to trust? These questions point to a different understanding of change in the international system than is normally considered in systemic IR. If the nature of individuals themselves, and therefore the nature of the practitioners of international politics, the substance of the first image "human nature," changes based on experience, and can be trained to change in specific ways, then an unaccounted and untheorized source of change in the international system may be in the first image. This type of change problematizes the notion of a static human nature and resonates with arguments that place the individual front and center in constituting, and replicating, the international system.[108]

Finally, research in quantum consciousness, which applies principles from quantum physics, psychology, and neuroscience to the philosophical problem of other minds, among others, suggests some fairly profound implications. For example, Wendt, in reviewing findings in quantum research and applying them to questions of social ontology and epistemology, argues that a new quantum approach to social interaction implies a new level of interconnectedness that belies a classical physics understanding of individuals, and individual minds, as discrete entities. This resonates strongly with the argument in this book that individual minds are not necessarily all that separate and unconnected. Indeed as Wendt argues, rather than individuals with brains existing as separate quantities, with an unsurpassable gulf between the two, "a quantum theory of vision . . . suggests there is a *non*-local connection between minds-in-action, and as such that in mind-reading our minds are not fully separable in the first place."[109] While the argument put forth in this book has been solidly on the classical side of the ledger from a physics perspective, it may well be that the more we learn about quantum theory, the more the claims "that human beings are not fully separable,"[110] and "we are in a very good position to know other human minds,"[111] receive substantial support and may revolutionize the way we think about interpersonal interaction.

In the end, successfully communicating intentions is critical to the formation of stable and peaceful relationships, both in international politics and daily life. The absence of such an ability is one key reason why violence often ensues, either in the form of a security dilemma or

[108] Wendt 2010.    [109] Wendt 2015, 233.    [110] Wendt 2015, 233.
[111] Wendt 2015, 285.

misperception about the other's aims and desires. If face-to-face diplomacy is able to provide decision-makers with a better understanding of each other's intentions, and thereby minimize misunderstanding and misperception while providing the foundation for trust-building, then the value of face-to-face diplomacy is difficult to overstate. While clearly not a panacea or foolproof method for good relations, as this book has demonstrated, there is, it turns out, a very good reason to see *value* in the "strange matters" that can be read from the face.

# Bibliography

Ackerman, Spencer and Franklin Foer. 2003. "The Radical." *The New Republic*, December 1.

Adams, R. J. Q. 1993. *British Politics and Foreign Policy in the Age of Appeasement, 1935–39*. Palo Alto, CA: Stanford University Press.

Adelman, Ken. 2014. *Reagan at Reykjavik: Forty-Eight Hours That Ended the Cold War*. New York, NY: Broadside Books.

Adler, Emanuel. 2005. *Communitarian International Relations: The Epistemic Foundations of International Relations*. Abingdon, UK: Routledge.

Adler, Emanuel and Vincent Pouliot. 2011a. *International Practices*. Cambridge, UK: Cambridge University Press.

Adler, Emanuel and Vincent Pouliot. 2011b. "International Practices." *International Theory* 3(1):1–36.

Adler-Nissen, Rebecca. 2015. "Relationalism or why Diplomats Find International Relations Theory Strange." In *Diplomacy and the Making of World Politics*. Ole Jacob Sending, Vincent Pouliot, and Iver B. Neumann (eds), 284–308. Cambridge, UK: Cambridge University Press.

Adler-Nissen, Rebecca and Vincent Pouliot. 2014. "Power in Practice: Negotiating the International Intervention in Libya." *European Journal of International Relations* 20(4):889–911.

Adolphs, Ralph. 2010. "Conceptual Challenges and Directions for Social Neuroscience." *Neuron* 65(6):752–67.

Adomeit, Hannes. 2006. "Gorbachev's Consent to Unified Germany's Membership in NATO." *Working Paper: Research Unit Russia/CIS Stiftung Wissenschaft Und Politik German Institute for International and Security Affairs*. Available: www.swp-berlin.org/fileadmin/contents/products/arbeitspapiere/Consent_to_Nato_ks.pdf.

Allport, Gordon W. 1954. *The Nature of Prejudice*. Cambridge, MA: Perseus Books.

Ames, Daniel R. and Lara K. Kammrath. 2004. "Mind-Reading and Metacognition: Narcissism, Not Actual Competence, Predicts Self-Estimated Ability." *Journal of Nonverbal Behavior* 28(3):187–209.

Amodio, David M. and Chris D. Frith. 2006. "Meeting of Minds: The Medial Frontal Cortex and Social Cognition." *Nature Reviews Neuroscience* 7(4):268–77.

Anderson, Jeffrey. 1999. *German Unification and the Union of Europe: The Domestic Politics of Integration Policy*. Cambridge, UK: Cambridge University Press.

Anderson, Mary. 2013. "Art and Inter-Religious Dialogue." In *The Wiley-Blackwell Companion to Inter-Religious Dialogue*. Catherine Cornille (ed), 99–116. West Sussex: John Wiley & Sons. 99–116.

Antonietti, Alessandro and Antonella Corradini. 2013. "Mirroring Mirror Neurons in an Interdisciplinary Debate." *Consciousness and Cognition* 22(3):1092–94.

Ansell, Chris and Alison Gash. 2007. "Collaborative Governance in Theory and Practice." *Journal of Public Administration Research and Theory* 18(4):543–71.

Ascher, Abraham. 2012. *Was Hitler a Riddle?: Western Democracies and National Socialism*. Palo Alto, CA: Stanford University Press.

Austin, John. 1979. *Philosophical Papers*, L., J. O. Urmson, and G. J. Warnock (eds). Oxford, UK: Oxford University Press.

Baird, Amee D., Ingrid E. Scheffer, and Sarah J. Wilson. 2011. "Mirror Neuron System Involvement in Empathy: A Critical Look at the Evidence." *Social Neuroscience* 6(4):327–35.

Balakrishnan, P. V., Pete Nye, and Jill M. Purdy. 2000. "The Impact of Communication Media on Negotiation Outcomes." *The International Journal of Conflict Management* 11(2):162–87.

Baker, James Addison and Thomas M. DeFrank. 1995. *The Politics of Diplomacy: Revolution, War, and Peace, 1989–1992*. New York, NY: G.P. Putnam's Sons.

Barnett, Correlli. 1972. *The Collapse of British Power*. New York, NY: William Morrow & Company.

Baron-Cohen, Simon. 2011. *The Science of Evil on Empathy and the Origins of Cruelty*. New York, NY: Basic Books.

Barry, Bruce and Erin M. Rehel. 2014. "Lies, Damn Lies, and Negotiation: An Interdisciplinary Analysis of the Nature and Consequences of Deception at the Bargaining Table." *Handbook of Research in Conflict Management*. Oluremi B. Ayoko, Neal M. Ashkanasy, Karen A. Jehn (eds), 343–62. Cheltenham, UK: Edward Elgar.

Bar-Tal, Daniel. 1998. "Societal Beliefs in Times of Intractable Conflict: The Israeli Case." *International Journal of Conflict Management* 9(1):22–50.

Beck, Robert J. 1989. "Munich's Lessons Reconsidered." *International Security* 14(2):161–91.

Bederman, David. 2001. *International Law in Antiquity*. Cambridge, UK: Cambridge University Press.

Begin, Menachem. 1977. *The Revolt: Story of the Irgun*. London: W.H. Allen
1979. *White Nights: The Story of a Prisoner in Russia*. New York, NY: Harper & Row.

Bell, Duncan. 2006. "Beware of False Prophets: Biology, Human Nature and the Future of International Relations Theory." *International Affairs* 82(3):493–510.
2015. "In Biology We Trust: Biopolitical Science and the Elusive Self." In *Human Beings in International Relations*. Daniel Jacobi and Annette Freyberg-Inan (eds), 113–31. Cambridge, UK: Cambridge University Press.

Bendersky, Joseph W. 2000. *A History of Nazi Germany: 1919–1945*. Chicago, IL: Burnham Publishers.

Bercovitch, Jacob. 1986. "International Mediation: A Study of the Incidence, Strategies and Conditions of Successful Outcomes." *Cooperation and Conflict* 21(3):155–68.

Beschloss, Michael R. 1991. *The Crisis Years: Kennedy and Khrushchev, 1960–1963*. New York, NY: Edward Burlingame Books.

Beschloss Michael and Strobe Talbott. 1993. *At the Highest Levels: The Inside Story of the Cold War*. New York, NY: Little, Brown & Company.

Bially Mattern, Janice. 2011. "A Practice Theory of Emotion for International Relations." *International Practices*. Adler, Emanuel and Vincent Pouliot (eds), 63–86. Cambridge, UK: Cambridge University Press.

Bjola, Corneliu and Marcus Holmes. 2015. *Digital Diplomacy: Theory and Practice*. New York, NY: Routledge.

Blaney, David and Naeem Inayatullah. 1996. "Knowing Encounters: Beyond Parochialism in International Relations Theory." In *The Return of Culture and Identity in IR Theory*. Yosef Lapid and Friedrich Kratochwil (eds), 65–84. Boulder, CO: Lynne Rienner.

Blanton, Thomas. 2010. "U.S. Policy and the Revolutions of 1989." In *Masterpieces of History: The Peaceful End of the Cold War in Europe, 1989*. Svetlana Savranskaya, Thomas Blanton, and Vladislav Martinovich Zubok (eds), 49–98. Budapest, HU: Central European University Press.

Blanton, Thomas and Svetlana Savranskaya. 2011. "Reykjavik: When Abolition Was Within Reach." *Arms Control Today* 41(8):46–51.

Bleiker, Roland. 2000. *Popular Dissent, Human Agency, and Global Politics*. Cambridge, UK: Cambridge University Press.

2004. "Alternatives to Peacekeeping in Korea: The Role of Non-State Actors and Face-to-Face Encounters." *International Peacekeeping* 11(1):143–59.

2005. *Divided Korea: Toward a Culture of Reconciliation*. Minneapolis, MN: University of Minnesota Press.

2009. *Aesthetics and World Politics*. Basingstoke, UK: Palgrave Macmillan.

2010. "Negotiating with Nuclear North Korea? The Nuclear Question and Inter-Korean Relations." *Critique Internationale* 4(49):21–36.

Bleiker, Roland and Emma Hutchison. 2008. "Fear No More: Emotions and World Politics." *Review of International Studies* 34(1):115–35.

Bloom, Paul. 2016. *Against Empathy: The Case for Rational Compassion*. New York, NY: HarperCollins Publishers.

Bohl, Vivian and Nivedita Gangopadhyay. 2014. "Theory of Mind and the Unobservability of Other Minds." *Philosophical Explorations* 17(2):203–22.

Bombari, Dario, Marianne Schmid Mast, Tobias Brosch, and David Sander. 2013. "How Interpersonal Power Affects Empathic Accuracy: Differential Roles of Mentalizing vs. Mirroring?" *Frontiers in Human Neuroscience* July 2013(7) Article 375, 1–6.

Bond, Charles F., Adnan Omar, Urvashi Pitre, Brian R. Lashley, Lynn M. Skaggs, and C. T. Kirk. 1992. "Fishy-Looking Liars: Deception Judgment from Expectancy Violation." *Journal of Personality and Social Psychology* 63(6):969–77.

Bonini, Luca, Pier Francesco Ferrari, and Leonardo Fogassi. 2013. "Neurophysiological Bases Underlying the Organization of Intentional Actions and the Understanding of Others' Intention." *Consciousness and Cognition* 22(3):1095–104.

Booth, Ken and Nicholas Wheeler. 2008. *The Security Dilemma: Fear, Cooperation, and Trust in World Politics*. Basingstoke, UK: Palgrave Macmillan.

Bozo, Frédéric. 2009. "'Winners' and 'Losers': France, the United States, and the End of the Cold War." *Diplomatic History* 33(5):927–56.

Brands, H. W. 2015. *Reagan: The Life*. New York, NY: Knopf Doubleday Publishing Group.

Brooks, Stephen G. and William C. Wohlforth. 2002. "American Primacy in Perspective." *Foreign Affairs* 81(4):20–33.

    2003. "Economics Constraints Towards the End of the Cold War." In *Cold War Endgame*. William Wohlforth (ed), 273–312. University Park, PA: The Pennsylvania State University Press.

Brown, Archie. 1996. *The Gorbachev Factor*. Oxford, UK: Oxford University Press.

Bruneau, Emile G., Nicholas Dufour, and Rebecca Saxe. 2012. "Social Cognition in Members of Conflict Groups: Behavioural and Neural Responses in Arabs, Israelis and South Americans to Each Other's Misfortunes." *Philosophical Transactions of the Royal Society B: Biological Sciences* 367(1589):717–30.

Brzezinski, Zbigniew K. 1985. *Power and Principle: Memoirs of the National Security Advisor 1977–1981*. New York, NY: Farrar, Straus and Giroux.

Bull, Hedley. 1977. *The Anarchical Society: A Study of Order in World Politics*. Basingstoke, UK: Palgrave Macmillan.

Buller, David B. and Judee K. Burgoon. 1996. "Interpersonal Deception Theory." *Communication Theory* 6(3):203–42.

Bush, George H. W. and Brent Scowcroft. 1998. *A World Transformed*. New York, NY: Alfred A. Knopf.

Byman, Daniel L. and Kenneth M. Pollack. 2001. "Let Us Now Praise Great Men: Bringing the Statesman Back in." *International Security* 25(4): 107–46.

Cacioppo, John T. and Gary G. Berntson. 2004a. *Essays in Social Neuroscience*. Cambridge, MA: MIT Press.

    2004b. *Social Neuroscience: Key Readings*. New York, NY: Psychology Press.

Cacioppo, John T., Louis G. Tassinary, and Gary Berntson. 2007. *Handbook of Psychophysiology*. Cambridge, UK: Cambridge University Press.

Carter, Jimmy. 1995. *Keeping Faith: Memoirs of a President*. Fayetteville, AR: University of Arkansas Press.

    2009. *We Can Have Peace in the Holy Land: A Plan That Will Work*. New York, NY: Simon and Schuster.

Carter, Jimmy and Don Richardson. 1998. *Conservations with Carter*. Boulder, CO: Lynne Rienner Pub.

Carter, Jimmy and James H. Laue. 1991. *A Conversation on Peacemaking with Jimmy Carter, June 7, 1991*. Washington, D.C.: National Institute for Dispute Resolution.

Cetina, Karin Knorr, Eike von Savigny, and Theodore R. Schatzki. 2001. *The Practice Turn in Contemporary Theory*. London, UK: Routledge.

Chamberlain, Austen and Robert C. Self. 1995. *The Austen Chamberlain Diary Letters: The Correspondence of Sir Austen Chamberlain with His Sisters Hilda and Ida, 1916–1937*. Cambridge, UK: Cambridge University Press.

Chartrand, Tanya L. and John A. Bargh. 1999. "The Chameleon Effect: The Perception–behavior Link and Social Interaction." *Journal of Personality and Social Psychology* 76(6):893.

Chartrand, Tanya L., William W. Maddux, and Jessica L. Lakin. 2005. "Beyond the Perception-Behavior Link: The Ubiquitous Utility and Motivational Moderators of Nonconscious Mimicry." *The New Unconscious*. Ran Hassin, James Uleman, and John Bargh (eds), 334–61. Oxford, UK: Oxford University Press.

Checkel, Jeffrey T. 2001. "Why Comply? Social Learning and European Identity Change." *International Organization* 55(3):553–88.

Chernyaev, Anatoly C. 2000. *My Six Years with Gorbachev*. Robert English and Elizabeth Tucker (eds). University Park, PA: Penn State Press.

Chollet, Derek H. and James M. Goldgeier. 2003. "Once Burned, Twice Shy? The Pause of 1989." *Cold War Endgame: Oral History, Analysis, Debates*. William C. Wohlforth (ed), 141–74. University Park, PA: Penn State Press. 141–74.

Christov-Moore, Leonardo, Taisei Sugiyama, Kristina Grigaityte and Marco Iacoboni. 2016. "Increasing Generosity by Disrupting Prefrontal Cortex." *Social Neuroscience* 12(2):174–81.

Churchland, Patricia S. 2011. *Braintrust: What Neuroscience Tells Us about Morality*. Princeton, NJ: Princeton University Press.

Cikara, Mina, Emile G. Bruneau, and Rebecca R. Saxe. 2011. "Us and Them Intergroup Failures of Empathy." *Current Directions in Psychological Science* 20(3):149–53.

Clark, Phil. 2010. *The Gacaca Courts, Post-Genocide Justice and Reconciliation in Rwanda: Justice without Lawyers*. New York, NY: Cambridge University Press.

Collins, Randall. 2004. *Interaction Ritual Chains*. Princeton, NJ: Princeton University Press.

Constantinou, Costas M. 2006. "On Homo-Diplomacy." *Space and Culture* 9(4):351–64.

Constantinou, Costas M. and James Der Derian. 2010. *Sustainable Diplomacies*. Basingstoke, UK: Palgrave Macmillan.

Constantinou, Costas M., Pauline Kerr, and Paul Sharp. 2016. "The SAGE Handbook of Diplomacy." Thousand Oaks, CA: SAGE Publications Ltd.

Coolidge, Frederick L., Felicia L. Davis, and Daniel L. Segal (2007). Understanding madmen: A DSM-IV assessment of Adolf Hitler. *Individual Differences Research* 5(1)30–43.

Copeland, Dale C. 2006. "The Constructivist Challenge to Structural Realism: A Review Essay." In *Constructivism and International Relations: Alexander Wendt and His Critics*. Stefano Guzzini and Anna Leander (eds), 1–20. London: Routledge.

2011. "Rationalist Theories of International Politics and the Problem of the Future." *Security Studies* 20(3):441–50.

Corradini, Antonella and Alessandro Antonietti. 2013. "Mirror Neurons and Their Function in Cognitively Understood Empathy." *Consciousness and Cognition* 22(3):1152–61.

Cosmides, Leda and John Tooby. 1992. "Cognitive Adaptations for Social Exchange." *The Adapted Mind*: Evolutionary Psychology and the Generation of Culture, J. Barkow, L. Cosmides, and J. Tooby (eds), 163–228. New York, NY: Oxford University Press.

Costigliola, Frank. 2012. "Roosevelt's Lost Alliances: How Personal Politics Helped Start the Cold War." Princeton, NJ: Princeton University Press.

Crawford, Neta. 2014. "Institutionalizing Passion in World Politics: Fear and Empathy." *International Theory* 6(3):535–57.

Crowe, William J. 2001. *The Line of Fire: From Washington to the Gulf, the Politics and Battles of the New Military.* New York, NY: Simon and Schuster.

Dalton, Hugh. 1957. *The Fateful Years: Memoirs, 1931–1945.* London, UK: Frederick Muller, Ltd.

Dapretto, Mirella, Mari S. Davies, Jennifer H. Pfeifer, Ashley A. Scott, Marian Sigman, Susan Y. Bookheimer, and Marco Iacoboni. 2006. "Understanding Emotions in Others: Mirror Neuron Dysfunction in Children with Autism Spectrum Disorders." *Nature Neuroscience* 9(1):28–30.

Davis, James W., and William C. Wohlforth. 2004. "German Unification." In *Ending the Cold War: Interpretations, Causation and the Study of International Relations.* Richard K. Herrmann and Richard Ned Lebow (eds), 131–57. New York, NY: Palgrave Macmillan US.

Dayan, Moshe. 1981. *Breakthrough: A Personal Account of the Egypt-Israel Peace Negotiations.* New York, NY: Alfred A. Knopf.

Decety, Jean. 2011. "The Neuroevolution of Empathy." *Annals of the New York Academy of Sciences* 1231(1):35–45.

DePaulo, Bella M., James J. Lindsay, Brian E. Malone, Laura Muhlenbruck, Kelly Charlton, and Harris Cooper. 2003. "Cues to Deception." *Psychological Bulletin* 129(1):74–118.

Derian, James Der. 1987. "Mediating Estrangement: A Theory for Diplomacy." *Review of International Studies* 13(2):91–110.

De Vignemont, Frederique and Tania Singer. 2006. "The Empathic Brain: How, When and Why?" *Trends in Cognitive Sciences* 10(10):435–41.

Dobrynin, Anatoly. 1995. *In Confidence: Moscow's Ambassador to America's Six Cold War Presidents (1962–1986).* New York, NY: Times Books, Random House.

Doidge, Norman. 2007. *The Brain That Changes Itself: Stories of Personal Triumph from the Frontiers of Brain Science.* New York, NY: Penguin Books.

Doty, Roxanne Lynn. 1997. "Aporia: A Critical Exploration of the Agent-Structure Problematique in International Relations Theory." *European Journal of International Relations* 3(3):365–92.

Duncan, Starkey and Donald W. Fiske. 1977. *Face-to-Face Interaction: Research, Methods, and Theory.* Sydney, Australia: Halsted Press.

Eden, Sir Anthony. 1962. *The Eden Memoirs: Facing the Dictators*. 1st edition. London, UK: Cassell & Co.

Edkins, Jenny. 2015. *Face Politics*. New York, NY: Taylor & Francis.

Ekedahl, Carolyn and Melvin A. Goodman. 2010. *Wars of Eduard Shevardnadze*. University Park, PA: Penn State Press.

Ekman, Paul. 1992. "An Argument for Basic Emotions." *Cognition and Emotion* 6(3–4): 169–200.

2009. *Telling Lies*. New York, NY: W. W. Norton & Company.

Ekman, Paul and Maureen O'Sullivan. 1991. "Who Can Catch a Liar?" *American Psychologist* 46(9):913–20.

Ekman, Paul and Erika L. Rosenberg. 1997. *What the Face Reveals: Basic and Applied Studies of Spontaneous Expression Using the Facial Action Coding System (FACS)*. Oxford, UK: Oxford University Press.

Elfenbein, Hillary Anger and Nalini Ambady. 2002. "Is There an in-Group Advantage in Emotion Recognition?" *Psychological Bulletin*, 128(2):243–49.

Elster, Jon. 1983. *Explaining Technical Change: A Case Study in the Philosophy of Science*. Cambridge, UK: Cambridge University Press.

1998. "A Plea for Mechanisms." In *Social Mechanisms: An Analytical Approach to Social Theory*. Peter Hedström and Richard Swedberg (eds), 45–73. Cambridge, UK: Cambridge University Press.

Engel, Jeffrey A. 2009. *The Berlin Wall: The Revolutionary Legacy of 1989*. Oxford, UK: Oxford University Press.

English, Robert D. 2000. *Russia and the Idea of the West: Gorbachev, Intellectuals, and the End of the Cold War*. New York, NY: Columbia University Press.

Etkin, Amit, Christopher Pittenger, H. Jonathan Polan, and Eric R. Kandel. 2005. "Toward a Neurobiology of Psychotherapy: Basic Science and Clinical Applications." *The Journal of Neuropsychiatry & Clinical Neurosciences* 17(2):145–58.

Evangelista, Matthew. 2002. *Unarmed Forces: The Transnational Movement to End the Cold War*. Ithaca, NY: Cornell University Press.

Faber, David. 2009. *Munich, 1938: Appeasement and World War II*. New York, NY: Simon & Schuster.

Fahmy, Ismail. 1983. *Negotiating for Peace in the Middle East*. Kent, UK: Croom Helm.

Fearon, James D. 1994. "Domestic Political Audiences and the Escalation of International Disputes." *The American Political Science Review* 88(3):577–92.

Fearon, James D. and Alexander Wendt. 2002. "Rationalism v. Constructivism: A Skeptical View." *Handbook of International Relations*. Walter Calsnaes, Thomas Risse, and Beth Simmons (eds), 52–72. London, UK: Sage.

Fierke, Karin M. 2003. "Breaking the Silence: Language and Method in International Relations." In *Language, Agency, and Politics in a Constructed World*. Francois Debrix (ed), 66–86. North Castle, NY: M.E. Sharpe.

Fierke, Karin M. and Antje Wiener. 1999. "Constructing Institutional Interests: EU and NATO Enlargement." *Journal of European Public Policy* 6(5):721–42.

Finklestone, Joseph. 1996. *Anwar Sadat: Visionary Who Dared*. London: Frank Cass.

Finnemore, Martha. 2003. "The Purpose of Intervention: Changing Beliefs about the Use of Force." Ithaca, NY: Cornell University Press.

Fischer, Beth A. 1997. *The Reagan Reversal: Foreign Policy and the End of the Cold War*. Columbia, MI: University of Missouri Press.

Fisher, Roger and William Ury. 1983. *Getting to Yes: Negotiating Agreement Without Giving In*. New York, NY: Penguin Books.

Forsberg, Tuomas. 1999. "Power, Interests and Trust: Explaining Gorbachev's Choices at the End of the Cold War." *Review of International Studies* 25(4):603–21.

Frank, Robert H. 1988. *Passions Within Reason: The Strategic Role of the Emotions*. New York, NY: W.W. Norton.

Frank, Mark G. and Paul Ekman. 1997. "The Ability to Detect Deceit Generalizes across Different Types of High-Stake Lies." *Journal of Personality and Social Psychology* 72(6):1429–39.

Frantz, Roger. 2004. *Two Minds: Intuition and Analysis in the History of Economic Thought*. New York, NY: Springer Science & Business Media.

Frieden, Jeffry. 1999. "Actors and Preferences in International Relations." In *Strategic Choice and International Relations*. David A. Lake and Robert Powell (eds), 39–76. Princeton, NJ: Princeton University Press.

Frith, Christopher D. and Daniel M. Wolpert. 2004. *The Neuroscience of Social Interaction: Decoding, Imitating, and Influencing the Actions of Others*. New York, NY: Oxford University Press.

Gaddis, John Lewis. 2005. *The Cold War: A New History*. New York, NY: Penguin Press.

Gaddis, John Lewis. 1991. "Toward the Post-Cold War World." *Foreign Affairs* 70(2):102–22.

Gallese, Vittorio. 2001. "The Shared Manifold Hypothesis. from Mirror Neurons to Empathy." *Journal of Consciousness Studies* 8(5–7):33–50.

Gallese, Vittorio, Luciano Fadiga, Leonardo Fogassi, and Giacomo Rizzolatti. 1996. "Action Recognition in the Premotor Cortex." *Brain* 119(2):593–610.

Gallese, Vittorio and Alvin Goldman. 1998. "Mirror Neurons and the Simulation Theory of Mind-Reading." *Trends in Cognitive Sciences* 2(12):493–501.

Garrard, Peter, Vassiliki Rentoumi, Christian Lambert, and David Owen. 2014. "Linguistic Biomarkers of Hubris Syndrome." *Cortex, Language, Computers and Cognitive Neuroscience* 55(June):167–81.

Garthoff, Raymond L. 1994. *Detente and Confrontation: American-Soviet Relations from Nixon to Reagan, Revised Edition*. Washington, D.C: Brookings Institution Press.

Gates, Robert. 1996. *From the Shadows: The Ultimate Insider's Story of Five Presidents and how They Won the Cold War*. New York, NY: Simon and Schuster.

Gendler, Tamar Szabó. 2008. "Alief and Belief." *Journal of Philosophy* 105(10):634–63.

Gerring, John. 2007. *Case Study Research: Principles and Practices*. Cambridge, UK: Cambridge University Press.

Gertler, Brie. 2003. *Privileged Access: Philosophical Accounts of Self-Knowledge*. New York, NY: Ashgate Publishing.

Giordano, Gabriel A., Jason S. Stoner, Robyn L. Brouer, and Joey F. George. 2007. "The Influences of Deception and Computer-Mediation on Dyadic Negotiations." *Journal of Computer-Mediated Communication* 12(2):362–83.

Glad, Betty. 1980. *Jimmy Carter: In Search of the Great White House*. New York, NY: W.W. Norton.

2009. *An Outsider in the White House: Jimmy Carter, His Advisors, and the Making of American Foreign Policy*. Ithaca, NY: Cornell University Press.

Glaser, Charles L. 2010. *Rational Theory of International Politics: The Logic of Competition and Cooperation*. Princeton, N.J: Princeton University Press.

Glaser, Charles L. and Chaim Kaufmann. 1998. "What Is the Offense-Defense Balance and Can We Measure It?" *International Security* 22(4): 44–82.

Glenberg, Arthur M. 2011a. "Introduction to the Mirror Neuron Forum." *Perspectives on Psychological Science* 6(4):363–68.

2011b. "Positions in the Mirror Are Closer Than They Appear." *Perspectives on Psychological Science* 6(4):408–10.

Goddard, Stacie E. 2015. "The Rhetoric of Appeasement: Hitler's Legitimation and British Foreign Policy, 1938–39." *Security Studies* 24(1):95–130.

Goffman, Erving. 1959. *The Presentation of Self in Everyday Life*. New York, NY: Anchor Books.

Goldgeier, James M. and Michael McFaul. 2003. *Power and Purpose: U.S. Policy toward Russia After the Cold War*. Washington, D.C: Brookings Institution Press.

Goldgeier, James M. and P. E Tetlock. 2001. "Psychology and International Relations Theory." *Annual Review of Political Science* 4(1):67–92.

Goldman, Alvin I. 2006. *Simulating Minds: The Philosophy, Psychology, and Neuroscience of Mindreading*. New York, NY: Oxford University Press.

Goldman, Alvin I. and Lucy C. Jordan. 2013. "Mindreading by Simulation: The Roles of Imagination and Mirroring." *Understanding Other Minds: Perspectives from Developmental Social Neuroscience*. Simon Baron-Cohen, Michael Lombardo, and Helen Tager-Flusberg (eds), 448–67. Oxford, UK: Oxford University Press.

Goldstein, Erik. 2012. "Neville Chamberlain, the British Official Mind and the Munich Crisis." *The Munich Crisis, 1938: Prelude to World War II*. Abingdon, UK: Routledge.

Goldstein, Joshua S. and John R. Freeman. 1990. *Three-Way Street: Strategic Reciprocity in World Politics*. University of Chicago Press.

Goleman, Daniel. 2005. *Emotional Intelligence: Why It Can Matter More Than IQ*. New York, NY: Bantam Books.

Goleman, Daniel, Annie McKee, and Richard E. Boyatzis 2002. *Primal Leadership: Realizing the Power of Emotional Intelligence*. Boston, MA: Harvard Business Review Press.

Gorbachev, Mikhail Sergeevich. 1996. *Memoirs*. New York, NY: Doubleday.

Gordis, Daniel. 2014. *Menachem Begin: The Battle for Israel's Soul*. New York, NY: Schocken.

Görtemaker, Manfred. 1994. *Unifying Germany, 1989–1990*. New York, NY: St. Martin's Press.

Grachev, Andrei. 2008. *Gorbachev's Gamble: Soviet Foreign Policy and the End of the Cold War.* Cambridge, UK: Polity.

Greenstein, Fred I. 2009. *The Presidential Difference: Leadership Style from FDR to Barack Obama.* Princeton, NJ: Princeton University Press.

Grèzes, Julie, Chris Frith, and Richard E. Passingham. 2004. "Brain Mechanisms for Inferring Deceit in the Actions of Others." *The Journal of Neuroscience* 24(24):5500–05.

Groth, Alexander. 1964. "On the Intelligence Aspects of Personal Diplomacy." *Orbis* 7:833–49.

Gunnell, Justin J. and Stephen J. Ceci. 2010. "When Emotionality Trumps Reason: A Study of Individual Processing Style and Juror Bias." *Behavioral Sciences & the Law* 28(6):850–77.

Gutsell, Jennifer N. and Michael Inzlicht. 2010. "Empathy Constrained: Prejudice Predicts Reduced Mental Simulation of Actions during Observation of Outgroups." *Journal of Experimental Social Psychology* 46(5):841–45.

2011. "Intergroup Differences in the Sharing of Emotive States: Neural Evidence of an Empathy Gap." *Social Cognitive and Affective Neuroscience* 7(5):596–603.

Haidt, Jonathan. 2001. "The Emotional Dog and Its Rational Tail: A Social Intuitionist Approach to Moral Judgment." *Psychological Review* 108(4): 814–34.

Haines, Gerald K. and Robert E. Leggett. 2003. *Watching the Bear: Essays on CIA's Analysis of the Soviet Union.* Washington, D.C.: Government Printing Office.

Hall, Todd H. and Andrew A. G. Ross. 2015. "Affective Politics after 9/11." *International Organization* 69(4):847–79.

Hall, Todd and Keren Yarhi-Milo. 2012. "The Personal Touch: Leaders' Impressions, Costly Signaling, and Assessments of Sincerity in International Affairs." *International Studies Quarterly* 56(3):560–73.

Hare, Robert D. 2003. *Manual for the Revised Psychopathy Checklist.* Toronto, ON, Canada: Multi-Health Systems.

Hari, Riitta and Miiamaaria V. Kujala. 2009. "Brain Basis of Human Social Interaction: From Concepts to Brain Imaging." *Physiological Reviews* 89(2):453–79.

Haroush, Keren and Ziv M. Williams. 2015. "Neuronal Prediction of Opponent's Behavior during Cooperative Social Interchange in Primates." *Cell* 160(6):1233–45.

Head, Naomi. 2012. "Transforming Conflict: Trust, Empathy, and Dialogue." *International Journal of Peace Studies* 17(2):33–55.

Hedström, Peter and Richard Swedberg. 1996. "Social Mechanisms." *Acta Sociologica* 39(3):281–308.

Herrmann, Richard K. and Jong Kun Choi. 2007. "From Prediction to Learning: Opening Experts' Minds to Unfolding History." *International Security* 31(4):132–61.

Herrmann, Richard K. and Richard Ned Lebow. 2004. *Ending the Cold War: Interpretations, Causation, and the Study of International Relations.* New York, NY: Palgrave Macmillan.

Herrmann, Richard K. and Michael P. Fischerkeller. 1995. "Beyond the Enemy Image and Spiral Model: Cognitive-Strategic Research after the Cold War." *International Organization* 49(3):415–50.

Hey, Nigel. 2006. *The Star Wars Enigma: Behind the Scenes of the Cold War Race for Missile Defense*. Washington, D.C.: Potomac Books, Inc.

Hickok, Gregory. 2014. *The Myth of Mirror Neurons: The Real Neuroscience of Communication and Cognition*. New York, NY: W. W. Norton & Company.

Hirst, David and I. Beeson. 1981. *Sadat*. London, UK: Faber and Faber.

Hochschild, Arlie. 1979. Emotion work, feeling rules, and social structure. *American Journal of Sociology* 85:551–75.

Hoffman, Aaron M. 2006. *Building Trust: Overcoming Suspicion In International Conflict*. Albany, NY: SUNY Press.

Hollis, Martin. 1998. *Trust Within Reason*. Cambridge, UK: Cambridge University Press.

Holmes, Alison R. and J. Simon Rofe. 2016. *Global Diplomacy: Theories, Types, and Models*. Boulder, CO: Westview Press.

Holmes, Marcus. 2011. "Something Old, Something New, Something Borrowed: Representations of Anarchy in International Relations Theory." *International Relations of the Asia-Pacific* 11(2):279–308.

2013. "The Force of Face-to-Face Diplomacy: Mirror Neurons and the Problem of Intentions." *International Organization* 67(4):829–61.

2014. "International Politics at the Brain's Edge: Social Neuroscience and a New 'Via Media.'" *International Studies Perspectives* 15(2):209–28.

2015. "Believing This and Alieving That: Theorizing Affect and Intuitions in International Politics." *International Security Quarterly* 59(4):706–20.

2016. "You Never Get a Second Chance to Make a First Impression? First Encounters and Face-Based Threat Perception." *Journal of Global Security Studies*.

Holmes, Marcus and Costas Panagopoulos. 2014. "The Social Brain Paradigm and Social Norm Puzzles." *Journal of Theoretical Politics* 26(3):384–404.

Holmes, Marcus and David Traven. 2015. "Acting Rationally without Really Thinking: The Logic of Rational Intuitionism in International Relations Theory." *International Studies Review* 17(3):414–40.

Holmes, Marcus and Keren Yarhi-Milo. 2017. "The Psychological Logic of Peace Summits: How Empathy Shapes Outcomes of Diplomatic Negotiations." *International Studies Quarterly* 61(1):107–22.

Holmes, Marcus and Nicholas J. Wheeler. 2017. "Time for Jimmy Carter to go Back to North Korea." *The Diplomat* May 11.

Holsti, Ole R. 1962. "The Belief System and National Images: A Case Study." *Journal of Conflict Resolution* 6(3):244–52.

Hopf, Ted. 1991. "Polarity, The Offense Defense Balance, and War." *The American Political Science Review* 85(2):475–93.

2010 "The Logic of Habit in International Relations." *European Journal of International Relations* 16(4):539–61.

Horgan, Terence and James Woodward. 1985. "Folk Psychology Is Here to Stay." *The Philosophical Review* 94(2):197–226.

Horowitz, Michael C., Allan C. Stam, and Cali M. Ellis. 2015. *Why Leaders Fight*. New York, NY: Cambridge University Press.

Hsee, Christopher K., Elaine Hatfield, and John G. Carlson. 1990. "The Effect of Power on Susceptibility to Emotional Contagion." *Cognition and Emotion* 4(4):327–40.

Humphrey, Nicholas K. 1976. "The Social Function of Intellect." *Growing Points in Ethology* 303–17.

Hurley, Susan. 2008. "The Shared Circuits Model (SCM): How Control, Mirroring, and Simulation Can Enable Imitation, Deliberation, and Mindreading." *Behavioral and Brain Sciences* 31(01):1–22.

Hutchings, Robert L. 1997. *American Diplomacy and the End of the Cold War: An Insider's Account of US Diplomacy in Europe, 1989–1992*. Washington, D.C.: Woodrow Wilson Center Press.

Hutchings, Roberts. 2015. "American Diplomacy and the End of the Cold War in Europe." In *Foreign Policy Breakthroughs Cases in Successful Diplomacy*. Robert Hutchings and Jeremi Suri (eds), 148–72. New York, NY: Oxford University Press.

Hutchison, Emma. 2016. *Affective Communities in World Politics*. Cambridge, UK: Cambridge University Press.

Hutchison, Emma and Roland Bleiker. 2008. "Emotional Reconciliation: Reconstituting Identity and Community after Trauma." *European Journal of Social Theory* 11(3):385–403.

  2013. "Reconciliation." In *The Routledge Handbook of Peacebuilding*. Roger Mac Ginty (ed), 81–91. New York, NY: Routledge.

  2014. "Theorizing Emotions in World Politics." *International Theory* 6(3):491–514.

Hyland, Philip, Daniel Boduszek, and Krzysztof Kielkiewicz, K. 2011. Psycho-Historical Analysis of Adolf Hitler: the Role of Personality, *Psychopathology and Development. Psychology and Society* 4(2):58–63.

Iacoboni, Marco. 2008. *Mirroring People: The New Science of How We Connect with Others*. New York, NY: Farrar Straus & Giroux.

  2009a. "Imitation, Empathy, and Mirror Neurons." *Annual Review of Psychology* 60:653–70.

  2009b. "Neurobiology of Imitation." *Current Opinion in Neurobiology* 19(6):661–65.

Iacoboni, Marco and Mirella Dapretto. 2006. "The Mirror Neuron System and the Consequences of Its Dysfunction." *Nature Reviews. Neuroscience* 7(12):942–51.

Ickes, William John. 1997. *Empathic Accuracy*. William Ickes (ed). New York, NY: Guilford Press.

Imai, Kosuke, Dustin Tingley, and Teppei Yamamoto. 2013. "Experimental Designs for Identifying Causal Mechanisms." *Journal of the Royal Statistical Society: Series A (Statistics in Society)* 176(1):5–51.

Inzlicht, Michael, Jennifer N. Gutsell, and Lisa Legault. 2012. "Mimicry Reduces Racial Prejudice." *Journal of Experimental Social Psychology* 48(1):361–65.

Jackson, Robert L. 1991. "Friend's Suicide Saddens Retired Adm. Crowe: Military: 'We Grew to Be Quite Close,' Former Joint Chiefs Chairman Says of Soviet Marshal Akhromeyev." *Los Angeles Times*, August 26. Available: http://articles.latimes.com/1991-08-26/news/mn-938_1_former-joint-chiefs.

Jacob, Pierre and Marc Jeannerod. 2005. "The Motor Theory of Social Cognition: A Critique." *Trends in Cognitive Sciences* 9(1):21–25.

Jackson, Patrick Thaddeus and Daniel H. Nexon. 1999. "Relations Before States: Substance, Process and the Study of World Politics." *European Journal of International Relations* 5(3):291–332.

Jarausch, Konrad H. 1994. *The Rush to German Unity*. New York, NY: Oxford University Press.

Jay, Martin. 2010. *The Virtues of Mendacity: On Lying in Politics*. Charlottesville, VA: University of Virginia Press.

Jedrzejewicz, Waclaw. 1968. *The Papers and Memoirs of Jozef Lipski, Ambassador of Poland, Diplomat in Berlin 1933–1939*. New York, NY: Columbia University Press.

Jeffery, Renee. 2014. "The Promise and Problems of the Neuroscientific Study of Individual and Collective Emotions." *International Theory* 6(3):584–89.

Jervis, Robert. 1970. *The Logic of Images in International Relations*. New York, NY: Columbia University Press.

   1976. *Perception and Misperception in International Politics*. Princeton, NJ: Princeton University Press.

   1978. "Cooperation under the Security Dilemma." *World Politics* 30(2):167–214.

   2013. "Do Leaders Matter and How Would We Know?" *Security Studies* 22(2):153–79.

Jiang, Jing, Bohan Dai, Danling Peng, Chaozhe Zhu, Li Liu, and Chunming Lu. 2012. "Neural Synchronization during Face-to-Face Communication. *The Journal of Neuroscience* 32(45):16064–69.

Johnson, Gaynor. 2013. *The Foreign Office and British Diplomacy in the Twentieth Century*. New York, NY: Routledge.

Jonason, Peter K., Minna Lyons, Holly M. Baughman, and Philip A. Vernon. 2014. "What a Tangled Web We Weave: The Dark Triad Traits and Deception." *Personality and Individual Differences* 70:117–19.

Kahneman, Daniel. 2003. "A Perspective on Judgment and Choice: Mapping Bounded Rationality." *American Psychologist* 58(9):697–720.

Kahneman, Daniel and Amos Tversky. 1979. "Prospect Theory: An Analysis of Decision Under Risk." *Econometrica* 47(2):263–91.

Kamel, Mohamed Ibrahim. 1986. *The Camp David Accords*. Abingdon, UK: Kegan Paul International.

Kelman, Herbert C. 2005. "Building trust among enemies: The central challenge for international conflict resolution." *International Journal of Intercultural Relations* 29(6):639–50.

Kennedy, Paul M. 1989. *Strategy and Diplomacy 1870–1945*. London: Harper-collins.

Kennedy, John F. 1960. The Strategy of Peace. Allan Nevins (ed). New York, NY: Harper Brothers.

Keohane, Robert O. 1984. *After Hegemony: Cooperation and Discord in the World Political Economy*. Princeton, NJ: Princeton University Press.

1993. "Institutional Theory and the Realist Challenge after the Cold War." In *Neorealism and Neoliberalism: The Contemporary Debate*. David A. Baldwin (ed), 269–300. New York, NY: Columbia University Press.

Kershaw, Ian. 2000. *Hitler, 1936–45*. New York, NY: W. W. Norton & Company.

Kertzer, Joshua D. 2016. *Resolve in International Politics*. Princeton, NJ: Princeton University Press.

Keysers, Christian. 2011. *The Empathic Brain*. Amsterdam, NL: Social Brain Press.

2015. "The Strawman in the Brain." *Science* 347(6219):240.

Keysers, Christian. and Valeria Gazzola. 2007. "Integrating Simulation and Theory of Mind." *Trends in Cognitive Sciences* 11(5):194–96.

2009. "Expanding the Mirror: Vicarious Activity for Actions, Emotions, and Sensations." *Current Opinion in Neurobiology* 19(6):666–71.

Keysers, Christian, Marc Thioux, and Valeria Gazzola. 2013. "Mirror Neuron System and Social Cognition." In *Understanding Other Minds: Perspectives from Developmental Social Neuroscience*. Simon Baron-Cohen, Michael Lombardo, and Helen Tager-Flusberg (eds). Oxford, UK: Oxford University Press.

Khong, Yuen Foong. 1992. *Analogies at War: Korea, Munich, Dien Bien Phu, and the Vietnam Decisions of 1965*. Princeton, NJ: Princeton University Press.

Kirkpatrick, Ivone 1959. *The Inner Circle: The Memoirs of Ivone Kirkpatrick*. London, UK: Macmillan.

Kissinger, Henry. 1994. *Diplomacy*. New York, NY: Simon and Schuster.

Kleiboer, Marieke. 1998. *The Multiple Realities of International Mediation*. Boulder, CO: Lynne Rienner.

Klein, Kristi J. K. and Sara D. Hodges. 2001. "Gender Differences, Motivation, and Empathic Accuracy: When It Pays to Understand." *Personality and Social Psychology Bulletin* 27(6):720–30.

Kort, Michael. 2014. *The Soviet Colossus: History and Aftermath*. New York, NY: Routledge.

Krebs, Ronald R. and Patrick T. Jackson. 2007. "Twisting Tongues and Twisting Arms: The Power of Political Rhetoric." *European Journal of International Relations* 13(1):35–66.

Kressel, Neil J. 1992. "Review." *Political Psychology* 13 (4): 805–10.

Krueger, Joel. 2012. "Seeing mind in action." *Phenomenology and the Cognitive Sciences* 11(2):149–73.

Kurtzer, Daniel C., Scott B. Lansensky, William B. Quandt, Steven L. Spiegel, and Shibley Z. Telhami. 2013. *The Peace Puzzle: America's Quest for Arab-Israeli Peace, 1989–2011*. Ithaca, NY: Cornell University Press.

Kydd, Andrew. 2000. "Trust, Reassurance, and Cooperation." *International Organization* 54(02):325–57.

2005. *Trust and Mistrust in International Relations*. Princeton, NJ: Princeton University Press.

Lange, Thomas and Geoff Pugh. 1998. *The Economics of German Unification: An Introduction*. New York, NY: Edward Elgar Pub.

Langleben, Daniel D., Dan F. X. Willard, and Jane C. Moriarty. 2012. "Brain Imaging of Deception." In *Neuroimaging in Forensic Psychiatry*. Joseph R. Simpson (ed), 215–36. West Sussex, UK: John Wiley & Sons, Ltd.

Larres, Klaus. 2002. *Churchill's Cold War: the Politics of Personal Diplomacy*. New Haven, CT: Yale University Press.

Larson, Deborah Welch. 2000. *Anatomy of Mistrust: U.S.-Soviet Relations during the Cold War*. Ithaca, NY: Cornell University Press.

Layne, Christopher. 2008. "Security Studies and the Use of History: Neville Chamberlain's Grand Strategy Revisited." *Security Studies* 17(3):397–437.

Lazar, Sara W., Catherine E. Kerr, Rachel H. Wasserman, Jeremy R. Gray, Douglas N. Greve, Michael T. Treadway, and Metta McGarvey. 2005. "Meditation Experience Is Associated with Increased Cortical Thickness." *Neuroreport* 16(17):1893–97.

Lebow, Richard Ned. 2003. *The Tragic Vision of Politics: Ethics, Interests and Orders*. Cambridge, UK: Cambridge University Press.

   2014. *Constructing Cause in International Relations*. New York, NY: Cambridge University Press.

Lebow, Richard Ned and Janice Gross Stein. 2004. "Understanding the End of the Cold War as a Non-Linear Confluence." In *Ending the Cold War: Interpretations, Causation and the Study of International Relations*. Richard K. Herrmann and Richard Ned Lebow (eds), 189–217. New York, NY: Palgrave Macmillan.

Lee, Jin Joo, W. Bradley Knox, Jolie B. Wormwood, Cynthia Breazeal, and David DeSteno. 2013. "Computationally Modeling Interpersonal Trust." *Frontiers in Psychology* 4 (December).

Leffler, Melvyn P. and Odd Arne Westad. 2010. *The Cambridge History of the Cold War*. Cambridge, UK: Cambridge University Press.

Lettow, Paul. 2005. *Ronald Reagan and His Quest to Abolish Nuclear Weapons*. New York, NY: Random House.

Lévesque, Jacques. 1997. *The Enigma of 1989: The USSR and the Liberation of Eastern Europe*. Translated by Keith Martin. Berkeley, CA: University of California Press.

Lockwood, Patricia L., Geoffrey Bird, Madeleine Bridge, and Essi Viding. 2013. "Dissecting Empathy: High Levels of Psychopathic and Autistic Traits Are Characterized by Difficulties in Different Social Information Processing Domains." *Frontiers in Human Neuroscience* 7:760.

Lutz, Antoine, Lawrence L. Greischar, Nancy B. Rawlings, Matthieu Ricard, and Richard J. Davidson. 2004. "Long-Term Meditators Self-Induce High-Amplitude Gamma Synchrony during Mental Practice." *Proceedings of the National Academy of Sciences of the United States of America* 101(46):16369–73.

Mahoney, James. 2015. "Process Tracing and Historical Explanation." *Security Studies* 24(2):200–18.

Mann, James. 2009. *The Rebellion of Ronald Reagan: A History of the End of the Cold War*. New York, NY: Penguin.

Mansbridge, Jane J. 1983. *Beyond Adversary Democracy.* Chicago, IL: University of Chicago Press.

Marangoni, Carol, Stella Garcia, William Ickes, and Gary Teng. 1995. "Empathic Accuracy in a Clinically Relevant Setting." *Journal of Personality and Social Psychology* 68(5):854–69.

Massie, Suzanne. 2013. *Trust But Verify: Reagan, Russia and Me.* 1st edition. Rockland, Maine: Hearttree Press.

Matlock, Jack. 1996. *Autopsy on an Empire: The American Ambassador's Account of the Collapse of the Soviet Union.* New York, NY: Random House.

2004. *Reagan and Gorbachev: How the Cold War Ended.* New York, NY: Random House.

McCourt, David. M. 2016. "Practice Theory and Relationalism." *International Studies Quarterly.* 60:475–85.

McDermott, Rose. 2004a. *Political Psychology in International Relations.* Ann Arbor, MI: University of Michigan Press.

2004b. "The Feeling of Rationality: The Meaning of Neuroscientific Advances for Political Science." *Perspectives on Politics* 2(04):691–706.

2009. "Mutual Interests: The Case for Increasing Dialogue between Political Science and Neuroscience." *Political Research Quarterly* 62(3): 571–83.

2014. "The Body Doesn't Lie: A Somatic Approach to the Study of Emotion in World Politics." *International Theory* 6(3):557–62.

McDonough, Frank. 1998. *Neville Chamberlain, Appeasement, and the British Road to War.* Manchester, UK: Manchester University Press.

2011. *The Origins of the Second World War: An International Perspective.* Frank McDonough (ed). London, UK: Bloomsbury Publishing.

Mearsheimer, John. 1994. "The False Promise of International Institutions." *International Security* 19(3):5–49.

2001. *The Tragedy of Great Power Politics.* New York, NY: W. W. Norton & Company.

2011. *Why Leaders Lie: The Truth About Lying in International Politics.* Oxford University Press, USA.

2014. "Why the Ukraine Crisis Is the West's Fault." *Foreign Affairs* September/October Issue.

Mehrabian, Albert. 1972. *Nonverbal Communication.* Chicago, IL: Aldine-Atherton.

1981. *Silent Messages: Implicit Communication of Emotions and Attitudes.* Belmont, CA: Wadsworth Publishing Company.

Mercer, Jonathan. 2005. "Rationality and Psychology in International Politics." *International Organization* 59(1):77–106.

2010. "Emotional Beliefs." *International Organization* 64(01):1–31.

2014. "Feeling like a State: Social Emotion and Identity." *International Theory* 6(03):515–35.

Merkl, Peter H. 2010. *German Unification in the European Context.* University Park, PA: Penn State University Press.

Michel, Torsten. 2009. "Pigs can't fly, or can they? Ontology, scientific realism and the metaphysics of presence in international relations." *Review of International Studies* 35(2):397–419.

2012. "Trust, Rationality and Vulnerability in International Relations." *The vulnerable subject: Beyond Rationalism in International Relations*. Amanda Beattie and Kate Schick (eds). Palgrave.

Mitzen, Jennifer. 2013. *Power in Concert: The Nineteenth-Century Origins of Global Governance*. Chicago, IL: University of Chicago Press.

Mitzen, Jennifer and Randall L. Schweller. 2011. "Knowing the Unknown Unknowns: Misplaced Certainty and the Onset of War." *Security Studies* 20(1):2–35.

Moens, Alexander. 1991. "American Diplomacy and German Unification." *Survival* 33(6):531–45.

Montague, P. Read, Gregory S. Berns, Jonathan D. Cohen, Samuel M. McClure, Giuseppe Pagnoni, Mukesh Dhamala, and Michael C. Wiest. 2002. "Hyperscanning: Simultaneous fMRI during Linked Social Interactions." *NeuroImage* 16(4):1159–64.

Monteiro, Nuno P. 2014. *Theory of Unipolar Politics*. New York, NY: Cambridge University Press.

Moramarco, Rossella, Cynthia Kay Stevens, and Pierpaolo Pontrandolfo. 2013. "Trust in Face-to-Face and Electronic Negotiation in Buyer-Supplier Relationships: A Laboratory Study." *Behavioral Issues in Operations Management* 49–81.

Morrow, James D. 1999. "The Strategic Setting of Choices: Signaling, Commitment, and Negotiation in International Politics." *Strategic Choice and International Relations*. David A. Lake and Robert Powell (eds), 77–114. Princeton, NJ: Princeton University Press.

Morris, Benny. 2001. *Righteous Victims: A History of the Zionist-Arab Conflict, 1881–1998*. New York, NY: Knopf Doubleday Publishing Group.

Morris, Michael W. and Dacher Keltner. 2000. "How emotions work: An analysis of the social functions of emotional expression in negotiations." *Review of Organizational Behavior* 22:1–50.

Mukamel, Roy, Arne D. Ekstrom, Jonas Kaplan, Marco Iacoboni, and Itzhak Fried. 2010. "Single-Neuron Responses in Humans during Execution and Observation of Actions." *Current Biology* 20(8):750–56.

Murray, Henry A. 1943. *Analysis of the Personality of Adolph Hitler*. Washington, D.C.: Office of Strategic Services.

Naftali, Timothy. 2007. *George H. W. Bush: The American Presidents Series: The 41st President, 1989–1993*. Arthur M. Schlesinger and Sean Wilentz (eds). New York, NY: Times Books.

Naquin, Charles E. and Gaylen D. Paulson. 2003. "Online Bargaining and Interpersonal Trust." *The Journal of Applied Psychology* 88(1):113–20.

Neumann, Iver B. 2003. "The English School on Diplomacy: Scholarly Promise Unfulfilled." *International Relations* 17(3):341–69.

2005. "To Be a Diplomat." *International Studies Perspectives* 6(1):72–93.

2008. "The Body of the Diplomat." *European Journal of International Relations* 14(4):671–95.

2012. *At Home with the Diplomats: Inside a European Foreign Ministry*. Ithaca, NY: Cornell University Press.

Neville, Neville. 2007. "The Foreign Office and Britain's Ambassadors to Berlin, 1933–39." *Contemporary British History* 18(3):110–29.

Newhouse, John. 1989. *War And Peace In The Nuclear Age*. New York, NY: Knopf.

Nexon, Daniel H. 2009. "The Balance of Power in the Balance." *World Politics* 61(2): 330–59.

Nicolson, Sir Harold. 1939. *Diplomacy*. Washington DC: Institute for the Study of Diplomacy, reprinted 1988.

Norwich, John Julius. 2007. *The Duff Cooper Diaries*. London: Orion Publishing.

Oberdorfer, Don. 1992. *The Turn: How the Cold War Came to an End, the United States and the Soviet Union, 1983–90*. London, UK: Jonathan Cape Ltd.

    1998. *From the Cold War to a New Era: The United States and the Soviet Union, 1983–1991*. Baltimore, MD: Johns Hopkins University Press.

Okdie, Bradley M., Rosanna E. Guadagno, Frank J. Bernieri, Andrew L. Geers, and Amber R. Mclarney-Vesotski. 2011. "Getting to Know You: Face-to-Face versus Online Interactions." *Computers in Human Behavior* 27(1):153–59.

O'Mahoney, Joseph. 2015. "Why Did They Do That?: The Methodology of Reasons for Action." *International Theory* 7(02):231–62.

Osgood, Charles E. 1962. "An Alternative to War or Surrender." Champaign, IL: University of Illinois Press.

O'Sullivan, Maureen. 2005. "Emotional Intelligence and Deception Detection: Why Most People Can't 'read' Others, but a Few Can." *Applications of Nonverbal Communication* 215–53.

Owen, David and Jonathan Davidson. 2009. "Hubris Syndrome: An Acquired Personality Disorder? A Study of US Presidents and UK Prime Ministers over the Last 100 Years." *Brain* 132(5):1396–406.

Palazhchenko, Pavel. 1997. *My Years with Gorbachev and Shevardnadze*. University Park, PA: Penn State Press.

    2007. "A Perspective From Moscow." In *Turning Points in Ending the Cold War*, Kiron K. Skinner (ed), *vii–xvii*. Stanford, CA: Hoover Institution Press.

Pettigrew, Thomas F. and Linda R. Tropp. 2006. "A Meta-Analytic Test of Intergroup Contact Theory." *Journal of Personality and Social Psychology* 90(5):751–83.

    2013. *When Groups Meet: The Dynamics of Intergroup Contact*. New York, NY: Psychology Press.

Pentland, Alex. 2008. *Honest Signals: How They Shape our World*. Cambridge, MA: MIT Press.

Pfiffner, James P. 2013. "The Paradox of President Reagan's Leadership." *Presidential Studies Quarterly* 43(1):81–100.

Phipps, Sir Eric and Gaynor Johnson. 2004. *Our Man in Berlin: The Diary of Sir Eric Phipps 1933–37*. Washington, D.C.: Potomac Books, Incorporated.

Plokhy, Serhii. 2010. *Yalta: The Price of Peace*. London, UK: Penguin Books.

    2014. *The Last Empire: The Final Days of the Soviet Union*. London, UK: Basic Books.

Porter, Stephen and Leanne ten Brinke. 2008. "Reading between the Lies Identifying Concealed and Falsified Emotions in Universal Facial Expressions." *Psychological Science* 19(5):508–14.

Post, Jerrold M. 2004. *Leaders and Their Followers in a Dangerous World: The Psychology of Political Behavior*. Ithaca, NY: Cornell University Press.

Pouliot, Vincent. 2007. "Sobjectivism: Toward a Constructivist Methodology." *International Studies Quarterly* 51(2):359–84.

2008. "The Logic of Practicality: A Theory of Practice of Security Communities." *International Organization* 62(02):257–88.

2010. *International Security in Practice: The Politics of NATO-Russia Diplomacy.* Cambridge, UK: Cambridge University Press.

2011. "Diplomats as permanent representatives: the practical logics of multilateral pecking order." *International Journal* 66(3):543–61.

2016. *International Pecking Orders: The Politics and Practice of Multilateral Diplomacy.* Cambridge, UK: Cambridge University Press.

Pouliot, Vincent and Jérémie Cornut. 2015. "Practice Theory and the Study of Diplomacy: A Research Agenda." *Cooperation and Conflict* 50(3):297–315.

Princen, Thomas. 1991. "Camp David: Problem-Solving or Power Politics as Usual?" *Journal of Peace Research* 28(1):57–69.

Putnam, Robert D. 1988. "Diplomacy and Domestic Politics: The Logic of Two-Level Games." *International Organization* 42(03):427–60.

2001. *Bowling Alone: The Collapse and Revival of American Community.* New York, NY: Touchstone Books by Simon & Schuster.

Quandt, William B. 1986a. *Camp David: Peacemaking and Politics.* Washington, D.C.: Brookings Institution Press.

1986b. "Camp David and Peacemaking in the Middle East." *Political Science Quarterly* 101(3):357–77.

Ragin, Charles C. 2009. *Redesigning Social Inquiry: Fuzzy Sets and Beyond.* Chicago, IL: University of Chicago Press.

Raiffa, Howard. 1982. *The Art and Science of Negotiation.* Cambridge, MA: Belknap Press of Harvard University Press.

Ramachandran, V. S. 2011. *The Tell-Tale Brain: A Neuroscientist's Quest for What Makes Us Human.* Gurugram, India: W. W. Norton & Company.

Ramsay, Kristopher W. 2011. "Cheap Talk Diplomacy, Voluntary Negotiations, and Variable Bargaining Power." *International Studies Quarterly* 55(4):1003–23.

Rathbun, Brian. 2007. "Uncertain about Uncertainty: Understanding the Multiple Meanings of a Crucial Concept in International Relations Theory." *International Studies Quarterly* 51(3):533–57.

2009. "It Takes All Types: Social Psychology, Trust, and the International Relations Paradigm in Our Minds." *International Theory* 1(03):345.

2012. *Trust in International Cooperation: International Security Institutions, Domestic Politics, and American Multilateralism.* New York, NY: Cambridge University Press.

2014. *Diplomacy's Value: Creating Security in 1920s Europe and the Contemporary Middle East.* Ithaca, NY: Cornell University Press.

Reagan, Ronald. 1990. *An American Life.* New York, NY: Simon and Schuster.

2007. *The Reagan Diaries.* New York, NY: HarperCollins Publishers.

Renshon, Jonathan. 2009. "When Public Statements Reveal Private Beliefs: Assessing Operational Codes at a Distance." *Political Psychology* 30(4):649–61.

Reynolds, David. 2009. *Summits: Six Meetings That Shaped the Twentieth Century.* London, UK: Allen Lane.

Rhodes, Richard. 2007. *Arsenals of Folly: The Making of the Nuclear Arms Race.* New York, NY: Knopf Doubleday Publishing Group.

Ringmar, Erik. 2014. "The Search for Dialogue as a Hindrance to Understanding: Practices as Inter-Paradigmatic Research Program." *International Theory* 6(1):1–27.

Ripsman, Norrin M. and Jack S. Levy. 2007. "The Preventive War That Never Happened: Britain, France, and the Rise of Germany in the 1930s." *Security Studies* 16(1):32–67.

2008. "Wishful Thinking or Buying Time? The Logic of British Appeasement in the 1930s." *International Security* 33(2):148–81.

Risse, Thomas. 1997. "The Cold War's Endgame and German Unification." *International Security* 21(4):159–85.

2000. "Let's Argue!": Communicative Action in World Politics." *International Organization* 54(1):1–39.

Rizzolatti, Giacomo and Leonardo Fogassi. 2014. "The Mirror Mechanism: Recent Findings and Perspectives." *Philosophical Transactions of the Royal Society B: Biological Sciences* 369(1644):20130420–20130420.

Rizzolatti, Giacomo and Laila Craighero. 2004. "The Mirror-Neuron System." *Annual Review of Neuroscience* 27:169–92.

Rizzolatti, Giacomo and Corrado Sinigaglia. 2006. "Mirror Neurons and Motor Intentionality." *Functional Neurology* 22(4):205–10.

Rockmann, Kevin W. and Gregory B. Northcraft. 2008. "To Be or Not to Be Trusted: The Influence of Media Richness on Defection and Deception." *Organizational Behavior and Human Decision Processes* 107(2): 106–22.

Roosevelt, Franklin Delano. 1950. *Public Papers of the Presidents of the United States: F.D. Roosevelt, 1944–1945, Volume 13.* Best Books.

Rosato, Sebastian. 2015. "The Inscrutable Intentions of Great Powers." *International Security* 39(3):48–88.

Rosenbaum, H. D. and A. Ugrinsky. 1994. *The Presidency and Domestic Policies of Jimmy Carter.* Westport, CT: Greenwood Pub Group.

Rosenwein, Barbara H. 2005. "Worrying about Emotions in History." *The American Historical Review* 107(3):821–45.

Ross, Dennis. 2008. *Statecraft: And How to Restore America's Standing in the World.* New York, NY: Farrar, Straus and Giroux.

Ross, Andrew. 2014. *Mixed Emotions: Beyond Fear and Hatred in International Conflict.* Chicago, IL: University of Chicago Press.

Ruzicka, Jan and Nicholas J. Wheeler. 2010. "The Puzzle of Trusting Relationships in the Nuclear Non-Proliferation Treaty." *International Affairs* 86(1):69–85.

Sachar, Howard M. 1976/2000. *A History of Israel: From the Rise of Zionism to Our Time.* New York, NY: Knopf.

Sadat, Anwar. 1978. *Anwar El Sadat: In Search of Identity an Autobiography.* 1st edition. New York, NY: Harpercollins.

Safty, Adel. 1992. *From Camp David to the Gulf: Negotiations, Language & Propaganda, and War.* Montreal, Canada: Black Rose Books Ltd.

Sakharov, Andrei D. 1991. *Moscow And Beyond, 1986 To 1989.* Translated by Antonina Bouis. 1st edition. New York, NY: Alfred A. Knopf.

Saltoun-Ebin, Jason. 2013. *Dear Mr. President . . . : Reagan/Gorbachev and the Correspondence That Ended the Cold War*. United States: CreateSpace Independent Publishing Platform.

Sanders, Sol. 2008. "The record on face-to-face diplomacy by top U.S. leaders? Damnably disastrous." *The World Tribune*, February 18, 2008. Available: http://www.worldtribune.com/worldtribune/WTARC/2008/s2_22.html.

Sarotte, Mary Elise. 2009. *1989: The Struggle to Create Post-Cold War Europe*. Princeton, NJ: Princeton University Press.

Sasley, Brent E. 2011. "Theorizing States' Emotions." *International Studies Review* 13(3):452–76.

Saunders, Elizabeth. 2011. *Leaders at War: How Presidents Shape Military Interventions*. Ithaca, NY: Cornell University Press.

    2017. "No Substitute for Experience: Presidents, Advisers, and Information in Group Decision-Making." *International Organization* 71(S1): S219–S47.

Saunders, Elizabeth and James Lebovic. 2016. "The Diplomatic Core: The Determinants of High-Level US Diplomatic Visits, 1946–2010." *International Studies Quarterly* 60(1):107–23.

Savranskaya, Svetlana, Thomas Blanton, and Vladislav Martinovich Zubok. 2010. *Masterpieces of History: The Peaceful End of the Cold War in Eastern Europe, 1989*. Budapest, HU: Central European University Press.

Savranskaya, Svetlana. 2010. "The Logic of 1989: The Soviet Peaceful Withdrawal from Eastern Europe." In *Masterpieces of History: The Peaceful End of the Cold War in Europe, 1989*. Svetlana Savranskaya, Thomas Blanton, and Vladislav Martinovich Zubok (eds), 1–48. Budapest, HU: Central European University Press.

Savranskaya, Svetlana and Thomas Blanton. 2017. *The Last Superpower Summits: Gorbachev, Reagan, and Bush*. Budapest, HU: Central European University Press.

Schafer, Mark. 2000. "Issues in Assessing Psychological Characteristics at a Distance: An Introduction to the Symposium." *Political Psychology* 21(3):511–27.

Schelling, Thomas C. 1966. "Arms and Influence." *New Haven: Yale University*.

Schilbach, Leonhard, Bert Timmermans, Vasudevi Reddy, Alan Costall, Gary Bente, Tobias Schlicht, and Kai Vogeley. 2013. "Toward a Second-Person Neuroscience." *The Behavioral and Brain Sciences* 36(4):393–414.

Schmid Mast, Marianne, Klaus Jonas, and Judith A. Hall. 2009. "Give a Person Power and He or She Will Show Interpersonal Sensitivity: The Phenomenon and Its Why and When." *Journal of Personality and Social Psychology* 97(5):835–50.

Schmidt, Manfred G. and Gerhard A. Ritter. 2012. *The Rise and Fall of a Socialist Welfare State: The German Democratic Republic*. 2013 edition. Berlin; London: Springer.

Schmidt, Paul. 1951. *Hitler's Interpreter*. Basingstoke, UK: Macmillan.

Schulte-Rüther, Martin, Hans J. Markowitsch, Gereon R. Fink, Martina Piefke. 2007. "Mirror Neuron and Theory of Mind Mechanisms Involved in Face-to-Face Interactions: A Functional Magnetic Resonance Imaging Approach to Empathy." *Journal of Cognitive Neuroscience* 19(8):1354–72.

Schwartz, Jeffrey M. and Sharon Begley. 2003. *The Mind and the Brain: Neuroplasticity and the Power of Mental Force*. New York, NY: Harper Perennial.

Schweizer, Peter. 2003. *Reagan's War: The Epic Story of His Forty-Year Struggle and Final Triumph Over Communism*. New York, NY: Knopf Doubleday Publishing Group.

Self, Robert C. 2006. *Neville Chamberlain: A Biography*. Farnham, UK: Ashgate Pub Co.

Shapiro, Ian. 2002. "Problems, Methods, and Theories in the Study of Politics, or What's Wrong with Political Science and What to Do about It." *Political Theory* 30(4):596–619.

Sharp, Paul. 2009. *Diplomatic Theory of International Relations*. New York, NY: Cambridge University Press.

Shay, R. P. 1977. *British Rearmament in the Thirties: Politics and Profits*. Princeton, NJ: Princeton University Press.

Shultz, George Pratt. 1993. *Turmoil and Triumph: My Years as Secretary of State*. New York, NY: Scribner's.

2013. *Issues on My Mind: Strategies for the Future*. Stanford, CA: Hoover Institution Press.

Singer, Tania. 2006. "The Neuronal Basis and Ontogeny of Empathy and Mind Reading: Review of Literature and Implications for Future Research." *Neuroscience & Biobehavioral Reviews* 30(6):855–63.

Singer, Tania, Ben Seymour, John O'Doherty, Holger Kaube, Raymond J. Dolan, and Chris D. Frith. 2004. "Empathy for Pain Involves the Affective but not Sensory Components of Pain." *Science* 303(5661):1157–62.

Singer, Tania, Ben Seymour, John P. O'Doherty, Klaas E. Stephan, Raymond J. Dolan and Chris D. Frith. 2006. "Empathic neural responses are modulated by the perceived fairness of others." *Nature* 439:466–69.

Skinner, Kiron K. 2008. *Turning Points in Ending the Cold War*. Stanford, CA: Hoover Institution Press Publication.

Snodgrass, Sara E., Marvin A. Hecht, and Robert Ploutz-Snyder. 1998. "Interpersonal Sensitivity: Expressivity or Perceptivity?" *Journal of Personality and Social Psychology* 74(1):238–49.

Snyder, Jack and Erica D. Borghard. 2011. "The Cost of Empty Threats: A Penny, Not a Pound." *American Political Science Review* 105(03):437–56.

Solms, Mark and Oliver Turnbull. 2010. *Brain and the Inner World: An Introduction to the Neuroscience of Subjective Experience*. New York, NY: Other Press, LLC.

Spektor, Matias, Nicholas J. Wheeler, and Dani Nedal. 2015. "Witnesses to Nuclear Rapprochement: Key Junctures." In *The Origins of Nuclear Cooperation: A Critical Oral History Between Argentina and Brazil*. Rodrigo Mallea, Matias Spektor, and Nicholas J. Wheeler (eds), 14–25. Rio de Janeiro, BR: Woodrow Wilson International Center for Scholars and the FGV School of Social Sciences.

Spohr, Kristina. 2000. "German Unification: Between Official History, Academic Scholarship, and Political Memoirs." *The Historical Journal* 43(3):869–88.

Sporer, Siegfried Ludwig. 2001. "Recognizing Faces of Other Ethnic Groups: An Integration of Theories." *Psychology, Public Policy, and Law* 7(1):36.

Spunt, Robert P., Ajay B. Satpute, and Matthew D. Lieberman. 2011. "Identifying the What, Why, and How of an Observed Action: An fMRI Study of Mentalizing and Mechanizing during Action Observation." *Journal of Cognitive Neuroscience* 23(1):63–74.

Stedman, Andrew David. 2011. *Alternatives to Appeasement: Neville Chamberlain and Hitler's Germany*. New York, NY: I.B.Tauris.

Stent, Angela E. 2000. *Russia and Germany Reborn: Unification, the Soviet Collapse, and the New Europe*. Princeton, NJ: Princeton University Press.

Stinson, Linda and William Ickes. 1992. "Empathic Accuracy in the Interactions of Male Friends versus Male Strangers." *Journal of Personality and Social Psychology* 62(5):787.

Storper, Michael and Anthony J. Venables. 2004. "Buzz: Face-to-Face Contact and the Urban Economy." *Journal of Economic Geography* 4(4):351–70.

Strong, Robert A. 2000. *Working in the World: Jimmy Carter and the Making of American Foreign Policy*. Baton Rouge, LA: LSU Press.

Szabo, Stephen F. 1992. *The Diplomacy of German Unification*. New York, NY: St Martin's Press.

Tang, Shiping. 2009. "The Security Dilemma: A Conceptual Analysis." *Security Studies* 18(3):597–623.

Taylor, Telford. 1979. *Munich: The Price of Peace*. Garden City, N.Y: Doubleday.

Telhami, Shibley. 1992. "Evaluating Bargaining Performance: The Case of Camp David." Political Science Quarterly, 629–53.

1992. *Power and Leadership in International Bargaining: The Path to the Camp David Accords*. New York, NY: Columbia University Press.

Tetlock, Philip E. 1998. "Social Psychology and World Politics." *Handbook of Social Psychology* 4:868–914.

Thorpe, D. R. 2011. *Eden: The Life and Times of Anthony Eden First Earl of Avon, 1897–1977*. London, UK: Random House.

Thompson, Lori Foster and Michael Coovert. 2003. "The effects of computer conferencing on perceived confusion, satisfaction and postdiscussion accuracy." *Group Dynamics: Theory, Research, and Practice* 7(2):135–51.

Tooze, Adam. 2008. *The Wages of Destruction: The Making and Breaking of the Nazi Economy*. London, UK: Allen Lane.

Trager, Robert F. 2017. *Diplomacy: Communication and the Origins of the International Order*. Cambridge, UK: Cambridge University Press.

Tummolini, Luca and Cristiano Castelfranchi. 2006. "The Cognitive and Behavioral Mediation of Institutions: Towards an Account of Institutional Actions." *Cognitive Systems Research, Cognition, Joint Action and Collective Intentionality*, 7:307–23.

Umilta, Maria Alessandra, Evelyne Kohler, Vittorio Gallese, Leonardo Fogassi, Luciano Fadiga, Christian Keysers, and Giacomo Rizzolatti. 2001. "I Know What You Are Doing: A Neurophysiological Study." *Neuron* 31(1):155–65.

Valley, Kathleen L, Joseph Moag, and Max H Bazerman. 1998. "'A Matter of Trust': Effects of Communication on the Efficiency and Distribution of Outcomes." *Journal of Economic Behavior & Organization* 34(2):211–38.

Vance, Cyrus R. 1917–2002. 1983. *Hard Choices: Critical Years in America's For-eign Policy*. New York, NY: Simon and Schuster.

Van Evera, Stephen. 1998. "Offense, Defense, and the Causes of War." *International Security* 22(4):5–43.

Van Zant, Alex B. and Laura J. Kray. 2014. "'I Can't Lie to Your Face': Minimal Face-to-Face Interaction Promotes Honesty." *Journal of Experimental Social Psychology* 55:234–38.

Vrij, Aldert, Hayley Evans, Lucy Akehurst, and Samantha Mann. 2004. "Rapid judgements in assessing verbal and nonverbal cues: their potential for deception researchers and lie detection." *Applied Cognitive Psychology* 18(3):283–96.

Waltz, Kenneth N. 1979. *Theory of International Politics*. 1 edition. New York, NY: McGraw Hill.

Weinberg, Gerhard L. 2013. *Hitler's Foreign Policy 1933–1939: The Road to World War II*. New York, NY: Enigma Books.

Weinberger, Caspar. 1990. *Fighting for Peace 7 Critical Years in the Pentagon*. New York, NY: Grand Central Publishing.

Weizman, Ezer. 1981. *The Battle for Peace*. New York, NY: Bantam Books.

Wendt, Alexander. 1999. *Social Theory of International Politics*. Cambridge, UK: Cambridge University Press.

    2005. "Social Theory as Cartesian Science: An Auto-Critique from a Quantum Perspective." *Constructivism and International Relations: Alexander Wendt and His Critics*. S. Guzzini & A. Leander (eds), 178–216. Oxon, UK: Routledge.

    2010. "Flatland: Quantum Mind and the International Hologram." *New Systems Theories of World Politics*. M. Albert, L-E. Cederman & A. Wendt (eds). Basingstoke, UK: Palgrave.

    2015. *Quantum Mind and Social Science: Unifying Physical and Social Ontology*. Cambridge, UK: Cambridge University Press.

Wheeler, Nicholas J. 2007. "Trust Building between enemies in the nuclear Age." Unpublished Manuscript.

    2013. "Investigating Diplomatic Transformations." *International Affairs* 89(2):477–96.

    2018. *Trusting Enemies*. Oxford, UK: Oxford University Press.

Wilson, James Graham. 2014. *The Triumph of Improvisation*. Ithaca, NY: Cornell University Press.

Wilson David S., Near David and Miller Ralph R. 1996. "Machiavellianism: a synthesis of the evolutionary and psychological literatures." *Psychological Bulletin* 119(2):285–99.

Wilson, Robert A. and Lucia Foglia. 2011. "Embodied Cognition." In *The Stanford Encyclopedia of Philosophy*. Edward N. Zalta (ed).

Wohlforth, William C. 1996. *Witnesses to the End of the Cold War*. Baltimore, MD: The Johns Hopkins University Press.

Wohlforth, William C. 2011. "No One Loves a Realist Explanation." *Internationesal Politics* 48(4):441–59.

Wright, Lawrence. 2014. *Thirteen Days in September: Carter, Begin, and Sadat at Camp David*. London, UK: Knopf Doubleday Publishing Group.

Xu, Xiaojing, Xiangyu Zuo, Xiaoying Wang, and Shihui Han. 2009. "Do You Feel My Pain? Racial Group Membership Modulates Empathic Neural Responses." *The Journal of Neuroscience* 29(26):8525–29.

Yarhi-Milo, Keren. 2013. "In the Eye of the Beholder: How Leaders and Intelligence Organizations Assess Intentions." *International Security* 38(1):7–51.

2014. *Knowing the Adversary: Leaders, Intelligence, and Assessment of Intentions in International Relations*. Princeton, NJ: Princeton University Press.

Yun, Kyongsik. 2013. "On the Same Wavelength: Face-to-Face Communication Increases Interpersonal Neural Synchronization." *Journal of Neuroscience* 33(12):5081–82.

Zahavi, Dan. 2008. "Simulation, Projection and Empathy." *Consciousness and Cognition* 17(2):514–22.

Zaki, Jamil, Jochen Weber, Niall Bolger, and Kevin Ochsner. 2009. "The Neural Bases of Empathic Accuracy." *Proceedings of the National Academy of Sciences* 106(27):11382–87.

Zartman, I. William. 1985. *Ripe for Resolution: Conflict and Intervention in Africa*. New York, NY: Oxford University Press.

1986. "Ripening Conflict, Ripe Moment, Formula and Mediation," In *Perspectives on Negotiation*. D. Ben-Dahmane & J. McDonald (eds). Washington, D.C.: Government Printing Office.

Zehfuss, Maja. 2002. *Constructivism in International Relations*. Cambridge, UK: Cambridge University Press.

Zelikow, Philip. 1995. "NATO Expansion Wasn't Ruled Out." *The New York Times*, August 10.

Zelikow, Philip and Condoleezza Rice. 1995. *Germany Unified and Europe Transformed: A Study in Statecraft*. Cambridge, MA: Harvard University Press.

Zubok, Vladislav and Constantine Pleshakov. 1996. *Inside the Kremlin's Cold War: From Stalin to Khrushchev*. Collingdale, PA: Diane Publishing Company.

# Index